Die Familie Mendelssohn
und ihre Gräber vor dem Halleschen Tor

The Mendelssohn Family
and Their Graves at Hallesches Tor

Herausgegeben vom Evangelischen Friedhofsverband Berlin Stadtmitte
und von der Mendelssohn-Gesellschaft e.V.

nicolai

Widmung von Karl Wilhelm Ramler am Postament der Tassaert-Büste von Moses Mendelssohn.

Dedication by Karl Wilhelm Ramler on the pedestal of Tassaert's bust of Moses Mendelssohn: *"Moses Mendelssohn / born in Dessau / in the year 1729 / by Jewish parents / wise like Socrates / loyal to the faith of his fathers / like him he taught immortality and he immortalized himself like him."*

Inhalt
Contents

Vorwort
Foreword

When the first descendant of Moses Mendelssohn was buried in the *Dreifaltigkeitsfriedhof* cemetery just outside the city gate known as Hallesches Tor, there was disagreement among the relatives as to whether or not a cross should be placed on his grave. The dispute was probably less about the deceased's confessional affiliation than about ensuring a simple and clean design. That was in 1836, and in the end, the departed – former City Councilor Abraham Mendelssohn Bartholdy – was interred in a "grave of honor" granted by the City of Berlin. Since that time, the five separate cemeteries clustering around Hallesches Tor have been amalgamated into a funereal complex of unique historical significance. Here one can find the resting places of six generations of the Mendelssohn family, with stone crucifixes or marble and granite headstones. While some graves are no longer extant, others have been rediscovered only recently and restored. Many friends of the Mendelssohn family form part of this necropolis, such as the salon hostess Henriette Herz and the intellectual Rahel Varnhagen. Like many of her contemporaries, Madame Varnhagen was not convinced that death had been given a sufficiently precise definition, and so instructed that she should be laid to rest, at least for a longer period of time, in a crypt rather than in the ground.

That the many Mendelssohn stories told at the Hallesches Tor have become the subject of a permanent exhibition is the happy result of the collaboration among three partners. The first of these is Evangelischer Friedhofsverband Berlin Stadtmitte. The Association of Protestant Cemeteries in Central Berlin has always had as its mission to make its memorial gardens interesting and, indeed, inviting to the public in the interests of giving a new impetus to funerary culture. Another is the Mendelssohn-Gesellschaft e.V., a society researching and disseminating the lives and stories of the Mendelssohns, which has long had its eye on these graveyards in Kreuzberg, where no less than 28 descendants of Moses Mendelssohn are buried along with their spouses and among their friends. Last but not least: the Berlin Senate Department for Cultural Affairs, which inspired the other two partners to work together and thus to preserve this part of the city's heritage.

Funded by subsidies from the Stiftung Deutsche Klassenlotterie Berlin (Foundation of the Berlin Lottery) and the Stiftung Historische Friedhöfe (Foundation for Historical Cemeteries), along with endowments and volunteer work contributed by members of the Mendelssohn-Gesellschaft, the project was realized in three years' time. On November 3, 2013, the

Als der erste Nachkomme Moses Mendelssohns auf dem Dreifaltigkeitsfriedhof vor dem Halleschen Tor beerdigt war, stritten die Angehörigen darüber, ob ein Kreuz auf seinem Grab stehen sollte. Dabei ging es vielleicht weniger um das Bekenntnis als um die Schlichtheit der Gestaltung. Das war 1836, der Verstorbene – Stadtrat Abraham Mendelssohn Bartholdy – erhielt schließlich ein Ehrengrab der Stadt Berlin. Fünf Friedhöfe vor dem Halleschen Tor sind seit damals zu einer einzigartigen historischen Gräberlandschaft zusammengewachsen. An Ruhestätten der Mendelssohn-Familie aus sechs Generationen stehen nun steinerne Kreuze, Marmor- und Granitsteine; manche Gräber existieren nicht mehr, andere sind vor kurzem erst wieder entdeckt und jetzt restauriert worden. Auch Freunde der Mendelssohn-Familie zählen zu dieser Friedhofswelt, die Salonière Henriette Herz gehört dazu und die Intellektuelle Rahel Varnhagen, der wie vielen Zeitgenossen die Präzision menschlicher Todesdefinition nicht geheuer war – weshalb sie für sich verfügt hatte, dort zunächst einmal längere Zeit lieber in einer Gruft zu ruhen als unter der Erde.

Daß aus all den Geschichten, die vor dem Halleschen Tor überliefert werden, während der vergangenen Jahre eine Ausstellung entstanden ist, verdanken wir der glücklichen Kooperation dreier Partner. Dem Evangelischen Friedhofsverband Berlin Stadtmitte war und ist es ein Anliegen, seine historischen Friedhofsanlagen der Öffentlichkeit so interessant und, jawohl, einladend zu präsentieren, daß die Kultur der Grabpflege neu angeregt wird. In der Mendelssohn-Gesellschaft e.V., die Geschichten der Nachkommen Moses Mendelssohns erforscht und verbreitet, hatte man wiederum schon längst ein besonderes Augenmerk auf die Kreuzberger Friedhöfe am Mehringdamm gerichtet, wo 28 Mendelssohn-Nachfahren mit ihren Partnern und Freunden die letzte Ruhe gefunden haben. Die Senatskulturverwaltung schließlich vermittelte inspirierend, zur Rettung des historischen Berliner Erbes, zwischen dem Verein und dem Verband.

Getragen durch Mittel der Stiftung Deutsche Klassenlotterie Berlin und der Stiftung Historische Friedhöfe sowie durch finanzielle und ehrenamtliche Beiträge aus der Mendelssohn-Gesellschaft konnte das Projekt innerhalb von drei Jahren realisiert werden. Am 3. November 2013 wurde in der ehemaligen Friedhofskapelle auf dem Dreifaltigkeitsfriedhof die Ausstellung „Die Familie Mendelssohn und ihre Gräber vor dem Halleschen Tor" eingeweiht, unter Anwesenheit von zahlreichen Nachkommen Moses und Fromet Mendelssohns.

exhibition "The Mendelssohn Family and Their Graves at Hallesches Tor" housed in the former graveyard chapel of the Dreifaltigkeitsfriedhof was officially inaugurated, with numerous descendants of Moses and Fromet Mendelssohn in attendance.

This catalogue of the permanent exhibit offers visitors – as well as those who have been unable to visit it in person – a beautiful compendium of the images shown there, as well as the German documentary texts with their complete English translations (rather than the abbreviated versions found on the exhibit plaques). Moreover, the catalogue is the most comprehensive illustrated history available on this prominent German-Jewish dynasty that contributed so much to the development of Berlin, the Kingdom of Prussia, and Germany as a whole. We wish to thank all the institutions and private individuals whose commitment and contributions have allowed this extraordinary family history of achievement, rupture, and reconciliation to be told in such an impressive and uplifting way.

Berlin, March 2015

Pastor Jürgen Quandt, Managing Director of Evangelischer Friedhofsverband Berlin Stadtmitte

André Schmitz, Chairman of Mendelssohn-Gesellschaft e.V.

Der Katalog zu dieser Dauerausstellung bietet künftig deren Besuchern und allen, die den Weg dorthin noch nicht geschafft haben, eine prächtige Zusammenfassung des Bilderpanoramas und die Dokumentation der deutschen Texte mit englischer Übersetzung, welche gedruckt sogar in voller Länge (nicht gekürzt, wie auf den Ausstellungstafeln) erscheint. Das Buch ist darüber hinaus auch der umfassendste Bildband zur Geschichte dieser großen deutschen Familie jüdischer Herkunft, der Berlin, Preußen und Deutschland viel verdankt. Wir danken allen Institutionen und Personen, die es durch ihren Einsatz und ihre Beiträge ermöglicht haben, daß diese besondere Geschichte des Neubeginns, der Trennungen und des Zusammenfindens so eindrucksvoll und ermutigend erzählt werden kann.

Berlin, im März 2015

Pfarrer Jürgen Quandt, Geschäftsführer des Evangelischen Friedhofsverbandes Berlin Stadtmitte

André Schmitz, Vorsitzender der Mendelssohn-Gesellschaft e.V.

CATHARINE HENRIETTE
CECILIE SCHELSKE
GEB. MENDELSSOHN-BARTHOLDY
PAULINE LUISE A
MENDELSSOHN BA
GEB. HEINE
GEBOREN
ZU
BERLIN
AM
22. MAERZ
1814.

Die Familie Mendelssohn und ihre Gräber vor dem Halleschen Tor
The Mendelssohn Family and Their Graves at Hallesches Tor

"On the Immortality of the Soul"

This was the title of the bestseller of 1767 that made Moses Mendelssohn famous. He had first set foot in Berlin twenty-four years earlier, probably entering the city through the south-eastern gate to the city called the Hallesches Tor. In the 19th century, a number of memorial plaques were mounted on the façade of Moses' birth house in Dessau and to his family's first town home at Spandauer Strasse 68, in the Marienviertel district of Berlin. The biggest of these plaques, an engraved stone tablet, was all that remained after the building was torn down in 1886; it was eventually affixed to the building next door in 1911. By 1945, the whole block lay in ruins and was demolished and the plaque was believed to have been destroyed. Until 1988, that is, when it was found, broken and covered by rubble, in the boiler room of the Jewish Community Center on Oranienburger Strasse. The Centrum Judaicum has kindly loaned this stone memorial plaque to the Mendelssohn-Gesellschaft for the current exhibition. It reads: "In this house Moses Mendelssohn b. 1729 in Dessau d. 1789 in Berlin lived and gained immortality."

As artists, bankers, and scholars, the descendants of Moses Mendelssohn exerted a profound influence on German-Jewish history. Scattered across three cemeteries near Hallesches Tor are the final resting places of no less than twenty-eight of these descendants and their spouses, as well as those of many of their contemporaries and allies in the common struggle for civic progress. The biographies of the Mendelssohns are filled with wrenching change, deep friendships, grim ordeals and illustrious careers. They tell of the search for truth, social advancement, and the passion for music and art; but also of persecution, exile, and the courage to start anew. Its protagonists include shining talents and black sheep, hopeful educators, and groundbreaking modernizers, looking toward the future yet beholden to a long tradition. In short, it is nothing less than a panorama of modern times – as seen through the eyes of one very special German-Jewish family from Berlin.

„Über die Unsterblichkeit der Seele“

ging der Bestseller von 1767, durch den Moses Mendelssohn berühmt geworden war. 24 Jahre zuvor hatte er Berlin erstmals, wohl durch das Hallesche Tor, betreten. An seinem Dessauer Geburtshaus sowie am ersten Haus seiner Familie im Berliner Marienviertel sind während des 19. Jahrhunderts mehrere Gedenktafeln angebracht worden. Die größte blieb das einzige Relikt des Wohnhauses Spandauer Straße 68. Der Bau ist 1886 abgerissen, die Tafel 1911 am Nachbarhaus angebracht worden. Mit dem Abriß des Ruinen-Areals nach 1945 schien sie verloren, wurde dann 1988 im Heizungskeller der Jüdischen Gemeinde an der Oranienburger Straße wiedergefunden – hinter Gerümpel verborgen und zerbrochen. Das Centrum Judaicum hat den Erinnerungsstein der Mendelssohn-Gesellschaft für diese Ausstellung als Leihgabe überlassen. Der Text der Tafel lautet: "In diesem Hause lebte und wirkte Unsterbliches Moses Mendelssohn geb. 1729 in Dessau gest. 1786 in Berlin".

Moses' Nachkommen prägten als Künstler, Bankiers und Gelehrte die deutsch-jüdische Geschichte. 28 von ihnen und ihre Partner ruhen auf drei Friedhöfen am Halleschen Tor, ebenso manche Mitstreiter für die gemeinsam wahrgenommene bürgerliche Verantwortung. Biographien der Mendelssohns handeln von Aufbrüchen, Freundschaften, Zerreißproben, Karrieren, von Wahrheitssuche, Erfolgen, von der Passion für Musik und Kunst, von Verfolgung, Flucht, Mut zum Neuanfang. Sie zeigen das Panorama der Neuen Zeit: große Talente, schwarze Schafe, hoffnungsvolle Erzieher, traditionsbewußte Modernisierer – eine Berliner Familie in Deutschland.

Ehemalige Friedhofskapelle, in der die Ausstellung auf dem Dreifaltigkeitsfriedhof am Halleschen Tor in Berlin Kreuzberg gezeigt wird.
Former graveyard chapel, housing the exhibition on *Dreifaltigkeitsfriedhof* cemetery at Hallesches Tor in Berlin Kreuzberg.

Moses Mendelssohn · 1729 (1728) Dessau – 1786 Berlin

When the Dessau Talmud student Mausche, son of the Torah scribe Mendel, followed his revered teacher Rabbi Fränkel to Berlin in 1743, Jewish community leaders viewed the arrival of the 14-year-old warily. Under the scrutiny of Prussian authorities, the last thing they needed was for an impoverished Jew to settle in Berlin. The autodidact from Anhalt had a thirst for knowledge; he learned old and new Western languages and mastered High German and the European scholarly canon, which provoked conflict with community leaders who favored cultural separatism. His constant study under trying conditions from childhood on had ruined his health. He helped to secure his status as a resident by obtaining a position as a tutor for the textile manufacturer Bernhard Isaak. Soon, he began working as a bookkeeper for Bernhard, swiftly rising to become the managing director and, finally, a partner in the firm. In this way, Moses Mendelssohn – the self-made intellectual chose this civil name for himself – earned his family's livelihood. He also won the right of residence in Berlin thanks to his service for state-subsidized silk production.

His acquaintance with the publisher Friedrich Nicolai and the writer Gotthold Ephraim Lessing developed into a trio of young friends whose debates, critical reviews, essays, and published discussions made cultural history. They were the triumvirate of the Berlin Enlightenment. Moses' marriage at 32 to Fromet, the daughter of a Hamburg merchant, produced ten children, six of whom survived. A best-selling author, Moses scored a hit with his "Phädon: on the Immortality of the Soul," a topic of great interest to his contemporaries. A transformational cultural figure, his translation of the Torah into German paved the way for his co-religionists to learn the language of the Christian majority society and participate in its literature and art. He urged them to break out of the intellectual ghetto. A modernizer, he counseled Jewish communities that found themselves torn between tradition and assimilation with the majority society; he also advised Prussian officials who were interested in reducing discrimination. As an observant and faithful Jew, he helped to reconcile the revealed laws of Judaism with enlightened reason.

When the theologian Lavater called on the philosopher to have himself baptized as a Christian, the "worldly sage" Moses rebuffed him. However, the public debate that this provocation ignited triggered a nervous disorder that plagued him for seven years. His charismatic personality and integrity became famous throughout Europe. When the "Jew of Berlin" died at the age of 56, Berlin's entire Jewish community was joined by many Christian friends in paying their final respect.

Als der Dessauer Talmudschüler Mausche, Sohn des Synagogendieners Mendel, im Jahr 1743 seinem verehrten Lehrer Rabbi Fränkel hinterherreist, erfolgt der Eintritt des Vierzehnjährigen nach Berlin unter kritischer Beobachtung jüdischer Gemeindevertreter. Die haben, auf Befehl der preußischen Obrigkeit, am Zuzug von Hungerleidern wenig Interesse. Der bildungshungrige Autodidakt aus Anhalt eignet sich alte und neue Sprachen des Abendlandes an, das Hochdeutsche und den europäischen Bildungskanon – was Konflikte mit Gemeindeführern provoziert, die auf kulturelle Abgrenzung setzen. Das Lernen unter strapaziösen Bedingungen hat schon von Kindheit an seine Gesundheit ruiniert. Sein Aufenthaltsstatus verbessert sich durch eine Hauslehrer-Stelle beim Textilfabrikanten Bernhard Isaak, in dessen Firma er bald als Buchhalter wirkt, zum Geschäftsführer, schließlich zum Teilhaber, zum Eigentümer aufrückt. So sichert Moses Mendelssohn – diesen bürgerlichen Namen nimmt der Selfmade-Intellektuelle an – seiner Familie den Lebensunterhalt. Und sich selbst das Bleiberecht: aufgrund seiner Verdienste um die staatlich geförderte Seidenproduktion.

Aus Mendelssohns Bekanntschaft mit dem Verleger Friedrich Nicolai und dem Dichter Gotthold Ephraim Lessing entsteht ein Freundestrio junger Männer, deren Dispute, Rezensionen, Aufsätze und publizierte Diskussionsforen Kulturgeschichte machen – das Dreigestirn der Berliner Aufklärung. Aus der Eheschließung des 32jährigen Moses mit der Hamburger Kaufmannstochter Fromet gehen zehn Kinder hervor, sechs überleben. Der Bestsellerautor Moses trifft mit seinem „Phädon. Über die Unsterblichkeit der Seele" ein Thema, das den Zeitgenossen am Herzen liegt. Der Kulturtransformator ebnet Glaubensgenossen durch Thora-Übersetzungen den Weg zur Sprache ihrer christlichen Umgebung, zu ihrer Literatur und Kunst. Er motiviert zum Aufbruch aus dem geistigen Ghetto. Der Modernisierungshelfer berät jüdische Gemeinden im Konflikt zwischen Tradition und Anpassung an die Mehrheitsgesellschaft; auch preußische Beamte, denen der Abbau von Diskriminierungen wichtig ist. Der Philosoph vereinbart als gläubiger Jude Gesetzesoffenbarung und aufgeklärte Vernunftreligion.

Die Aufforderung des Theologen Lavater, sich taufen zu lassen, weist der „Weltweise" Moses zurück – doch löst eine nun anhebende öffentliche Debatte um diese Provokation bei ihm eine siebenjährige Nervenkrankheit aus. Seine charismatische, integre Persönlichkeit wird europaweit berühmt. Als „der Jude von Berlin" 56jährig stirbt, gibt ihm, mit christlichen Freunden, Berlins ganze jüdische Gemeinde das Geleit.

Moses Mendelssohn. Gemälde von Johann Christoph Frisch (1786).
Moses Mendelssohn. Painting of Johann Christoph Frisch (1786).

Mendelssohns Geburtshaus in Dessau.
Öl auf Leinwand.

The house in Dessau where Mendelssohn was born.
Oil on canvas.

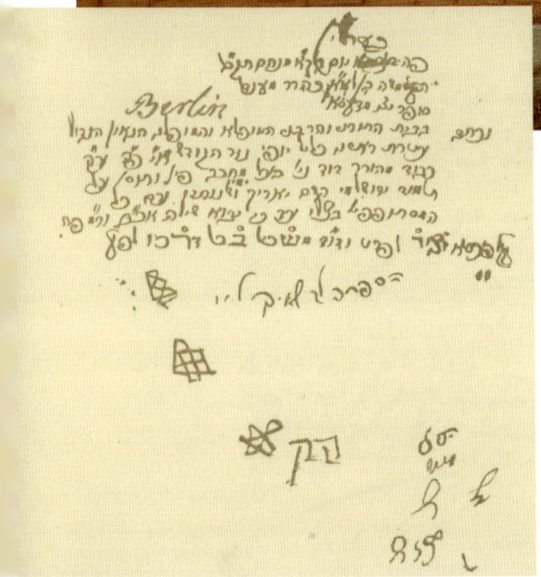

„Gott mache seine Tage und Jahre lang mit denen, die sich in seinem Schatten bergen ...".
Widmung des 14jährigen Mausche Dessau für Rabbi Fränkel in einem Buch, 21. August 1742.

"May God make his days and years long for those who take refuge in his shadow..."
Dedication from the 14-year-old Mausche Dessau in a book for Rabbi Fränkel on August 21, 1742.

Geschäftsjournal Mendelssohns
aus der Seidenfabrik Bernhard, Januar 1779.

Mendelssohn's business diary
from the Bernhard silk factory, January 1779.

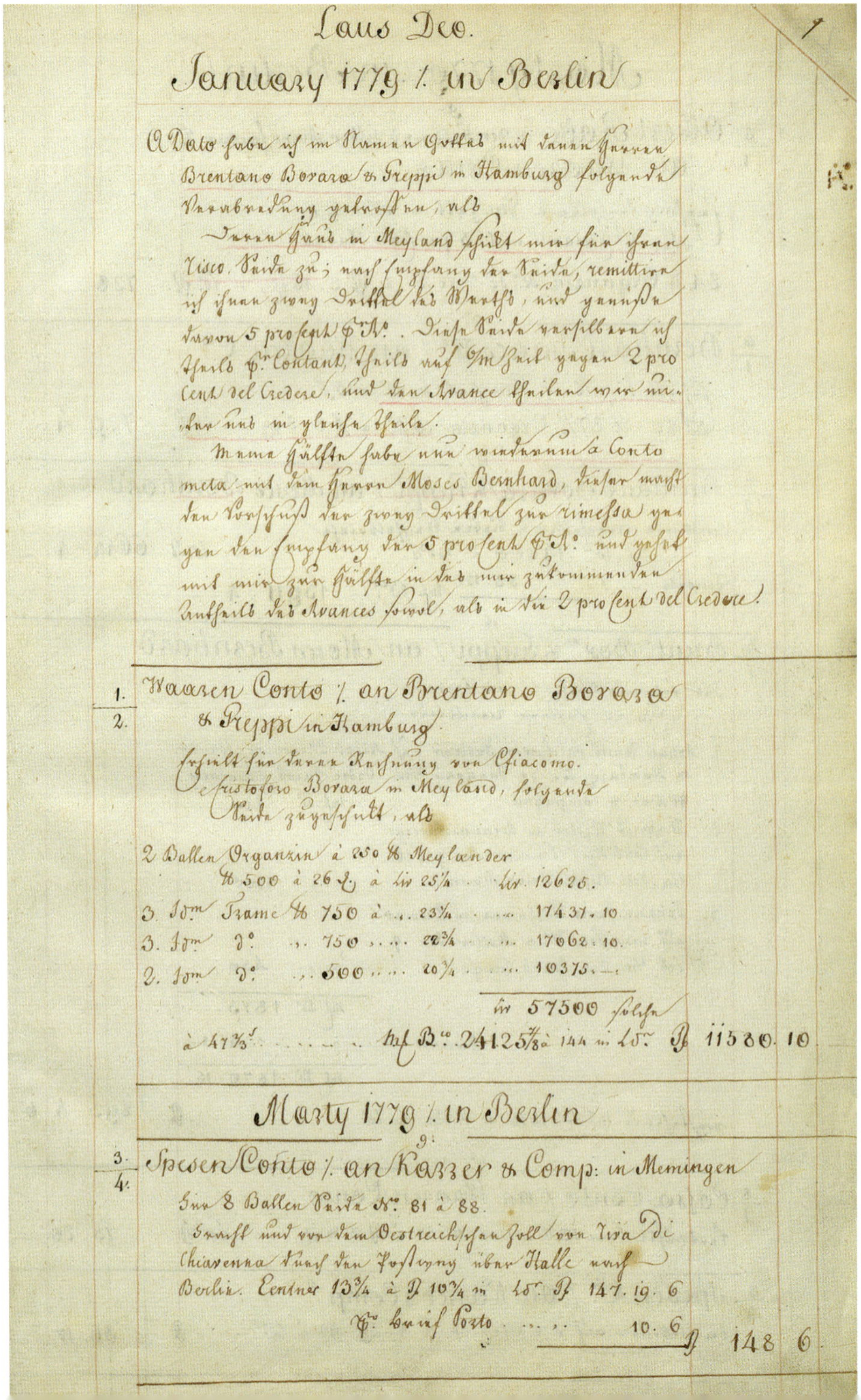

Laus Deo.

January 1779 / in Berlin

Waaren Conto / an Brentano Borara & Greppi in Hamburg

Marty 1779 / in Berlin

Spesen Conto / an Kazzer & Comp: in Memingen

Taschenuhr von Moses Mendelssohn
aus dem Nachlaß seines Sohnes
Nathan (1781 – 1852).

Moses Mendelssohn's pocket watch,
from the estate of his son
Nathan (1781 – 1852).

Moses Mendelssohn
am Tor zu Potsdam.
Stich (1792) von
Johann M.S. Lowe
nach einer Zeichnung von
Daniel Chodowiecki.

Moses Mendelssohn
at the city gates
of Potsdam.
Engraving (1792) by
Johann M.S. Lowe
based on a drawing by
Daniel Chodowiecki.

Siegel Moses Mendelssohns (um 1766).

Moses Mendelssohn's seal (c. 1766).

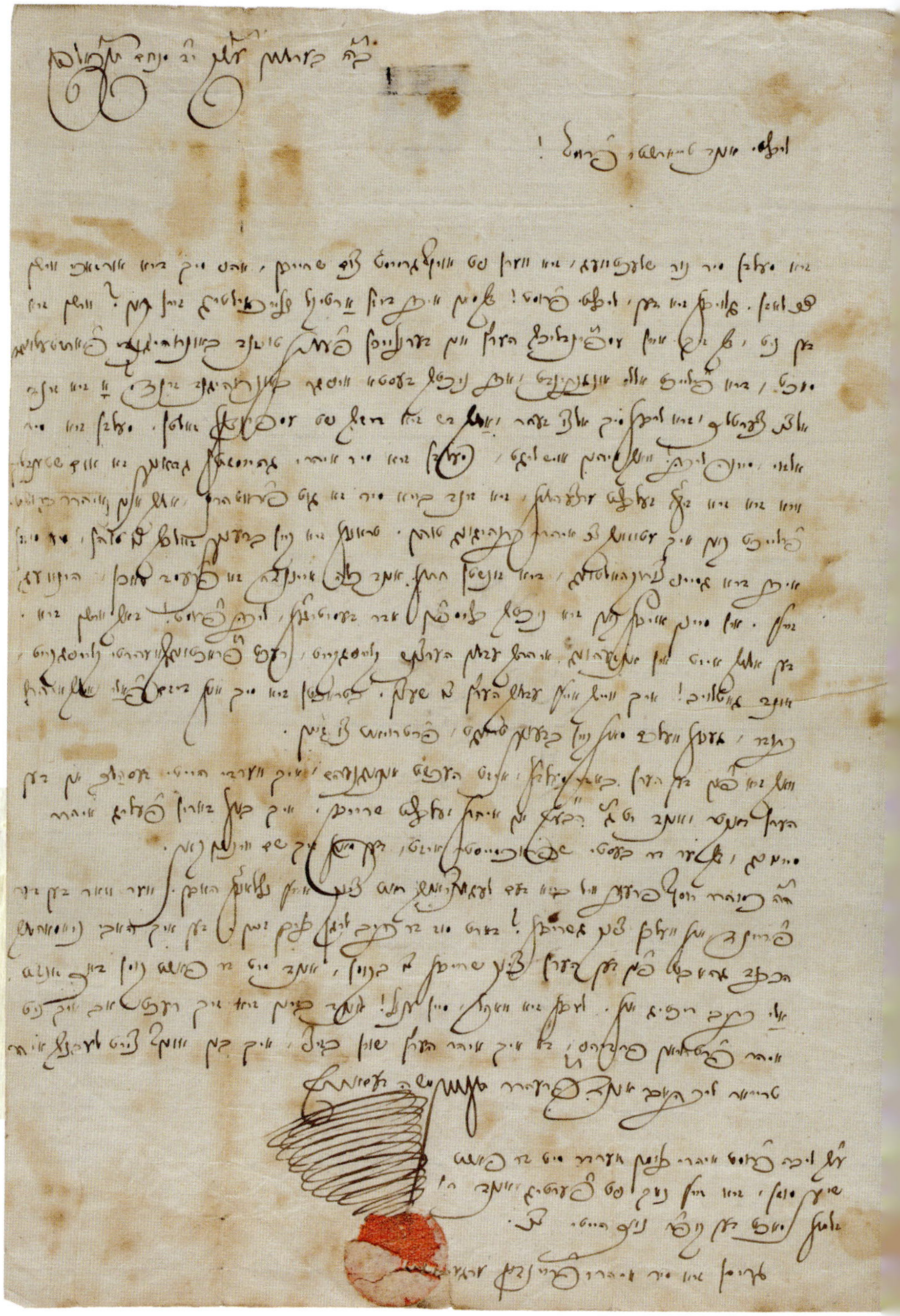

Moses Mendelssohn,
Brief an Fromet Gugenheim, 14. August 1761.

Moses Mendelssohn,
letter to Fromet Gugenheim, August 14, 1761.

Grabstein von Moses Mendelssohn auf dem ehemaligen
jüdischen Friedhof in Berlin in der Großen Hamburger Straße.
Druck (o.J.) nach einer Kupfervignette
von Daniel Chodowiecki (1788).

Moses Mendelssohn's gravestone in the former
Jewish cemetery on Grosse Hamburger Strasse in Berlin.
Print (undated) based on a copper plate engraving
by Daniel Chodowiecki (1788).

Fromet Mendelssohn, geb. Gugenheim · 1737 Hamburg – 1812 Berlin

Fromet Gugenheim was related to famous merchant families from Vienna and Hamburg. When the charming and learned, but humpbacked, Berlin textile merchant Moses Mendelssohn courted the 24-year-old with an interest in literature in 1761, her nearly bankrupt father Abraham happened to be on a business trip. Although they were an uneven match, they chose one another for love, skirting an official arranged marriage. Sixty-seven letters from their courtship and engagement are preserved. They speak of her education, honesty, emotions, friendships and relationships, problems with relatives, gifts exchanged, and preparations for the wedding on June 22, 1762 in Berlin. The lovers' relationship was spirited and founded on a principle of partnership, and this is as evident from this part of their correspondence as it is from the correspondence of Fromet's that is preserved from the period of their marriage.

As a mother, lady of the household, and hostess, Fromet was the strong, intelligent woman behind the philosopher, Moses, who attracted an array of partners, students, and acquaintances in his dual profession as a philosopher and silk manufacturer but was often overtaxed. Fromet bore him through many crises. She lost four children at early ages and raised six to adulthood; she never recovered from the loss of her eldest daughter Brendel, who left her Jewish husband and the Jewish faith. After Moses' death in 1786, the widowed Fromet obtained the right of residence for herself and her children. She bought their house, sold it, and moved in with her favorite daughter Recha in Neustrelitz. At the beginning of the new century, she moved back to her native Hamburg with her divorced daughter Recha and Recha's ex father-in-law, the long-time family friend Nathan Meyer.

Her wedding dress, which the couple had converted into a Torah curtain *(Parochet)* and donated to a Berlin synagogue, she now gave to the Altona synagogue. As a widow, she showed an undiminished zest for life, enjoying card games and comedies at the theater. She was the nucleus of her family, which had largely followed her back to Hamburg. She died five days after the edict proclaiming the emancipation of the Jews of Prussia was issued.

Fromet Gugenheim ist mit berühmten Hamburger und Wiener Kaufleuten verwandt. Als der charmante, gelehrte, aber bucklige Berliner Textilhändler Moses Mendelssohn 1761 in Altona um die literaturinteressierte 24Jährige wirbt, weilt deren fast bankrotter Vater Abraham gerade auf Geschäftsreise. Das ungleiche Liebespaar Fromet und Moses entscheidet sich füreinander, jenseits offizieller Heiratsvermittlung. Erhalten sind 67 Brautbriefe des Verlobten, die von Bildungsprojekten für die Freundin handeln, von Aufrichtigkeit, Gefühlen, Freundschaft und Beziehungen, von Verwandtschaftsproblemen, gegenseitigen Geschenken, von Vorbereitungen der Berliner Hochzeit am 22. Juni 1762. Die temperamentvolle Partnerschaft der Verliebten läßt sich an diesem Teil der Korrespondenz ebenso erkennen wie später an Fromets überlieferten Ehebriefen.

Als Mutter, Haushaltschefin und Gastgeberin ist sie die starke, kluge Persönlichkeit hinter dem Philosophen, der im Doppelberuf, als Seidenfabrikant und Philosoph, verschiedenste Partner, Schüler und Bekannte anzieht, dabei aber die eigenen Kräfte überstrapaziert. Fromet trägt ihn durch viele Krisen. Sie verliert vier Kinder früh, sechs zieht sie groß. Den Verlust der ältesten Tochter Brendel, die ihren jüdischen Mann und das Judentum verläßt, verwindet sie nicht. Nach dem Tod des Moses (1786) erhält seine Witwe für sich und ihre Kinder das Bleiberecht. Sie erwirbt ihr Wohnhaus; verkauft es; zieht zu ihrer Lieblingstochter Recha nach Neustrelitz. Mit der geschiedenen Recha und deren Ex-Schwiegervater, dem langjährigen Familienfreund Nathan Meyer, und mit ihrem Sohn Joseph aus Berlin kehrt sie am Anfang des neuen Jahrhunderts in ihre Heimatstadt zurück.

Ihr Hochzeitskleid, das die Eheleute um 1775, umgearbeitet zu einem Thoravorhang, einem Berliner Bethaus gestiftet hatten, schenkt sie nun der Altonaer Synagoge. Als lebensfrohe Witwe, der das Kartenspiel und Komödienbesuche gefallen, bildet sie die Mitte ihrer großteils nach Hamburg gefolgten Familie. Sie stirbt fünf Tage nach der Verkündigung des Emanzipationsedikts für die Juden in Preußen.

Fromet Mendelssohn. Miniatur (um 1767).
Fotomechanische Reproduktion.

Fromet Mendelssohn. Miniature (c. 1767).
Photo-mechanical reproduction.

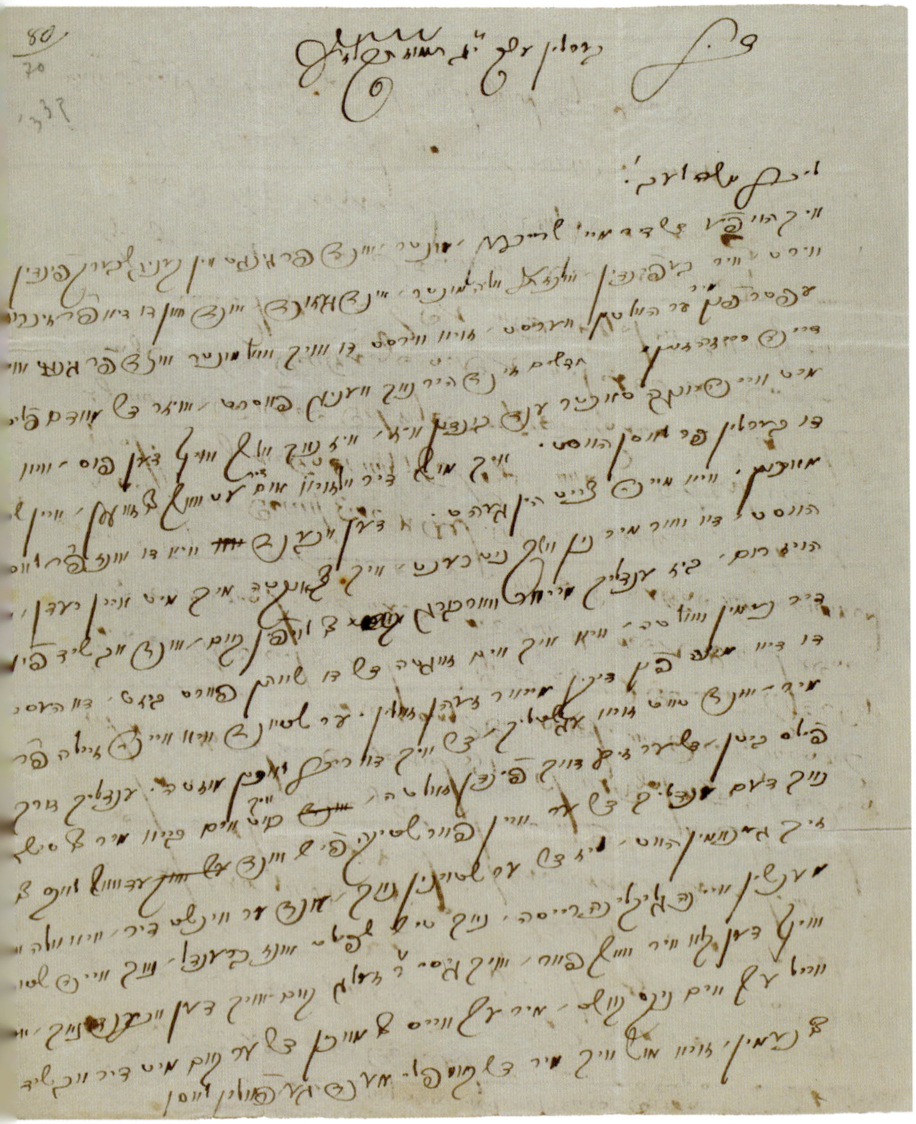

Fromet Mendelssohn: Brief an den Ehemann, 18. Juli 1777.
Das Schreiben bereitet ihr „die erste vergnügte Stunde“ seit Moses’ Abreise.

Fromet Mendelssohn: Letter to her husband dated July 18, 1777.
She writes that working on the letter has given her the “first joyful hour” since Moses’ departure.

Thoravorhang, Berlin 1774 – 1775, Seide, Leinen, bestickt.
Umgearbeitet aus dem Brautkleid Fromet Gugenheims.

Torah Curtain *(Parochet)*, Berlin 1774 – 1775, silk, linen, embroidered.
Made from the wedding dress of Fromet Gugenheim.

Silhouette Fromet Mendelssohns aus einem
Stammbucheintrag Mendelssohns für Herz Homberg.

Silhouette of Fromet Mendelssohn from an entry
in the family album for Herz Homberg.

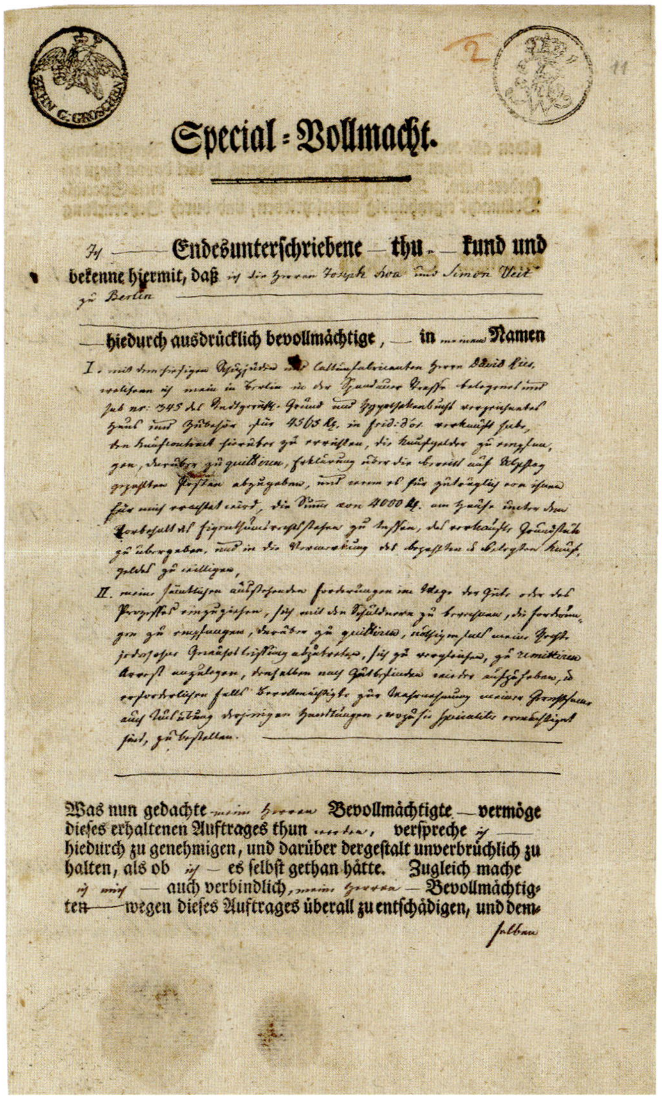

Special=Vollmacht.

Ich Endesunterschriebene thu kund und bekenne hiermit, daß ich den Herren Joseph Veit und Simon Veit zu Berlin

hiedurch ausdrücklich bevollmächtige, in meinem Namen

I. [illegible]

II. [illegible]

Was nun gedachte meine Herren Bevollmächtigte vermöge dieses erhaltenen Auftrages thun werden, verspreche ich hiedurch zu genehmigen, und darüber dergestalt unverbrüchlich zu halten, als ob ich es selbst gethan hätte. Zugleich mache ich mich auch verbindlich, meine Herren Bevollmächtigten wegen dieses Auftrages überall zu entschädigen, und denselben

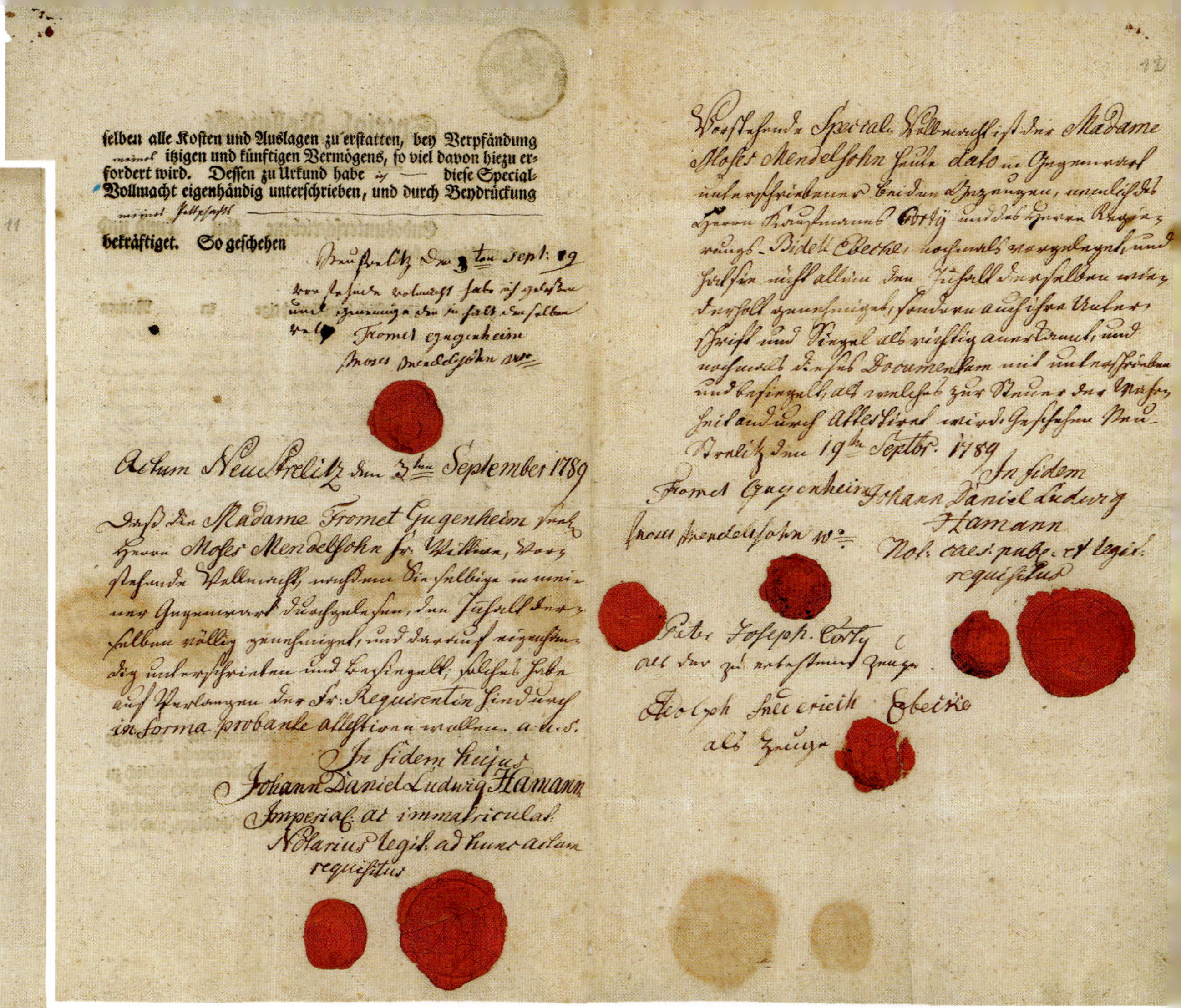

selben alle Kosten und Auslagen zu erstatten, bey Verpfändung meines itzigen und künftigen Vermögens, so viel davon hiezu erfordert wird. Dessen zu Urkund habe ich diese Special-Vollmacht eigenhändig unterschrieben, und durch Beydrückung meines Pettschafts bekräftiget. So geschehen Neustrelitz den 3ten Sept. 89

[illegible]
Fromet Gugenheim
Moses Mendelssohn Wwe.

Actum Neustrelitz den 3ten September 1789

[illegible]

In fidem [illegible]
Johann Daniel Ludwig Hamann
Imperial. at immatriculat.
Notarius legit. ad haec actum requisitus

[illegible] Neustrelitz den 19ten Septbr. 1789

Fromet Gugenheim
Moses Mendelssohn Wwe.

In fidem
Johann Daniel Ludwig Hamann
Not. caes. publ. et legit. requisitus

Peter Joseph Corty als dazu erbetener Zeuge

Adolph Friedrich Ebecke als Zeuge

Fromet Mendelssohn erteilt Simon Veit die Vollmacht, das Berliner Haus zu verkaufen, Neustrelitz 1789.

Fromet Mendelssohn grants Simon Veit power of attorney to sell the family house in Berlin, Neustrelitz 1789.

Lessing und Lavater als Gäste im Haus Moses Mendelssohns. Ölgemälde auf Leinwand von Moritz Daniel Oppenheim (1856).

Lessing and Lavater as guests at the home of Moses Mendelssohn. Oilpainting on canvas of Moritz Daniel Oppenheim (1856).

Dorothea Schlegel, geb. Mendelssohn, gesch. Veit · 1764 Berlin – 1839 Frankfurt / Main

Brendel, Moses' eldest daughter, was also his favorite. Her mother Fromet made sure that she wrote letters well, played piano beautifully, and understood French theater. At the age of sixteen, she married Simon Veit, her father's business partner and friend. Later, she fled this marriage to a banker for a life of literary salons and close alliances with friends. Some portraits from these years show her with her hair modestly covered according to Jewish tradition, while in others she boldly flaunts uncovered hair. She chose the name Dorothea (from Goethe's "Hermann and Dorothea"). An encounter with the cultural philosopher Friedrich Schlegel, who would later portray their relationship in his roman a clef, "Lucinde," changed her life. She left the father of her sons and her family. She considered reconciling with her widowed mother but never did. After her divorce in 1799, she lived in the commune of early Romantics in Jena. In Paris in 1804, she converted to Schlegel's Protestant faith and married him. She claimed that Moses Mendelssohn appeared to her during her baptism. She was the first of her family to leave behind the patriarch's Jewish legacy. Her own awakenings and wanderings reflected the turn of an epoch, the tensions between the Enlightenment, Idealism, and Romanticism, the upheaval of the old regime and the emergence of the revolutionary period, the transition from the age of Napoleon to the Restoration.

As a translator and author, she supported her brilliant husband. She was the driving force behind the couple's joint conversion to Catholicism in 1808 in Cologne. She did not learn to appreciate her ex-husband's generosity of heart until after their split. Veit found it difficult to accept the conversion of his children (1810), which Dorothea had pursued energetically. For two decades, she lived in Vienna, where her husband, elevated to the nobility, was employed as a court secretary. She visited her sons, the painters Jonas (Johannes) and Philipp, in Rome, where they were both affiliated with the Nazarene movement. She combined a Romantic conception of art with a missionary Catholicism. After Friedrich's death (1829), she lived in Frankfurt am Main, where her son Philipp was director of the museum. Her contact with other members of the family, be they Catholics, Jews, or Protestants, grew warmer over the years, but she never returned to Berlin.

Brendel, die Älteste, ist Moses' Lieblingstochter. Mutter Fromet paßt auf, daß sie gute Briefe schreibt, schön Klavier spielt, französisches Theater versteht. Mit sechzehn heiratet sie Simon Veit, Vaters Geschäftspartner und Freund. Aus dieser Bankiers-Ehe flieht sie in Literatursalons und Freundschaftsbünde. Porträts jener Jahre zeigen sie mal nach jüdischem Brauch mit züchtiger Kopfbedeckung, mal gewagt mit offenem Haar. Sie nennt sich Dorothea (nach Goethes „Hermann und Dorothea"). Die Begegnung mit dem Kulturphilosophen Friedrich Schlegel, der beider Liebesbeziehung im Schlüsselroman „Lucinde" ausstellen wird, verändert ihr Leben. Sie verläßt den Vater ihrer Söhne, ihre Familie. Überlegungen, sich mit der verwitweten Mutter zu versöhnen, bleiben unrealisiert. Nach ihrer Scheidung 1799 lebt sie in der Jenaer Frühromantiker-Kommune, konvertiert 1804 in Paris zur evangelischen Konfession Friedrich Schlegels, den sie heiratet. Bei der Taufe sagt sie, sei ihr Moses Mendelssohn erschienen. Als Erste der Familie hat sie das jüdische Vermächtnis des Stammvaters hinter sich gelassen. Ihre Aufbrüche und Wandlungen spiegeln auch die Epochenbrüche zwischen Aufklärung, Idealismus und Romantik, die Umwälzungen vom alten Regime zur Revolutionsemphase, von der Napoleon-Zeit zur Restauration wider.

Als Übersetzerin und Autorin unterstützt sie die intellektuelle Produktivität ihres Gatten; beim gemeinsamen Übertritt zur katholischen Kirche, 1808 in Köln, ist sie treibende Kraft. Das große Herz ihres Ex-Mannes, dem es nicht leicht fällt, die von Dorothea forcierte Konversion seiner Kinder (1810) zu akzeptieren, erkennt sie erst spät. Zwei Jahrzehnte wohnt sie in Wien, wo der nobilitierte Schlegel als Hofsekretär angestellt wurde, besucht in Rom ihre Söhne Jonas (Johannes) und Philipp, die Nazarener-Maler. Ihr romantisches Kunstverständnis verbindet sich mit ihrem missionarischen Katholizismus. Nach Friedrichs Tod (1829) lebt sie in Frankfurt (Main), wo Philipp Museumsdirektor ist. Ihre Kontakte mit anderen Katholiken, Juden oder Protestanten der Familie gewinnen an Herzlichkeit. Doch nach Berlin kehrt sie nie mehr zurück.

Dorothea Veit.
Öl auf Leinwand von Anton Graff (um 1790).

Dorothea Veit.
Oil on canvas by Anton Graff (c. 1790).

Im Salon von Abraham Abramson, v.l.n.r.:
Charlotte Schadow, Madame Abramson, Abraham Abramson, Brendel Veit, August Wilhelm Schlegel, Marianne Schadow. Zeichnung (1794).

At the salon of Abraham Abramson (l-r):
Charlotte Schadow, Madame Abramson, Abraham Abramson, Brendel Veit, August Wilhelm Schlegel, Marianne Schadow. Drawing (1794).

Simon Veit (1754 – 1819).
Öl auf Leinwand
von Johannes Veit.

Simon Veit (1754 – 1819).
Oil on canvas
by Johannes Veit.

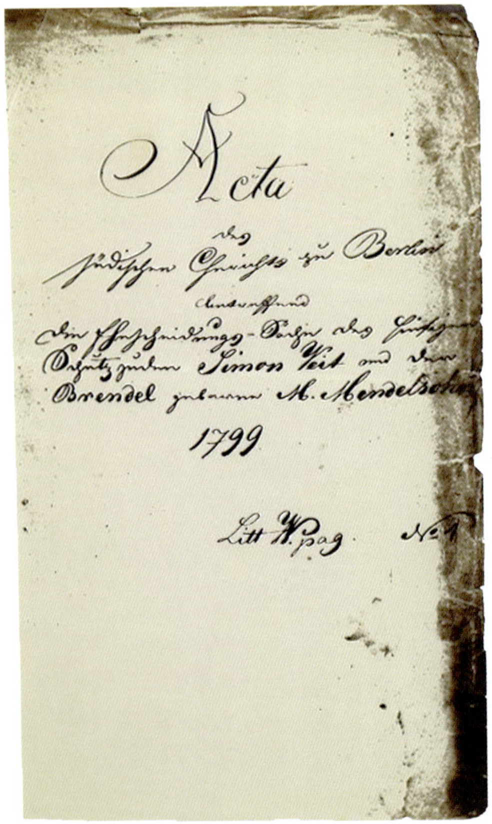

Acta
des
jüdischen Gerichts zu Berlin
betreffend
die Ehescheidungs-Sache des Schutz-Juden Simon Veit und der Brendel geborne M. Mendelsohn
1799
Litt W. pag. No.

Scheidungsurkunde
für Simon und Brendel Veit.

Certificate of divorce
for Simon and Brendel Veit.

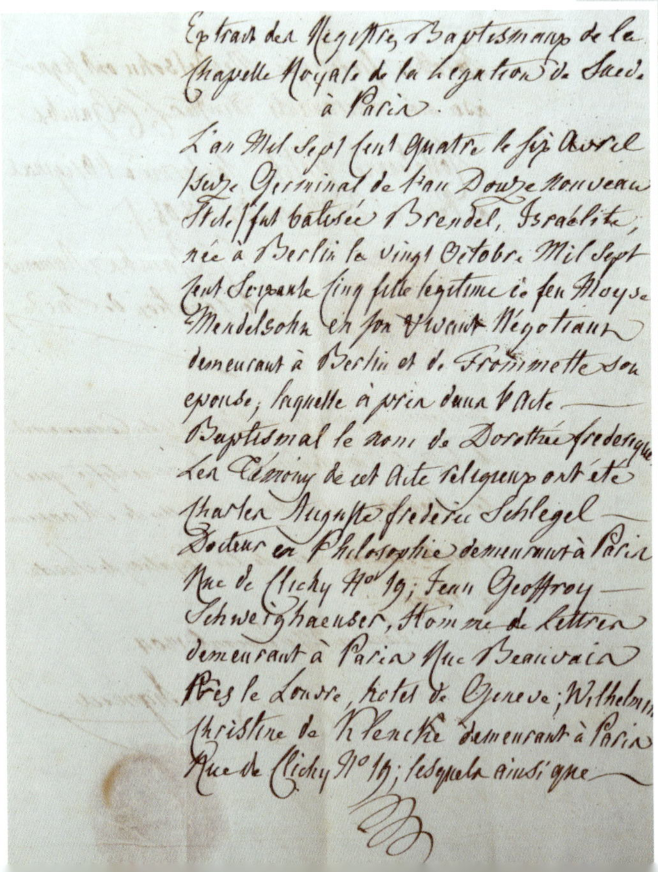

Extrait des Registres Baptismaux de la Chapelle Royale de la Légation de Suède à Paris.
L'an Mil Sept Cent Quatre le six Avril (seize Germinal de l'an Douze nouveau Style) fut baptisée Brendel, Israélite, née à Berlin le vingt Octobre Mil Sept Cent Soixante Cinq fille légitime de feu Moyse Mendelsohn en son vivant Négociant demeurant à Berlin et de Fromette son epouse, laquelle a pris dans l'Acte Baptismal le nom de Dorothée Frederique. Les Témoins de cet Acte religieux ont été Charles Auguste Frederic Schlegel Docteur en Philosophie demeurant à Paris Rue de Clichy No 19; Jean Geoffroy Schweighaeuser, Homme de lettres demeurant à Paris Rue Beauvais près le Louvre, hotel de Genève; Wilhelmine Christine de Klencke demeurant à Paris Rue de Clichy No 19; lesquels ainsi que

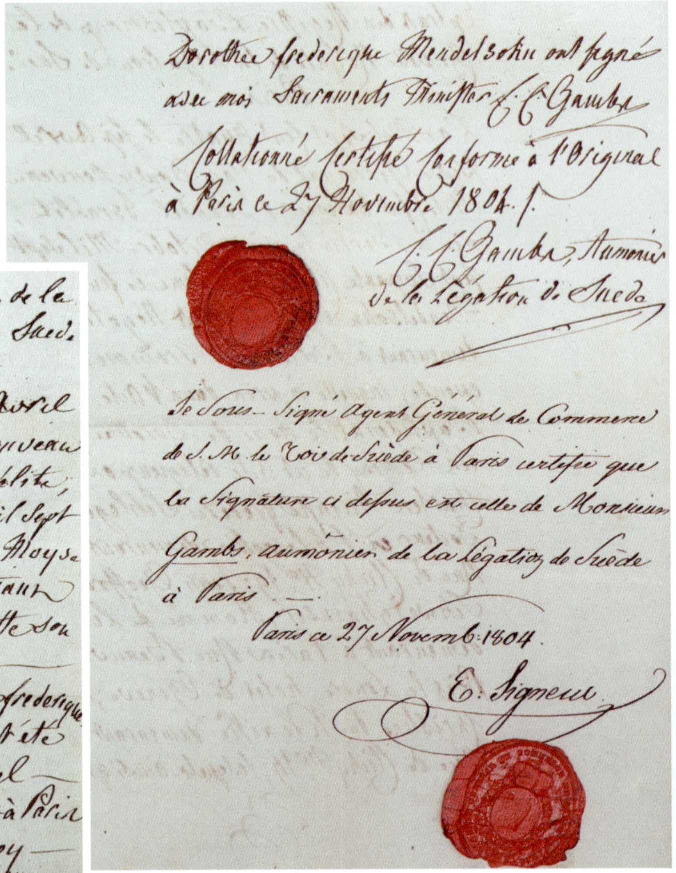

Dorothée Frederique Mendelsohn ont signé avec moi Sacraments Minister C. C. Gambs
Collationné Certifié Conforme à l'Original à Paris ce 27 Novembre 1804.
C. C. Gambs, Aumônier de la Légation de Suède
Je Sous-Signé Agent Général de Commerce de S. M. le Roi de Suède à Paris certifie que la Signature ci dessus est celle de Monsieur Gambs, aumônier de la Légation de Suède à Paris —
Paris ce 27 Novemb. 1804.
E. Signeul

Taufurkunde Dorothea Mendelssohns
vom 8. April 1804 in Paris, beglaubigte
Abschrift vom 27. November 1804.

Baptismal certificate of Dorothea Mendelssohn
dated April 8, 1804 in Paris, notarized copy
dated November 27, 1804.

„Geschichte des ave maria's in der Grünangergaße."
Zwei Nachbarsfrauen haben eine Anekdote Dorothea Schlegels aus ihrer Wiener Zeit festgehalten und illustriert: wie sich bei den gemeinsamen Mahlzeiten der Katholikin der heitere Wechsel zwischen Gebeten und Konversation vollzieht.

"The story of the Ave Marias in Grünangergasse."
An anecdote by Dorothea Schlegel (relating how prayer and conversation would alternate cheerfully at a shared meal with fellow Catholics), as written down and illustrated by two of her neighbors.

Friedrich Schlegel (1772 – 1829).
Kohlezeichnung von Philipp Veit (um 1810).

Friedrich Schlegel (1772 – 1829).
Charcoal drawing of Philipp Veit (c. 1810).

Dorothea von Schlegel, umgeben von ihrem Sohn, dem Maler Philipp Veit, dessen Gattin und Enkeln. Zeichnung von Franz Brentano.

Dorothea von Schlegel surrounded by her son, the painter Philipp Veit along with his wife, and her grandchildren. Drawing by Franz Brentano.

Wilhelm Stein.
Kleiderstoff
68
K. Conrad.
Friseur.
Sammet
Seiden-
Waaren.
Specialität
Shlipse
Cravatten.
Wilhelm Stein.
R. Giese
Klempnerei
Reparaturen
Wiener
Rasir
&
Haarschneide
Salon
Rasir- Frisir-
arschneide &
Shampoonir-
Salon.
K.Conrad.
Wiener
Rasir
&
Frisir
Salon

Exkurs · Haus der Mendelssohns Spandauer Straße 68
The Mendelssohn's Home at Spandauer Strasse 68

Just steps from the Gothic Marienkirche in the densely-built old town of Berlin is the house at Spandauer Strasse 68. Before 1762, the publisher Nicolai, the journalist Mylius, and the dramatist Lessing all spent time living here. Moses and Fromet Mendelssohn moved into the three-story, 17th-century building after their wedding on June 22, 1762.

The neighborhood around Spandauer Strasse was home to various milieus and religions. Karl Wilhelm Ramler, a writer and friend of Moses, also lived in the area, as did the parents of the future composer Meyerbeer. Rahel Levin (married name: Varnhagen) was born nearby. Around the corner, on Bischofstrasse, was the Bernhard silk factory, where Mendelssohn worked. In the house at Spandauer Strasse 68, the couple lived together with their children, Brendel, Recha, Joseph, Jette, Abraham, and Nathan, with Fromet's stepmother, Vogel Gugenheim, and three tutors, the mathematicians Abraham Wolff and Moses Metz Ensheim and the Hebrew poet Hartwig Wessely. In this house, Moses collaborated on translation projects and led discussions about reforms. Visitors seeking advice, friends, and intellectual sparring partners came and went; among them many fellow Jews but also a pastor's daughter, a monk in crisis, and Christian allies. The house became a hub for Enlightenment thinkers and a laboratory of German-Jewish friendship. After the patriarch's death, this textile merchant's second office was the starting point of the Mendelssohn bank.

The eldest son, Joseph, sold the property around 1800 to family friends, the Veits, before he moved to Hamburg. Later it was owned by the Lessing and Lesser families. In 1886, a hotel complex was built on the site. It was torn down after World War II. The marble plaque dedicated to Mendelssohn remains preserved above the door. The Israeli sculptor Micha Ullman designed a monument for the historic lot at the corner of Karl-Liebknecht-Strasse and Spandauer Strasse to commemorate this unique site of the Berlin Enlightenment.

Wenige Schritte von der gotischen Marienkirche, im dicht bebauten Alt-Berlin, steht das Haus Spandauer Straße 68. Vor 1762 wohnten hier zeitweise der Verleger Nicolai, der Publizist Mylius, der Dramatiker Lessing. Nach ihrer Hochzeit am 22. Juni 1762 beziehen Moses und Fromet Mendelssohn das dreistöckige Gebäude aus dem 18. Jahrhundert.

Um die Spandauer Straße erstreckt sich ein Quartier diverser Milieus und Religionen. Hier lebt auch Karl Wilhelm Ramler, ein Schriftsteller-Freund von Moses, hier steht das Elternhaus des späteren Komponisten Meyerbeer, hier wird Rahel Levin (verheiratet: Varnhagen) geboren. Um die Ecke, in der Bischofstraße, liegt die Seidenfabrik Bernhard, der Arbeitsplatz Mendelssohns. In der Spandauer Straße 68 lebt das Ehepaar mit den Kindern Brendel, Recha, Joseph, Jette, Abraham und Nathan, mit Fromets Stiefmutter Vogel Gugenheim und den Hauslehrern, den Mathematikern Abraham Wolff und Moses Metz Ensheim, dem hebräischen Dichter Hartwig Wessely. Hier realisiert Moses im Team Übersetzungsprojekte, leitet Diskussionen über Reformen. Ratsuchende, Freunde, intellektuelle Sparringspartner gehen ein und aus; Glaubensgenossen, auch eine Pfarrerstochter, ein Mönch in der Krise, christliche Mitstreiter. Das Haus wird zum Treffpunkt für Aufklärer, zum Labor jüdisch-deutscher Freundschaften. Nach dem Tod des Stammvaters entwickeln sich hier, wo der Textilkaufmann sein zweites Büro hatte, Anfänge des Bankhauses Mendelssohn.

Die Immobilie verkauft der Älteste Joseph im Jahr 1800, vor seinem Wegzug nach Hamburg, den befreundeten Veits. Später gelangt sie in den Besitz der Familien Lessing und Lesser. 1886 entsteht auf dem Gelände des Hauses ein Hotelkomplex, der nach dem II. Weltkrieg abgerissen wird. Erhalten ist die marmorne Gedenktafel an Mendelssohn über dem Türsturz. Zur Erinnerung an diesen einzigartigen Ort der Berliner Aufklärung hat der israelische Bildhauer Micha Ullman für die historische Parzelle an der Ecke Karl-Liebknecht-Straße / Spandauer Straße ein Denkmal entworfen.

Haus Spandauer Straße 68 (später 33), vor 1886.
Spandauer Strasse 68 (later 33), before 1886.

Silhouetten von Brendel, Joseph und Abraham Mendelssohn, aus einem Stammbucheintrag Mendelssohns für den Hauslehrer Herz Homberg.

Silhouettes of Brendel, Joseph and Abraham Mendelssohn from an entry for the Mendelssohns in the family album of the tutor Herz Homberg.

Die Erbfolge der Mendelssohn-Kinder wird 1789 in das Hypothekenbuch eingetragen.

The order of succession for Mendelssohn's heirs is entered into the mortgage register in 1789.

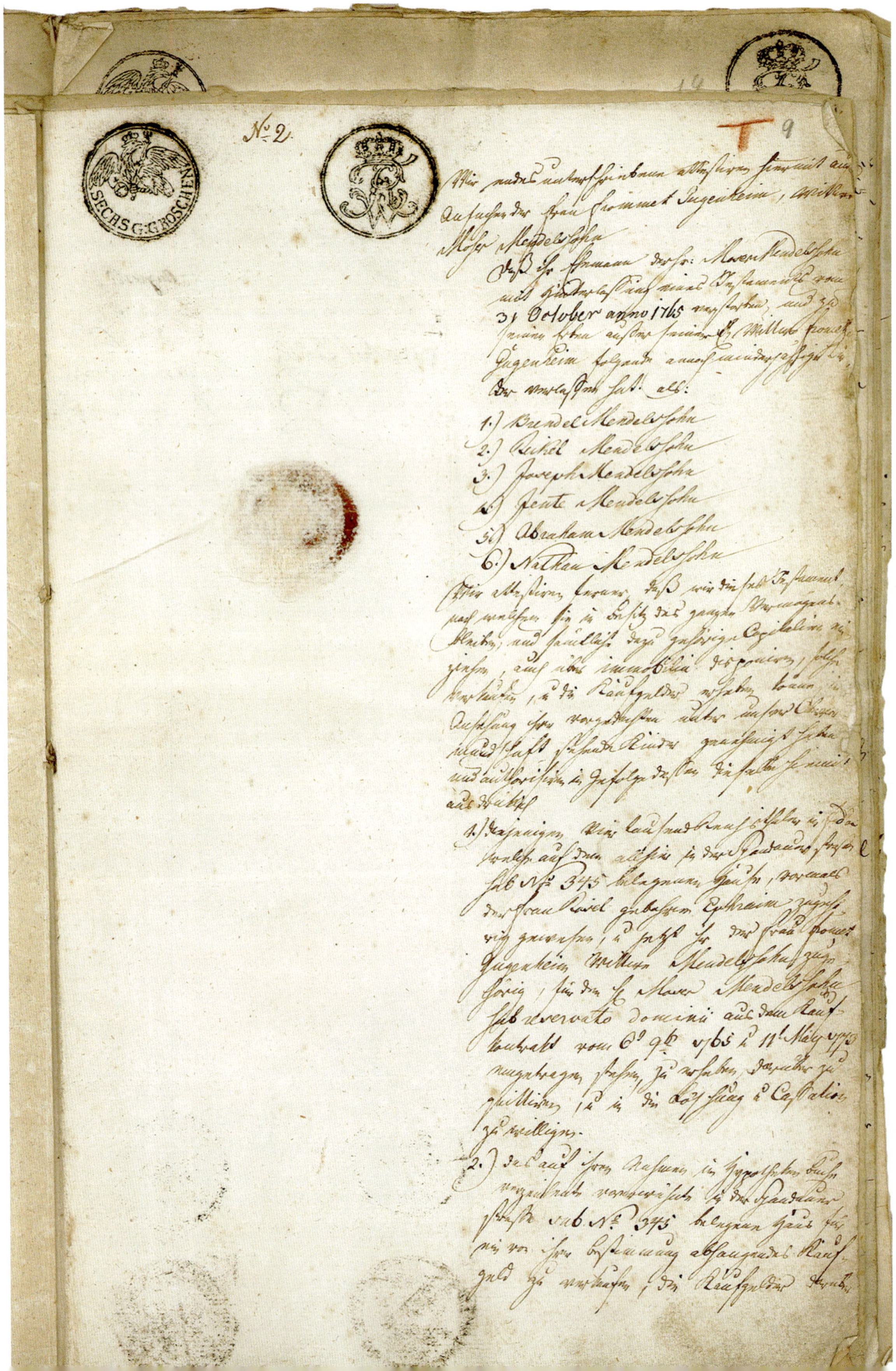

SECHS G: GROSCHEN

No 2

1.) Brendel Mendelssohn
2.) Reikel Mendelssohn
3.) Joseph Mendelssohn
4.) Jente Mendelssohn
5.) Abraham Mendelssohn
6.) Nathan Mendelssohn

Die zwei Meter breite Marmortafel wurde 1829, zum 100. Geburtstag Moses Mendelssohns, über dem Türsturz des Hauses Spandauer Straße 68 angebracht. Zu dieser Zeit war es noch unüblich, Denkmäler und Gedenksteine für bürgerliche Personen aufzustellen.

The marble plaque, two meters wide, was mounted above the door lintel of the building at Spandauer Strasse 68 to commemorate the 100th birthday of Moses Mendelssohn in 1829. In those days, it was still quite unusual to devote memorial stones or plaques to commoners.

Hypothekenvertrag Moses Mendelssohns von 1765: Beleihung der Spandauer Straße 68 mit 4000 Reichstalern.

Mortgage agreement of Moses Mendelssohn from 1765: Mortgage in the amount of 4,000 Reichstaler for Spandauer Strasse 68.

Joseph Mendelssohn · 1770 Berlin – 1848 Berlin

When Joseph Mendelssohn was born in Berlin, Jewish families still had to pay special taxes for the "addition" of a second son. Yet when the many-faceted philanthropist and respected banker died, his company Mendelssohn & Co. had long become one of the Prussian state's most important business partners.

His father had taught Joseph, together with his older brother Mendel Abraham, who only lived to the age of six, and involved him in the Torah translation project. He also took part in workshop discussions "on the existence of God" (1785). In 1791, still employed as a bookkeeper by Itzig's company, he was member of a circle of young followers of the Enlightenment, who strove to emulate his late father by their "Foundation 1791." In the following year, he and like-minded fellows initiated the "Society of Friends," a progressive alliance of young Jews who opposed reactionary interpretation of tradition in the Jewish community. He was the only son of Moses who did not leave the faith. He anonymously authored a biography of his father for an edition of the philosopher's works edited by his own son Georg Benjamin in 1843.

He never was able to become a scholar in his own right; Prussia only tolerated "useful" Jews. The banker did spend his gray years pursuing his hobby of philological studies and published his own research on Dante. He was respected by partners, competitors, and politicians as a strong and dependable business man. Between 1800 and 1811, he lived with his family in Hamburg, where he was soon joined by his business partner and younger brother Abraham and his family. They eventually returned to the Spree, fleeing from French customs. During the Napoleonic wars, their company, Mendelssohn & Co., expanded by engaging in dealings with the French occupiers of Europe, money transfers for Prussian occupation troops, and transactions related to French reparations. Away from the office, Joseph Mendelssohn was a philanthropist who enjoyed summers at his estate in the wine-making village of Horchheim near Koblenz.

In 1793, he had married Henriette Meyer of Neustrelitz, whose father Nathan had been a court agent in Mecklenburg and one of Moses Mendelssohn's best friends. Later, when he played the role of head of the family himself, a bitter conflict remained unreconciled; his partnership with Abraham ended after seventeen years in 1821 and they remained separated by an enduring tension. Still, his relatives considered the patriarch an exemplary educator and were impressed by his close relationships to both of his sons, Georg Benjamin and Alexander. While they chose different faiths, their relationship to their parents and to one another remained strong.

Als Joseph Mendelssohn in Berlin geboren wird, müssen jüdische Familien für das „Ansetzen" ihres zweiten Sohnes noch Sondersteuern zahlen. Als der vielfältige Stifter und angesehene Bankchef stirbt, ist seine Firma Mendelssohn & Co. längst zum wichtigen Geschäftspartner für den preußischen Staat geworden.

Gemeinsam mit dem älteren Mendel Abraham, der nur sechs Jahre alt werden sollte, war Joseph durch den Vater unterrichtet, in das Projekt Thora-Übersetzung einbezogen worden. Auch an den Werkstatt-Gesprächen „über das Daseyn Gottes" (1785) hatte er teilgenommen. 1791 gehört er, noch als Buchhalter der Firma Itzig, zu einem Zirkel von Aufklärungsjüngern, die mit ihrer „Stiftung 1791" dem Vorbild seines verstorbenen Vaters nacheifern. Im Folgejahr initiieren er und Gesinnungsgenossen die „Gesellschaft der Freunde", einen Fortschrittsbund junger Juden, der sich zum Schulterschluß gegen rückschrittliche Traditionsauslegung zusammenfindet. Als einziger Sohn des Moses verläßt Joseph die Synagoge nicht. Für eine Werkausgabe des Vaters, die sein Sohn Georg Benjamin 1843 ediert, verfaßt er anonym die Biographie des Philosophen.

Gelehrter hatte er nicht werden dürfen, Preußen duldete nur „nützliche" Juden. Seinem philologischen Hobby geht der ergraute Bankier in späten Jahren noch nach, publiziert eigene Dante-Forschungen. Unter Partnern, Konkurrenten und Politikern respektiert man ihn als starken, verläßlichen Kaufmann. 1800 bis 1811 leben er und bald auch sein Kompagnon, der jüngere Bruder Abraham, samt ihren Familien in Hamburg. Auf der Flucht vor dem französischen Zoll sind sie schließlich an die Spree zurückgekehrt. Ihr Mendelssohn-Bankhaus expandiert während der Napoleonischen Kriege: durch Geschäfte mit Europas französischen Besatzern, durch Geldtransfers für die preußischen Besatzungstruppen, beim Abwickeln französischer Reparationen. Abseits des Kontors weiß Joseph als Wohltäter und Sommerfrischler auf seinem Gut im Weinbauerndorf Horchheim bei Koblenz das Leben zu genießen.

Geheiratet hatte er 1793 Henriette Meyer aus Neustrelitz, deren Vater Nathan, Hofagent in Mecklenburg, einer der besten Freunde Moses Mendelssohns ist. Später, als Joseph selbst den Familienchef gibt, bleibt ein bitterer privater Konflikt für ihn ungelöst: Seine siebzehnjährige Sozietät mit Abraham endet 1821, die Spannung der ungleichen Brüder dauert weiter an. Zugleich beeindruckt der Patriarch die Verwandtschaft als Erzieher, durch seine innige Beziehung zu beiden Söhnen, Georg Benjamin und Alexander. Deren Konfessionswege trennen sich, ohne daß ihre Eintracht mit den Eltern und untereinander zerbricht.

Joseph Mendelssohn (1770 – 1848), Bankier. Grisaille.
Joseph Mendelssohn (1770 – 1848), banker. Grisaille.

Stiftungsring (1791).

Foundation ring (1791).

Henriette Mendelssohn,
geb. Meyer (1776 – 1862).
Öl auf Leinwand.

Henriette Mendelssohn,
née Meyer (1776 – 1862).
Oil on canvas.

Alexander Mendelssohn (1798 – 1871).
Pastell von Franz Krüger.

Alexander Mendelssohn (1798 – 1871).
Pastel by Franz Krüger.

Georg Benjamin Mendelssohn (1794 – 1874).
Pastell (um 1850).

Georg Benjamin Mendelssohn (1894 – 1874).
Pastel (c. 1850).

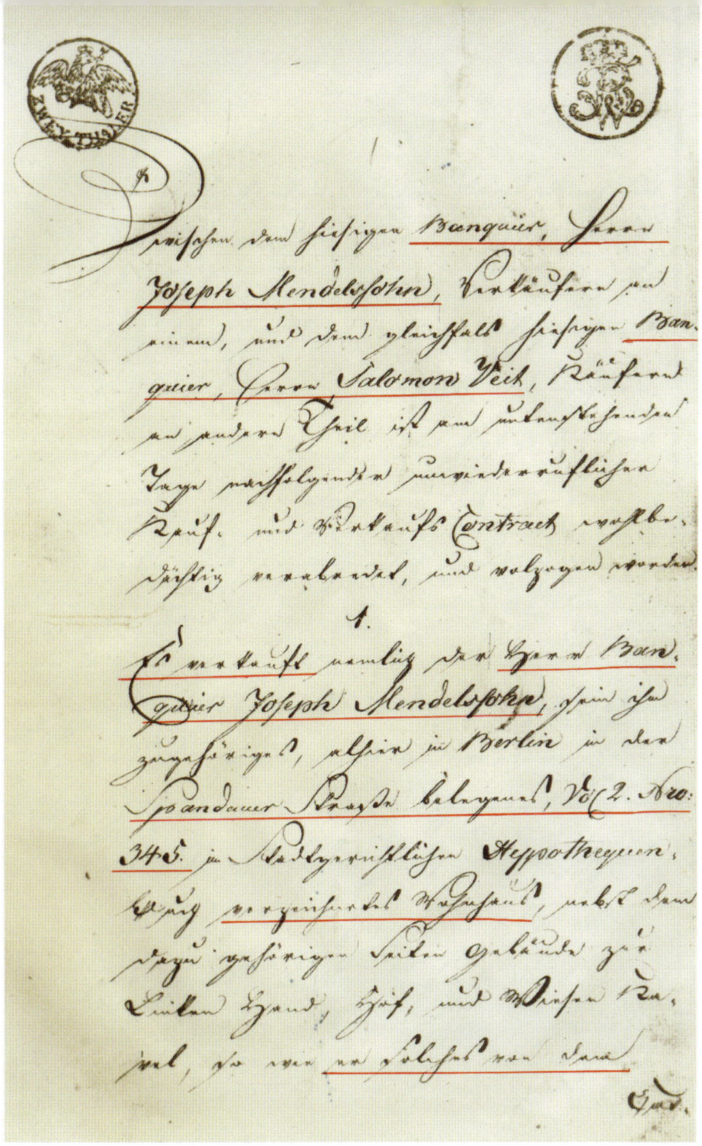

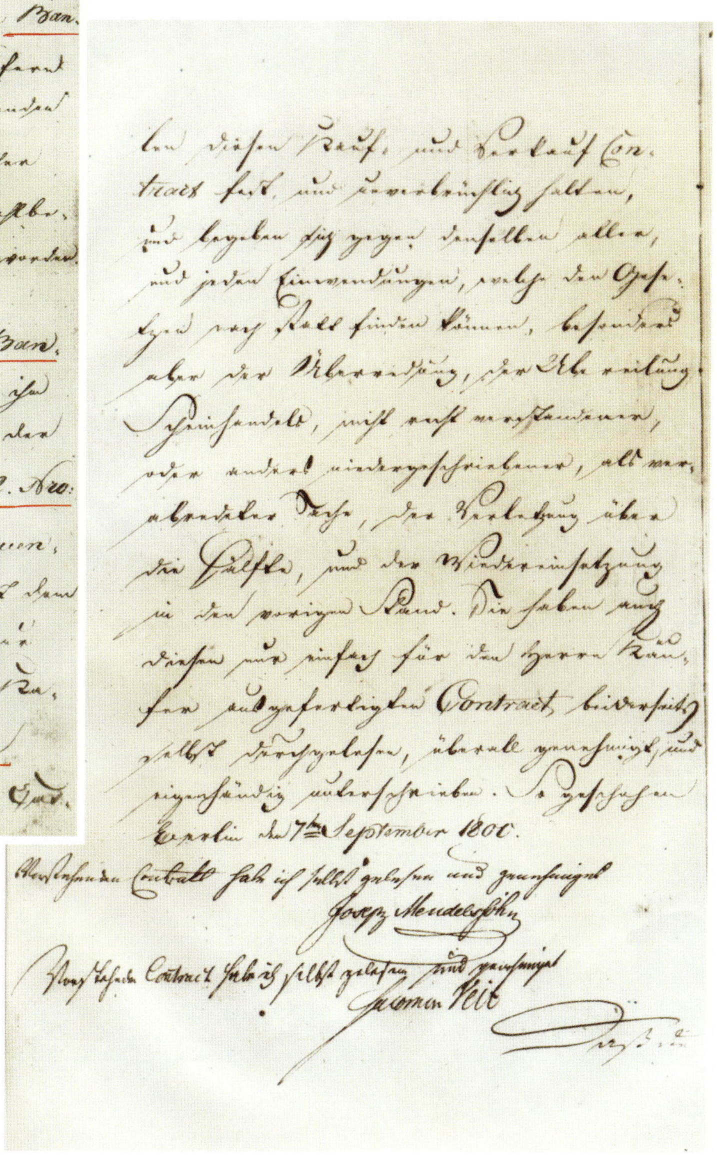

Vertrag zum Verkauf des Hauses Spandauer Straße an Salomon Veit, 7. September 1800.

Contract for the sale of the house at Spandauer Strasse 68 to Salomon Veit, dated September 7, 1800.

Das rechte Rheinufer in Horchheim bei Koblenz mit dem Gutshaus Joseph Mendelssohns.

The right bank of the Rhine in Horchheim near Koblenz and the manor house of Joseph Mendelssohn.

Die beiden Pädagogen.

Ouverture.

in einem Act.

Exkurs · Erzieherinnen und Pädagogik in den Familien Mendelssohn und Hensel
Educators and Pedagogy in the Mendelssohn and Hensel Families

Two of Moses and Fromet's daughters earned their livings as educators. One of Mendelssohn's contacts was Johann Basedow, who directed a school in Dessau with the mission of molding useful young people in the spirit of the Enlightenment. Mendelssohn was an adviser to the Berlin Jewish Free School *(Freyschule)*, which imparted knowledge and values to children of various religions and social milieus. The young Felix Mendelssohn's musical comedy mocking "Die beiden Pädagogen" (The Two Pedagogues), hints at the fact that Basedow's concept of social utility and Pestalozzi's concept of an empathetic approach to educating the individual were the topic of considerable debate and discussion within the families of Moses' sons.

Fromet's favorite daughter Recha (1767 – 1831) moved from Strelitz to Altona after the marriage arranged by her father ended in divorce. In Altona, she operated an educational institution for Jewish girls located on the Palmaille with support from her daughter Betty (1793 – 1850). Jette (1775 – 1831), who is said to have resembled her misshapen father (no image of her exists), rejected the overtures of admirers and chose to become a governess. She began her pedagogical career as a lady's companion in Vienna and then lived with her brother Abraham in a rear courtyard building of their employer, Fould. She hosted salons and began providing daycare for a group of girls, whom she fed and educated. She was tortured by loneliness, as her intimate letters to Karl August Varnhagen von Ense attest. In 1812, she converted to Catholicism and took the name Henriette Maria in order to work for a rich general. She became a devout Catholic. However, it is said that both she and her sister Recha took the Enlightenment ideals of their father to heart.

Luise Hensel (1798 – 1876), the most beautiful sister of the pastor's son Wilhelm Hensel, turned down proposals of marriage from the poets Clemens Brentano and Wilhelm Müller, the composer Ludwig Berger, and Ernst Ludwig Gerlach, who would later become Bismarck's teacher, to devote her life to Christ as a Catholic convert. Her spiritual influence on her brother Wilhelm irritated his future in-laws, the Mendelssohns. Luise sought and found a succession of new charity projects: the construction of a hospital in Coblenz, education and nursing work in Aachen, Cologne, Dresden, and Paderborn. She cared for her mother in the house of the Mendelssohn Bartholdy and Hensel family. Her poems "Müde bin ich, geh zur Ruh" (I am tired, now I rest) are better known than those of her sister Minna (1802 – 1893), who ran an orphanage at the Elisabethstift in Pankow from 1851 to 1876, for which she received Medal of the Order of Louise.

Zwei Töchter von Moses und Fromet werden Erzieherinnen, um ihren Lebensunterhalt zu verdienen. Mit Johann Basedow, der an einer Dessauer Schule im Sinne der Aufklärung nützliche junge Menschen formt, ist Mendelssohn in Kontakt. Die Berliner Freyschule, in der Kinder verschiedener Religionen und Milieus Wissen und Werte vermittelt bekommen, wird durch ihn beraten. Daß später in den Familien seiner Söhne Basedows Nützlichkeits-Konzept und Pestalozzis einfühlsame Individualerziehung kontrovers diskutiert werden, läßt das spöttische Singspiel des jungen Felix Mendelssohn „Die beiden Pädagogen“ vermuten.

Fromets Lieblingstochter Recha (1767 – 1831) zieht, nachdem ihre durch den Vater arrangierte Heirat mit Scheidung endet, von Strelitz nach Altona: um dort auf der Palmaille, unterstützt von Tochter Betty (1793 – 1850), ein Erziehungsinstitut für jüdische Mädchen zu betreiben. Jette (1775 – 1831), die ihrem verwachsenen Vater ähnlich sehen soll (ein Bild existiert nicht), weist Verehrer-Anträge ab, wählt den Gouvernanten-Beruf: Sie beginnt ihre pädagogische Laufbahn als Gesellschafterin in Wien, wohnt in Paris mit dem Bruder Abraham im Hinterhof des gemeinsamen Arbeitgebers Fould, wird zur Salon-Gastgeberin und sammelt als Tagesmutter Mädchen um sich, die sie versorgt und bildet. Einsamkeit quält sie, was ihre innigen Briefe an Karl August Varnhagen von Ense zeigen. Als Henriette Maria konvertiert sie 1812 zur katholischen Kirche, um im Haus eines reichen Generals angestellt zu werden, entwickelt sich dabei zur überzeugten Katholikin. Doch heißt es von ihr wie von Recha, beide Töchter hätten das Aufklärungsideal ihres Vaters verinnerlicht.

Luise Hensel (1798 – 1876), die schönste Schwester des Pastorensohns Wilhelm Hensel, gibt den Dichtern Clemens Brentano und Wilhelm Müller, dem Komponisten Ludwig Berger und Ernst Ludwig Gerlach, dem späteren Lehrer Bismarcks, einen Korb: um als katholische Konvertitin das eigene Leben dem Bräutigam Christus zu weihen. Ihr spiritueller Einfluß auf den Bruder Wilhelm irritiert dessen künftige Schwiegereltern Mendelssohn. Luise sucht und findet immer neue karitative Projekte: beim Aufbau eines Krankenhauses in Koblenz, bei Erziehungs- und Pflegeaufgaben in Aachen, Köln, Dresden, Paderborn. Im Haus der Familien Mendelssohn Bartholdy und Hensel pflegt sie ihre Mutter. Ihre Dichtungen („Müde bin ich, geh zur Ruh“) sind bekannter als die Verse ihrer ebenfalls poetisch aktiven Schwester Minna (1802 – 1893), die von 1851 bis 1876 im Elisabethstift in Pankow ein Waisenhaus leitet und dafür mit dem Luisenorden ausgezeichnet wird.

Overtüre und Streitgesang „Pestalozzi“ contra „Basedow“ aus: „Die beiden Pädagogen“, Singspiel von Felix Menddelssohn (1821) nach Eugène Scribes Komödie „Les deux Précepteurs“.

Overture and a debate set to song, "Pestalozzi" vs. "Basedow" from: "Die beiden Pädagogen" (The Two Pedagogues), musical comedy by Felix Mendelssohn (1821) based on Eugène Scribe's comedy "Les deux Précepteurs."

Henriette (Maria) Mendelssohn am 1. August 1818 aus Viry an ihre Schwägerin Lea Mendelssohn Bartholdy in Berlin:
„ ... Fanny's Meisterstück 24 Präludien auswendig zu lernen und Ihre Beharrlichkeit sie einstudiren zu lassen, haben mich starr und stumm vor Erstaunen gemacht und ich habe nur die Sprache wiedergefunden, um allen Menschen dies ungeheure Gelingen mitzutheilen. Nachdem ich aber Ihnen und Fanny meine ungetheilte Bewunderung zuerkannt, muß ich doch gestehn daß ich das Unternehmen strafbar finde, die Anstrengung ist zu groß ..."

Henriette (Maria) Mendelssohn, writing from Viry to her in-law Lea Mendelssohn Bartholdy in Berlin on August 1, 1818:
"... Learning to play Fanny's masterpiece *24 Preludes* from memory and her insistence that I do so have left me speechless and astonished. I have only regained the power of speech to tell the world of this incredible accomplishment. Now that I have expressed my unreserved admiration to you and Fanny, however, I must admit that I found the undertaking punishing. The strain is too great..."

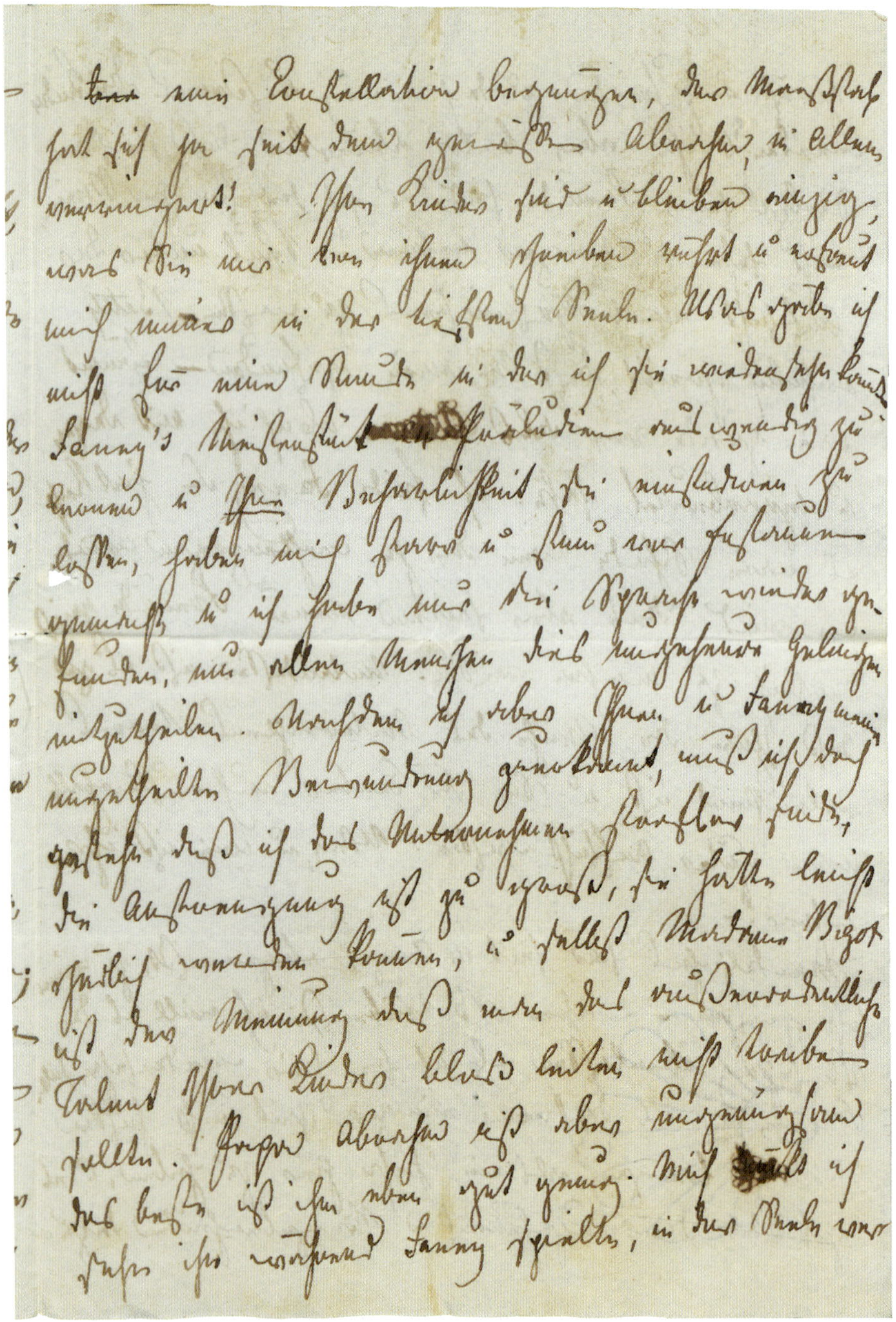

Recha Meyer, geb. Mendelssohn. Gouache (um 1790).
Recha Meyer, née Mendelssohn. Gouache (c. 1790).

Betty Beer, geb. Meyer. Stich von E. Meyer (1852).
Betty Beer, neé Meyer. Engraving by E. Meyer (1852).

Luise Hensel. Zeichnung von Wilhelm Hensel, Bleistift auf Karton (1828).

Luise Hensel. Drawing by Wilhelm Hensel, pencil on cardboard (1828).

Elisabethstift in Pankow zur Zeit Minna Hensels.

The Elisabethstift in Pankow during the time of Minna Hensel.

Minna Hensel, Zeichnung von Wilhelm Hensel (1819).

Minna Hensel, drawing by Wilhelm Hensel (1819).

Abraham Mendelssohn (Bartholdy) · 1776 Berlin – 1835 Berlin

"I used to by my father's son, but now I am my son's father." That is how Moses' middle son summed up his own identity dilemma and the conflicts that shaped his life.

He was born in 1776, the second-to-last of six surviving children. He was nine years old when his father died. A half-orphan, Abraham Moses Mendelssohn found a sense of belonging at the home of the composer and mason Karl Friedrich Zelter. At sixteen, he was a member of Zelter's *Sing-Akademie*, which performed Christian sacred music. Along with his brother Joseph, he allied himself to the Jewish "Society of Friends." He would like to have become a singer. In Paris, he learned the banking trade and became an opera fan. He returned to Berlin as his brother's new business partner because Lea Salomon, a granddaughter of the court banker Itzig, would not marry him as a mere employee. The couple spent the early years of their marriage in Hamburg, and their first children were born there. For a decade, he contemplated how best to protect his family from discrimination. Should they emigrate to France? Should they convert? His mother-in-law was opposed to both options. In 1816, he had his children baptized, and in 1821 he withdrew from the long-standing business partnership with his Jewish brother. In 1822, he and his wife Lea converted in Frankfurt (Main). Henceforth, his name was Abraham Ernst Mendelssohn Bartholdy.

History would remember the passionate father, difficult head of the household, and luckless businessman for his engagement in the education of his two child prodigies and the financing of their house concerts. He was also criticized by later generations for discouraging his daughter, Fanny, from pursuing a career as a professional musician. One disturbing document that illustrates how he strove to assimilate and struggled with his own father's long shadow is a letter forming part of the "name dispute" in which he urges his son, Felix, his beloved *alter ego*, to drop the name Mendelssohn and go by Bartholdy alone. "With the name of Mendelssohn, you are a Jew *eo ipso*, and that will not help you at all, for one because it is not true." He died in 1835 at the age of 58 as an unpaid city official in charge of care for the poor. He was the first descendant of Moses to be buried in the Trinity Cemetery.

„Früher war ich der Sohn meines Vaters, jetzt bin ich der Vater meines Sohnes." So hat der mittlere Sohn des Moses seine Identitätsfrage und eigene Lebenskonflikte auf den Punkt gebracht.

Geboren wird er 1776 als vorletztes von sechs überlebenden Kindern. Als der Vater stirbt, ist er neun. Im Haus des Komponisten und Maurers Karl Friedrich Zelter findet Abraham Moses Mendelssohn, der Halbwaise, Anschluß. Mit sechzehn gehört er zu Zelters Sing-Akademie, die christliche Sakralmusik pflegt. Mit dem Bruder Joseph verkehrt er in der jüdischen Gesellschaft der Freunde. Gern wäre er wohl Sänger geworden. In Paris lernt er das Bankgeschäft, wird zum Opernfan. Nach Berlin kehrt er als neuer Teilhaber seines Bruders zurück: weil Lea Salomon, eine Enkelin des Hoffinanziers Itzig, ihn als Angestellten nicht heiraten würde. In Hamburg, wo das Paar erste Ehejahre verbringt, werden seine ersten Kinder geboren. Ein Jahrzehnt lang erwägt er, wie die Familie vor Diskriminierung zu bewahren wäre: durch Emigration nach Frankreich? Durch Glaubenswechsel? Schwiegermutter Bella Salomon lehnt beides ab. 1816 läßt er seine Kinder taufen, 1821 verläßt er die Sozietät mit dem jüdischen Bruder. 1822 konvertiert er selbst mit seiner Frau Lea in Frankfurt (Main), heißt nun Abraham Ernst Mendelssohn Bartholdy.

Die Nachwelt wird den leidenschaftlichen Vater, schwierigen Hausherrn und glücklosen Geschäftsmann als engagierten Erzieher zweier Wunderkinder und Finanzier ihrer Hauskonzerte würdigen, aber seine Abwehr einer Profi-Karriere für Tochter Fanny kritisieren. Als verstörendes Dokument seiner Assimilations-Bemühung und seiner Auseinandersetzung mit dem Schatten des Vaters hinterläßt er den Brief zum „Namensstreit", die Aufforderung an Felix, sein geliebtes Alter ego, sich nur noch Bartholdy zu nennen: „Heißt du Mendelssohn so bist du eo ipso ein Jude, und das taugt dir nichts, schon weil es nicht wahr ist." Der 1835 mit 58 Jahren am Schlaganfall verstorbene, unbesoldete Stadtrat für Armenpflege ruht in einem Ehrengrab, als erster Nachkomme des Moses auf dem Dreifaltigkeitsfriedhof.

Abraham Mendelssohn Bartholdy (1829).
Zeichnung von Wilhelm Hensel.

Abraham Mendelssohn Bartholdy (1829).
Drawing by Wilhelm Hensel.

Neumühlen mit Martensmühle (1845).
Kolorierte Lithographie. Sommerwohnsitz der Familie Abraham Mendelssohn in Hamburg.
Hier wurde Felix gezeugt und vom Vater im Kinderwagen geschoben.

Neumühlen with the Martens Mill (1845).
Color lithograph. Summer residence of Abraham Mendelssohn's family in Hamburg.
Felix was conceived here and pushed in a pram by his father.

Abraham Mendelssohn Bartholdy beim Kartenspiel. Zeichnung von Wilhelm Hensel.

Abraham Mendelssohn Bartholdy playing cards. Drawing by Wilhelm Hensel.

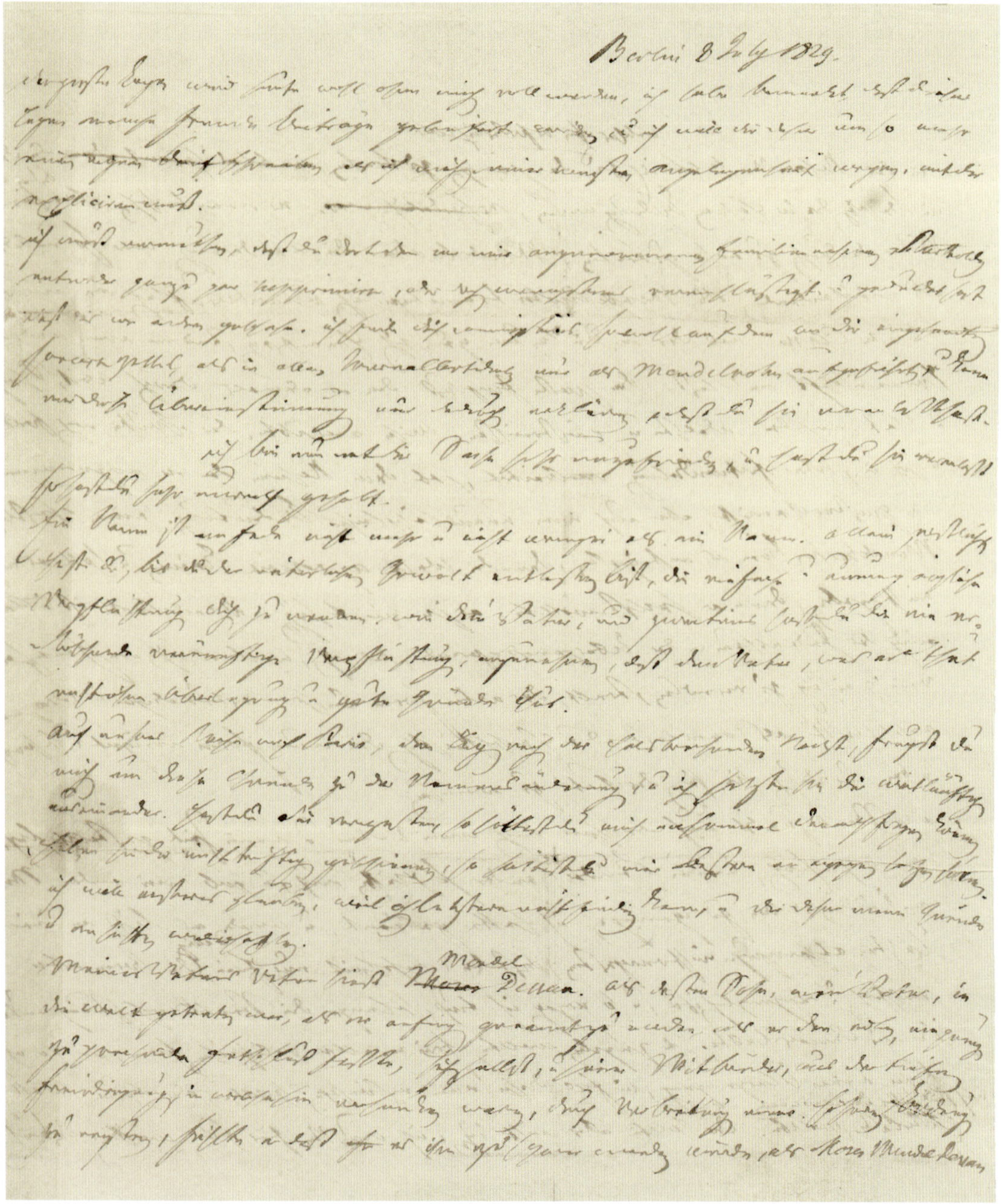

Berlin 8 July 1829.

Brief zum Namensstreit mit dem Sohn Felix, 8. Juli 1829.

Letter to his son Felix addressing the "name dispute," July 8, 1829.

Recksches Palais, Leipziger Straße 3,
ab 1825 Wohnsitz der Mendelssohn Bartholdys.

Recksches Palais, Leipziger Strasse 3,
Residence of the Mendelssohn Bartholdys beginning in 1825.

Pendule. Geschenk des Vaters zur Hochzeit von
Fanny und Wilhelm Hensel am 3. Oktober 1829.

Pendant. A gift to Fanny and Wilhelm Hensel from
Fanny's father on their wedding day, October 3, 1829.

Nathan Mendelssohn · 1781 Berlin – 1852 Berlin
Arnold Mendelssohn · 1817 Neiße – 1854 Bayazid (Türkei)

Of all the Mendelssohns, Nathan possessed the greatest technical talent. From the minor principality of Strelitz, where he had moved with his widowed mother, he left to pursue his education in London and Paris. He returned to Berlin and established a workshop for the manufacture of scientific instruments that won the endorsement of no less a figure than Alexander von Humboldt. Nathan's plans to establish himself as a weapons manufacturer in France, and later East Prussia, never came to fruition. During the wars of liberation against Napoleon, Lieutenant Mendelssohn was in demand as an adviser to arms makers. After his departure from the army, he launched a mining project in Bad Reinerz, which failed. His banker brothers invested to save the project, to no avail. The creative inventor had to feed his family somehow, so he took work as a tax official in Silesia and later as an auditor in Berlin. On the side, he founded a polytechnic society and registered foreign patents in Prussia.

In 1809, Nathan and his wife Henriette Hitzig of the Itzig family were baptized. Seven of their children died young. Their daughter Ottilie married the mathematician Eduard Kummer, and their son Wilhelm became a railroad machinist.

Their eldest surviving son, Arnold, took piano lessons from his cousin, Felix, studied medicine, and treated the poor in Berlin's slums. Inspired by his rich, socialist-oriented friend Ferdinand Lassalle, he became a radical salon communist, which devastated his loyalist father. A theft he committed for a client of Lassalle's made him a wanted criminal.In 1848, the year of the revolution, the courts decided to make an example of him. Humboldt vouched for him with the King, who commuted the sentence of the black sheep of the Mendelssohn family from imprisonment to exile. He spent his exile years in the Near East, working as a mountain doctor in Lebanon and founding a hospital in Jerusalem. He converted to Catholicism to win support from the Latin Patriarch of Jerusalem. Finally, he became a physician in the Ottoman military and reported on the Crimean War for English and German papers in his "Levantine Letters." Then, he succumbed to a typhus infection. The exact location of his grave, "at the foot of Mount Ararat" (Ferdinand Lassalle) is unknown.

Nathan ist das technische Talent der Mendelssohns. Aus dem Zwergfürstentum Strelitz, wohin er mit seiner verwitweten Mutter gezogen war, bricht er auf zu Bildungsreisen nach London und Paris. Für die Werkstatt des nach Berlin zurückgekehrten Instrumentenbauers macht Alexander von Humboldt Reklame. Pläne Nathans, sich in Frankreich oder später in Ostpreußen als Waffenfabrikant zu etablieren, scheitern. Während der Befreiungskriege gegen Napoleon ist Leutnant Mendelssohn als Berater für Rüstungsschmieden gefragt. Nach dem Abschied aus der Armee beginnt er ein Bergbauprojekt in Bad Reinerz, das durch Investitionen der Bankiersbrüder nicht zu retten ist. Der kreative Erfinder muß irgendwie seine Familie ernähren, als Steuerbeamter in Schlesien, als Stempelrevisor in Berlin. Nebenher gründet er eine Polytechnische Gesellschaft, meldet ausländische Patente für Preußen an.

1809 hatte sich Nathan, wie seine Braut Henriette Hitzig aus der Itzig-Familie, taufen lassen. Sieben Kinder sterben früh. Tochter Ottilie heiratet den Mathematiker Eduard Kummer, Sohn Wilhelm wird Maschinist bei der Eisenbahn.

Der älteste Überlebende, Arnold, erhält Klavierstunden vom Cousin Felix, studiert Medizin, arbeitet in Berliner Slums als Armenarzt. Er radikalisiert sich als Salonkommunist, animiert durch den reichen, sozialistisch orientierten Freund Ferdinand Lassalle; zur Bestürzung seines staatstreuen Vaters. Sein Diebstahl für eine Mandantin Lassalles macht ihn zum gesuchten Kriminellen. Im Revolutionsjahr 1848 statuiert die Justiz an ihm ein Exempel. Auf Fürsprache von Humboldt wandelt der König die Zuchthausstrafe des schwarzen Schafs der Familie in Verbannung um. Im orientalischen Exil wirkt er als libanesischer Bergdoktor, als Krankenhausgründer in Jerusalem; wird katholisch, um die Unterstützung des Lateinischen Patriarchen zu erhalten. Zuletzt ist er osmanischer Militärarzt, berichtet in seinen „Levantischen Briefen" für deutsche und englische Blätter aus dem Krimkrieg. Dann eine Typhusinfektion. Sein Grab „am Fuß des Berges Ararat" (Ferdinand Lassalle) ist unbekannt.

Der junge Nathan Mendelssohn. Miniatur.
The young Nathan Mendelssohn. Miniature.

Bildnis eines Unbekannten (vermutlich Arnold Mendelssohn). Öl auf Leinwand von Philipp Veit.
Portrait of an unknown person (probably Arnold Mendelssohn). Oil on canvas by Philipp Veit.

Anzeige Alexander von Humboldts
für Nathan Mendelssohns Instrumente.
„Gilberts Annalen“ (1806).

Advertisement in which Alexander von Humboldt
endorses Nathan Mendelssohn's instruments.
"Gilbert's Annals," (1806).

[362]

IX.

ANZEIGE
astronomischer, geometrischer und physikalischer Instrumente.

Unter den mannigfaltigen Ursachen, welche im nördlichen Deutschland den Fortschritten des ausübenden Theils mathematischer Wissenschaften entgegen stehen, ist eine der grössten die Schwierigkeit, sich genaue astronomische und geometrische Instrumente zu verschaffen. Ich schmeichle mir in dieser Hinsicht, dem arbeitenden Theile des scientifischen Publicums einen nicht unangenehmen Dienst zu erweisen, wenn ich demselben anzeige, dass sich ein vortrefflicher Künstler, der in London und Paris sich unter vorzüglichen Meistern gebildet, Herr Nathan Mendelssohn, (Sohn des berühmten Moses Mendelssohn,) in Berlin niedergelassen hat. Seine Arbeiten bedürfen meiner Empfehlung nicht, und ich begnüge mich, in dieser Anzeige nur die Gegenstände zu nennen, auf welche dieser junge Künstler bereits in dem gegenwärtigen Zustande seiner Werkstatt Bestellungen annehmen kann.

a. Bordaische Multiplicationskreise von 4 bis 8 Zoll, mit achromatischen Fernröhren, nach Art derer, welche zur französischen, schwedischen und thüringischen Gradmessung gedient haben. Vierzöllige Kreise ohne Vernierschrauben kosten mit Stativ 15 Friedrichsd'or, mit den Vernierschrauben 20 Friedrichsd'or; dieselben mit silbernem Limbus von 30″ zu 30″ getheilt $24\frac{1}{2}$ Friedrichsd'or.

b. Teodolite von 4 bis 8 Zoll Durchmesser kosten von 15 bis 40 Friedrichsd'or.

Repoussé-Doppelgehäuse-Spindeluhr „des Vaters Moses Mendelssohn“ aus Nathans Nachlaß. Hergestellt von der Londoner Fa. Joseph Rose & Sons (1765 – 1784). Der Erfinder Nathan meldete selbst Patente zur Uhrenverbesserung an. Sein Sohn Arnold bat aus der Verbannung, ihm die Uhr des Moses zu vererben.

A verge watch in a repoussé double case that belonged to "Father, Moses Mendelssohn" from Nathan's estate. Manufactured by the London firm of Joseph Rose & Sons (1765 – 1784). An inventor, Nathan registered patents for the improvement of clocks himself. During his exile, Nathan's son Arnold asked him to bequeath Moses' watch to him.

Manifest Arnold Mendelssohns aus dem Gefängnis,
veröffentlicht im „Spartacus“, Juni 1849.

Arnold Mendelssohn's prison manifesto,
published in "Spartacus," June 1849.

Spartacus.

Wochenzeitung für sociale Fragen.

Beilage zur Neuen Bonner Zeitung.

Redigirt von J. Kinkel.

Nr. 23.	Montag den 18. Juni	1849.

„Tief und ernstlich denkende Menschen haben gegen das Publikum einen bösen Stand.“

Göthe.

m. Die Tauschbank.

Letzter Brief aus dem Gefängniß.*)

Bürger Kinkel! Noch einmal und vorläufig das letztemal muß ich Sie bitten, mir die Spalten Ihres Blattes zu meinen Aufsätzen zu leihen, weil mir grade nach dem Untergange der Proudhon'schen Volksbank, den ich beim Schluß meines letzten erfuhr und mittheilte, noch Einiges übrig bleibt zu sagen, was ich, da das Ende jener Bank für mich unerwartet kam, der Praxis überlassen zu müssen glaubte, während ich heut vorziehe, den Arbeitern, die ihr Blatt lesen, weil sie auf jenes Institut Hoffnungen setzten, jetzt auseinanderzusetzen, daß und wie unsre Ordnung auf den Prinzipien der Proudhon'schen Tausch- und Volksbank beruht, und daß trotzdem, daß jenes Institut aus was immer für einer Ursache aufgelöst worden ist, wir früher oder später darauf zurückkommen müssen, wenn wir die sociale Republik gründen wollen, die bei uns in dem alten übervölkerten Europa so nothwendig geworden ist, daß wir dießmal die Ehre haben werden den Amerikanern im Fortschritt vorauszugehen, nicht weil wir größere Talente zu Freiheit und Fortschritt hätten als sie, sondern weil die alte, bürgerliche Ordnung, die amerikanische Republik, aus Mangel an Land, welches unter dem alten Regime des Eigenthums, d. h. außerhalb der Association kultivirbar wäre, bei uns unmöglich geworden ist.

Uebrigens faßt Proudhon seine Verbannung, wie ich sehe, humoristisch genug auf, da er verspricht, als commis voyageur für die Volksbank im Ausland zu wirken. Ich möchte ihm zurufen, daß er in dieser Beziehung ganz ruhig sein kann, er hat commis voyageurs im Auslande, und wenn auch nicht Alle so klug wie er sind, einer festen Anstellung, wie man sie ihm in Paris zu geben beabsichtigte, aus dem Wege gegangen zu sein, so schadet das gar nichts, ein ordentlicher Commis weiß überall Geschäfte zu machen, sogar im Gefängniß; und überdieß will man ja nicht einmal in dem intelligenten Frankreich die Association friedlich einführen, die Herren Rentiers und Bourgeois haben nun einmal einen verwöhnten Magen, sie wollen den Revolutionsfisch nicht ohne Sauce essen; nun, sie werden Sauce bekommen; sie haben die Association nicht gratis haben wollen, jetzt werden sie, und zwar theuer, dafür bezahlen müssen.

Ich habe in meinem letzten Schreiben auseinandergesetzt, wie durch die Einführung des direkten Tausches zwischen den Producenten die Uebermacht des Kapitals als Geld, welche durch den Verkehr entstanden ist und täglich entsteht, zu Falle gebracht wird. Proudhon's Absicht war nun die, verschiedene Arbeiterassociationen mit einander durch den Tausch in Verbindung zu setzen, wozu sich natürlich die der sogenannten kleinen Industrie angehörigen am ersten eigneten, als da sind Bäcker, Köche, Schuster, Schneider, Tischler, Maurer u. s. f., weil grade die diesen Klassen angehörigen Arbeiter zusammen eine Körperschaft bildeten, in welcher sich die Mitglieder die ersten Lebensbedürfnisse zu dem „kostenden Preise“ garantirten. Zur Be-

*) Wir wünschen nicht, daß dieses überhaupt der letzte Brief unseres geehrten Mitarbeiters sei: aber der letzte aus dem Gefängniß ist es, denn in diesen Tagen hat er seine Freiheit erlangt. Die Red.

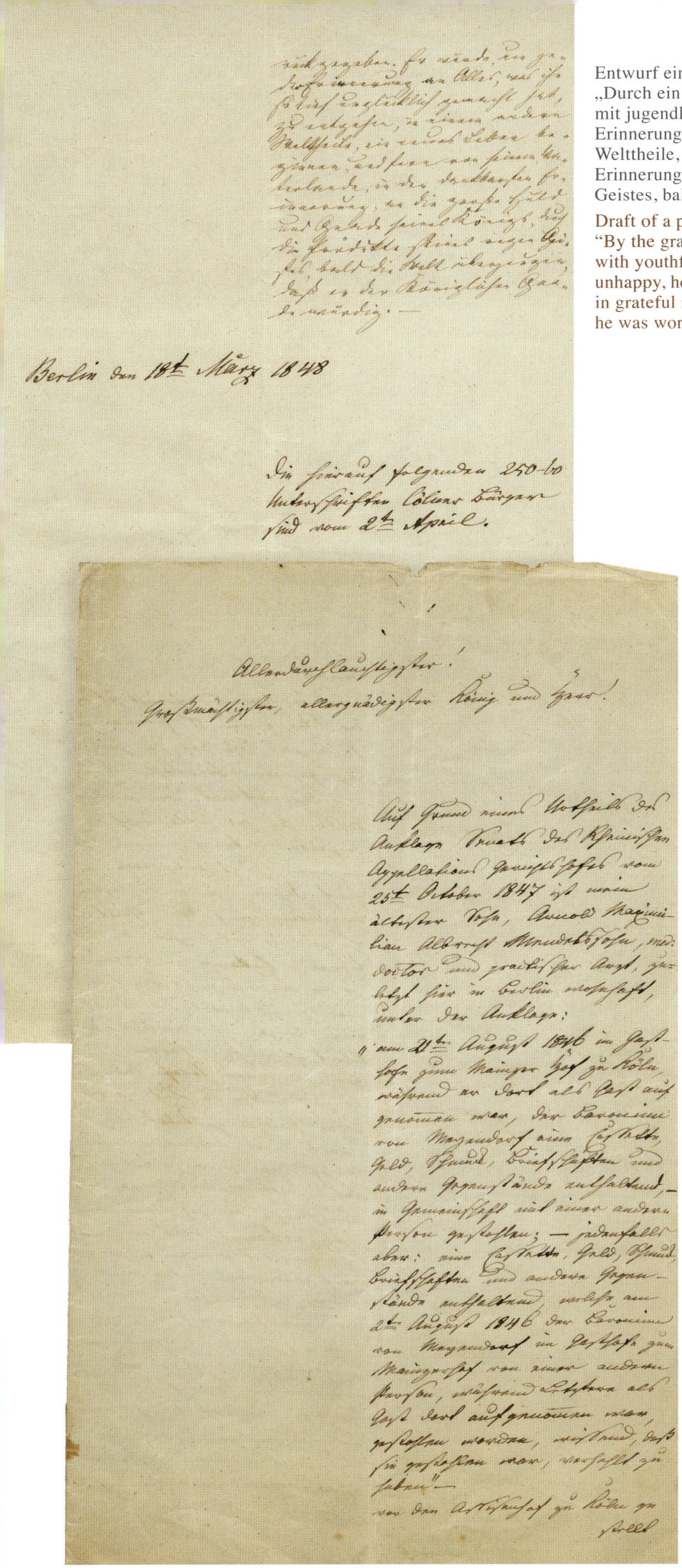

Entwurf eines Begnadigungsgesuchs Nathan Mendelssohns für seinen Sohn, 18. März 1848: „Durch ein huldreiches Königliches Wort, würde mein Sohn der Wissenschaft, für die er mit jugendlicher Begeisterung zu leben begonnen hatte, zurückgegeben. Er würde, um jeder Erinnerung an Alles, was ihn so tief unglücklich gemacht hat, zu entgehen, in einem andern Welttheile, ein neues Leben beginnen, und fern von seinem Vaterlande, in der dankbarsten Erinnerung, an die große Huld und Gnade seines Königs, durch die Produkte seines regen Geistes, bald die Welt überzeugen, daß er der Königlichen Gnade würdig."

Draft of a petition for pardon by Nathan Mendelssohn for his son, March 18, 1848: "By the grace of a royal decree, my son might be returned to science, for which he lived with youthful enthusiasm. In order to escape the memory of all that has made him so deeply unhappy, he would begin a new life in another part of the world, and, far from his fatherland, in grateful memory of the grace and mercy of his King, he would soon show the world that he was worthy of that royal grace through the inventions of his active mind."

Letztes Wohnhaus Nathan Mendelssohns, Johannisstraße 3 in Berlin. Foto von Karl Brandmann (1913).

The final residence of Nathan Mendelssohn at Johannisstrasse 3 in Berlin. Photo of Karl Brandmann (1913).

1842

Fanny Hensel, geb. Mendelssohn · 1805 Hamburg – 1847 Berlin

Fanny was the first sign of musical genius in the Mendelssohn family. Her mother Lea recognized immediately that his first-born possessed "Bach's fugue fingers." As a child, she practiced the piano so intensely that her relatives grew concerned. When the family moved to Berlin, she received musical training along with her brother, who was nicknamed "Cantor." For many years, she was her brother's artistic confidant. Nevertheless, her father seemed convinced that music should not become her profession. Felix also discouraged his sister: in order to be a professional composer, he warned, one may not simply compose now and again, but must regularly edit one's works. A pianist, conductor, impresaria, and the most important woman composer of the 19th century, Fanny became the *spiritus rector* of the Sunday Concerts whose beginnings could be traced back to her grandmother's home on Hackescher Markt around 1820. They continued (with interruptions) for nearly a quarter century in the Garden Hall of the *Reckscher Palais* on Leipziger Strasse.

Wilhelm Hensel, the dashing former soldier who had served in the Wars of Liberation, encouraged his wife not to give up her musical productivity to avoid private conflicts under any circumstances. The painter had met the 17-year-old Fanny at the court ball Lalla Rukh, where he was drawing portraits of Prussian high society in costume. Fanny, the ironic banker's daughter, and Wilhelm, a pastor's son with Catholic ambitions, came from very different milieus. In order to prevent Fanny from being infected by the penniless artist's "superstition," her parents insisted that they cut off contact for five years. During this time, the man still hoping to become their son-in-law was awarded a fellowship by the Prussian King to study in Rome, where he became associated with the artists of the Nazarene movement. When Fanny and Wilhelm were married on October 3, 1829 in the Berlin Parochialkirche, the Mendelssohn family was joined to a family without Jewish heritage for the first time without the bride and groom leaving Berlin as a consequence. Fanny, ever self-critical, played several demanding roles at once. She was a mother to her son Sebastian, a wife as well as back office to her artist husband, and a composer. Her husband's studio was next to the Garden Hall, where she presented Berlin's best private concert series featuring local and visiting artists for friends and high society. Her sudden death at a rehearsal for one of the Sunday Concerts was the first in a series of deaths that hit the family hard. The house and garden at Leipziger Strasse 3 were sold. It was the end of an era.

Mit ihr zeigt sich musikalisches Genie erstmals in der Mendelssohn-Familie. Fannys Mutter Lea erkennt an ihrer Erstgeborenen sofort „Bachsche Fugenfinger". So intensiv übt das Kind Klavier, daß die Verwandtschaft sich Sorgen macht. Musikerausbildung erhält sie, mit dem Umzug der Familie nach Berlin, wie ihr Bruder; für den stellt sie – Spitzname Kantor – über lange Zeit die künstlerische Vertrauensperson dar. Dennoch scheint der Vater überzeugt, daß Musik nicht ihr Beruf werden darf. Auch Felix bremst die Schwester: Um Profi-Komponist zu sein, müsse man mehr als ab und an regelmäßig Werke edieren. Die Pianistin, Dirigentin, Impresaria und bedeutendste Komponstin des 19. Jahrhunderts wird zum Spiritus rector jener Sonntagsmusiken, deren Anfänge bis ins Haus der Großmutter am Hackeschen Markt um 1820 zurückgehen; die (mit Unterbrechungen) fast ein Vierteljahrhundert im Gartensaal des Reckschen Palais an der Leipziger Straße fortgesetzt werden.

Wilhelm Hensel, der fesche ehemalige Befreiungskrieger, hatte schon seine Braut bestärkt, ihre musikalische Produktivität keinesfalls zur privaten Konfliktvermeidung aufzugeben. Begegnet waren sich die Siebzehnjährige und der Maler im Umfeld des Hoffestes Lalla Rookh, bei dem Hensel Preußens verkleidete High Society porträtiert. Die ironische Bankierstochter und der Pastorensohn mit katholischen Ambitionen kommen aus sehr verschiedenen Milieus. Damit Fanny nicht von dem „Aberglauben" des brotlosen Künstlers angesteckt werde, bestehen ihre Eltern auf einer fünfjährigen Kontaktsperre: In dieser Zeit kommt ihr Schwiegersohn in spe als römischer Stipendiat des preußischen Königs den Nazarener-Künstlern nahe. Mit der Heirat von Fanny und Wilhelm am 3. Oktober 1829 in der Berliner Parochialkirche verbinden sich erstmals Mendelssohns und eine Familie nichtjüdischer Herkunft: ohne daß die Getrauten in der Folge Berlin verlassen. Fanny, die Selbstkritische, erfüllt als Ehefrau und Mutter ihres Sohnes Sebastian sowie als *back office* ihres Künstlergatten und als Tonsetzerin mehrere strapaziöse Rollen zugleich. Neben dem Gartensaal, in dem sie für Freunde und die vornehme Gesellschaft, für die lokale und die durchreisende Künstler-Szene Berlins bestes privates Konzertprogramm realisiert, befindet sich das Atelier ihres Mannes. Ihr plötzlicher Tod bei der Probe zu einer Sonntagsmusik ist der Auftakt für weitere einschneidende familiäre Todesfälle; Haus und Garten Leipziger Straße 3 werden verkauft. Abschied von einer Epoche.

Fanny Hensel.
Öl auf Leinwand von Moritz Daniel Oppenheim (1842).

Fanny Hensel.
Oil on canvas by Moritz Daniel Oppenheim (1842).

Fanny und Felix Mendelssohns Hamburger Geburtshaus in der Großen Michaelis-Straße.

The house on Grosse Michaelis Strasse in Hamburg where Fanny and Felix Mendelssohn were born.

Fanny Hensel am Flügel. Skizze von Wilhelm Hensel.

Fanny Hensel at the piano. Sketch by Wilhelm Hensel.

Familiengruppe: Wilhelm, Fanny und Sebastian. Zeichnung von Wilhelm Hensel.

Family group: Wilhelm, Fanny and Sebastian. Drawing by Wilhelm Hensel.

In der Parochialkirche (Innenraum um 1884) heiratete Fanny Mendelssohn Bartholdy 1829, hier spielten sie und Bruder Felix Orgel.

Fanny Mendelssohn Bartholdy was married in the Parochialkirche (interior c. 1884) in 1829, where she and her brother Felix played organ.

„Musik für die Toten der Cholera-Epidemie“ (1833) von Fanny Hensel, No. 9. Trauerchor.

“Musik für die Toten der Cholera-Epidemie” (Music for the Dead of the Cholera Epidemic) (1833) by Fanny Hensel, No. 9. Funeral Chorus.

Fanny Hensel auf dem Totenbett. Bleistiftzeichnung auf Karton von Wilhelm Hensel (1847).

Fanny Hensel on her deathbed. Drawing by Wilhelm Hensel, pencil drawing on cardboard (1847).

Fanny Hensels Musikzimmer neben dem Gartensaal, Leipziger Straße 3. Aquarell von Julius Helfft (1849).

Fanny Hensel’s music room next to the Garden Hall at Leipziger Strasse 3. Watercolor by Julius Helfft (1849).

Felix Mendelssohn Bartholdy · 1809 Hamburg – 1847 Leipzig

"Felix has a strong voice and sings all day," is how his seven-year-old sister describes the three-year-old in a letter to friends in Hamburg in 1812. Felix, Fanny and the rest of the family had moved from there back to Berlin, the Mendelssohn's old hometown. Here, Felix, the eldest son of Abraham and Lea Mendelssohn, attended Dr. Messow's Elementary School near Gendarmenmarkt Square. His education continued with a comprehensive home-tutoring program based on the classical canon but also including drawing, physical education, piano and violin lessons, and studies in composition with the director of the *Sing-Akademie*. Then the move to live with grandmother Mendelssohn in her house at Hackescher Markt. Her home eventually became the venue for regular Sunday recitals, where the two *Wunderkinder* showed off their musical skills to friends and acquaintances, accompanied by instrumentalists hired by their father. By this time, young Felix was already writing humorous verse in classical meters and composing privately performed lyrical dramas, symphonies and chamber music. After their child prodigy had been warmly received by Goethe in Weimar and Cherubini in Paris, the parents were more convinced than ever that the boy should become an artist – ideally, a famous opera composer. As Felix' talent matured, the Sunday recitals held by the Mendelssohn Bartholdys (as the family was now known) in the garden room of their newly acquired town home (*Recksches Palais*, Leipziger Strasse 3) became a *de rigeur* event on Berlin's social calendar. Before long, Felix had produced his first masterpiece with the "Overture to a Midsummer Night's Dream." The dream of composing opera came to naught, unfortunately, after his first (and only) such work proved a flop with audiences. Yet his rediscovery and conducting of the St. Matthew's Passion by Bach was heralded as a milestone. Travelling to England for the first time in 1829 allowed young Felix to strike out on his own, while his grand educational tour of Europe in 1830/1831 provided formative experiences and impressions.

The refusal to appoint him as director at Berlin's *Sing-Akademie*, probably due to his Jewish ancestry, reinforced his disenchantment with his hometown. Before long he was able to establish himself as a musical director/conductor in his own right at the Düsseldorf theater and at the Leipziger Gewandhaus orchestra. His charm and good breeding meant that he was well-liked wherever he went. After the death of his revered father (1835), Felix finally felt emboldened to marry and start a family of his own. His bride would come from a Frankfurt-based Huguenot family. Devoted to his family yet also driven to excel, Mendelssohn took on an enormous workload. Travelling back and forth between Leipzig and Berlin as

„Felix hat eine starke Stimme und singt den ganzen Tag," schreibt seine siebenjährige Schwester 1812 über den Dreijährigen an Freunde in Hamburg. Von dort ist die Familie in ihre Ursprungsstadt an die Spree zurückgezogen. Der Stammhalter Abraham und Lea Mendelssohns besucht Dr. Messows Elementarschule im Quartier am Gendarmenmarkt, später folgen ein breitgefächerter Hauslehrereinsatz, das klassische Bildungsprogramm, Zeichen- und Sportunterricht, Geigen- und Klavierlektionen, Kompositionskunde beim Direktor der Sing-Akademie. Dann der Umzug in Großmutters Haus am Hackeschen Markt: Hier finden erste Sonntagsmusiken im Bekanntenkreis als Übungsforum der Wunderkinder statt, begleitet von Instrumentalisten, die der Vater bezahlt. Felix schreibt ein spöttisches Heldenepos im antiken Versmaß, komponiert private Singspiele, Sinfonien und Kammermusik. Die Vorführung des begabten Sprößlings bei Goethe in Weimar und bei Cherubini in Paris bestätigt den Eindruck der Eltern: dieses Talent muß Künstler werden, am besten Opernstarkomponist. Nach dem Umzug ins neuerworbene Recksche Palais, Leipziger Straße 3, entwickeln sich die Sonntagsmusiken im großen Gartensaal als gesellschaftliche Events der Mendelssohn Bartholdys (wie die Familie jetzt heißt). Felix liefert, mit der Ouvertüre zum „Sommernachtstraum", sein erstes Meisterstück. Seine erste (und letzte) Oper wird zum Publikumsflop, seine Aufführung der Matthäus-Passion ein Ereignis. Seine erste Englandreise 1829 gerät zur Abnabelung, zum Triumph, seine große europäische Bildungsreise 1830/1832 dient der Zukunfts-Orientierung.

Daß die Sing-Akademie zu Berlin das vitale Genie jüdischer Herkunft nicht als Direktor will, verstärkt Felix' Abneigung gegen die Heimatstadt. Als städtischer Musikdirektor in Düsseldorf und am Leipziger Gewandhaus steht der junge Dirigent auf eigenen Füßen. Seine soziale Kompetenz macht den Götterliebling zum Sympathieträger. Nach dem Tod des mit Anhänglichkeit verehrten Vaters (1835) traut er sich zu heiraten. Seine Frau stammt aus einer Frankfurter Hugenotten-Familie. Er ist nun auch engagierter Familienvater mit enormem Arbeitspensum, schreibt 5000 Briefe in seinem Leben; zerreißt sich im nochmaligen Hin und Her zwischen Leipzig und Berlin, zwischen Komponieren, Institutionsleitung, Häuslichkeit und Erholungs- oder Arbeitsreisen. Er wird, besonders in England, das er mehrfach besucht, berühmtester Tonsetzer seiner Zeit, entwickelt in respektvoller Auseinandersetzung mit Bach und Beethoven eigenen Stil in allen Genres außer dem Musiktheater, wird ein Pionier der Musikerausbildung. Noch Generationen später haben Nachgeborene, aufgrund antijüdischer

Felix Mendelssohn Bartholdy im Alter von zwölf Jahren.
Ölskizze von Karl Joseph Begas d.Ä. (1821).

Felix Mendelssohn Bartholdy at the age of twelve.
Oil sketch by Karl Joseph Begas the Elder (1821).

well as abroad to meet his directorial obligations, he also had to find time to compose, to manage the institutions entrusted to him, to spend leisure and vacation time with his family, and to write letters (some 5,000 over his lifetime!). In England, which he visited often, he was hailed as the leading composer of his day. Steeped in the great German musical tradition from Bach to Beethoven, Mendelssohn was able to develop his own style in practically all genres (except musical theatre), and became a pioneering figure in musical education. Long afterwards, widespread anti-Semitic prejudice would cause his music to be dismissed as light-weight. His death at the age of only 38, just six months after his beloved sister Fanny, is easily romanticized as the end of a comet that fell from the heavens too soon.

Polemik, den Diffamierten als leichtgewichtigen Glückspilz unterschätzt. Der Tod des 38Jährigen, ein halbes Jahr nach dem der geliebten Schwester, verklärt seine Biographie zur romantischen Kometenbahn.

Der zwölfjährige Felix Mendelssohn und Karl Friedrich Zelter bei Goethe in Weimar. Kupferstich in der „Gartenlaube“ (1867) nach einer Zeichnung von Carl Friedrich Doepler.

The twelve-year-old Felix Mendelssohn and Karl Friedrich Zelter visiting Goethe in Weimar. Copper engraving in the “Gartenlaube journal” (1867) after a drawing by Carl Friedrich Doepler.

Felix Mendelssohn Bartholdy.
Gemälde von Theodor Hildebrandt (1835).

Felix Mendelssohn Bartholdy.
Portrait by Theodor Hildebrandt (1835).

Cécile Mendelssohn Bartholdy, geb. Jeanrenaud (1817 – 1853).
Öl auf Leinwand von Eduard Magnus (1845).

Cécile Mendelssohn Bartholdy, née Jeanrenaud (1817 – 1853).
Oil on canvas by Eduard Magnus (1845).

Aus dem gemeinsamen Tagebuch der Hochzeitsreise von
Felix und Cécile Mendelssohn Bartholdy (1837): Kutschfahrt.

From the joint honeymoon diary kept by
Felix and Cécile Mendelssohn Bartholdy (1837): carriage ride.

„Hochzeitsmarsch“ von
Felix Mendelssohn Bartholdy (1842).
Aus „Ein Sommernachtstraum“ op. 61.

“Wedding March” by
Felix Mendelssohn Bartholdy (1842).
From “A Mid-Summer Night’s Dream” Opus 61.

Felix Mendelssohn Bartholdy:
Wohnstube der Leipziger Wohnung mit seiner Frau Cécile
und den Kindern Carl und Marie.
Aquarell (1840).

Felix Mendelssohn Bartholdy:
In the Living Room of his Leipzig flat with his wife Cécile
and children Carl and Marie.
Watercolor (1840).

Nachkommen Daniel Itzigs und die Mendelssohn-Familie
The Descendants of Daniel Itzig and the Mendelssohn Family

During the Seven Years' War (1756 – 1763), Moses Mendelssohn received a lucrative offer from the banker of the Prussian court, Daniel Itzig (1723 – 1799): Would he become Itzig's partner in order to lend a better public image to the inflationary production of coins that the King had approved? Mendelssohn refused, but was still feted as a welcome guest by Itzig, a lover of music and the arts, in the latter's sumptuous town home. This is where Moses became acquainted with Karl Friedrich Zelter, the musician, master builder and admirer of one of the daughters of moneyer Ephraim, as well as with Itzig's daughters Bella Salomon (1749 – 1824) and Sara Levy (1761 – 1854). Their brother Isaac Daniel Itzig (1750 – 1806) and his brother-in-law David Friedländer were later to bankroll the Jewish Free School (*Jüdische Freyschule*) inspired by Moses Mendelssohn. Joseph Mendelssohn, who later became a banking partner of Friedländer's son Moses (1774 – 1840), began his career as a businessman in the firm owned by Itzig.

A love of music – especially for that of Bach – was inculcated in the family by Bella Salomon, grandmother of the Mendelssohn Bartholdy children, as well as by Sara Levy, who was a member of the *Sing-Akademie*, a pianist, a student of Friedemann Bach, and a patron of Carl Philipp Emanuel Bach. As a strictly observant Jew who rejected her baptized son and initially disinherited her baptized grandchildren, Bella certainly had an impact on the family history – also through her bequest to her son-in-law Abraham, which gave him the means to acquire the *Reckschen Palais*. The widow of a prominent banker, Sara Levy established a cultural and intellectual salon (at the later site of the National Gallery) that she would maintain for five decades, turning it into a Berlin institution.

Soon after the death of family patriarch Daniel (1799), Julius Eduard (H)Itzig (1780 – 1849) became the first nephew to accept baptism, and subsequently entered the judicial service. His Christianized name was assumed by his sister Henriette (1781 – 1845) who, after becoming a Protestant in 1809, tied the knot with Nathan, the youngest of the Mendelssohn boys. Many of her children died early in what was a marriage dogged by ill luck. Julius Eduard became famous as a drinking companion of E.T.A. Hoffmann and as crime-story author. He also published travelogues written by his cousin Jacob (1774 – 1825). A son of Bella Salomon, Jacob became a Lutheran in 1805 in order to join the diplomatic service, taking the name Jacob Ludwig Salomon Bartholdy (after the so-called *Meierei Bartholdy*, his family's summer estate). Just one year earlier, Jacob's impressively educated sister Lea (1777 – 1842), a piano student of Bach disciple J.P. Kirnberger, had married Abraham Mendelssohn. The pair converted in 1822. Lea's niece

Während des Siebenjährigen Krieges (1756 – 1763) erhält Moses Mendelssohn ein lukratives Angebot des Hofbankiers Daniel Itzig (1723 – 1799): Er als Partner möge der von Itzig umgesetzten, königlich gebilligten, inflationären Münzproduktion ein besseres Image geben. Trotz seiner Weigerung ist Mendelssohn im Palais der musik- und kunstbegeisterten Itzigs ein angesehener Gast. Karl Friedrich Zelter, der Musiker, Baumeister und Verehrer einer Tochter des Münzjuden Ephraim, begegnet dem Moses bei Gesellschaften dort ebenso, wie die Itzig-Tochter Bella, verh. Salomon (1749 – 1824) und ihre Schwester Sara, verheiratete Levy (1761 – 1854). Deren Bruder Isaac Daniel Itzig (1750 – 1806) stiftet mit seinem Schwager David Friedländer die von Mendelssohn inspirierte Jüdische Freyschule. Joseph Mendelssohn, später als Bankier ein Sozius des Friedländer-Sohnes Moses (1774 – 1840), beginnt seine Kaufmannslaufbahn in der Firma Itzig.

Bella Salomon, die Großmutter der Mendelssohn Bartholdy-Kinder, und Sara Levy als Mitglied der Sing-Akademie, Pianistin, Schülerin von Friedemann und Mäzenin von Carl Philipp Emanuel Bach, bringen Bach-Begeisterung in die Mendelssohn-Familie. Bella beeinflußt als gläubige Jüdin, die ihren getauften Sohn verstößt und getaufte Enkel zunächst enterbt, die Familiengeschichte – aber auch mit ihrem Erbe, das dem Schwiegersohn Abraham Mittel zur Erwerbung des Reckschen Palais verschafft. Sara Levy wird mit ihrem Salon, den die Bankiers-Witwe über fünf Jahrzehnte am späteren Ort der Nationalgalerie führt, eine Berliner Institution.

Bald nach dem Tod des Patriarchen Daniel (1799) läßt sich Julius Eduard (H)Itzig (1780 – 1849) als erster Enkel taufen und tritt in den Justizdienst ein. Seinen Christennamen übernimmt Schwester Henriette (1781 – 1845): Sie wird 1809 evangelisch, heiratet Nathan, den jüngsten Mendelssohn-Sohn. Viele ihrer Kinder sterben früh: eine von Unglück überschattete Ehe. Julius Eduard wird berühmt als Zechkumpan E.T.A. Hoffmanns und Krimi-Autor. Zudem verlegt er Reiseberichte seines Cousins Jacob (1774 – 1825), eines Sohnes Bella Salomons. Der war 1805 als Jacob Ludwig Salomon Bartholdy – benannt nach der Meierei Bartholdy, dem Sommergut seiner Familie – lutherisch geworden: um in die Diplomatie einzusteigen. Ein Jahr zuvor hatte Jacobs beeindruckend gebildete Schwester Lea (1777 – 1842), eine Klavierschülerin des Bach-Schülers Kirnberger, Abraham Mendelssohn geheiratet. Das Paar konvertiert 1822. Leas Nichte Marianne Seeligmann (1799 – 1880) dagegen, die Ehefrau des Bankiers Alexander Mendelssohn, wird als letzte Jüdin der Familie auf dem Friedhof Schönhauser Allee begraben.

Daniel und Miriam Itzig, geb. Wulff. Pastelle von Joseph Friedrich d'Arbes (1787).
Daniel and Miriam Itzig, née Wulff. Pastel by Joseph Friedrich d'Arbes (1787).

Marianne Seeligmann (1799 – 1880), wife of banker Alexander Mendelssohn, was the last female member to be buried as a Jew on the Schönhauser Allee Cemetery.

Friedrich Hitzig (1811 – 1891), a son of Julius Eduard, became one of Berlin's most industrious architects of the 19th century. After tearing down his family's old *palais* on the Burgstrasse, he built the new Berlin stock exchange in its place – as well as the new Reichsbank at the end of Jägerstrasse, not far from the Mendelssohn bank.

Friedrich Hitzig (1811 – 1891), ein Sohn Julius Eduards, schaffensstarker Berliner Architekt des 19. Jahrhunderts, wird das vormalige Palais seiner Familie an der Burgstraße abreißen, dort die neue Börse errichten – und die Reichsbank am Ende der Jägerstraße, nahe der Mendelssohn-Bank.

Palais Itzig in der Burgstraße.
The Palais Itzig on the Burgstrasse.

Bella Salomon, geb. Itzig. Miniatur.
Bella Salomon, née Itzig. Miniature.

Tasse mit Unterschale, mit Porträt Isaac Daniel Itzig und Darstellung seines Schöneberger Freigutes. Königliche Porzellan-Manufaktur (um 1790).

Cup and saucer with portrait of Isaac Daniel Itzig and a representation of his freehold in Schöneberg. Königliche Porzellan-Manufaktur (c. 1790).

„La Métairie de M. Itzig“. Stich von Christoph J. W. Haller von Hallerstein (1801). Die Meierei Bartholdy, das Naturparadies der Jugendzeit für Lea Salomon, wurde zum Namensgeber für den getauften Bruder Jacob und für ihren Mendelssohn'schen Familienzweig.

"La Métairie de M. Itzig." Engraving by Christoph J. W. Haller von Hallerstein (1801). The Bartholdy "Dairy Farm" (Meierei), a natural paradise where the young Lea Salomon spent blissful hours as a child, was adopted as a namesake by the baptized Jacob brothers for their branch of the Mendelssohn family.

Lea Mendelssohn Bartholdy. Zeichnung von Wilhelm Hensel (1823).
Lea Mendelssohn Bartholdy. Drawing by Wilhelm Hensel (1823).

Familie Alexander Mendelssohn, mit Marianne, geb. Seeligmann.
Fotokopie einer Zeichnung von Wilhelm Hensel (1832).
Family of Alexander Mendelssohn, with Marianne, née Seeligmann.
Photocopy of a drawing by Wilhelm Hensel (1832).

Julius Eduard Hitzig.
Aquarellierte Bleistiftzeichnung von Franz Krüger.
Julius Eduard Hitzig.
Water-colorized pencil drawing by Franz Krüger.

Marianne Mendelssohn, geb. Seeligmann.
Marianne Mendelssohn, née Seeligmann.

Johannes Veit

Jonas (Johannes) Veit · 1790 Berlin – 1854 Rom
Philipp Veit · 1793 Berlin – 1877 Mainz

Their brothers Moses and Abraham died young. Their parents, Simon Veit and Brendel, née Mendelssohn, separated in 1799. Philipp moved with his mother and stepfather Friedrich Schlegel to Jena, to join a local community of Romantic artists and writers. Jonas stayed behind with his father in Berlin and learned the merchant's trade from his uncle Abraham Mendelssohn in Hamburg. Both became painters and, having internalized the religious zeal of their mother, accepted baptism in Vienna in 1810. Serving as a soldier in the German wars of liberation from Napoleon, Philipp befriended the poet Joseph von Eichendorff. In Rome, Philipp and Johannes (Jonas' new Christian name) joined the so-called "Nazarenes," a brotherhood of German painters who wanted to reinvigorate Christian-themed painting with their Romantic spirit. Philipp married the 13-year-old daughter of his innkeeper and started a large family. Called back to Frankfurt to head the Städel Museum, he came into ideological conflict with his colleagues due to his conservative artistic outlook. In 1848, a year of revolutionary upheaval, he painted the giant figure of Germania to adorn the Frankfurt's Paulskirche church, where the National Assembly was meeting. In 1853, he became Director of Mainz' Fine Paintings Collection (Gemäldesammlung). His works were commissioned by, amongst others, the Vatican, the King of Prussia, and the cathedrals of Frankfurt and Mainz.

In 1821, his brother Johannes tied the knot in Berlin. His bride Flora Riess, a convert from Judaism to Catholicism, moved with him to Rome. Even more of a brooding introvert than his younger brother, Johannes often made life difficult for himself. His best-known work, "The Adoration of the Shepherds" (1819), originally displayed in Berlin's St. Hedwig's Cathedral, did not survive World War II. This first grandson of Moses Mendelssohn was buried in Rome, in the baroque cathedral of Il Gesù, the mother church of the Jesuit Order.

Ihre beiden Brüder Moses und Abraham sterben früh. Ihre Eltern Simon Veit und Brendel, geb. Mendelssohn, trennen sich 1799. Philipp zieht mit der Mutter und dem Stiefvater Schlegel in die Jenaer Romantiker-Kommune. Jonas bleibt beim Vater in Berlin, beginnt eine Kaufmannslehre beim Onkel Abraham Mendelssohn in Hamburg. Beide werden Maler, folgen dem religiösen Eifer ihrer Mutter, lassen sich 1810 in Wien taufen. Philipp befreundet sich als Soldat im Befreiungskrieg mit dem Dichter von Eichendorff. In Rom gehören Johannes, wie sich der Getaufte nun nennt, und Philipp zu den Nazarenern, denen es als katholische Romantiker um die Erneuerung der sakralen Malerei geht. Philipp heiratet die 13jährige Tochter seiner Wirtsleute, gründet eine große Familie.

Als Direktor des Städel-Museums nach Frankfurt berufen, gerät er dort wegen seiner konservativen Kunstauffassung in ideologische Konflikte mit Kollegen. 1848 malt er für die Nationalversammlung in der Paulskirche die monumentale Germania. 1853 wird er Direktor der Gemäldesammlung in Mainz. Für den Vatikan, den preußischen König, den Frankfurter und den Mainzer Dom hat er Aufträge realisiert.

Sein Bruder Johannes hatte 1821 in Berlin Flora Riess geheiratet, die zuvor vom Judentum zum katholischen Bekenntnis gewechselt war. Er zieht mit ihr nach Rom. Der Ältere ist, mehr noch als sein Bruder, ein Grübler, der es sich schwer macht. Sein bekanntestes Werk „Anbetung der Hirten" (1819) übersteht in der Berliner St. Hedwigs-Kathedrale den II. Weltkrieg nicht. Sein Grab fand der erste Enkel Moses Mendelssohns in der barocken Hauptkirche der Jesuiten, Il Gesù zu Rom.

Philipp Veit: Selbstporträt. Öl auf Leinwand (um 1816).
Philipp Veit: Self-portrait. Oil on canvas (c. 1816).

Bildnis des Johannes Veit. Zeichnung von Philipp Veit (1820).
Portrait of Johannes Veit. Drawing by Philipp Veit (1820).

„Germania". Gemälde Philipp Veits für die Nationalversammlung in der Paulskirche (1848).

"Germania" painting by Philipp Veit for the National Assembly in Frankfurt's Paulskirche (1848).

Philipp Veit.
Wandgemälde an der Bavaria am Schillerplatz in Frankfurt am Main von Wilhelm Steinhausen (1884).

Philipp Veit.
Wall mural for the Bavaria Statue on Schillerplatz in Frankfurt am Main by Wilhelm Steinhausen (1884).

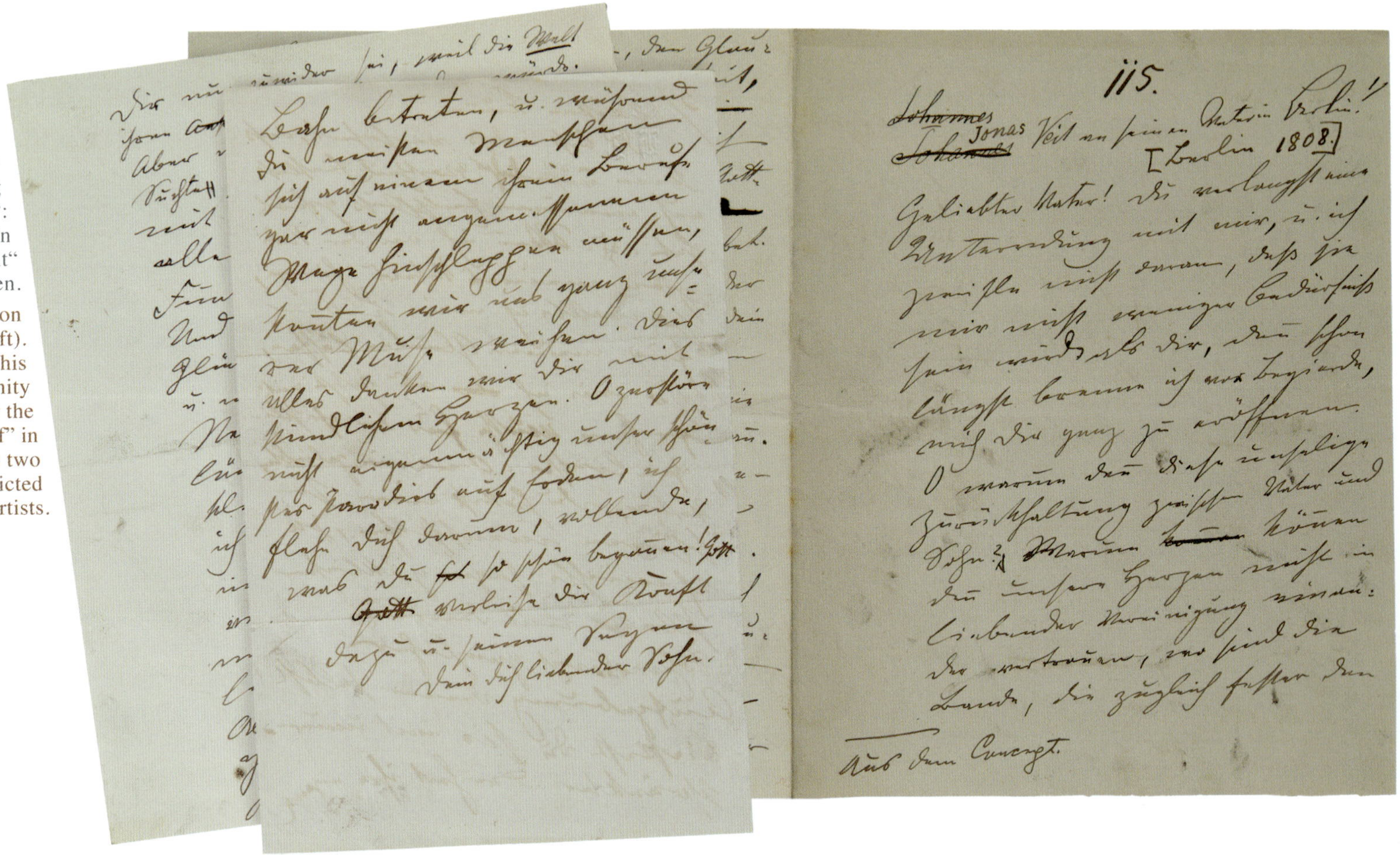

115.

~~Johannes~~ Jonas Veit an seinen Vater in Berlin!
[Berlin 1808.]

Geliebter Vater!

Aus dem Concept.

Jonas Veit: Brief an Simon Veit, Berlin 1808 (Entwurf). Der Sohn bekennt sich zum Christentum und dankt dem Vater für die „Aufgebung Deiner selbst": daß beide Brüder in „unumschränkter Freiheit" Künstler werden dürfen.

Jonas Veit: Letter to Simon Veit, Berlin 1808 (draft). The son declares his adherence to Christianity and thanks his father for the "sacrifice of your own self" in that he had given the two brothers "unrestricted freedom" to become artists.

Grab von Philipp Veit auf dem Hauptfriedhof Mainz.

Grave of Philipp Veit in Mainz.

Grab von Johannes Veit, der durch Gesinnung und Bilder „seine Verehrung Gottes vorzüglich ausdrückte“, in der Kirche Il Gesù.

The grave of Johannes Veit in the Church of the Gesù. Infused with a sense of spirituality, Veit's paintings were praised for "giving outstanding expression to the worship of God."

Paul Mendelssohn-Bartholdy · 1812 Berlin – 1874 Berlin
Ernst (von) Mendelssohn-Bartholdy · 1846 Berlin – 1909 Dresden

The youngest child of Abraham and Lea Mendelssohn Bartholdy, Paul grew up in the shadow of his composer siblings. A decent cellist, he was more cut out for the business world, and soon earned the family nickname "Prokura Paul" reminiscent of corporate officers. With partners of his father Abraham, where he learned the banking trade in London and Paris, he sees no future. Paul thus became an employee of his uncle Joseph's firm, which his father had left eleven years before. By 1838, he had worked his way up to partner, thereby bringing the banking firm back into the ownership of both branches of the family – which was to remain the case until 1938. Eager to promote the bank's business activities in Czarist Russia, Paul built up an extensive network of contacts to St. Petersburg. Serving as Otto von Bismarck's financial advisor, he gave the Iron Chancellor the financial "all-clear" to go to war with Austria in 1866. Paul had a headstrong, independent streak. After becoming engaged to Albertine Heine, for example – a banker's daughter baptized only a few years before – he kept this fact a secret. Feeling the need to set himself apart from his famous brother Felix, he added a hyphen to his name. Later, he got entangled in a protracted dispute with Carl, his orphaned nephew and former legal ward, concerning the uncensored publication of various family documents.

Ernst Moses Felix, as he was known after baptism, was the first son and heir of Paul and Albertine. Shortly after the US Civil War had ended, the "upright Prussian" and direct descendant of Moses Mendelssohn visited the "New World." Following the death of his uncle, Franz von Mendelssohn Sr, he became Senior Director of Mendelssohn & Co, but his managerial style caused tension. He married into the Warschauer banking family and strove for a noble title, which he ultimately attained. Counted among William II's highly influential Kaiserjuden (court Jews), he advanced into the ranks of the ruling class. He indulged his appetite for power and prestige by building a palatial urban residence on Jägerstrasse, and by acquiring the Börnicke Manor, a noble country estate. A generous public donor and benefactor, he was Berlin's richest taxpayer by the time of his death.

Der jüngste Sprößling Abraham und Lea Mendelssohn Bartholdys steht im Schatten seiner Komponisten-Geschwister. Er spielt gut Cello, ist aber für den Kaufmannsberuf bestimmt; wird Prokura-Paul genannt. Bei Partnern des Vaters Abraham in London und Paris, wo er das Bankgeschäft lernt, sieht er für sich keine Zukunft. In die Firma des Onkels Joseph, die Abraham elf Jahre zuvor verlassen hatte, tritt er nun als Angestellter ein. Mit seinem Aufstieg zum Sozius (1838) ist das Bankhaus wieder im Besitz beider Familienzweige, was bis 1938 so bleiben wird. Als Förderer des Rußlandgeschäftes baut Paul Kontakte nach St. Petersburg aus. Als Finanzberater Bismarcks gibt er grünes Licht für den Krieg von 1866. Eigene Wege hatte er bei seiner lange verheimlichten Verlobung mit der wenige Jahre zuvor getauften Bankierstochter Albertine Heine verfolgt. Von dem berühmten Bruder grenzt er sich ab durch den Bindestrich im eigenen Doppelnamen. Als ehemaliger Vormund seines verwaisten Neffen Carl gerät er mit diesem in Streit über die unzensierte Veröffentlichung von Familiendokumenten.

Ernst Moses Felix, wie seine Taufnamen lauten, ist der Stammhalter von Paul und Albertine. Kurz nach dem Bürgerkrieg in den USA besucht er, als „guter Preuße“ und erster Nachkomme des Moses, die Neue Welt. Nach dem Tod Franz von Mendelssohn d. Ä. (1889) wird er Seniorchef von Mendelssohn & Co, sein Führungsstil provoziert Spannungen. Er heiratet ein in die Bankiersfamilie Warschauer, wird auf eigenes Betreiben nobilitiert und zu den „Kaiserjuden“ Wilhelms II. gezählt, avanciert zum Mitglied im Herrenhaus. Sein Sinn für Macht und Repräsentanz drückt sich aus durch den Bau eines Stadtpalais in der Jägerstraße und durch die Erwerbung des Rittergutes Börnicke. Zuletzt gilt der großzügige Stifter als reichster Steuerzahler Berlins.

Paul Hermann Mendelssohn-Bartholdy. Gemälde (1842) von Eduard Magnus (Replik).
Paul Hermann Mendelssohn-Bartholdy. Painting (1842) by Eduard Magnus (replica).

Ernst Mendelssohn-Bartholdy. Gemälde von Ludwig Passini (um 1885).
Ernst Mendelssohn-Bartholdy. Painting by Ludwig Passini (c. 1885).

„Decoration eines Zimmers im Hause des Herrn Paul Mendelssohn-Bartholdy. Entwurf von Martin Gropius für das Haus des Bankiers in der Französischen Straße.“

“Decoration for a room in the house of Mr. Paul Mendelssohn-Bartholdy.” Design by Martin Gropius for the banker's house on Französische Strasse.

Carl Mendelssohn Bartholdy, geb. 1838 in Leipzig, gest. 1897 in Königsfelden (Schweiz), porträtiert von B. Laurens.

Karl Mendelssohn Bartholdy, b. 1838 in Leipzig, d. 1897 in Königsfelden (Switzerland). Portrait by B. Laurens.

Albertine Mendelssohn-Bartholdy (1814 – 1879) als Braut. Öl auf Leinwand von August Theodor Kaselowsky (1835). Paul, der Bruder des Komponisten Felix, heiratete seine mit elf Jahren getaufte Verlobte aus der jüdischen Familie Heine am 27. Mai 1835 in der Berliner Marienkirche, nahe dem ersten Haus der Familie Mendelssohn an der Spandauer Straße.

Albertine Mendelssohn-Bartholdy (1814 – 1879) as a bride. Oil on canvas by August Theodor Kaselowsky (1835). On May 27, 1835 Paul Mendelssohn, the brother of composer Felix, married a member of the Jewish Heine clan who had been baptized at the age of eleven. The ceremony was held in Berlin's *Marienkirche* church, close to the Mendelssohn's first house on Spandauer Strasse.

Adelswappen Ernst von Mendelssohn-Bartholdy, nobiltiert 1896. Der Kranich mit dem Stein ist das Wappen der Mendelssohns, die Taube mit dem Zweig gehört zum Wappen von Börnicke.

Coat of arms of Ernst von Mendelssohn-Bartholdy, ennobled in 1896. The crane grasping the pebble is from the Mendelssohn coat of arms, while the dove with the branches is from the Börnicke manorial crest.

Ernst Mendelssohn Bartholdys Stadtpalais Jägerstraße 52.

Ernst Mendelssohn Bartholdy's town villa at Jägerstrasse 52.

Das Rittergut Börnicke.

Börnicke Manor.

Honoring the memory of the family patriarch Moses Mendelssohn became a matter of pride and filial piety for his descendants. Among Moses' children, Joseph was especially active in this regard; from an early age, he championed the philosopher's achievements among the progressive circles he frequented.

When, in 1820, the marble bust of Moses no longer had a worthy setting in the Jewish Free School *(Jüdische Freyschule)*, it was leased to the Mendelssohn family for 15 gold talers a year and placed in the ancestral gallery of the family bank at Jägerstrasse 51. Here, the heads of the banking house in the second, third, and fourth generation would proudly give visitors a tour of their family history. In their private quarters as well, the Mendelssohns liked to give pride of place to representations of their ancestors as a way of staying in touch with their identity. A sense of continuity and reverence for the past were also expressed in the family's choice of first (Christian) names. For it was common practice, during the period of Jewish conversions, to adopt Christian names that could be linked back to the old Jewish ones, e.g. Zippora = Cäcilie.

After Paul Mendelssohn-Bartholdy's first-born child Pauline died at the age of 19 due to an undetermined illness (in 1863), she was immortalized in a life-size painting by the artist Julius Schrader. This work would later serve as backdrop for a group portrait showing Paul's family assembled in the salon of their residence on Französische Strasse. (In this case the artist was Ludwig Passini, who had married into the related Warschauer family.) Since the group portrait is intended for Paul's daughter Käthe as a wedding gift, she is not shown, but her presence in spirit is symbolized by her letter, which is being read to the family members beneath the eyes of Pauline's painted image. The message conveyed is one of family togetherness and unity.

Telling the story of their origins became a preoccupation for many of Moses' descendants, especially in their later years. Thus, the scholar of international law Albrecht Mendelssohn Batholdy and the Cellist Francesco von Mendelssohn each drafted books on the family history during their time in exile as emigrants. Or take Gustav Mendelssohn-Bartholdy, a nephew of Felix' brother Paul: For a long time, it was thought that he had disappeared without a trace in Argentina sometime in 1914. Then came an unexpected sign of life: In 1943, his Spanish translation of Sebastian Hensel's family chronicle, "Félix Mendelssohn Bartholdy: La Historia de Su Vida y de Su Familia," was issued by the Buenos Aires publisher Compañia Editora del Plata.

In der Verehrung der Nachkommen für den Stammvater verbinden sich Stolz und Pietät. Unter Moses' Kindern engagiert sich vor allem Joseph, bereits als junger Mann im aufgeklärten Freundeskreis, für die Würdigung des Philosophen. Als um 1820 die Marmorbüste des Moses in der Jüdischen Freyschule keinen würdigen Platz mehr findet, wird sie den Mendelssohn-Bankiers für jährlich 15 Taler Gold überlassen und im Ahnensaal des Hauses Jägerstraße 51 aufgestellt. Dort zeigen Firmenchefs der zweiten, dritten, vierten Generation die Parade ihrer Vorgänger. Auch in den Privatwohnungen gehört die identitätsstiftende Vorfahren-Galerie zur repräsentativen Einrichtung. Kontinuität und Verehrung drücken sich ebenso in der Wahl von Vornamen aus, die in der Familie eingeführt sind. Zu Zeiten der Konversion gibt es christliche Vornamen, die als Chiffren für abgelegte jüdische Namen zu deuten sind, z.B. Zippora = Cäcilie.

Als Paul Mendelssohn-Bartholdy 1863 seine Erstgeborene Pauline im Alter von 19 Jahren aufgrund eines ungeklärten Krankheitsdramas verliert, porträtiert Julius Schrader die Verstorbene posthum in Lebensgröße. Später wird der bei den verwandten Warschauers eingeheiratete Maler Ludwig Passini Pauls Familie gemeinsam – im Salon ihres Hauses an der Französischen Straße vor diesem großen Gemälde – als Gruppenbild festhalten. Die Anwesenheit der Tochter Käthe, der man das Gemälde zur Hochzeit schenken will, ist durch einen Brief abgebildet, welcher unter Paulines Augen verlesen wird: Die Familie ist versammelt und hält zusammen.

Den Antrieb, von der eigenen Herkunft zu erzählen, verspüren etliche Moses-Nachkommen in ihren späteren Jahren. Der Völkerrechtler Albrecht Mendelssohn Bartholdy und der Cellist Francesco von Mendelssohn entwerfen als Emigranten Bücher zur Familiengeschichte. Gustav Mendelssohn-Bartholdy, ein Enkel des Felix-Bruders Paul, galt ab 1914 als in Argentinien verschollen. 1943 erscheint seine Übersetzung der Familienbiographie von Sebastian Hensel „Félix Mendelssohn Bartholdy: la historia de su vida y de su familia" in der Compañia Editora del Plata.

◂ Ahnensaal im Stammhaus der Mendelssohn-Bank, Jägerstraße 51.
◂ Ancestral gallery in the original headquarters of the Mendelssohn bank, Jägerstrasse 51.

Pauline Mendelssohn-Bartholdy.
Ölgemälde von Julius Schrader (1863).

Pauline Mendelssohn-Bartholdy.
Oil painting by Julius Schrader (1863).

I can't make up my silly mind, to whom I should dedicate this first book of mine.

Off hand I would say:

To the one and only A.B.C.

But on the other hand I have to consider:

THE MENDELSSOHN'S

So, on second thought:

To my unbelievable Mother Giulietta von Mendelssohn-Gordigiani and to my nutty sister Eleonora.

THE MENDELSSOHNS

Prelude

Chapter One and Interlude I.

MOSES, THE PHILOSOPHER (and the others: Lessing, Kant, LaFater, King Frederick, the Great, etc.)

Chapter Two

HIS CHILDREN: Dorothy, Joseph, Abraham (Mendelssohn-Bartholdy), Henrietta, Rachel, Nathan (and the others).

Chapter Three

FELIX MENDELSSOHN-BARTHOLDY, the Composer (and the others); Goethe, Schumann, Wagner, Chopin, Napoleon, and especially his sister Fanny Hensel.

Chapter Four

THE OTHERS: (The uninteresting Mendelssohns: Betty, Arnold, Ottilie, Wilhelm, Benjamin, Alexander, Margarethe, Herman, Adolph, Franz, Wilhelm, Alexandrine, Pauline, Katherine, Ernest, Gotthold, Fanny.

Chapter Five

JOSEPH JOACHIM, the violinist and composer (and the others): Clara Schulmann, Hans von Buelow, Enole Biarnez-Mendelssohn, Max Bruch, Brahms, etc.

Chapter Six

ELEANORA DUSE (And She Alone)

Chapter Seven

MY PARENTS (and the others), Pablo Casals, Nickisch, Chamberlain, D'Annunzio, Sarah Bernhardt, Kaiser Wilhelm II, King Victor Emanuel, Benedict XIII, etc.

Francesco von Mendelssohn entwirft 1943/1944 in Texas eine Familienchronik, die er seiner „durchgeknallten" Schwester und seiner „unglaublichen" Mutter widmet. Kapitel 8 bis 12 sollten Künstlerkollegen, den letzten und den aktuellen Weltkrieg, das Exil und verrückte Amerikaner behandeln.

While in Texas in 1943/1944, Francesco von Mendelssohn drafted a family chronicle that he dedicated to his "bonkers" sister and his "incredible" mother. Chapters 8 to 12 were to cover his circle of artist friends, the World War I and (still ongoing) World War II, his life in exile, and a number of crazy American characters he had met along the way.

Paul und Albertine Mendelssohn-Bartholdy mit ihren Kindern Fanny, Ernst und Gotthold (rechts). Fotografie eines Ölgemäldes von Ludwig Passini (um 1868).

Paul and Albertine Mendelssohn-Bartholdy with their children Fanny, Ernst and Gotthold (right). Photograph of an oil painting by Ludwig Passini (c. 1868).

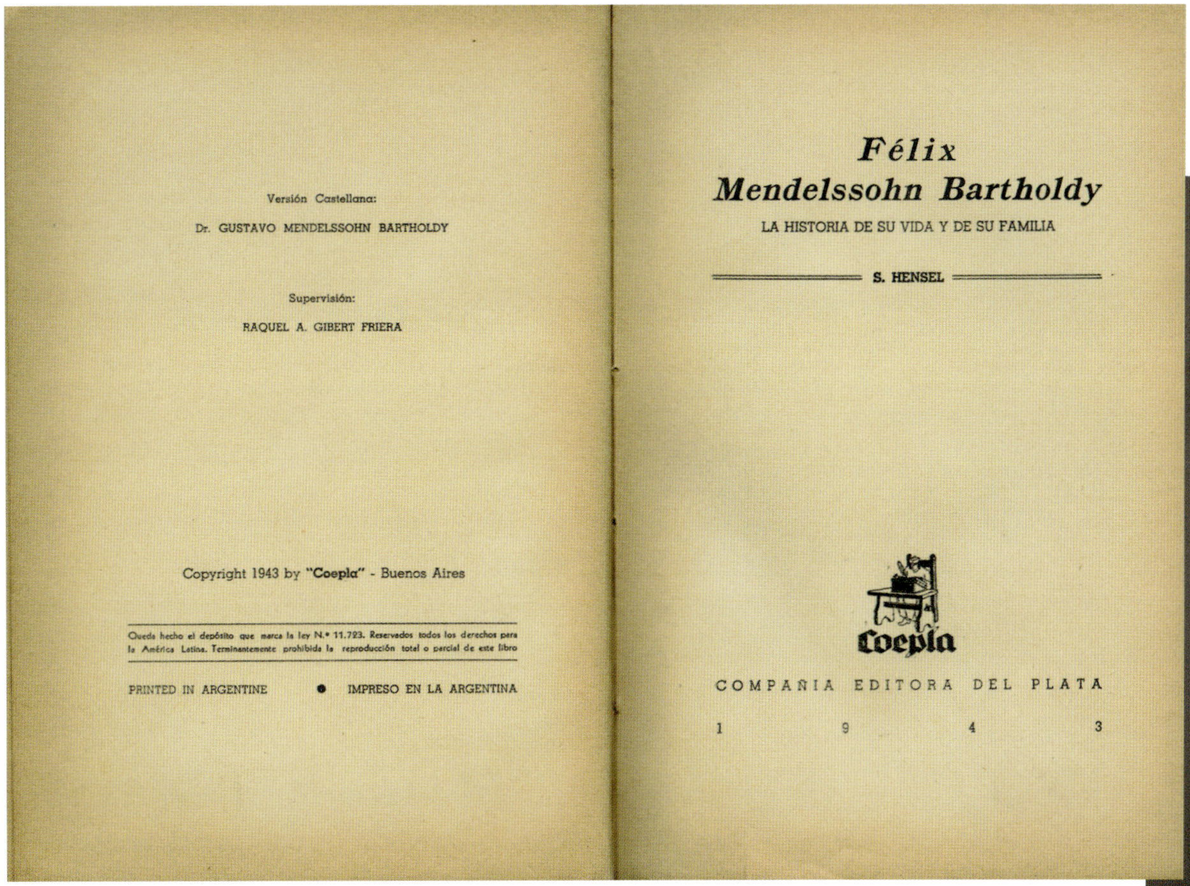

Versión Castellana:

Dr. GUSTAVO MENDELSSOHN BARTHOLDY

Supervisión:

RAQUEL A. GIBERT FRIERA

Copyright 1943 by "Coepla" - Buenos Aires

Queda hecho el depósito que marca la ley N.º 11.723. Reservados todos los derechos para la América Latina. Terminantemente prohibida la reproducción total o parcial de este libro

PRINTED IN ARGENTINE • IMPRESO EN LA ARGENTINA

Félix
Mendelssohn Bartholdy

LA HISTORIA DE SU VIDA Y DE SU FAMILIA

S. HENSEL

Coepla

COMPAÑIA EDITORA DEL PLATA

1 9 4 3

„Félix Mendelssohn Bartholdy: la historia de su vida y de su familia“.
Gustav Mendelssohn-Bartholdys spanische Übersetzung von Sebastian Hensels „Die Familie Mendelssohn“, erschienen 1943 in Buenos Aires.

Félix Mendelssohn Bartholdy: "La Historia de Su vida y de Su Familia."
Gustav Mendelssohn-Bartholdy's Spanish translation of Sebastian Hensel's "Die Familie Mendelssohn," published in 1943 in Buenos Aires.

Gustav Mendelssohn-Bartholdy
(1877 – 1961).

Wohnzimmer der Familie Sebastian Hensel in Berlin-Westend.

Living room of Sebastian Hensel and family in Berlin-Westend.

Franz (von) Mendelssohn · 1829 Berlin – 1889 Berlin
Enole (von) Mendelssohn, geb. Biarnez · 1827 Bordeaux – 1889 Berlin

Hermann, the son and heir of Alexander Mendelssohn, had no interest in becoming a bank director, so he set up shop as a publisher in Leipzig instead. Adolph, Alexander's second son, died at the age of 25, followed shortly thereafter by his infant son Stephan. Alexander's third son, Franz, had wanted to go into farming: now he had no choice but to work for the family bank.

Franz Mendelssohn decided to marry his brother's widow Enole, whose father was a major wine merchant in Bordeaux. A singer and pianist, Enole made music-making and fine living an integral part of life of Jägerstrasse 51. The couple became friends with Clara Schumann, a customer of the family bank who occasionally lived and gave piano recitals in their home, as well as with the famous violinist Joseph Joachim. In 1854, Franz became a partner of Mendelssohn & Co, and the firm's senior director twenty years later. Building on the business legacy left by his father Alexander and his uncle Paul, Franz expanded the bank's activities in Russia, while also investing in railroad projects and on the international financial markets. These endeavors eventually brought social recognition: In 1888, during the brief 99-day-reign of Kaiser Frederick III, Franz was given a title, which ennoblement he accepted only subject to receiving consent from Bismarck. As his coat of arms, Franz proposed a crane grasping a pebble, a symbol of ever-watchful responsibility that the bank's founder, Joseph Mendelssohn, had adopted as his seal. But the College of Heralds felt they knew better and designed a more embellished crane surrounded by the grapes of the family vineyards in Horchheim near Coblenz.

Franz and Enole had two sons, Robert and Franz II, with whom they had a loving relationship. Franz died only six weeks after his spouse, at the age of 60.

Hermann, der Stammhalter von Alexander Mendelssohn, will kein Bankenchef werden; er geht als Verlagsbuchhändler nach Leipzig. Alexanders zweiter Sohn Adolph stirbt mit 25 Jahren, bald auch dessen kleiner Sohn Stephan. Alexanders dritter Sohn Franz hatte Landwirt werden wollen: Nun muß er in das Bankhaus einsteigen.

Franz Mendelssohn heiratet Enole, die Witwe seines Bruders, ihr Vater ist Weingroßkaufmann in Bordeaux. Die Sängerin und Pianistin verschafft der Hausmusik und dem guten Leben einen Platz in der Jägerstraße 51. Das Paar ist befreundet mit Clara Schumann, einer Kundin des Bankhauses, die gelegentlich hier wohnt und musiziert, und mit dem Geiger Joseph Joachim. Franz wird 1854 Teilhaber von Mendelssohn & Co und 1874 Seniorchef. Im Sinne der Vorgänger, seines Vaters Alexander und seines Onkels Paul, baut er die Geschäfte mit Rußland, Eisenbahnprojekte und Einsätze auf dem internationalen Geldmarkt aus. Er erwirbt sich den Respekt der Politik: Während der kurzen Regierungszeit des 99-Tage-Kaisers wird er von Friedrich geadelt (1888) – und akzeptiert nur unter der Bedingung, daß Bismarck zustimmt. Als Adelswappen schlägt er den Kranich mit dem Stein vor, ein Symbol der Verantwortung, das Joseph, der Bankgründer, sich als Siegel gewählt hatte. Gegenüber seinem schlichten Entwurf plädiert das Heroldsamt für einen verschnörkelten Kranich samt den Trauben des Familienweinguts in Horchheim bei Koblenz.

Mit den beiden Söhnen Robert und Franz d.J. haben die Eltern ein zärtliches Verhältnis. Franz stirbt sechs Wochen nach seiner Frau im Alter von 60 Jahren.

Enole von Mendelssohn, geb. Biarnez.
Enole von Mendelssohn, née Biarnez.

Franz von Mendelssohn.

Adolph Mendelssohn (1826 – 1851),
erster Ehemann von Enole Biarnez. Ölgemälde.

Adolph Mendelssohn (1826 – 1851),
first husband of Enole Biarnez. Oil painting.

Enole Biarnez mit ihrer Mutter. Gemälde.

Enole Biarnez with her mother. Painting.

Enole von Mendelssohn musiziert mit ihren Söhnen
Robert und Franz (links).

Enole von Mendelssohn playing music with her sons
Robert and Franz (left).

Anice, das Weingut der Familie Biarnez bei Bordeaux. Aquarell Sebastian Hensels für sein Märchen „Zugvögel“.

Anice, the vineyard of the Biarnez family in Bordeaux. Watercolor by Sebastian Hensel for his fairy tale “Zugvögel” (Birds of Passage).

Die Reise wurde sehr gemüthlich, nicht mit der sonst üblichen Eile der Zugvögel gemacht. Gleich am Ufer des Meeres hielten sie sich einige Tage auf, und lernten dies ihnen ganz neue Element kennen. Im Meer schwammen schwarze Delphine, bunte fliegende Fische erhoben sich schaarenweis in die Luft, und wurden von kreischenden schneeweissen Möven verfolgt. Auch einen grossen Sturm erlebten sie am Strande, wo die Wellen haushoch heranrollten, und die Schiffe ängstlich den Hafen aufsuchten um nicht zerschlagen zu werden und unterzugehen. Und eines Abends leuchtete das Meer, als wäre es voll lauter Flammen; das waren aber nur unzählige Wasserthierchen, die so glühten wie unsre Leuchtwürmer.

Dann flogen unsre Vögel über das Meer, und den alten Weg vom vorigen Jahr durch Spanien, wo alles jetzt in einem Frühlingsblüthenmeer prangte, und über die hohen Pyrenäen und eines Morgens kamen sie wohlbehalten in Anice wieder an; denn Vögel die einmal einen Weg gemacht haben, finden ihn unfehlbar wieder, und verirren sich nie, selbst in der dunkelsten Nacht und im stärksten Sturm.

Wappen Franz von Mendelssohns, erste Version.

The coat of arms of Franz von Mendelssohn, first version.

Sebastian Hensel · 1830 Berlin – 1898 Berlin-Westend

The only son of Fanny and Wilhelm Hensel, he inherited his father's aptitude for painting, yet decided not to become an artist like his parents. His chosen path: farming. A watershed in the young man's life came on May 14, 1847 with the sudden death of his mother, followed only six months later by that of his uncle Felix. For Sebastian, who reacted to the loss by becoming seriously ill, this marked the end of an idyllic childhood of garden concerts and hours spent in his father's atelier in the temple to the muses at Leipziger Strasse.

During the revolutionary upheavals of 1848, Sebastian cast his lot with the rebels, a rebuke to the conservative politics of his father Hensel, who was painter to the Prussian court. After studying agricultural science in Southwestern Germany, he acquired the Grossbarthen estate near Königsberg, and married into a Russian-Jewish patrician family, the von Adelsons. Since his wife Julie could not abide the local climate, Sebastian agreed to move back to Berlin and start a business career. The year was 1872, the start of the Gründerzeit, when German industry was modernized by leaps and bounds. His first job was to manage the luxury hotel Kaiserhof, but that burned down shortly after its grand opening. He then became director of a company that managed market halls, and of another one constructing apartment buildings, but had to suffer a number of bitter reversals. The offspring of his extended family delighted in the children's books he wrote and illustrated. Sebastian probably left his greatest mark as the official clan biographer who "invented" the Mendelssohn saga by compiling a family chronicle from selected documents and anecdotes. It was intended for private use at first, but became something of a cultural milestone once it was published, conveying to the reading public an idealized view of a well-to-do, bourgeois German family that happened to have Jewish roots. Sebastian's Mendelssohn family chronicle went through no less than twenty-two editions, the last one appearing in 1933.

Der einzige Sohn von Fanny und Wilhelm Hensel erbt das zeichnerische Talent des Vaters. Aber beeindruckt von seinen Künstlereltern entscheidet er sich für den eigenen Weg, Landwirt zu werden. Der plötzliche Tod seiner Mutter am 14. Mai 1847 trifft Sebastian Hensel als dramatischer Lebenseinschnitt, gefolgt vom Tod des Onkels Felix sechs Monate später. Für ihn, der mit einer schweren Krankheit auf den Verlust reagiert, bedeutet das Abschied: von einer Kindheit zwischen Gartensaal-Konzerten und väterlichem Atelier – das Ende des Musentempels Leipziger Straße.

Während der Revolution von 1848 schlägt sich der Sproß des royalistischen Hofmalers Hensel auf die Seite der Rebellenbürger. Nach seiner Landwirtschafts-Ausbildung in Südwestdeutschland wird er Besitzer des Gutes Großbarthen bei Königsberg, heiratet ein in die russisch-jüdische Patrizierfamilie von Adelson. Kehrt, weil seine Frau Julie das Klima nicht verträgt, 1872 zur Gründerzeit nach Berlin zurück. Auf diversen Manager-Posten – als Chef der bald nach der Eröffnung abgebrannten Luxusherberge Kaiserhof, als Direktor einer Markthallen- und einer Wohnungsbaugesellschaft – erlebt er bittere Niederlagen. Den Nachwuchs seiner Verwandtschaft beglückt er als Autor und Illustrator von Kinderbüchern. Kulturgeschichte schreibt der fünffache Vater und Clan-Biograph als „Erfinder" der „Mendelssohns": Seine zunächst für den privaten Gebrauch zusammengestellte, dann bis 1933 zweiundzwanzig Mal aufgelegte Familienchronik aus Dokumenten und Erzählungen vermittelt dem deutschen Bürgertum das verklärte Inbild einer bürgerlichen deutschen Familie jüdischer Herkunft.

Sebastian Hensel. Fotografie aus den 1890er Jahren.
Sebastian Hensel. Photograph from the 1890s.

Fanny Hensel mit ihrem Sohn Sebastian auf dem Arm. Öl auf Leinwand (um 1832) von Wilhelm Hensel. Ausschnittstudie zu dem 1908 in der Berliner Garnisonkirche verbrannten Gemälde „Christus vor Pilatus“.

Fanny Hensel holding her son Sebastian. Oil on canvas (c. 1832) by Wilhelm Hensel. Excerpt from a study for "Christ Before Pilate," a painting destroyed by fire in Berlin's *Garnisonkirche* church in 1908.

Julie von Adelson. Zeichnung von Wilhelm Hensel. Widmung: „Nicht in Deinem Album, sondern in Deinem Herzen einen Platz einzunehmen, ist Wunsch und das Streben Deiner getreuen Tochter Julie Adelson.“

Julie von Adelson. Drawing by Wilhelm Hensel. Dedication: "To find a place not in your album, but in your heart – the wish and quest of your faithful daughter Julie Adelson."

St. Marta. Zeichnung Sebastian Hensels aus dem Italienreise-Tagebuch von 1839/1840.

St. Marta. Drawing by Sebastian Hensel from his Italian travel diary of 1839/1840.

Ansicht des Großbarthener Gutshauses. Zeichnung von Sebastian Hensel.

View of the Grossbarthen manor house. Drawing by Sebastian Hensel.

„Die Familie Mendelssohn" von Sebastian Hensel. Der Frontispiz zeigt den Mathematiker Peter Gustav Lejeune Dirichlet, den Ehemann der Tante Rebecka, geb. Mendelssohn, die für den Halbwaisen Sebastian zur mütterlichen Freundin wurde. Erstausgabe von 1879, Bd. III.

"The Mendelssohn Family" by Sebastian Hensel. The frontispiece shows mathematician Peter Gustav Lejeune Dirichlet, the husband of "Aunt Rebecka" (née Mendelssohn), who became a motherly friend to the half-orphaned Sebastian. First edition of 1879, Vol. III.

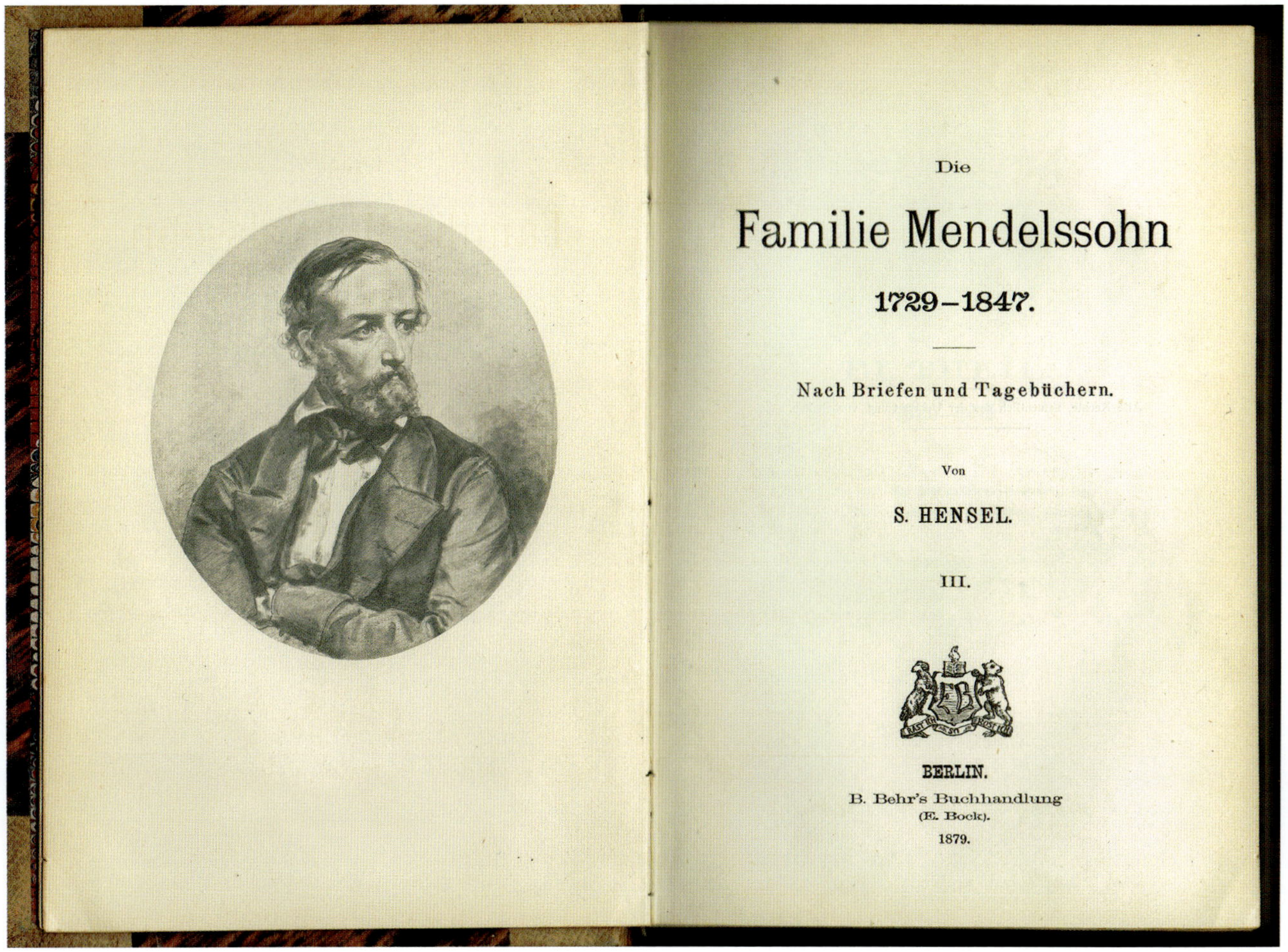

Die

Familie Mendelssohn

1729–1847.

Nach Briefen und Tagebüchern.

Von

S. HENSEL.

III.

BERLIN.

B. Behr's Buchhandlung

(E. Bock).

1879.

Paul Mendelssohn Bartholdy · 1841 Leipzig – 1880 Berlin

The youngest son of composer Felix Mendelssohn, Paul was a likeable character appreciated by all. After the death of their parents, Paul and his brother Carl were separated from their sisters, who were taken in by their Huguenot relations in Frankfurt. The two boys, meanwhile, were given into the charge of their uncle Paul, the Berlin banker. While the strict upbringing of their caretaker drove the older brother to rebel, Paul kept a more positive attitude and ostensibly came away untraumatized. Despite breaking off his schooling at the *Gymnasium* for a business apprenticeship in Leipzig, he eventually got his school-leaving degree. He went on to study chemistry in Heidelberg, joining the Allemania patriotic student fraternity just like his brother. He served in the 1866 Austro-Prussian War and, one year later, exchanged marriage vows with his niece twice removed, Else Oppenheim. Her family had ties to the banking house of Robert Warschauer & Co., as did the chemist Carl Alexander Martius. The two men became partners and founded an aniline factory, subsidized by the long-established company Kunheim & Co, situated on the Spree River in the Rummelsburg area of Berlin. In 1873, the factory was merged with the chemical plant Dr. Jordan in Treptow. Paul became the first Managing Director of the Aktiengesellschaft für Anilinfabrikation (Corporation for Aniline Production), later to be become known throughout the world as "Agfa." The idyllic marriage between Paul and his beautiful wife came to an abrupt end when Else died only five months after the birth of their son Otto. At the same time, the Agfa factories were booming. When the Franco-Prussian War broke out in 1871, Paul served as a lieutenant. His second wife, Enole, was the sister of the late Else. The couple had two girls and two boys. Those who knew Paul averred that he must have inherited his musical talent from his father; a dyed-in-the-wool Beethoven fan, he never missed a Berlin performance of the master's opera "Fidelio." Paul Mendelssohn suffered a fatal heart attack at the age of only 39, and so did not live to see his company grow into a global giant.

Er ist der jüngste Sohn des Komponisten Felix: ein Sympathieträger, dem die Herzen zufliegen. Nach dem Tod beider Eltern waren die Brüder Carl und Paul von ihren Schwestern, die bei der Frankfurter Hugenotten-Verwandtschaft bleiben, getrennt worden. Die Jungen wachsen auf beim Berliner Onkel Paul, dem Bankier. Während Konflikte mit diesem strengen Vormund den älteren Bruder in die Rebellion treiben, trägt Paul, der Positive, offenbar keinen Schaden davon. Er bricht das Gymnasium für eine Kaufmannslehre in Leipzig ab, holt das Abitur nach. Studiert Chemie in Heidelberg, ist Burschenschaftler bei der Allemania wie sein Bruder. Er nimmt teil am österreichisch-preußischen Krieg (1866) und heiratet im Folgejahr die Nichte zweiten Grades Else Oppenheim, deren Familie mit der Warschauer-Bank verbunden ist – wie ebenso der Chemiker Carl Alexander Martius. Mit ihm gründet Paul an der Rummelsburger Spree, unterstützt durch die eingesessene Firma Kunheim & Co., eine Anilinfabrik, die 1873 mit der in Treptow übernommenen Chemischen Fabrik Dr. Jordan zusammengeführt wird. Er ist erster Generaldirektor der Actiengesellschaft für Anilinfabrikation = Agfa. Die kurze Ehe des Traumpaares endet fünf Monate nach der Geburt seines Sohnes Otto mit dem Tod der schönen Frau. Die Fabriken boomen. Paul zieht als Leutnant in den 1871er-Krieg gegen Frankreich. Er heiratet Enole, die Schwester der verstorbenen Else. Zwei Töchter, zwei Söhne werden geboren. Seine Musikalität habe er vom Vater geerbt, sagen die, die ihn kennen. Als Beethoven-Fan versäumt er keinen „Fidelio" in Berlin. Er stirbt, 39 Jahre alt, am Herzinfarkt. Den Aufstieg seiner Fabrik zum Weltkonzern hat er nicht mehr erlebt.

Paul Mendelssohn Bartholdy (um 1870).
Paul Mendelssohn Bartholdy (c. 1870).

Else Mendelssohn Bartholdy, geb. Oppenheim (1844 – 1868).
Gemälde von Hanno Rhomberg.

Else Mendelssohn Bartholdy, née Oppenheim (1844 – 1868).
Portrait by Hanno Rhomberg.

Als Lieutenant der Landwehr-Kavallerie.
Von 1870/1871 hat sich in Pauls Satteltasche ein
Konvolut Heimatpost erhalten.

As a cavalry lieutenant in the Landwehr militia.
A bundle of letters from home written in 1870/1871
was preserved in Paul's saddlebag.

Enole (Nono) Mendelssohn Bartholdy, geb. Oppenheim (1855 – 1939).

Enole (Nono) Mendelssohn Bartholdy, née Oppenheim (1855 – 1939).

Spektrograph, gewidmet
dem Chemie-Doktoranden
Paul Mendelssohn Bartholdy.

Spectrograph, dedicated to
the doctoral student in chemistry
Paul Mendelssohn Bartholdy.

Gräber von Enole, Paul und Else Mendelssohn Bartholdy
auf den Friedhöfen vor dem Halleschen Tor.

Graves of Enole, Paul and Else Mendelssohn Bartholdy
on the cemeteries near Hallesches Tor.

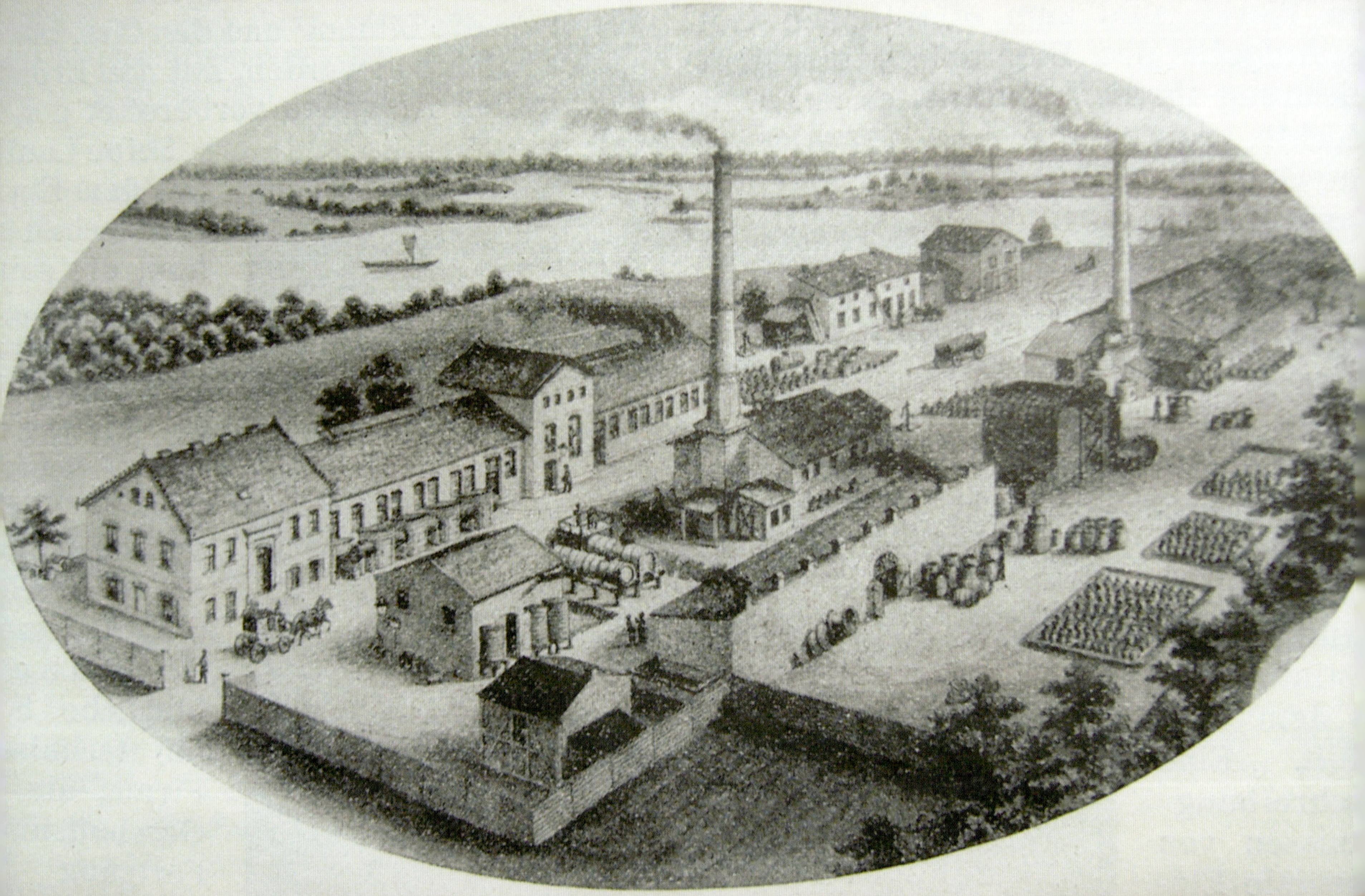

Exkurs · Nachkommen Moses Mendelssohns in der Agfa und bei der I.G. Farben
The Descendants of Moses Mendelssohn at Agfa and I.G. Farben

During the lifetime of its founder, Paul Mendelssohn Bartholdy (1841 – 1880), the Aktiengesellschaft für Anilinfabrikation (Corporation for Aniline Production or "Agfa") manufactured dyes at its two Berlin plants in Rummelsburg and Treptow. The photography division was built up later by Paul's partner, Carl Alexander Martius, and Franz Oppenheim. A great-grandson of Moses Mendelssohn, Franz Oppenheim (1852 – 1929) became Chairman of Agfa's Managing Board in 1898. Before long, Afga had become a global corporation with branch locations in Wolfen (Germany), Moscow (Russia), Libau (Latvia) and Lyon (France), and was producing pharmaceuticals, aromas, photographic plates, film stock, and rayon fiber; in World War I, poison gas was turned out as well. In 1904, Oppenheim brought Agfa into a "tripartite pact" with Bayer and BASF. In 1925, the three giants were merged to become the massive conglomerate I.G. Farbenindustrie A.G., with Franz serving as a member of the Supervisory Board and Administrative Council. Franz's son Kurt Oppenheim (1886 – 1947) took on the commercial management of Agfa in 1919, after first having served as Managing Board Member of Kriegschemikalien AG (Military Chemicals Corporation). Starting in 1926, he would serve three years on the Executive Board of the newly created I.G. Farben. After a health-related, recuperational stay in Switzerland in 1930, he decided to move there permanently. In 1942, his luxurious villa on Berlin's *Kleiner Wannsee* lake was confiscated by the Gestapo.

Banker Otto von Mendelssohn Bartholdy, the eldest son of Agfa's founder Paul, was raised to the nobility in 1906. As Agfa's biggest stockholder, he sat on the company's Supervisory Board (as of 1908), and later on that of I.G. Farben (as of 1926). Otto was forced to give up his mandate by the Nazis in 1938; he emigrated to Switzerland in 1945. Otto's half-brother Paul Mendelssohn Bartholdy, Jr. (1879 – 1956) became a Director at I.G. Farben in 1925, overseeing the production of photographic plates in Berlin and of film rolls in Wolfen. Pushed out of the company by the Nazis in 1933, he took his family to England. In 1938, he was forced to sell the villa he had built in 1927 beside Berlin's Tiergarten Park. All of the shares held by Mendelssohn heirs were expropriated by the Third Reich.

I.G. Farben, the world's largest chemicals conglomerate, was Adolf Hitler's single biggest campaign contributor in the German elections of 1932. Later, the company was deeply involved in the Reich's re-armament, in the "death through work" regimen implemented at the concentration camps and, most notoriously, in the industrial-scale genocide of the gas chambers. At the Nuremberg Trials, 23 leading executives of the company were charged with war crimes; 12 of them received jail terms.

Zu Lebzeiten des Gründers Paul Mendelssohn Bartholdy (1841 – 1880) stellt die Aktiengesellschaft für Anilinfabrikation (Agfa) in Berlin-Rummelsburg und Treptow Farben her. Der Photo-Bereich kommt unter Carl Alexander Martius und Franz Oppenheim (1852 – 1929) hinzu. Dieser Ururenkel Moses Mendelssohns wird 1898 Vorstandsvorsitzender. Das Weltunternehmen hat Standorte in Wolfen, Moskau, Libau und Lyon, produziert Pharmazeutika, Riechstoffe, photographische Platten, Filme, Kunstseide; im Weltkrieg auch Giftgas. 1904 hat Oppenheim die Agfa mit Bayer und BASF in einem „Dreibund" zusammengeführt; 1925 geht sie in der „I.G. Farbenindustrie A.G." auf, deren Aufsichts- und Verwaltungsrat er angehört. Sein Sohn Kurt Oppenheim (1886 – 1947) war Vorstandsmitglied der „Kriegschemikalien AG"; 1919 übernimmt er die kaufmännische Leitung der Agfa, sitzt ab 1926 drei Jahre im Vorstand der I.G. Farben, bleibt 1930 nach einem Rekonvaleszenz-Aufenthalt in der Schweiz. 1942 wird seine Villa am Kleinen Wannsee von der Gestapo beschlagnahmt.

Der Bankier Otto von Mendelssohn Bartholdy, ältester – 1906 geadelter – Sohn des Agfa-Gründers, sitzt als Hauptaktionär ab 1908 im Agfa-Aufsichtsrat, ab 1926 in dem der I.G. Farben. 1938 wird er gezwungen, das Mandat niederzulegen, emigriert nach 1945 in die Schweiz. Sein Halbbruder Paul Mendelssohn Bartholdy d.J. (1879 – 1956) leitet als Direktor der I.G. Farben ab 1925 in Berlin die Produktion von Photoplatten, in Wolfen die von Rollfilm. 1933 drängt man ihn aus dem Amt, er geht mit der Familie nach England, wird 1938 zum Verkauf seiner 1927 erbauten Villa im Tiergarten gezwungen. Aktien der Mendelssohn-Nachkommen fallen an das Deutsche Reich.

Die I.G. Farben, der weltgrößte Chemiekonzern, hatte 1932 mit der höchsten Einzelspende der Industrie Hitlers Wahlkampf unterstützt, war an der Aufrüstung des „Dritten Reiches", an der „Vernichtung durch Arbeit" und am industriell organisierten Genozid beteiligt. In Nürnberg wurden wegen Kriegsverbrechen 23 leitende Angestellte angeklagt, zwölf erhielten Haftstrafen.

Aktiengesellschaft für Anilinfabrikation (Agfa) in Berlin-Rummelsburg (1877).
The Aktiengesellschaft für Anilinfabrikation (Agfa) in Berlin-Rummelsburg (1877).

Carl Alexander Martius, Mitbegründer der Agfa.
Carl Alexander Martius, co-founder of Agfa.

Paul Mendelssohn Bartholdy.
Stich aus der Veröffentlichung seines Nachrufes in „Berichte der Deutschen Chemischen Gesellschaft" (1880).

Paul Mendelssohn Bartholdy.
Engraving from his obituary published in the "Berichte der Deutschen Chemischen Gesellschaft" (Bulletins of the German Chemical Society) (1880).

Franz Oppenheim, Vorstandsvorsitzender der I.G. Farben.
Gemälde von Max Liebermann.

Franz Oppenheim, Chairman of the I.G. Farben Managing Board.
Painting by Max Liebermann.

Kurt Oppenheim,
Vorstandsmitglied der I.G. Farben.

Kurt Oppenheim,
Member of the I.G. Farben Managing Board.

Paul Mendelssohn Bartholdy d.J.,
Direktor der I.G. Farben.

Paul Mendelssohn Bartholdy Jr.,
Director at I.G. Farben.

Agfa-Werke der I.G. Farben in Treptow.
Luftaufnahme (um 1940).

The Agfa works of I.G. Farben in Treptow.
Aerial photograph (c. 1940).

Arnold Mendelssohn · 1855 Ratibor – 1933 Darmstadt

When Arnold was eight years old, his father Wilhelm, a mechanical railways engineer, died of the cholera he had contracted while volunteering at a military hospital. Arnold's mother decided to relocate with her four children from Silesia to Berlin, where they received financial assistance from the banker Alexander Mendelssohn. Young Arnold studied secular and ecclesiastical music and went on to work as organist and Protestant cantor at the Neue Evangelische Kirche in Bonn, and later in Bielefeld. German *Lieder*, which he had been encouraged to try his hand at by his composer friend Hugo Wolf, soon accounted for a large part of his musical output. In 1891, he was appointed Church Music Director in Darmstadt. A committed patriot, Arnold supported the morale of German troops during World War I by writing soldiers' ballads. He would eventually be recognized as the leading composer of Protestant sacred music during the first third of the 20th century.

Arnold was married to the graphic artist Maria Cauer. Like her husband, Maria came from a family of artists and educators and was related to the Itzigs. Tragically, three of the couple's children died young. Arnold suspected that he might be genetically responsible due to having married a relative, and was racked by persistent feelings of guilt. These dark emotions would inform much of his music, as in his opera "Elsi," for example. In 1912, his fourth child Dorothea fell ill with encephalitis, plunging him into an existential crisis. From now on, he would turn away from vocal music in favor of instrumental compositions. The renowned Wilhelm Furtwängler refused to conduct the premiere of Arnold's Third Symphony because he considered the work too "backward-looking." Undeterred, Arnold, who was teacher to the composer Paul Hindemith, continued to seek creative inspiration from older musical styles while toning down Romantic subjectivity. In 1928, Arnold was awarded the Beethoven Prize from the Prussian State Academy. A conservatively inclined oddball, he recorded innumerable critical reflections on modernism and tradition that he called "Gedanken und Grillen" (whims and ideas). He died in 1933, shortly after Hitler's rise to power, and five years after his wife.

Arnold's oratorium "Jonas," composed in 1932, has unfortunately been lost, since his Leipzig publisher refused to print it. His cantata for choir and string quartet "Die Seligpreisungen" (The Beatitudes) was premiered in the summer of 1933.

Als er acht ist, stirbt sein Vater Wilhelm, der Eisenbahn-Maschinenmeister, beim Freiwilligeneinsatz im Militärlazarett an der Cholera. Mutter Louise zieht mit ihren vier Kindern aus Schlesien nach Berlin, wo der Bankier Alexander Mendelssohn sie unterstützt. Ihr Sohn studiert Musik und Kirchenmusik. Als Organist und Kantor wirkt er an der Neuen Evangelischen Kirche in Bonn, später in Bielefeld. Sein Freund Hugo Wolf regt ihn zur Liedkomposition an, die bald breiten Raum in seinem Werk einnimmt. 1891 wird er nach Darmstadt als Kirchenmusikmeister berufen. Im ersten Drittel des 20. Jahrhunderts ist er der bedeutendste Komponist evangelischer Sakralmusik. Während des Ersten Weltkriegs unterstützt der Patriot Arnold die kaiserlichen Truppen als Verfasser von Soldatenliedern.

Verheiratet ist er mit der Grafikerin Maria Cauer, die einer Künstler- und Pädagogenfamilie entstammt, verwandt mit den Itzigs wie ihr Mann. Drei Kinder sterben früh, den Vater verfolgen Schuldgefühle: Aufgrund der eigenen Verwandten-Ehe fühlt er sich genetisch verantwortlich. Seine Oper „Elsi" ist von solch düsteren Überlegungen inspiriert. Als sein viertes Kind, Dorothea, 1912 an Gehirnhauterzündung erkrankt, gerät er in eine Lebenskrise. Von Vokalwerken wendet er sich verstärkt der Instrumentalmusik zu. Der Dirigent Furtwängler, dem sie zur Uraufführung vorliegt, lehnt seine dritte Sinfonie als rückwärtsgewandt ab. Auseinandersetzung mit alten Formen und die Rücknahme romantischer Subjektivität bleibt für Arnold, zu dessen Schülern auch Paul Hindemith zählt, das Thema seiner Kreativität. 1928 erhält er den Beethoven-Preis der Preußischen Staatsakademie. In tausenden Aphorismen, „Gedanken und Grillen" notiert der konservative Querkopf seine kritische Sicht auf Moderne und Tradition. Seine Frau hat er fünf Jahre überlebt, stirbt selbst kurz nach Hitlers Ernennung zum Reichskanzler.

Arnolds verschollenes Oratorium „Jonas" hatte Ende 1932 sein Leipziger Verlag nicht mehr drucken wollen. Seine Kantate mit Streichquartett „Die Seligpreisungen" wird im Sommer 1933 uraufgeführt.

Arnold Ludwig Mendelssohn. Zeichnung (1925).
Arnold Ludwig Mendelssohn. Drawing (1925).

„Wenn einst der letzte Schuß verhallt".
Friedensgedicht eines Frontsoldaten im Ersten Weltkrieg, vertont von Arnold Mendelssohn.

"When the Last Shot Has Died Away".
Pacifist poem by a front-line soldier in World War I, set to music by Arnold Mendelssohn.

Maria Louise Helene Mendelssohn, geb. Cauer (1861 – 1928). Ölgemälde.

Maria Louise Helene Mendelssohn, née Cauer (1861 – 1928). Oil painting.

Louise Mendelssohn, geb. Cauer (Mitte), später Ehefrau Wilhelm Mendelssohns und Mutter Arnolds, im Verwandtenkreis.
Oben rechts ihre Schwester Bertha Kummer, die nach dem Tod von Wilhelms Schwester Ottilie den verwitweten Mathematiker Eduard Kummer heiratete.
Rechts unten Clara Wilsing, geb. Hitzig.

Louise Mendelssohn, née Cauer (middle) amongst her relatives. She would later become the wife of Wilhelm Mendelssohn and mother of Arnold.
Upper right: Her sister Bertha Kummer, who married the mathematician Eduard Kummer after the death of his wife Ottilie, Wilhelm's sister.
Lower right: Clara Wilsing, née Hitzig.

„Drei Tonsätze" von Arnold Mendelssohn (1900).
Sein erstes kammermusikalisches Instrumentalwerk ist der Dank an den Bankiers-Neffen, der eine Opern-Uraufführung des Onkels im Theater des Westens unterstützt hatte.

"Three Compositions" by Arnold Mendelssohn (1900).
He composed this, his first piece of chamber music, as a thank-you to his banker nephew, who had subsidized the premiere of his opera at the Theater des Westens.

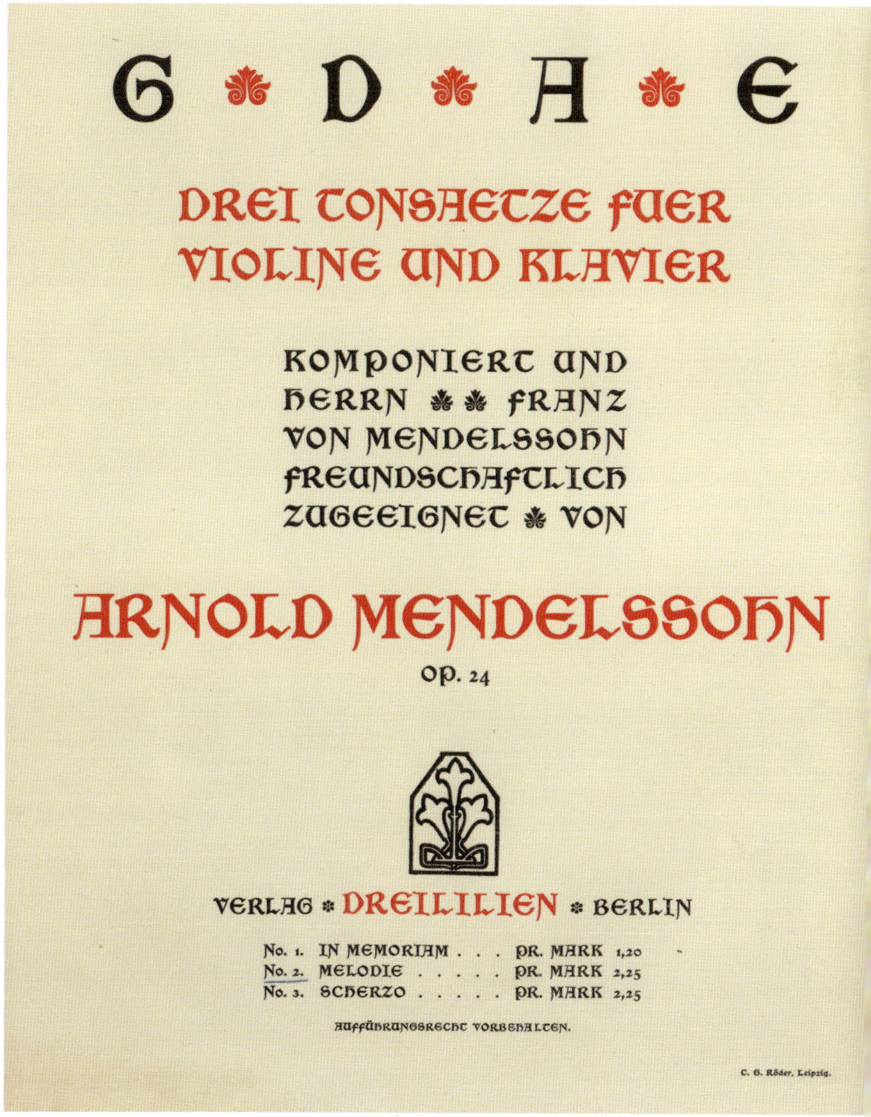

„Das Mädchen mit dem Tränenkrug". Die von Dorothea Mendelssohn (1890 – 1938) vor ihrer Einlieferung in eine Heilanstalt geschaffene Skulptur wurde auf dem Bessunger Friedhof in Darmstadt am Grab ihres Vaters aufgestellt.

"The Girl with the Pitcher of Tears." This sculpture, created by Dorothea Mendelssohn (1890 – 1938) before her commitment to a sanatorium, was placed by the grave of her father at the *Bessunger Friedhof* cemetery in Darmstadt.

Robert von Mendelssohn · 1857 Berlin – 1917 Berlin
Eleonora von Mendelssohn · 1900 Berlin – 1951 New York
Francesco von Mendelssohn · 1901 Berlin – 1972 New York

Banker Robert (von) Mendelssohn had a special bond with Italy. For one, he was a close friend of the Italian theater diva Eleonora Duse. In 1898, he was introduced to one of Eleanora's fans, the singer and pianist Giulietta Giordigiani (1871 – 1955), who would eventually become his wife. A passionate cellist, Robert purchased the Stradivari cello owned by late Italian virtuoso Alfredo Piatti. Together with Giulietta, he would perform on the instrument in outstanding musical soirees at their stately villa in Berlin's Grunewald suburb, where the guest list included the likes of Max Reinhardt, Max Planck, Albert Einstein, Samuel Fischer, and Joseph Joachim. A collector and patron of the arts, Robert was open to new artistic currents, yet well-connected in conservative political circles, serving as treasurer of the German Naval League and lending vocal support to German colonial policies. He was also chairman of a Jewish community foundation, as well as a sponsor of various other cultural and social institutions. Even before the passing of his uncle Ernst, whose leadership he had criticized, Robert became the Senior Director of the Mendelssohn & Co. banking house in 1908.

Robert and Giulietta had a son, Francesco, and a daughter, Eleonora, who was given the baptismal name of her godmother, the great Eleonora Duse. Growing up to become a successful actress in her own right, Eleonora worked with brilliant talents such as Fritz Kortner, Gustav Gründgens, and Max Reinhardt, who also became her lover. Francesco, meanwhile, became a cellist. He inherited the Piatti cello after the untimely death of his father and went on to play with the prestigious Klingler Quartet. He also worked as a theater director, bringing two plays by Ödön von Horváth to Berlin, for example. The two siblings gradually grew estranged from their mother Giulietta who, out of latent jealousy, had plotted to cause financial damage Eleonora Duse, a customer of the Mendelssohn bank. Giulietta, a party comrade of Benito Mussolini, took umbrage at her son Francesco's open homosexuality. After inheriting a fortune from their father, Eleonora and Francesco became the toast of Berlin during the Roaring Twenties, and their riotous escapades made them no strangers to scandal. Eleonora was to go through a series of marriages, first to pianist Edwin Fischer, then to a Hungarian riding champion, then, in the US, to the actor Rudolf Forster, and finally to the actor Martin Kosleck.

In 1935, the siblings escaped to New York but their lives gradually went downhill. While they generously assisted other emigrants,

Zu Italien hat Robert (von) Mendelssohn Beziehungen. Er ist mit Eleonora Duse, der Bühnendiva, befreundet; aus deren Fan-Zirkel wird dem Bankier 1898 seine Braut zugeführt, die Sängerin und Pianistin Giulietta Gordigiani (1871 – 1955). Er kauft als passionierter Cellist nach dem Tod des Virtuosen Alfredo Piatti dessen Stradivari-Cello; gibt mit Giulietta hervorragende Hauskonzerte. In seiner Grunewald-Villa sind Max Reinhardt, Max Planck, Albert Einstein, Samuel Fischer und Joseph Joachim zu Gast. Als Sammler und Mäzen ist er künstlerisch aufgeschlossen, politisch konservativ vernetzt: Schatzmeister des Flottenvereins, Befürworter der Kolonialpolitik, auch Vorsitzender einer Stiftung der Jüdischen Gemeinde, Förderer weiterer kultureller und sozialer Stiftungen. Noch vor dem Tod seines Onkels Ernst, dessen Führungsstil er kritisiert, wird er 1908 Seniorchef von Mendelssohn & Co.

Eleonora wird getauft auf den Namen ihrer Patin, der Duse. Als erfolgreiche Schauspielerin arbeitet sie mit Fritz Kortner, Gustav Gründgens und mit Max Reinhardt, dessen Geliebte sie wird. Francesco wird Cellist, erbt nach dem frühen Tod des Vaters das Piatti-Cello, spielt mit dem Klingler-Quartett. Als Regisseur realisiert er zwei Horváth-Uraufführungen. Die Beziehung der Geschwister zur Mutter, die der Duse – Kundin der Mendelssohn-Bank – aus später Eifersucht finanziell zu schaden weiß, verschlechtert sich. Im Berlin der *Roaring Twenties* machen die glamourösen Erben mit Eskapaden Furore. Giulietta, eine Parteigängerin Mussolinis, lehnt die Homosexualität ihres Sohnes ab. Eleonora heiratet den Pianisten Edwin Fischer, dann einen ungarischen Rittmeister; später in den USA den Schauspieler Rudolf Forster.

Im Exil ab 1935 verlieren Bruder und Schwester den Halt. Sie helfen anderen Emigranten, können beruflich kaum Fuß fassen, werden von einer Familienstiftung unterstützt. Francescos Plan, die Geschichte seiner Familie zu schreiben, geht über ein Konzept nicht hinaus. Die Leidenschaft der drogensüchtigen Eleonora gilt nun dem Dirigenten Toscanini. Ihren labilen Bruder, der wegen „aggressiver Homosexualität“ in Psychiatrien eingeliefert wird, möchte sie stärken. Ihre Anstrengungen, verkaufte Schätze der Kunstsammlung Roberts nach 1945 bei deutschen Gerichten zurückzugewinnen, schlagen fehl. Bald nach dem Start ihres einzigen Films, des Mafia-Dramas „Black Hand“, wenige Tage nach dem Suizidversuch ihres vierten Mannes Martin Kosleck,

Francesco, die 1920 verstorbene Schwester Angelica und Eleonora von Mendelssohn, mit ihrer Mutter Giulietta und dem Vater Robert.

Francesco, their sister Angelica (died 1920) and Eleonora von Mendelssohn with their mother Giulietta and father Robert.

they themselves had great difficulty in finding a livelihood, and eventually had to be supported by a family foundation. Francesco's plan to write his own family history never got beyond the concept stage. Eleonora, who had become addicted to drugs, had a stormy affair with conductor Arturo Toscanini. Although Eleonora tried to help her brother, he was eventually committed to psychiatric clinics for "aggressive homosexuality." Eleonora tried her best to recover some of the masterpieces in her father's art collection, which she claimed had been wrongfully sold off, but was rebuffed by the German courts. Just days after the attempted suicide of her fourth husband, Eleonora was found dead in her apartment. Her one and only film, the Mafia drama "Black Hand," had premiered only a short time before. Francesco, for his part, lived out his days under the care of the widow of his long-time psychiatrist. According to his will, his Piatti cello was sold and the proceeds given to a foundation to support aspiring young musicians.

wird Eleonora tot in ihrer Wohnung aufgefunden. Francesco lebt zuletzt bei der Witwe seines Psychiaters. Der Verkauf des Piatti-Cellos aus seinem Nachlaß fließt in eine Stiftung zur Förderung von Nachwuchsmusikern.

Eleonora von Mendelssohn (1900 – 1951), Schauspielerin.
Fotografie aus den 1940er Jahren.

Eleonora von Mendelssohn (1900 – 1951), actress.
Photograph from the 1940s.

Francesco von Mendelssohn, Bruno Eisner und Albert Einstein in der Berliner Wohnung des Physikers beim Musizieren (1927).

Francesco von Mendelssohn, Bruno Eisner, and Albert Einstein making music in the physicist's Berlin flat (1927).

ELEONORA DUSE

BILDNISSE UND WORTE

GESAMMELT, ÜBERSETZT UND HERAUSGEGEBEN VON

BIANCA SEGANTINI UND FRANCESCO VON MENDELSSOHN

1926

RUDOLF KAEMMERER VERLAG BERLIN

„Eleonora Duse. Bildnisse und Worte".
Gesammelt, übersetzt und herausgegeben von Bianca Segantini und Francesco von Mendelssohn (1926).

"Eleonora Duse: Bildnisse und Worte" (Images and Words). Collected, translated, and published by Bianca Segantini and Francesco von Mendelssohn (1926).

Das Piatti-Cello, gebaut von Antonio Stradivari (1720).

The Piatti cello, built by Antonio Stradivari (1720).

Francesco von Mendelssohn (Mitte) mit Varietékünstlern in der Berliner Scala.
Francesco von Mendelssohn (middle) with vaudeville performers at the *Berliner Scala* theater.

Der Regisseur Fritz Kortner und Eleonora von Mendelssohn (1928).

Theater director Fritz Kortner and Eleonora von Mendelssohn (1928).

Francesco und Eleonora von Mendelssohn mit Kurt Weill und Lotte Lenya bei der Ankunft in New York am 10. Oktober 1935. Rechts: Meyer Wolf Weisgal, ein zionistischer Theatermanager, der Max Reinhardt zu dem jüdischen Oratorium „The Eternal Road" (Musik: Kurt Weill, Libretto: Franz Werfel) angeregt hatte. An dieser bis dahin aufwendigsten Broadway-Produktion im Manhattan Opera House (UA 1937) sind Francesco als Regieassistent und Lotte Lenya als Sängerin beteiligt, Eleonora gibt zur Finanzierung ein Bankett.

Francesco and Eleonora von Mendelssohn with Kurt Weill and Lotte Lenya upon arriving in New York on October 10, 1935. Right: Meyer Wolf Weisgal, a theater manager and passionate Zionist who inspired Max Reinhardt to direct the Jewish oratorium "The Eternal Road" (music: Kurt Weill, libretto: Franz Werfel). Opening at the Manhattan Opera House in 1937, this was the most expensive Broadway production of its day and featured Francesco as Assistant Director and Lotte Lenya as one of the singers; Eleonora helped finance the show by throwing a backer's banquet.

Marie von Mendelssohn, geb. Westphal · 1867 Berlin – 1954 Berlin
Elisabeth Westphal · 1865 Berlin – 1942 Berlin
Ernst Westphal · 1871 Berlin – 1949 Kapstadt

Carl Westphal, a professor at the Charité, and Clara Mendelssohn, the youngest daughter of the Jewish banker Alexander, had seven children. Clara had been baptized at an early age. Marie, the fourth child, married her cousin Franz von Mendelssohn. After the death of her husband (1935) and the liquidation of the bank (1938), the family was driven out of their villa in the Grunewald neighborhood of Berlin in 1942. In order to be allowed to leave Germany for Stockholm, the widow had to fund a six-figure transfer from a Swedish bank to the SS.

Elisabeth, the unmarried third child, took care of her mother Clara. Her final residence was in Grunewald, at a pension for "non-Aryans." Her nephew, Robi von Mendelssohn, received indications from the SS that her deportation was imminent. There are differing reports about the 77-year-old's suicide, committed two weeks before her birthday. Some say she acted alone, while others suggest she had help from a nurse.

Ernst Westphal, the fifth child, a patriotic lawyer and combat veteran of World War I, was married to the daughter of the art maven James Simon. Deemed a „half-Jew," the Protestant Westphal faced a ban from the legal profession and dismissal from his post as a judge at the Potsdam District Court after Hitler came to power. In an internal memo from early March 1933, he protested against the flying of a banner with a swastika at his courthouse and was promptly forced into retirement. In 1940, the couple had to sell their house in Dahlem. They lost their next home in Schöneberg to a bomb, and they were arrested but later released. They moved to Moabit, where they lost yet another home to a bomb and were not allowed to use the air raid shelter. They were in constant danger of being deported. Their daughter Leni had gone to Palestine, and two of their other children lived in South Africa. In 1946, Ernst worked as a probate judge in Berlin-Lichtenberg. After a first suicide attempt, he and his wife emigrated to Cape Town, where the 77-year-old took his own life.

Der Charité-Professor Carl Westphal und Clara Mendelssohn, die früh getaufte Jüngste des jüdischen Bankchefs Alexander, haben sieben Kinder. Marie, die Viertälteste, heiratet ihren Cousin Franz von Mendelssohn. Nach dem Tod ihres Mannes (1935) und der Liquidation des Bankhauses (1938) wird die Familie aus ihrer Grunewald-Villa vertrieben. Für die Ausreise der Witwe nach Stockholm muß 1942 eine sechsstellige Devisen-Summe von einer schwedischen Bank an die SS gezahlt werden.

Elisabeth, die ledige Drittälteste, kümmert sich um ihre Mutter Clara. Zuletzt wohnt sie im Grunewald in einer Pension für nichtarische Personen. Der Neffe Robi von Mendelssohn erhält aus der SS Hinweise auf ihre nahende Deportation. Über den Suizid der 77Jährigen, der – mit Krankenschwesterhilfe oder allein – zwei Wochen vor ihrem Geburtstag stattfand, gibt es unterschiedliche Berichte.

Ernst, der Fünftälteste, ist ein patriotischer Jurist, Frontkämpfer, verheiratet mit einer Tochter des Mäzens James Simon. Als Potsdamer Amtsgerichtsrat droht dem evangelischen „Halbjuden" Westphal nach Hitlers Machtübernahme Berufsverbot. In einem internen Umlauf protestiert er Anfang März 1933 gegen die Hissung der Hakenkreuzfahne an seinem Dienstgebäude. Zwangsruhestand. 1940 muß das Ehepaar sein Haus in Dahlem verkaufen, wird in Schöneberg ausgebombt, verhaftet, entlassen, in Moabit ausgebombt, darf nicht in den Luftschutzkeller, lebt in ständiger Gefahr des Abtransports. Tochter Leni ist in Palästina, zwei weitere Kinder sind in Südafrika. 1946 arbeitet Ernst als Nachlaßrichter in Berlin-Lichtenberg. Suizidversuch. Er und seine Frau emigrieren nach Kapstadt. Dort nimmt sich der 77Jährige das Leben.

'herese (1877 – 1969), Elisabeth (1865 – 1942), Ernst (1871 – 1949), Anna (1864 – 1943),
Aarie (1867 – 1954), Alexander (1863 – 1943), Carl Westphal (1875 – 1937) (circa 1883).

Marie von Mendelssohn, geb. Westphal.
Marie von Mendelssohn, née Westphal.

Tennis-Ausflug: Drei Westphals mit Verwandten, die z.T. in den Folgejahren geadelt werden.
Westphals, Mendelssohn, und Simsons am Stadtrand von Charlottenburg (1885).

A tennis outing: three members of the Westphal family with relatives;
many would receive noble titles in the years to come.
The Westphals, Mendelssohns, and Simsons on the outskirts of Charlottenburg (1885).

Die Witwe Enole Mendelssohn Bartholdy; Fritz Simson; Hugo Oppenheim; Robert Mendelssohn;
Otto Mendelssohn Bartholdy; Ernst Mendelssohn-Bartholdy (mit Melone); Bernhard Simson;
Ludwig Passini und Tochter Marie (verh. Herrmann); Ernst Simson (sitzend); Elisabeth Westphal;
Paul Herrmann; Armie Simson; Marie Westphal; Lisbeth Simson; Anna Westphal;
Charly Horsfall, Enkel Alexander Mendelssohns.

Elisabeth Westphal und ihre Mutter Clara, geb. Mendelssohn (1840 – 1927).

Elisabeth Westphal and her mother, Clara, née Mendelssohn (1840 – 1927).

Ernst Westphal im Ersten Weltkrieg.

Ernst Westphal during World War I.

Die um 1900 erbaute Villa Franz und Marie von Mendelssohns, geb. Westphal, an der Herthastraße: 1939 zwangsverkauft, dann Nazi-Gästehaus, später Gestapo-Abhörstation. 1943 bombardiert. Aquarell.

The Herthastrasse villa of Franz and Marie von Mendelssohn (née Westphal), built around1900. Following a forced sale in 1939, the property became a guesthouse for the Nazi party. It was later used as a Gestapo listening post until 1943, when it was hit by bombs. Watercolor.

YAD VASHEM
MARTYRS' AND HEROES' REMEMBRANCE AUTHORITY
JERUSALEM

יד ושם
רשות־הזיכרון
לשואה ולגבורה
ירושלים

Jerusalem, 1 January 1973

Mrs. Greta Rapp
45 - 25 Kissens Blv.
Flushing, N, Y. 11355
U. S. A.

Dear Mrs. Rapp,

Re: Hensel Marie-Louise - Germany

I am happy to bring to your attention, that the Commission for the Righteous, has decided, at its last meeting on 10.12.72, to confer the late Marie Louise Hensel, its highest expression of honour, - a medal of honour with the right to plant a tree in the Avenue of the Righteous, on the Mount of Rememberance, Jerusalem.

Notification thereof shall be given to her sons by the Embassy of Israel in the near future.

Sincerely,
D. Rosen
Donia Rosen
Head of the Department
for the Righteous

JERUSALEM, HAR HAZIKARON, P.O.B. 84, CABLES: YAD VASHEM, TEL. 531202 ירושלים, הר הזיכרון, ת.ד. 84, מברקים: יד ושם, טל.

Marie-Louise Hensel, geb. Flothmann · 1894 Ems – 1942 Konstanz
Käthe Wach, geb. Mendelssohn-Bartholdy · 1876 Berlin – 1956 Orselina (CH)
Otto (von) Mendelssohn Bartholdy · 1868 Berlin – 1949 Basel
Ernst Leyden · 1891 Potsdam – 1980 Köln
Franz Mendelssohn · 1897 Potsdam – 1971 Freiburg i. Br.

In April 1918, Marie-Louise Flothmann married the tax attorney Albert Hensel, a great-grandson of the composer Fanny. In 1929 he was appointed *Professor Ordinarius* in Königsberg. Forced to retire due to an "Aryan clause" in the university policies, he died of a heart attack in 1933 in Pavia. His widow decided to help Jewish friends from Marburg flee in 1942. Caught trying to identify paths to the border near Überlingen, she was denounced and questioned. Fearful that she would endanger the lives of others by revealing information, she took her own life on August 31 after three days of interrogation by the Gestapo in Constance. The authorities in Marburg intended to deport her Jewish mother-in-law shortly thereafter, but members of the family raised objections and were able to prevent the deportation. In 1972, Marie-Louise Hensel was honored as "Righteous among the Nations" at Yad Vashem.

Käthe Wach was married in Dresden to her cousin Felix. After he protested against the demolition of the Mendelssohn Bartholdy monument in Leipzig, Felix was threatened by NSDAP functionaries. Their daughter, Susanne (1902 – 1992) was divorced by the star athlete Heinz Heigl, who feared his wife's heritage would damage his career in the Wehrmacht. According to oral reports, after Felix' death in 1943, his daughter and widow were interned in the Theresienstadt ghetto, but were released, thanks to the intervention of the Swedish royal family, and found refuge in Stockholm.

Otto von Mendelssohn Bartholdy, son of the founder of the Agfa company, which had been acquired by I.G. Farben, was deprived of his shares in the company in 1938, pushed out of the board, and forced to wear the yellow star. After the death of his "crossbreed" wife, Cécile, a cousin, he had to move out of his villa, the "Casa Bartholdy" in Potsdam and into the gardener's house. He was arrested and brought to the Gestapo headquarters for deportation. The president of Potsdam's government was able to secure his release. In 1945, when it became clear that Otto's expropriated estate would remain nationalized, he emigrated to Switzerland.

When Jenny Mendelssohn, née Leyden, died of old age in the Bethel Institution in 1944, her family suspected (incorrectly) that she had been a victim of the Nazi euthanasia program. Her husband, a grandson of the banker Alexander Mendelssohn, had died in 1935. In 1941, two of her sons and some grandchildren

Im April 1918 hatte Marie-Louise Flothmann den Steuerrechtler Albert Hensel geheiratet, einen Urenkel der Komponistin Fanny. Er wird 1929 in Königsberg Ordinarius; erliegt 1933 in Pavia, zwangsbeurlaubt aufgrund des Arierparagraphen, einem Herzleiden. Seine Witwe entschließt sich 1942 zur Fluchthilfe für jüdische Freunde aus Marburg. Bei Überlingen erkundet sie Wege an der Grenze, wird denunziert. Aus Angst, andere durch Geständnisse zu gefährden, nimmt sie sich am 31. August nach drei Tagen Verhör durch die Konstanzer Gestapo das Leben. In Marburg soll ihre jüdische Schwiegermutter kurz darauf deportiert werden, was Einsprüche aus der Familie verhindern können. 1972 wird Marie-Louise Hensel in Yad Vashem als „Gerechte unter den Völkern“ geehrt.

Käthe Wach ist in Dresden verheiratet mit ihrem Cousin Felix, der gegen den Abriß des Leipziger Mendelssohn Bartholdy-Denkmals protestiert. Darauf wird er von NSDAP-Funktionären bedroht. Tochter Susanne (1902 – 1992) läßt sich widerwillig von dem Star-Sportler Heinz Heigl scheiden, der seine Wehrmachtskarriere durch ihre Abstammung gefährdet sieht. Mündliche Berichte besagen, daß 1943, nach Felix Wachs Tod, dessen Tochter und Witwe im Ghetto Theresienstadt inhaftiert waren, von wo sie durch Intervention des schwedischen Königshauses entlassen wurden und nach Stockholm gelangten.

Otto von Mendelssohn Bartholdy, Sohn des Gründers der in den I.G. Farben aufgegangenen Agfa, wird 1938 seiner Konzern-Anteile beraubt und aus dem Aufsichtsrat gedrängt. Er trägt den gelben Stern, muß – nach dem Tod seiner „Mischlings-Ehefrau“ Cécile, einer Cousine – seine „Casa Bartholdy“ in Potsdam verlassen, ins Gärtnerhaus ziehen. Verhaftet wird er zur Deportation in die Gestapo-Zentrale verbracht. Potsdams Regierungspräsident erwirkt seine Freilassung. Als sich 1945 abzeichnet, daß Ottos enteigneter Besitz beschlagnahmt bleibt, emigriert er in die Schweiz.

Als Jenny Mendelssohn, geb. von Leyden, 1944 altersschwach in den Betheler Anstalten stirbt, vermutet ihre Familie (zu Unrecht), die Mutter sei ein Euthanasie-Opfer geworden. Ihr Mann Alexander, ein Enkel des Bankiers Alexander Mendelssohn, war 1935 gestorben. 1941 legen zwei ihrer Söhne und einige Enkel aus Angst den „jüdischen“ Vaternamen ab. Ihr Sohn Ernst Leyden wirkt mit an der Bewahrung des Kölner Bankhauses Sal. Oppenheim. Ihr Enkel Ernst fällt in Rußland. Ihr Sohn Franz

Marie-Loise Hensel (1894 – 1942).

Albert Hensel (1895 – 1933).

Ehrung Marie-Louise Hensels als „Gerechte unter den Völkern“ durch Yad Vashem.
Marie-Louise Hensel commemorated as "Righteous among the Nations" at Yad Vashem.

stopped using their father's "Jewish" surname out of fear. Her son Ernst Leyden helped to save the Cologne bank of Sal. Oppenheim. Her grandson Ernst fell in Russia. Her son Franz handed in his application for a name change belatedly. He hid his lineage with forged papers in order to secure his family's existence and his job in submarine construction.

reicht seinen Antrag auf Namensänderung zu spät ein. Er fälscht aber den eigenen Ahnennachweis, um die Existenz seiner Familie, seinen Arbeitsplatz im U-Bootbau zu sichern.

„Casa Bartholdy" in Potsdam.
The *Casa Bartholdy* in Potsdam.

Otto von Mendelssohn Bartholdy.

Brief zur Enteignung Otto Israels von Mendelssohn Bartholdy.
Letter expropriating Otto Israel von Mendelssohn Bartholdy.

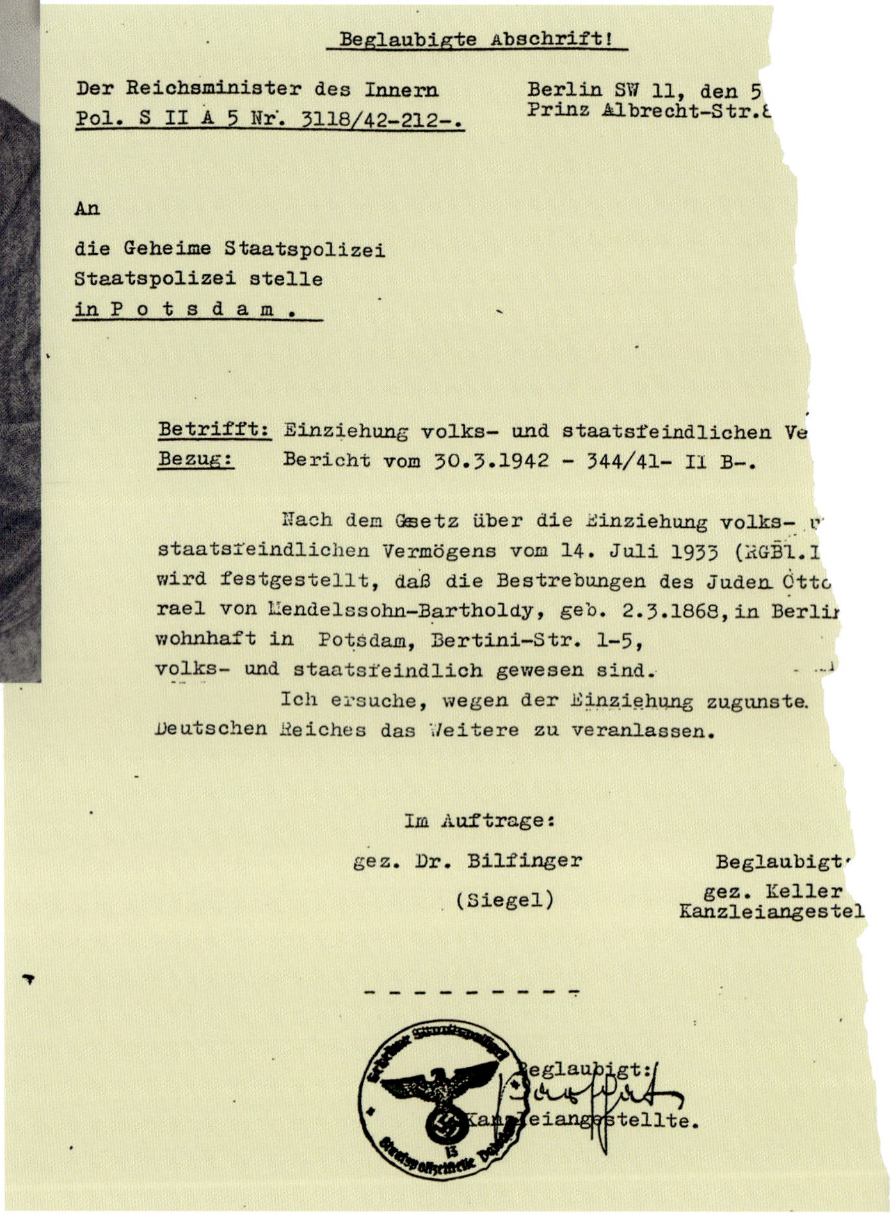

Beglaubigte Abschrift!

Der Reichsminister des Innern
Pol. S II A 5 Nr. 3118/42-212-.

Berlin SW 11, den 5
Prinz Albrecht-Str.8

An
die Geheime Staatspolizei
Staatspolizei stelle
in Potsdam.

Betrifft: Einziehung volks- und staatsfeindlichen Ve
Bezug: Bericht vom 30.3.1942 - 344/41- II B-.

Nach dem Gesetz über die Einziehung volks- u
staatsfeindlichen Vermögens vom 14. Juli 1933 (RGBl.I
wird festgestellt, daß die Bestrebungen des Juden Otto
rael von Mendelssohn-Bartholdy, geb. 2.3.1868, in Berlin
wohnhaft in Potsdam, Bertini-Str. 1-5,
volks- und staatsfeindlich gewesen sind.
Ich ersuche, wegen der Einziehung zugunste
Deutschen Reiches das Weitere zu veranlassen.

Im Auftrage:
gez. Dr. Bilfinger
(Siegel)

Beglaubigt
gez. Keller
Kanzleiangestel

Beglaubigt:
Kanzleiangestellte.

Käthe Wach (Mitte) und Marie von Mendelssohn (rechts) nach ihrer Ankunft im schwedischen Exil.
Käthe Wach (middle) and Marie von Mendelssohn (right) after their arrival in Sweden.

Adelswappen
Otto von Mendelssohn Bartholdys,
nobilitiert 1906.

Family crest of
Otto von Mendelssohn Bartholdy,
elevated to the nobility in 1906.

Die Geschwister
Ernst, Eva und Franz Mendelssohn
im Karneval (vor 1920).

The siblings
Ernst, Eva, and Franz Mendelssohn
at a carnival celebration (before 1920).

Hochzeit von Eva Irene Mendelssohn (1918 – 2001) und
Werner Meyer-Thode in Hamburg (1939).
Rechts der Brautvater, Marinebaurat Franz Mendelssohn (1887 – 1971).

Wedding photograph of Eva Irene Mendelssohn (1918 – 2001) and
Werner Meyer-Thode in Hamburg (1939).
On the right is the father of the bride, Franz Mendelssohn (1887 – 1971).

Franz von Mendelssohn · 1865 Berlin – 1935 Berlin

He collected the life-size novelty ape statues that Moses Mendelssohn was once forced to purchase as *Judenporzellan* – an arbitrary tax on Jews imposed by the Prussian state. He financed facsimile reprints of Mendelssohnian Judaica, and donated a marble copy of Tassaert's bust of his ancestor to the Jewish community. Yet Franz von Mendelssohn also sat on the Church Council of his protestant congregation. Among his children, his socially-engaged daughter, Lilli, was especially close to him. After Lilli, a violinist, and her husband, the composer Emil Bohnke, died in an accident (1928), their three children were raised by their grandparents.

After the death of his brother Robert (1917), Franz became the chief executive of the Mendelssohn bank but left the daily operation of the business to the partner Rudolf Loeb. In 1914, he became president of the Chamber of Commerce and Industry. In 1921, he became head of the Association of German Chambers of Commerce and Industry, where he gave many politicians in the fledgling Weimar Republic the chance to address the representatives of German Industry. In 1931, he led the Conference of International Chambers of Commerce. When the business leader had to step down due to ill health in 1931, the three organizations named him President Emeritus.

A loyal monarchist, he became a member of the Prussian *Herrenhaus* in 1913. During the Weimar era, he understood the importance of winning public trust in democracy. As a public citizen, he was an active supporter of the Kaiser Wilhelm Society promoting scientific research, the Kaiser Friedrich Museum Association, and the German Oriental Society. He sat on the General Council of the Reichsbank until 1933. Before a celebration at the International Chamber of Commerce, he received a call suggesting that he may prefer not to attend; the Führer was scheduled to make an appearance. He died three months before the Nuremberg Race Laws were passed.

Er sammelt jene lebensgroßen Ramsch-Affen, die einst Moses Mendelssohn als Judenporzellan hatte erwerben müssen. Er fördert Faksimile-Reprints Mendelssohnscher Judaica, schenkt der Jüdischen Gemeinde eine Marmor-Kopie der Tassaert-Büste seines Urahns. Franz von Mendelssohn sitzt auch im Kirchenrat seiner evangelischen Gemeinde. Unter seinen Kindern schlägt besonders die mit ihrer Musik sozial engagierte Lilli seiner Liebe zur Kunst, zum Einfach-Ursprünglichen nach. Als die Geigerin und ihr Mann, der Komponist Emil Bohnke, tödlich verunglücken (1928), wachsen ihre drei Waisen bei den Großeltern auf.

Nach dem Tod seines Bruders Robert (1917) war Franz Seniorchef des Bankhauses geworden. Das operative Geschäft überläßt er dem Sozius Rudolf Löb. Seit 1914 ist er Präsident der Industrie- und Handelskammer. 1921 rückt er an die Spitze des Deutschen Industrie- und Handelstages, bei dem er Politikern der jungen Republik Auftrittschancen gibt. 1931 leitet er die Konferenz der Internationalen Handelskammer. Nach dem gesundheitlich bedingten Abtreten des Wirtschaftsführers 1931 ernennen ihn die drei Organisationen zum Ehrenpräsidenten.

1913 war er als loyaler Monarchist Mitglied des Herrenhauses geworden. Zu Weimarer Zeiten weiß er als loyaler Republikaner um Vertrauen für die Demokratie zu werben. Er ist als Citoyen aktiv für die wissenschaftsfördernde Kaiser-Wilhelm-Gesellschaft, für den Kaiser-Friedrich-Museumsverein, für die Deutsche Orientgesellschaft. Bis 1933 sitzt er im Generalrat der Reichsbank. Vor einer Feier in der Internationalen Handelskammer erhält er einen Anruf, daß es ihm sicher angenehm sei, nicht zu erscheinen, der Führer werde wohl kommen. Er stirbt drei Monate vor Verabschiedung der Nürnberger Rassengesetze.

Franz von Mendelssohn. Öl auf Leinwand.
Franz von Mendelssohn. Oil on canvas.

Wohnzimmer mit Ahnenbildern im Palais an der Herthastraße.

Living room with portraits of ancestors in the *Palais* on Herthastrasse.

Die Eigentümer von Mendelssohn & Co als Quartett:
Der Seniorchef am Cello, Rudolf Löb am Flügel, Paul Kempner an der Flöte,
Paul von Mendelssohn-Bartholdy an der Geige.
Karikatur in der Betriebsfestzeitung von Mendelssohn & Co. (1926).

The partners of Mendelssohn & Co as a quartet:
The chief executive on the cello, Rudolf Loeb at the piano,
Paul Kempner on flute, and Paul von Mendelssohn-Bartholdy on violin.
Caricature in the company anniversary program. Mendelssohn & Co. (1926).

7 Uhr-Abendblatt

Einmalige Ausgabe (aus dem Vergnügungsfond) — Dieses Blatt gehört ausschließlich dem Hausherrn
Das Nicht-Erwünschte bitte zu durchstreichen! — Das Nicht-Erwünschte bitte zu durchstreichen!

Sensationelle Enthüllungen aus der Jägerstraße

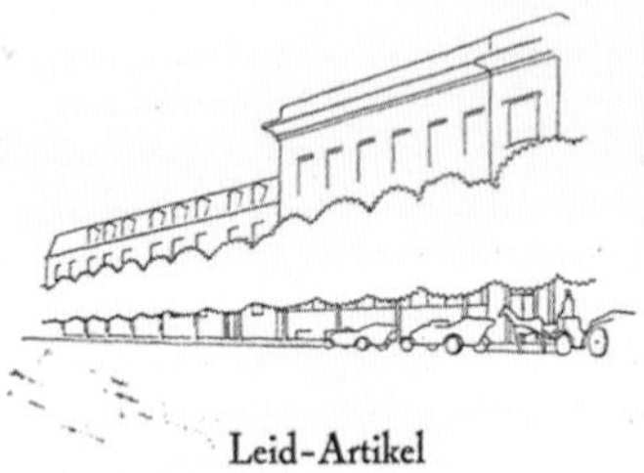

Leid-Artikel

Seit Tagen revoltiert's in meinem Schädel:
Wie leitartikelt man dies Blatt an's Licht?
Jedoch, trotz Nikotin und Kahlbaum Edel,
Die Muse streikte, es gelang mir nicht.
Mein Pegasus, einst hurtig, wie die Gemse,
— Moderne Technik ist gewiß recht weit —
Daß als Maschine er mit Vierradbremse
Noch nicht zu brauchen ist — — —
es tut mir leid!

Es tut mir leid, weil ja die Abonnenten
Im allgemeinen auf dem Standpunkt steh'n,
Daß sie für's Geld auch was erwarten könnten,
Und fürchten müssen, sich enttäuscht zu seh'n.
Besonders dann, wenn sie hier zu erwähnen
Wir nicht ergriffen die Gelegenheit.
Wir haben tiefstes Mitgefühl mit jenen
Und sagen frank und frei:
Sie tun uns leid!

Weit heikler liegt der Fall schon bei den andern,
Die unsre Lupe sich speziell erkor.
Sie könnten schwer gekränkt durch's Leben wandern,
Um Herz und Seele einen Trauerflor.
Ach, sie vergessen ganz, wie wir sie schätzen
So heute, wie gewiß noch lange Zeit,
Wir wollten ihnen keinen Schmerz versetzen,
Und wenn wir's doch getan,
so tut's uns leid!

Politik

Im Auswärtigen Amt, im Ministerium des Innern, im Polizei-Präsidium, herrschte in den gestrigen Abendstunden ungeheure Aufregung infolge der unerwarteten Nachricht von der Ankunft eines sehr hohen Herrn aus Holland. In den Wandelgängen hörte man abgerissene Worte: „Um Gotteswillen S.M.? — Unruhen? — Reichswehr? — Alarm? — Umfassende Vorsichtsmaßregeln?" —

Erst in den späten Abendstunden gelang es unserem U—L—K-Mitarbeiter festzustellen, daß es sich nicht um S.M., sondern um F.M. handelt, einen gleichfalls sehr hohen Herrn, der aus Amsterdam zu einer ganz privaten Festlichkeit hierher geeilt ist und von dessen Anwesenheit politische Verwicklungen nicht zu befürchten sind.

BANK-ABC

Der Abenhausen ist jetzt siebzig,
Der Arbeitsfimmel, na, der gibt sich.

Wer Beyer heißt, der ist zu preisen;
Doch wer wünscht Bullerjahn zu heißen?

Der Cohnheim tobt im Telefonreich,
Nicht jede Firma ist so Cohnreich.

Credit zu geben, ist gefährlich,
Consorten sind meist unentbehrlich.

Dem Degelow wird's heiß und kalt,
Der Dresel ist ein Rechtsanwalt.

Der Emuth blättert im Courier,
Der Elefant kann nichts dafür.

Wo Fehler sind, da sind auch Bucher,
Der Finder ist oft nur ein Sucher.

Ein Gaertner braucht nicht viel zu roden,
Sitzt er auf so gesundem Boden.

Tat Hilge mit dem Helm sich kleiden,
War's ohne Hochmuth und bescheiden.

O, Jahn, du hehres Turngestirn!
Ein Jahnel turnt mehr mit dem Hirn.

Der König steht im Kaufmannssold,
Der Kluge schwärmt für Schwarz-Rot-Gold.

Was Löffler heiter produziert,
Wird ernst von Leser kontrolliert.

Die Manovills sind stolz und echt,
Doch Mendelssohn klingt auch nicht schlecht.

Wär' Shakespeare noch, es hieß in jenem Fall:
Die Lerche war's, und nicht der Nachtigall.

Der Ostwald läßt's in Wien sich gut sein,
Nun wird der Anschluß bald akut sein.

Die Rechte zahlt, es pumpt die Linke,
Wo Pinkes sitzt, da gibt es Pinke.

Das Quatschen und das Quasseln quält
Den Mann, der fleißig Scheine zählt.

Bei Rohde häuft sich alles Mieße,
Rhabarber braucht oft auch ein Riese.

Im Sommerfeld und hier im Satz
Ist eine Sichel wohl am Platz.

Der Schumann schwärmt für Strauß und Liszt,
Weh dir, daß du ein Enkel bist!

Der Herr in seinem Schöpfungsweh
Schuf auch den Namen Trolldenier.

Man nennt ein Land verparadiest,
Wenn dort ein Urbach doppelt fließt.

Die Schwierigkeit beginnt mit V,
Miß Volkmann weiß das ganz genau.

Der Wallach wird wohl auch bald siebzig,
Wer so um sich besorgt ist, liebt sich.

Gleich nach dem W kommt nun das X,
Doch dafür weiß selbst Goethe nix.

Ein Zwillingspärchen doppelt frißt,
Stellmacher ist hier Spezialist.

Kammermusik in der Jägerstraße
Keine Spielnaturen und doch wundervolles Zusammenspiel

Franz von Mendelssohn (l.) 1930 beim Festbankett der Anwälte im Marmorsaal des Zoologischen Gartens, rechts der italienische Gesandte Luca Orsini Baroni. Schon der Bankgründer Joseph Mendelssohn hatte sich als Aktionär des Zoos an dessen Gründung beteiligt.

Franz von Mendelssohn (left) in 1930 at a gala dinner of attorneys in the Marble Hall of the Zoological Garden, right the Italian ambassador, Luca Orsini Baroni. The founder of the Mendelssohn bank, Joseph Mendelssohn, had been a founding shareholder of the zoo.

200. Geburtstag des Moses, 6. September 1929: Robert von Mendelssohn d.J. (l.), dessen Vater Franz mit Paul von Mendelssohn-Bartholdy (3. und 4. v.l.) in Dessau.

200th birthday anniversary of Moses on September 6, 1929 in Dessau: Robert von Mendelssohn, Jr. (left) and his father Franz with Paul von Mendelssohn-Bartholdy (3rd and 4th from the left).

Albrecht Mendelssohn Bartholdy · 1874 Karlsruhe – 1936 Oxford

As an enlightened political philosopher active in a crisis-ridden era, Albrecht was the 20th-century heir to the legacy of his great forebear Moses Mendelssohn. He was influenced by the liberal ideals of his unfortunate father Carl, a historian who had celebrated Europe's liberation movements and freedom fighters, but who was forced to spend his last decades in a psychiatric institution. While still in law school, the gifted young Albrecht published „Schmetterlinge" (Butterflies), a collection of poems. He also wrote librettos, composed *Lieder* and, as a professor, established a music festival in Würzburg in honor of the composer Max Reger. During World War I, Albrecht joined a pacifist initiative comprised of many prominent academics. At the post-war peace negotiations in Versailles, he served as a member of the German delegation's team of experts. Commissioned by the Weimar government to edit the diplomatic files pertaining to Germany's pre-1914 foreign policy, he concluded that he could not in good conscience comply with his superiors' wish to build a case rebutting Germany's guilt in starting the war.

He went on to publish the journal „Europäische Gespräche" (European Conversations) and, with financial assistance from the Warburg family, founded the Hamburger Institut für Auswärtige Politik (Hamburg Institute for Foreign Policy). The aim of both endeavors was to help strengthen the bonds that tied the fledgling German democracy to the family of nations. As Professor of International Law at the newly inaugurated University of Hamburg, he represented Germany at the League of Nations and before the affiliated Permanent Court of International Justice in The Hague.

Albrecht married his cousin Dora Wach (1875 –1949), with whom he adopted two girls. Once the Nazis came to power in Germany, he was forced out of his professorship and expelled from his faculty. In 1934, he decided to risk a perilous escape to England and was eventually, via Switzerland, followed by his family. This allowed him to also rescue the so-called "Green Books," the 27-volume collection of letters written to his famous grandfather Felix. In Oxford, where he obtained a teaching position, he chafed under the English appeasement policy towards Hitler, hoping in vain that a tyrannicide would intervene to free Germany from despotism. He died of stomach cancer not long after. His political testament, "The War and German Society," was published posthumously. Although barely legible, the gravestone of this pioneering German pacifist thinker can be found in the village churchyard of Clifton Hampden, high above the Thames River.

Er wird als politischer Aufklärer in der Krise der Moderne zum Erben seines Urahns Moses für das 20. Jahrhundert. Er fühlt sich dem liberalen Anspruch seines unglücklichen Vaters Carl verpflichtet, der als Historiker europäische Befreiungsbewegungen und Rebellengestalten gewürdigt hatte, aber letzte Lebensjahrzehnte in einer Anstalt verbrachte. Albrecht Mendelssohn Bartholdy veröffentlicht als Jura-Student den Gedichtband „Schmetterlinge", er schreibt Libretti, komponiert Lieder, gründet als Professor die Jenaer Max-Reger-Festspiele. Während des Ersten Weltkriegs schließt er sich einer pazifistischen Initiative prominenter Akademiker an. Bei Friedensvertragsverhandlungen in Versailles gehört er zur begleitenden deutschen Gutachter-Delegation. In der Weimarer Republik ediert er, beauftragt durch die Reichsregierung, Akten zur deutschen Außenpolitik vor 1914 – und erkennt, daß die gewünschte Widerlegung einer deutschen Kriegsschuld nicht möglich ist.

Mit seiner Zeitschrift „Europäische Gespräche" und durch die Gründung des von der Warburg-Familie unterstützten Hamburger Instituts für Auswärtige Politik will er ungelernten deutschen Demokraten die Staatenfamilie nahebringen. Der Ordinarius für Auslandsrecht an der neu gegründeten Universität der Hansestadt vertritt Deutschland beim Völkerbund und am Haager Gerichtshof.

Verheiratet ist Albrecht mit seiner Cousine Dora Wach (1875 – 1949), zwei Mädchen hat das Paar adoptiert. Nach Hitlers Wahl zum Reichskanzler wird er von seinem Lehrstuhl, aus seinem Institut gedrängt. Seine gefährliche Flucht, die Familie folgt ihm später über die Schweiz, führt 1934 nach England. Gerettet werden so auch die „Green Books", das 27bändige Konvolut von Briefen an seinen berühmten Großvater Felix. In Oxford, wo er einen Lehrauftrag erhält, leidet er unter der englischen Beschwichtigungspolitik gegenüber Hitler und hofft auf einen Tyrannenmord in Deutschland. Er stirbt an Magenkrebs. Posthum erscheint sein politisches Testament „The War and German Society". Der kaum zu entziffernde Grabstein dieses Pioniers der deutschen Friedensforschung steht auf dem Dorffriedhof von Clifton Hampden, hoch über der Themse.

Albrecht Mendelssohn Bartholdy als Student.
Albrecht Mendelssohn Bartholdy as a student.

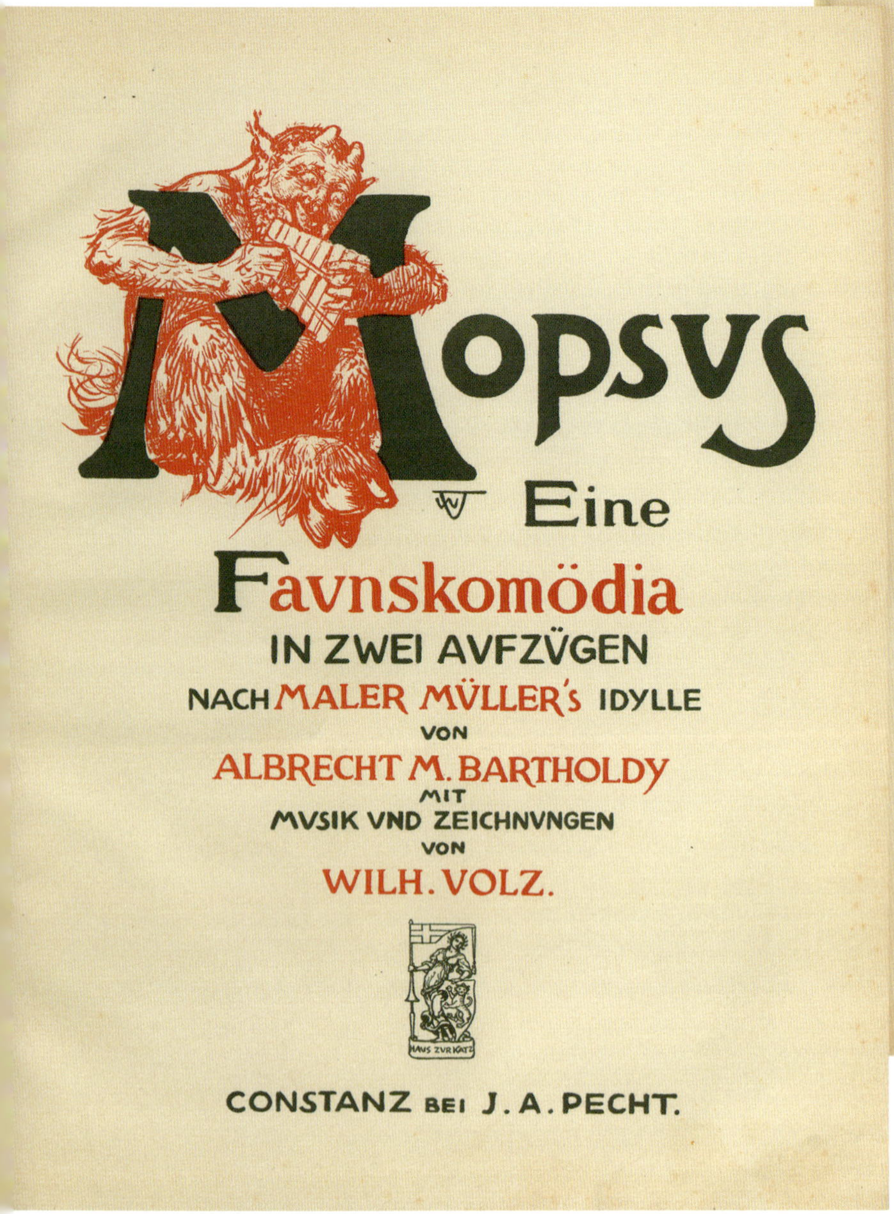

„Mopsus, eine Faunskomödie". Text Albrecht Mendelssohn Bartholdy, Musik und Illustrationen Wilhelm Volz (1898).

"Mopsus, or a Faun's Comedy." Text by Albrecht Mendelssohn Bartholdy, music and illustrations by Wilhelm Volz (1898).

Exlibris
Albrecht Mendelssohn Bartholdy.

Ex libris
Albrecht Mendelssohn Bartholdy.

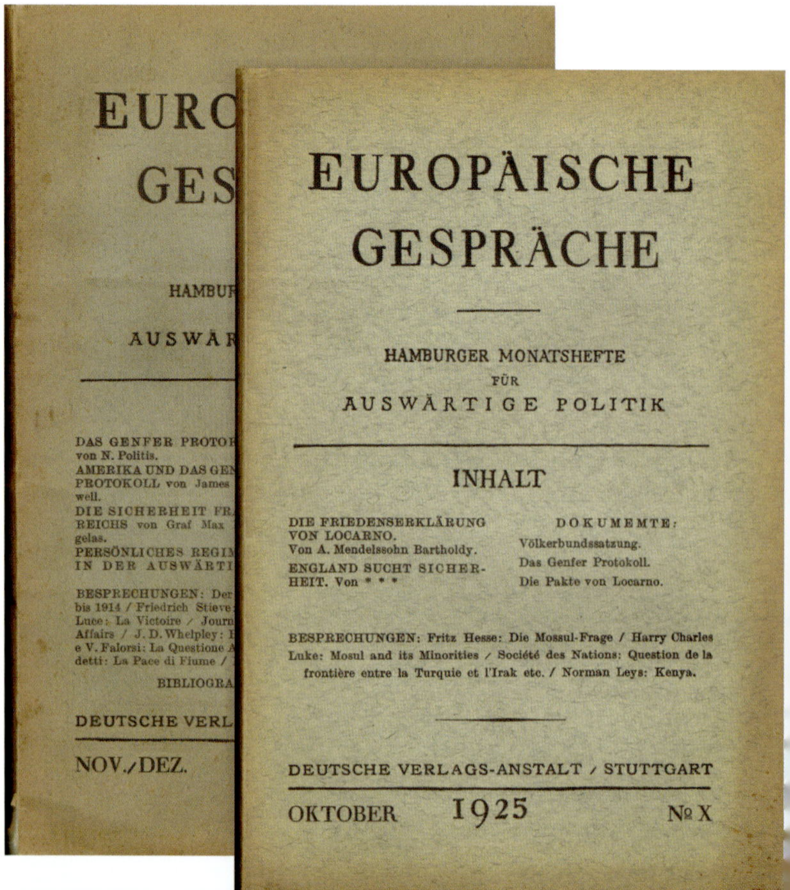

EUROPÄISCHE GESPRÄCHE

HAMBURGER MONATSHEFTE FÜR AUSWÄRTIGE POLITIK

INHALT

DIE FRIEDENSERKLÄRUNG VON LOCARNO. Von A. Mendelssohn Bartholdy.
ENGLAND SUCHT SICHERHEIT. Von * * *

DOKUMEMTE:
Völkerbundssatzung.
Das Genfer Protokoll.
Die Pakte von Locarno.

BESPRECHUNGEN: Fritz Hesse: Die Mossul-Frage / Harry Charles Luke: Mosul and its Minorities / Société des Nations: Question de la frontière entre la Turquie et l'Irak etc. / Norman Leys: Kenya.

DEUTSCHE VERLAGS-ANSTALT / STUTTGART

OKTOBER 1925 № X

„Europäische Gespräche", herausgegeben von Albrecht Mendelssohn Bartholdy.

"Europäische Gespräche" (European Conversations), published by Albrecht Mendelssohn Bartholdy.

Albrecht Mendelssohn Bartholdy mit Adoptivtochter
Lea (1916 – 2012), um 1920.

Albrecht Mendelssohn Bartholdy with his adopted daughter
Lea (1916 – 2012) around 1920.

Grabstätte Albrecht und
Dora Mendelssohn Bartholdys
in Clifton Hampden.

Gravesite of Albrecht and
Dora Mendelssohn Bartholdy
in Clifton Hampden.

Robert von Mendelssohn · 1902 Berlin – 1996 Worpswede

In spring of 1935, following the death of his father Franz von Mendelssohn and the latter's business partner Paul von Mendelssohn-Bartholdy, the fun-loving Robert suddenly had to take charge as head of both the family and the Mendelssohn bank. Despite being threatened, Robert refused to give in to an "offer" by the Nazi SS to "aryanize" the Mendelssohn brand by bringing on non-Jewish partners. But by 1938, Robert's partner Rudolf Loeb was negotiating with Deutsche Bank over the liquidation of Mendelssohn & Co. As his company was being unwound, Robert worked out of an office at the Deutsche Bank building on Mauerstrasse. He never believed the sardonic remark made in 1935 by a Jewish newspaper that he and his loved ones were to receive "honorary Aryan" status. Nevertheless, he had friends at high levels of the Nazi regime, who managed to protect him. In order to "improve his family's situation," as he put it, he volunteered for service in the German Wehrmacht (until becoming bedridden with a case of jaundice in 1936). At one point during the war, after returning to Germany from Stockholm, Robert was confronted with an interview that had been published in a British newspaper; in it, he had remarked that the war must almost be over, given that Jews were being inducted into the German army. Amazingly, it was not the Gestapo that called on him, but a German officer, who upbraided him for "shooting off at the mouth." Robert never confirmed the rumors that he served as a secret courier for the anti-Hitler resistance. What is certain is that he was able to bring his mother, via occupied Denmark, to safety in Sweden.

The Georgenhof estate in the idyllic highlands of the Swabian Alb, which the family had acquired as a summer estate just two years before, turned into a life-saving hideaway after 1933. In fact, twenty to thirty family members were able to take refuge at the Georgenhof during the dangerous years of World War II, as well as in the difficult period that followed. Towards the end of the war, Robert's first wife Lieselotte (née von Bonin) was taken away from the Georgenhof by the Gestapo, since the SS wanted to move in and occupy the property. Fortunately, an outraged neighbor in the village was able to secure her release by pulling strings with the local authorities. Robert was sometimes asked whether he felt the Mendelssohn bank should be re-established. He himself was against it, he would invariably reply. "At any rate, one is alive, and that's really the only thing one can say," is how he summed it up in 1989.

Als sein Vater Franz von Mendelssohn und dessen Sozius Paul von Mendelssohn-Bartholdy im Frühsommer 1935 sterben, fällt dem lebenslustigen Robert die Rolle des Familienchefs zu. Den Vorschlag eines SS-Vertreters, die Mendelssohn-Marke mit „arischen" Partnern zu erhalten, lehnt er trotz Drohungen ab. Firmenchef Rudolf Löb führt 1938 Auflösungsverhandlungen für Mendelssohn & Co. mit der Deutschen Bank; in deren Räumen an der Mauerstraße befindet sich dann Roberts Büro für das Bankhaus in Liquidation. Daß er und die Seinen, wie 1935 eine jüdische Zeitung schreibt, zu „Ehren-Ariern" ernannt werden sollten, hat er bezweifelt. Doch Bekannten im NS-Apparat gelingt es, ihn zu schützen. Freiwillig dient er (bis zur Gelbsuchterkrankung 1936) in der Wehrmacht, um die Situation seiner Familie, wie er sagt, zu verbessern. Als er während des Krieges aus Stockholm zurückkehrt, erscheint in England ein Interview von ihm zum baldigen Kriegsende, da bereits Juden zur Wehrmacht eingezogen würden. Doch statt der Gestapo behelligt ihn nur ein Offizier, der seine „Quatscherei" kritisiert. Berichte, er sei Widerstandskurier gewesen, hat er nicht bestätigt. Seine Mutter kann er über das besetzte Dänemark nach Schweden in Sicherheit bringen.

Der Georgenhof auf der Schwäbischen Alb, den die Familie als Sommergut 1931 erworben hatte, ist nach 1933 zur Zuflucht geworden. Dort wird Roberts erste Frau Lieselotte geb. von Bonin von einem beleidigten SS-Offizier aus Rache denunziert und zeitweise inhaftiert. Das Verfahren in Stuttgart führt ein Staatsanwalt, der dem Volksgerichtshof berichtet. Zwanzig bis dreißig Familienmitglieder finden in Kriegsjahren und danach auf dem Georgenhof Unterschlupf. Überlegungen, ob die Mendelssohn-Bank wiederherzustellen sei, lehnt Robert für sich schließlich ab. „Jedenfalls man lebt, das ist das Einzige, was man sagen kann," resümiert er 1989.

Robert und sein Vater Franz von Mendelssohn im Grunewald.
Robert and his father Franz von Mendelssohn in Grunewald.

Drei Generationen: Robert d.J. (r.), Großvater Franz d.Ä. (M.) und dessen Sohn Robert d.Ä. (l.).

Three generations: Robert Jr. (right), grandfather Franz the Elder (middle) and his son Robert the Elder (left).

Robert von Mendelssohn und seine Tochter Angelika vor dem Georgenhof (1950er Jahre).

Robert von Mendelssohn and his daughter Angelika in front of the Georgenhof (1950s).

Robert von Mendelssohn, seine Mutter Marie und seine älteste Tochter Angelika (um 1950).

Robert von Mendelssohn, his mother Marie and his oldest daughter Angelika (c. 1950).

Robert v. Mendelssohn d.J. (1902 – 1996)
mit seinen Kindern Angelika, Nora, Lili, Benjamin.

Robert v. Mendelssohn Jr. (1902 – 1996)
with his children Angelika, Nora, Lili, Benjamin.

Robert von Mendelssohn in Berlin (um 1990).

Robert von Mendelssohn in Berlin (c. 1990).

Eduard (von) Simson · 1810 Königsberg – 1899 Berlin, seine Nachfahren und die Mendelssohns

Eduard (von) Simson · 1810 Königsberg – 1899 Berlin, his Descendants and the Mendelssohns

The family burial plots of the Simsons are located on the cemeteries near Hallesches Tor.

Born into a Jewish family in Königsberg, Eduard Simson was baptized a Christian at the age of thirteen. He became a professor of law, and, in the revolutionary year of 1848, served as a delegate to the National Assembly that had convened in Frankfurt. By December of that same year, he had become the Assembly's president. In 1849, he headed the Assembly delegation that unsuccessfully offered Frederick William IV of Prussia the title of German Kaiser. Eduard Simson later presided over the Assembly of the North German Confederation, which met in the former Mendelssohn-Bartholdy Palais at Leipziger Strasse 3. In 1870, he travelled to Versailles at the head of delegation to once again petition the Prussian King to accept the title of Kaiser of a united Germany – offered this time by the German princes. The "Founding Father" of the German constitutional order (Jürgen Manthey), Eduard served as President of the Reichstag and later of the Reichsgericht (Imperial Court of Justice). In recognition of his achievements, he was ennobled by Frederick III in 1888, the same year in which Franz (von) Mendelssohn was so honored.

Eduard's nephew Ernst (1876 – 1941) was married to Martha Oppenheim (1882 – 1971), a great-great-granddaughter of Moses. He was a signatory to the Treaty of Versailles on behalf of the Weimar Republic and helped negotiate the Treaty of Rapallo on behalf of Germany as a state secretary. He went on to work as legal counsel for Agfa und I.G. Farben. In 1929, he joined the Society of Friends that Joseph Mendelssohn had founded in 1792. He emigrated to England in 1939. In the United States, Ernst von Simson's son Otto (1912 – 1993) became a professor of art history. After the war, he served as West Germany's first delegate to the UNESCO World Heritage Committee. Having returned to his old hometown of Berlin, he served as dean at the Freie Universität during the student protest movement of the late 1960s. Otto von Simson's sister Victoria, also known as "Vita" (1915 – 2011), was formatively influenced as a child by her grandparent's exquisite art collection in the Villa Oppenheim on Berlin's Lake Wannsee. Praised for her artistic talent by none other than Max Liebermann, she was allowed to become a painter. In 1938, she emigrated to New York City with her husband, businessman Gustav Petersen. Here, she moved in artistic circles that included her friends Jackson Pollack and Willem de Kooning, and was still actively teaching at the New York Studio School until shortly before her death.

Drei Familiengräber der von Simsons befinden sich auf den Friedhöfen vor dem Halleschen Tor.

In Königsberg läßt sich der jüdische Knabe Eduard mit dreizehn Jahren taufen. Er wird Jura-Professor und 1848 Abgeordneter für das Paulskirchen-Parlament, im Dezember Versammlungspräsident; steht an der Spitze jener Delegation, die Friedrich Wilhelm IV. 1849 vergeblich die Kaiserwürde anträgt. Im ehemaligen Palais der Mendelssohn Bartholdys, Leipziger Straße 3, leitet er die Versammlung des Norddeutschen Bundes und reist 1870 als Deputationsleiter nach Versailles: um König Wilhelm zu bitten, die von Deutschlands Fürsten angetragene Kaiserwürde anzunehmen. Der „erste deutsche Verfassungsvater" (Jürgen Manthey) wird Reichstags-, später Reichsgerichtspräsident und 1888, im selben Jahr wie Franz (von) Mendelssohn, durch Kaiser Friedrich geadelt.

Sein Enkel Ernst (1876 – 1941), verheiratet mit Martha Oppenheim (1882 – 1971), einer Urururenkelin des Moses, besiegelt für die Weimarer Republik den Versailler Vertrag, ist als Staatssekretär an den Verhandlungen von Rapallo beteiligt. Später arbeitet der Jurist für Agfa und I.G. Farben; tritt 1929 der Gesellschaft der Freunde bei, die Joseph Mendelssohn 1792 gegründet hatte. 1939 emigriert er nach England. Ernsts Sohn Otto (1912 – 1993) lehrt als Emigrant Kunstgeschichte in den USA, verteidigt als UNESCO-Vertreter der Bundesrepublik das Weltkulturerbe. Zurückgekehrt in seine Heimatstadt, ist er für die Freie Universität in den 68er Jahren ein streitbarer Dekan. Seine Schwester Viktoria, genannt Vita (1915 – 2011), war als Kind durch das Erlebnis der großelterlichen Kunstsammlung in der Oppenheim-Villa am Wannsee geprägt worden. Auf Max Liebermanns Urteil hin durfte sie Malerin werden. 1938 folgt sie dem Kaufmann Gustav Petersen nach New York, wo sie mit Jackson Pollock und Willem de Kooning befreundet ist und bis kurz vor ihrem Tod an der New York Studio School unterrichtet.

Eduard von Simson.
Druck nach Radierung (1886), Stich von Johann Lindner.

Eduard von Simson.
Print based on an etching (1886), engraving by Johann Lindner.

Dem preußischen König Friedrich Wilhelm IV. wird die deutsche Kaiserkrone angetragen (April 1849).
Die Deputation der Frankfurter Nationalversammlung unter dem Parlamentspräsidenten Eduard Simson am 3. April 1849 im Rittersaal des königlichen Schloßes in Berlin.
Holzstich.

Prussian King Frederick William IV being petitioned to accept the German imperial crown (April 1849).
The delegation of the Frankfurt National Assembly under the Presidency of Eduard Simson in the Great Hall of the Royal Palace in Berlin on April 3, 1849.
Wood engraving.

Eduard Simson bittet König Wilhelm von Preußen am 18. Dezember 1870 im Schloß von Versailles um die Annahme der Kaiserkrone.
Holzstich (1870/1871).

Eduard Simson appeals to King William I of Prussia to accept the imperial crown in the Palace of Versailles on December 18, 1870.
Wood engraving (1870/1871).

Hochzeit Ernst von Simsons mit Martha Oppenheim (1901).
The marriage of Ernst von Simson and Martha Oppenheim (1901).

Viktoria (Vita) Petersen,
geb. von Simson (um 1918).
Viktoria (Vita) Petersen,
née von Simson (c. 1918).

Otto von Simson.

Moses Mendelssohn (Seiten 7, 8 – 11, 13, 14, 15, 21, 23, 29, 33, 51, 65, 81, 124 – 127, 129 – 133, 135, 137, 138, 145, 149, 151, 157, 160, 169, 170, 175, 193, 217)
(6. September 1729, Dessau – 4. Januar 1786, Berlin)
oo 22. Juni 1762 in Berlin
Fromet Gugenheim (Seiten 9, 11, **12 – 14**, 15, 21, 23, 37, 157, 160, 211)
(6. Oktober 1737, Altona – 16. März 1812, Altona)

Brendel Mendelssohn (Seiten 13, 16 – 19, 21, 22, 135, 141, 142)
(24. Oktober 1764, Berlin – 3. August 1839, Frankfurt am Main)
oo 3. April 1783 in Berlin - 1. Ehe geschieden
Simon Veit (Seiten 15, 17, 18)
(25. Mai 1754, Berlin – 1. Oktober 1819, Berlin)
Änderung des Vornamens - Brendel > Dorothea
oo 6. April 1804 in Paris - 2. Ehe
Friedrich [von] Schlegel (Seiten 18, 142, 193)
(10. März 1772, Hannover – 12. Februar 1829, Dresden)

Jonas [Johannes] Veit (Seiten 56 – 59, 141, 142, 193 – 195)
(2. März 1790, Berlin – 18. Januar 1854, Rom)
oo 14. Februar 1821 in Berlin
Flora [Florina] Riess
(1. August 1797, Berlin – 21. April 1862, Rom)

Philipp Veit (Seiten 19, 56 – 59, 141, 142, 169, 173, 192 – 195)
(13. Februar 1793, Berlin – 18. Dezember 1877, Mainz)
oo 15. August 1820 in Rom
Carolina Caludinia **Pulini** (Seite 19)
(7. April 1807, Rom – 4. Dezember 1890, Mainz)

Recha [Reikl] Mendelssohn
(Seiten 13, 21, 22, 29, 30, 135)
(14. Juli 1767, Berlin – 23. April 1831, Berlin)
oo 1785 (geschieden)
Mendel Meyer
(? – 1832)
Namensänderung -
Mendel Meyer > Johann Martin Meyer (vor 1816)

Rebecka [Betty] Meyer
(Seiten 29, 30, 137)
(Oktober 1793, Berlin – 5. September 1850, Berlin)
oo 30. August 1818 in Berlin
Heinrich [Henoch] Beer
(6. Juli 1794, Berlin – 22. Oktober 1842, Berlin)

Mendel Abraham Mendelssohn (Seite 25)
(28. Januar 1769, Berlin – 20. September 1775, Berlin)

Joseph Mendelssohn
(Seiten 13, 21, 22, 24, 25, 27, 33, 37, 51, 65, 117, 135, 157, 161, 163, 169, 211, 214, 217)
(11. August 1770, Berlin – 24. November 1848, Berlin)
oo 13. Juni 1793 in Strelitz
Henriette [Hini] Meyer
(Seiten 25, 26)
(13. Februar 1776, Strelitz – 4. Dezember 1862, Berlin)

Georg Benjamin Mendelssohn
(Seiten 25, 26, 141, 169, 173, 211, 213, 215)
(16. November 1794, Berlin – 24. August 1874, Horchheim)
oo 20. Juli 1827 in Berlin
Rosamunde Ernestine Pauline Richter
(25. Juni 1804 – 22. Juni 1883, Horchheim)
Annahme von Betsy Thormann an Kindes statt
(1830 – 11. November 1905, Bonn)

Alexander Mendelssohn
(Seiten 25, 26, 55, 69, 85, 99, 135, 141, 178, 213, 215)
(19. September 1798, Berlin – 25. Oktober 1871, Berlin)
oo 14. Mai 1821 in Berlin
Marianne Seeligmann
(Seiten 51, 55, 145, 178)
(22. April 1799, Berlin – 20. Juni 1880, Charlottenburg)

Joseph Mendelssohn.
Öl auf Leinwand
von Wilhelm Ternite (1831).

Joseph Mendelssohn.
Oil on canvas
by Wilhelm Ternite (1831).

Dorothea (Brendel) Veit,
geb. Mendelssohn (1764 – 1839).
Pastell von
Joseph Friedrich August Darbes (1799).

Dorothea (Brendel) Veit,
née Mendelssohn (1764 – 1839).
Pastel by
Joseph Friedrich August Darbes (1799).

Henriette [Jette] Mendelssohn (Seiten 21, 22, 29, 30)
(23. August 1775, Berlin – 9. November 1831, Berlin)

Nathan (Carl Theodor Nathanael) **Mendelssohn** (Seiten 21, 22, 36 – 39, 51, 140, 141, 146, 163, 169, 181, 206 – 208)
(8. Dezember 1781, Berlin – 9. Januar 1852, Berlin)
oo 3. September 1809 in Berlin
Henriette Hitzig (Seiten 37, 51)
(27. März 1781, Berlin – 22. November 1845, Berlin)

Abraham Ernst Mendelssohn (Seiten 21, 22, 25, 32 – 35, 37, 41, 45, 51, 135, 137, 139, 157, 161, 169, 201, 211)
(10. Dezember 1776, Berlin – 19. November 1835, Berlin)
Namensänderung - Mendelssohn > Mendelssohn Bartholdy
oo 26. Dezember 1804 in Berlin
Lea Felicia Pauline Salomon (Seite 30, 33, 41, 43, 51, 54, 55, 61, 135, 139, 152, 211, 224, 227, 249, 252)
(15. März 1777, Berlin – 12. Dezember 1842, Berlin)

Fanny Cäcilie **Mendelssohn** (Seiten 33, 35, 40 – 43, 45, 47, 73, 74, 139, 141, 151, 173, 181, 197, 198)
(14. November 1805, Hamburg – 14. Mai 1847, Berlin)
Namensänderung - Mendelssohn > Mendelssohn Bartholdy
oo 3. Oktober 1829 in Berlin
Wilhelm Hensel (Seiten 29, 35, 41 – 43, 73, 74, 171, 175, 196 – 198)
(6. Juli 1794, Trebbin – 26. November 1861, Berlin)

Jakob Ludwig **Felix Mendelssohn** (Seiten 28, 29, 33, 34, 41, 42, 44 – 49, 73, 139, 140, 141, 147, 150, 197, 200, 213)
(3. Februar 1809, Hamburg – 4. November 1847, Leipzig)
Namensänderung - Mendelssohn > Mendelssohn Bartholdy
oo März 1837 in Frankfurt am Main
Cécile Sophie Charlotte **Jeanrenaud** (Seiten 45, 48, 49)
(10. Oktober 1817, Lyon – 25. September 1853, Frankfurt am Main)

Rebecka [Henriette] Mendelssohn Bartholdy (Seiten 141, 147, 175, 207)
(11. April 1811, Hamburg – 1. Dezember 1858, Göttingen)
oo 22. Mai 1832 in Berlin
Peter Gustav Lejeune Dirichlet (Seiten 175, 207)
(13. Februar 1805, Düren – 5. Mai 1859, Göttingen)

Paul Mendelssohn Bartholdy (Seiten 60 – 62, 65, 69, 139, 163, 167)
später Mendelssohn-Bartholdy
(30. Oktober 1812, Berlin – 21. Juli 1874, Berlin)
oo 31. Mai 1835 in Berlin
Pauline Louise **Albertine Heine** (Seiten 65, 66)
(22. März 1814, Berlin – 17. Juli 1879, Berlin)

Arnold Maximilian Albrecht **Mendelssohn** (Seiten 36 – 39, 141, 142 – 146, 173, 207)
(19. November 1817, Neiße – 1854, am 6. Oktober 1864 für tot erklärt)

Ottilie Ernestine **Mendelssohn** (Seiten 37, 207, 208)
(14. Juli 1819, Neiße – 30. Juli 1848, Breslau)
oo 24. April 1840
Ernst Eduard Kummer (Seite 37)
(29. Januar 1810, Sorau – 14. Mai 1893, Berlin)

Joseph Elias August **Wilhelm Mendelssohn** (Seiten 37, 85, 174, 175, 208)
(20. Juni 1821, Neiße – 14. September1866, Neiße)
oo 12. Dezember 1854 in Berlin
Louise Aimée Cauer (Seiten 85, 86, 87)
(2. März 1826, Berlin – 2. Juli 1894, Bonn)

Joseph Elias August Wilhelm Mendelssohn (1764 – 1839).

Joseph Elias August Wilhelm Mendelssohn (1764 – 1839).

Linie 2 Seite 123
Linie 3 Seite 123
Linie 4 Seite 123
Linie 5 Seite 123

Linie 1
Seite 120

Margarete Anna Henriette **Mendelssohn**
(Seite 55)
(17. April 1823, Berlin – 23. Juli 1890, Heidelberg)
oo 5. April 1843 in Berlin
Otto Georg Oppenheim
(2. Mai 1817, Königsberg – 27. November 1909, Berlin)

Paul Alexander Franz [von] Mendelssohn
(Seiten 55, 68 – 71, 114, 117, 163, 166, 178)
(25. Januar 1829, Berlin – 20. Februar 1889, Berlin)
oo 22. Oktober 1856 in Berlin (seine Schwägerin)
Marie Antoinette **Enole Biarnez**
(Seiten 68 – 71)
(6. Oktober 1827, Bordeaux – 3. Januar 1889, Berlin)

Wilhelm Bernhard Otto **Mendelssohn**
(22. April 1831, Berlin – 27. Juni 1892, Bonn)
oo 1. März 1856 in Oppeln
Klara Jonas
(Seite 95)
(27. Juni 1834, Oppeln – 25. April 1860, Rzuchow)

Clara Rosamunde Dorothea Mendelssohn
(Seiten 95, 97, 178)
(24. Juli 1840, Berlin – 3. Oktober 1927, Berlin)
oo 2. September 1862 in Berlin
Carl Friedrich Otto Westphal
(Seiten 94, 95)
(23. März 1833, Berlin – 27. Januar 1890, Kreuzlingen)

Robert Georg Alexander **[von] Mendelssohn** (Seiten 69, 88, 89, 96, 105, 114, 143)
(13. Dezember 1857, Berlin – 20. August 1917, Berlin)
oo 30. Januar 1898 in Berlin
Giulietta Gordigiani (Seiten 88, 89)
(17. Mai 1871, Florenz – 1955, Florenz)

Franz Pierre Walther **[von] Mendelssohn** (Seiten 69, 87, 95, 97, 104 – 107, 112 – 114, 143, 163, 167, 177, 179, 181, 216, 217)
(29. Juli 1865, Berlin – 13. Juni 1935, Berlin)
oo 4. März 1889 in Berlin seine Cousine
Marie Clara **Westphal** (Seiten 94 – 97, 113, 114)
(4. November 1867, Berlin – 7. November 1957, Berlin)

Otto **Franz Oppenheim** (Seiten 81, 146, 197, 201, 205)
(13. Juli 1852, Charlottenburg – 13. Februar 1929, Kairo)
oo 12. Juni 1881 in Berlin - 1. Ehe
Else [Elsbeth] Wollheim (Seite 148)
(26. November 1858, Berlin – 3. April 1904, Wannsee)
oo 1907 - 2. Ehe
Margarete Eisner (Seiten 201, 205)
(10. Oktober 1857, Berlin – 2. September 1935, Berlin)

Martha Enole **Oppenheim** (Seiten 117, 119)
(26. März 1882 – 10. Oktober 1971, Berlin)
oo 30. September 1901 in Wannsee
Ernst Bernhard Eduard **von Simson** (Seiten 96, 117, 119)
(7. April 1876, Berlin – 7. Dezember 1941, Oxford)
Enkel von Eduard [von] Simson (Seiten 116 – 118, 167)
(1810, Königsberg – 1899 Berlin)

Alexander Joseph Otto Mendelssohn (Seite 99)
(20. Dezember 1856, Rzuchow – 12. Juli 1935, Lippspringe)
oo 10. November 1885 in Berlin
Jenny von Leyden (Seite 99)
(22. März 1864, Berlin – 19. Juli 1944, Bielefeld)

Elisabeth Clara Henriette **Westphal**
(Seiten 94 – 97)
(25. September 1865, Berlin – 30. September 1942, Berlin)

Ernst Carl Siegfried **Westphal**
(13. Juni 1871, Berlin – 21. April 1949, Cape Town)
(Seiten 94, 95, 97, 211)
oo 11. Mai 1901 in Berlin
Helene Simon (1880 – 1965)
(Seite 95)

Robert [Robi] Franz Carl **von Mendelssohn** (Seiten 95, 107, 112 – 115, 216, 217)
(19. Februar 1902, Grunewald – 5. Juli 1996, Worpswede)
oo 25. Mai 1936 in Berlin - 1. Ehe (geschieden)
Lieselotte von Bonin - geschiedene von Gumberz-Rhontal
(8. Juli 1904, Mühlheim/Ruhr – 30. April 1997, Tübingen)
oo 19? - 2. Ehe
Traute Kistner
(11. Dezember 1944, Bremerhaven)

Linie 2 Seite 121

Linie 3 Seite 121

Linie 4 Seite 121

Ernst Moses Felix **[von] Mendelssohn-Bartholdy**
(Seiten 60, 61, 63, 66, 89, 96, 163, 213)
(13. Dezember 1846, Berlin – 25. Dezember 1909, Dresden)
oo 23. Januar 1875 in Berlin
Marie Alexandrine Warschauer
(29. August 1855, Berlin – 15. Oktober 1906, Berlin)

Carl Wolfgang Paul **Mendelssohn Bartholdy**
(Seite 49, 62, 77,109, 210, 211)
(7. Februar 1838, Leipzig – 23. Februar 1897, Windisch)
oo 21. Oktober 1872 in Karlsruhe
Mathilde von Merkl
(24. April 1848, Karlsruhe – 14. Juni 1937, Karlsruhe)

Paul Felix Abraham **Mendelssohn Bartholdy**
(18. Januar 1841, Leipzig – 17. Februar 1880, Berlin)
(Seiten 76 – 79, 81, 82, 165, 173)
oo 19. Mai 1867 in Berlin
Else Rosa Marianne Elisabeth **Oppenheim**
(Seiten 77 – 79)
(16. November 1844, Berlin – 20. August 1868, Heringsdorf)

Lili Fanny Henriette Elisabeth **Mendelssohn Bartholdy**
(Seite 77)
(19. September 1845, Leipzig – 15. Oktober 1910, Wilderswil)
oo 23. März 1870 in Frankfurt am Main
Adolf Gustav Eduard Louis **Wach**
(11. September 1843, Culm – 15. Oktober 1910, Leipzig)

Felix Gustav Adolf Wach
(19. April 1871, Frankfurt am Main – 21. August 1943, Dresden)
oo 6. März 1897 in Berlin seine Verwandte
Katharina [Käthe] von Mendelssohn-Bartholdy (Seiten 99, 102)
(24. September 1876, Berlin – 27. Juli 1956 in Orselina)

Otto Felix Paul **[von] Mendelssohn Bartholdy** (Seiten 77, 81, 96, 99 – 103)
(2. März 1868, Berlin – 26. Juli 1949, Basel)
oo 8. April 1893 in Baden seine Cousine
Cécile Euphrosine Elisabetha **Mendelssohn Bartholdy**
(15. Februar 1870, Freiburg im Breisgau – 22. Februar 1943, Potsdam)

Albrecht Carl Felix Adolf Wolfgang **Mendelssohn Bartholdy** (Seiten 65, 108 – 111, 149, 177, 197)
(25. Oktober 1874, Karlsruhe – 29. November 1936, Oxford)
oo 7. März 1905 in Leipzig seine Cousine
Dorothea Marie Anna Gustave Wach
(8. Juni 1875, Bonn – 18. August 1949, Oxford)

Eleonora Gabriella Marie Josepha **von Mendelssohn** (Seiten 88 – 91, 93)
(12. Januar 1900, Berlin – 24. Januar 1951, New York City)
oo 10. Juli 1919 in Berlin - 1. Ehe (geschieden am 1. Dezember 1925)
Edwin Fischer (Seite 89)
(6. Oktober 1886, Basel – 24. Januar 1960, Zürich)
oo 21. September 1927 in Vöcklabruck – 2. Ehe (geschieden am 5. Februar 1936)
Emmerich von Jeszenszky (Seite 89)
(1. Januar 1895, Budapest – 1981, Schörfling am Attersee)
oo 8. August 1938 in Santa Ana – 3. Ehe (geschieden am 11. Februar 1944)
Rudolf Forster (Seite 89)
(30. Oktober 1884, Gröbming – 26. Oktober 1968, Bad Aussee)
oo 1947 in Detroit – 4. Ehe
Martin Kosleck (Seite 89)
(24. März 1904, Barkotzen – 15. Januar 1994, Santa Monica)

Franz [Francesco] Otto Michele Herrmann **von Mendelssohn** (Seiten 65, 66, 88 / 89, 91 – 93)
(6. September 1901, Berlin – 22. September 1972, New York City)

Linie 5 Seite 121

Ludwig **Arnold Mendelssohn**
(Seiten 84 – 87, 141, 173)
(26. Dezember 1855, Ratibor – 18. Februar 1933, Darmstadt)
oo 12. November 1885 in Kreuznach
Maria Louise Helene Cauer
(Seite 85)
(3. Mai 1861, Kreuznach – 25. Dezember 1928, Darmstadt)

Ludwig Felix **Sebastian Hensel** (Seiten 65, 67, 72 – 75, 163, 171, 197, 208)
(16. Juni 1830, Berlin – 13. Januar 1898, Berlin)
oo 22. August 1856 in Cranz
Julie von Adelson (Seite 73)
(29. Februar 1836, Königsberg – 13. November 1901, Berlin)

Kurt Sebastian Wilhelm Hensel (Seiten 207, 209)
(29. Dezember 1861, Königsberg – 1. Juni 1941, Marburg)
oo 27. März 1887 in Berlin
Gertrud Hahn (Seite 181)
(4. August 1866, Berlin – 13. Februar 1954, Trautheim)

Albert Hensel (Seiten 98, 99, 210, 211)
(8. Februar 1895, Berlin – 18. Oktober 1933, Pavia)
oo 18. April 1918
Marie-Louise Flothmann (Seiten 98, 99, 181)
(8. November 1894, Ems – 31. August 1942, Konstanz)

Franz Victor Mendelssohn (Seiten 99, 101, 103, 181)
(25. Juli 1887, Potsdam – 17. Juli 1971, Freiburg im Breisgau)
oo 2. September 1915 in Berlin
Emma Martha Elli Wingendorf
(20. Mai 1892, Französisch Buchholz – 17. Dezember 1962, Freiburg im Breisgau)

Ernst Wilhelm Mendelssohn (Seiten 99, 101, 103)
(8. Oktober 1891, Potsdam – 20. November 1980, Köln)
Namensänderung, Mendelssohn > Leyden (1941)
oo 20. Oktober 1921 in Achim
Ursula Wiedenfeld
(18. November 1896, Wiesbaden – 14. Mai 1993, Köln)

Abhandlung
über die
Evidenz
in
Metaphysischen Wissenschaften,
welche den von der
Königlichen Academie der Wissenschaften in Berlin
auf das Jahr 1763. ausgesetzten Preis
erhalten hat,
von
Moses Mendelsohn
aus Berlin.

Nebst noch einer
Abhandlung
über dieselbe Materie, welche die Academie nächst der ersten
für die beste gehalten hat.

Berlin, bey Haude und Spener,
Königl. und der Academie der Wissenschaften Buchhändlern, 1764.

N° 3

Einleitung.

Man macht der Weltweisheit gemeiniglich den Vorwurf, daß in ihren Lehren niemals eine sonderliche Ueberzeugung zu hoffen wäre, weil in jedem Jahrhunderte neue Lehrgebäude empor kommen, schimmern und wieder vergehen. Die Gedichte, die Reden, die historischen und kritischen Schriften, die Bildsäulen und übrigen Kunststücke der Alten, werden noch in unsern Tagen als Meisterstücke bewundert, und zum Theil noch mit grösserm Nutzen studiret, als die Natur selbst. Allein die philosophischen Schriften der vorigen Zeiten, sind in unsern Tagen fast unbrauchbar gewor-

It is said that *Mausche mi Dessau* owed his hump and his stutter to the years he had spent hunched over without breathing properly as he studied the works of Moses Maimonides, the medieval religious sage. At the age of just ten, he had been accepted into the Talmudic scholars' circle of his teacher Fränkel, who was working on a new edition of Maimonides' magnum opus "Guide for the Perplexed," in which he reconciled religion and philosophy and that had long been out of print. By the time he set out for Berlin, the 13-year-old Mausche had already worked his way through both volumes. Settling in Prussia's capital and royal seat, he proceeded to work his way up from impoverished autodidact to the central figure of an influential intellectual network that spanned both the Jewish and Gentile worlds.

Moses Mendelssohn was well versed not only in the Torah and Talmud, but also in the classics of the Western philosophical canon. He expanded upon lines of enquiry that had been propounded by Leibniz and Christian Wolff with respect to logic, mathematics, religion, and the inner harmony of creation. He would eventually win a first prize from the Royal Academy for his treatise on "Evidence in the Metaphysical Sciences" (1763), beating out no less a competitor than Immanuel Kant. Moses Mendelssohn sought to combine experience and reason, while emphasizing the primacy of everyday experience as well as psychological aspects. His definition of the enlightened ideal, as described in his treatise "What is Enlightenment?" (1784) was more modern, less abstract than that of Kant, since it also included the aspect of education. Kant, the "Sage of Königsberg," treated Mendelssohn with admiration and respect when the latter came to visit him, but would later try to refute the ontological proof for the existence of God that Mendelssohn had offered in "Morning Lessons or Lectures on the Existence of G-d" (1785).

In his "Phaedon" (1767), a best-seller of its day, Moses updated Plato's re-telling of the dialogues of Socrates to reflect the concerns of his contemporary readership, while also adding his own moral-theological proof for the immortality of the soul. His writings on aesthetics were to have an influence on German literary giants such as Lessing, Schiller, and Kant. As a central figure of the Berlin Enlightenment, Moses worked closely with his friends Lessing and Nicolai to systematically spread the concepts of tolerance and of the universality of human rights by means of personal contacts, literary publications, public discourses and correspondence.

Seinen Buckel und sein Stottern soll *Mausche mi Dessau* dem verkrümmenden, lungenschwächenden Studium des Moses Maimonides verdanken: Mit zehn Jahren war er in den Talmud-Schülerkreis seines Lehrers Fränkel aufgenommen worden, der den „Führer der Unschlüssigen", das Hauptwerk dieses mittelalterlichen Religionsphilosophen, neu herausgibt – nachdem das Glauben und Vernunft verbindende Buch lange nicht zu haben war. Vor seinem Aufbruch nach Berlin arbeitet der dreizehnjährige Mausche beide Bände durch. In Preußens Residenzstadt entwickelt er sich vom bettelarmen Autodidakten zur Vermittlergestalt eines intellektuellen Netzwerkes.

Er kennt Thora und Talmud ebenso wie die Klassiker der abendländischen Philosophie. Er führt Denkansätze von Leibniz und Christian Wolff – über Logik, Mathematik, Religion und die Harmonie der Welt – weiter und gewinnt gegen Kant beim Wettbewerb der Königlichen Akademie den ersten Preis zur Fragestellung nach einer „Evidenz in den metaphysischen Wissenschaften" (1763). Dabei sucht er Erfahrung und Vernunft zu verbinden, betont den Primat der Alltagspraxis, psychologische Gesichtspunkte. Moses' Aufklärungsbegriff ist moderner, weniger abstrakt als der von Kant, da der Bildungsaspekt einbezogen wird („Ueber die Frage: Was heißt aufklären?", 1784). Der Königsberger ehrt Mendelssohn, als dieser ihn besucht, wird aber dessen ontologischen Gottesbeweis, dargelegt in „Morgenstunden oder Vorlesungen über das Daseyn Gottes" (1785), später widerlegen.

In seinem Bestseller „Phädon" (1767) aktualisiert Moses Platons Text über die Gespräche des Sokrates für die Fragen des zeitgenössischen Publikums; einen moraltheologischen Beweis zur Unsterblichkeit der Seele fügt er hinzu. Seine Schriften zur Ästhetik werden Lessing, Schiller und Kant beeinflussen. Als zentrale Figur der Berliner Aufklärung inspiriert er, im Freundestrio mit Lessing und Nicolai, durch Kontakte, Veröffentlichungen, Diskurse und Korrespondenzen die reflektierte Verbreitung des Toleranzgedankens und der Universalität der Menschenrechte.

Moses Mendelssohn: „Abhandlung über die Evidenz in Metaphysischen Wissenschaften", Berlin 1764.
Moses Mendelssohn: "Treatise on Evidence in the Metaphysical Sciences," Berlin 1764.

Christoph Friedrich Nicolai (1733 – 1811).
Öl auf Leinwand (1790) von Ferdinand Collmann
nach einer Vorlage (1783?) von Anton Graff.

Christoph Friedrich Nicolai (1733 – 1811).
Oil on canvas (1790) by Ferdinand Collmann
after an original (1783?) by Anton Graff.

Moses Mendelssohn. Miniatur, Tempera auf Elfenbein (um 1767).

Moses Mendelssohn. Miniature, tempera on ivory (c. 1767).

Gotthold Ephraim Lessing (1729 – 1781).
Die Zusammenarbeit zwischen Mendelssohn und dem Dramatiker und Aufklärer Lessing steht als glücklicher Freundschaftsauftakt am Beginn der gemeinsamen deutsch-jüdischen Geschichte.
Öl auf Leinwand (um 1767/1768)
von Anna Rosina de Gasc (1713 – 1783).

Gotthold Ephraim Lessing (1729 – 1781).
The partnership and friendship between Mendelssohn and the dramatist and enlightenment philosopher Lessing marked an auspicious beginning to a new phase of closer German-Jewish relations.
Oil on canvas (c. 1767/1768)
by Anna Rosina de Gasc (1713 – 1783).

Immanuel Kant (1724 – 1804).
Stich nach einem Gemälde von Johann Michael Siegfried Lowe (um 1784).

Immanuel Kant (1724 – 1804).
Engraving after a painting by Johann Michael Siegfried Lowe (c. 1784).

Gedenkmedaille aus Silber von Jakob Abraham / Abraham Abramson (1774).
Die Rückseite nennt das Geburtsjahr Mendelssohns und bezieht sich auf sein Buch über die Unsterblichkeit der Seele.

Commemorative silver medal by Jakob Abraham / Abraham Abramson (1774).
The obverse side shows Mendelssohn's date of birth and refers to his book on the immortality of the soul.

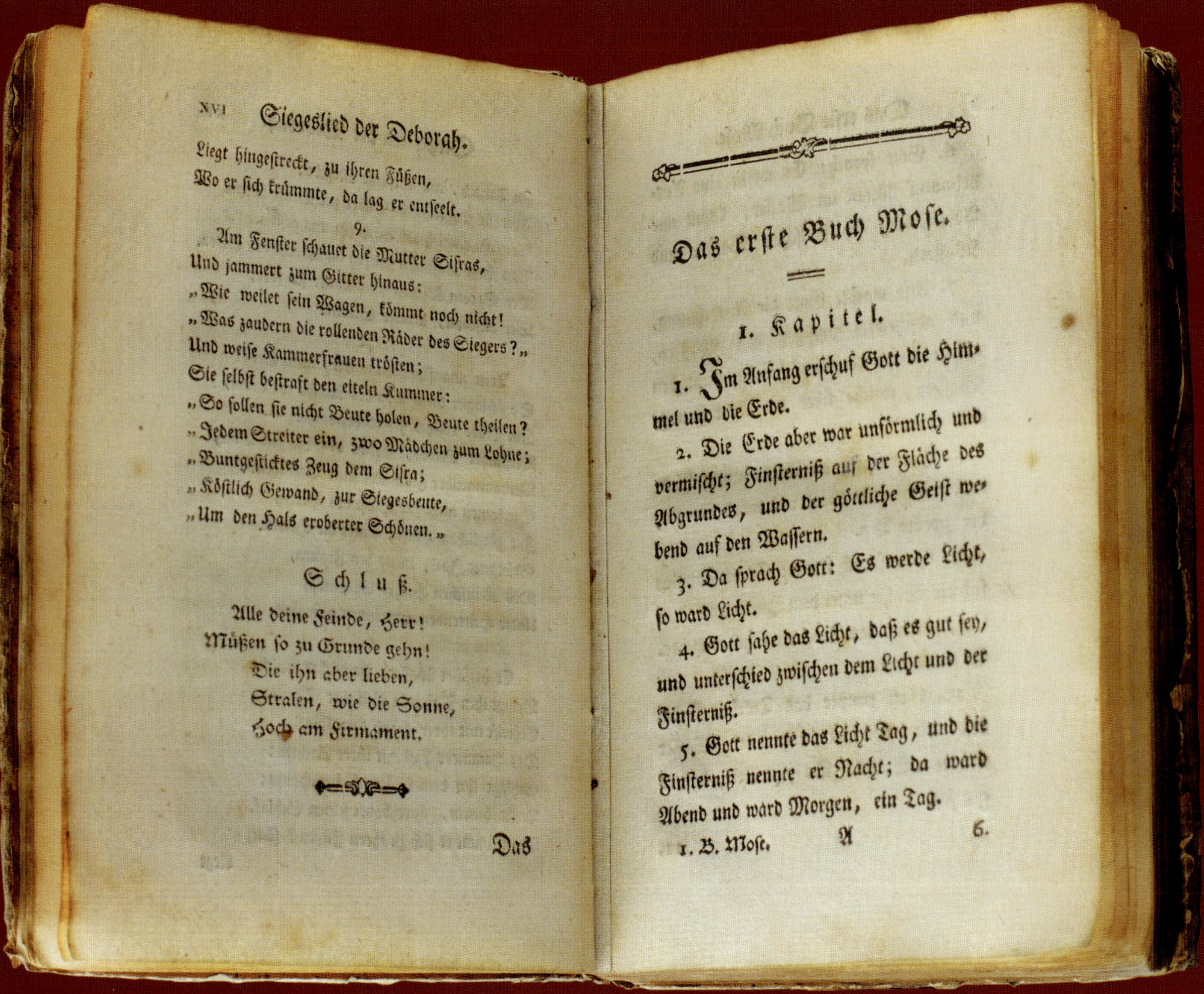
XVI Siegeslied der Deborah.
Liegt hingestreckt, zu ihren Füßen,
Wo er sich krümmte, da lag er entseelt.
9.
Am Fenster schauet die Mutter Sisras,
Und jammert zum Gitter hinaus:
„Wie weilet sein Wagen, kömmt noch nicht!
„Was zaudern die rollenden Räder des Siegers?„
Und weise Kammerfrauen trösten;
Sie selbst bestraft den eiteln Kummer:
„So sollen sie nicht Beute holen, Beute theilen?
„Jedem Streiter ein, zwo Mädchen zum Lohne;
„Buntgesticktes Zeug dem Sisra;
„Köstlich Gewand, zur Siegesbeute,
„Um den Hals eroberter Schönen.„
Schluß.
Alle deine Feinde, Herr!
Müßen so zu Grunde gehn!
Die ihn aber lieben,
Stralen, wie die Sonne,
Hoch am Firmament.
Das
Das erste Buch Mose.
1. Kapitel.
1. Im Anfang erschuf Gott die Him-
mel und die Erde.
2. Die Erde aber war unförmlich und
vermischt; Finsterniß auf der Fläche des
Abgrundes, und der göttliche Geist we-
bend auf den Wassern.
3. Da sprach Gott: Es werde Licht,
so ward Licht.
4. Gott sahe das Licht, daß es gut sey,
und unterschied zwischen dem Licht und der
Finsterniß.
5. Gott nennte das Licht Tag, und die
Finsterniß nennte er Nacht; da ward
Abend und ward Morgen, ein Tag.
1. B. Mose. A 6.

Intellectual pioneer of the pluralistic society

As a "worldly sage" and reformer, Moses exerted a huge influence on the Jewish community. Thus, he published German translations of the Torah and the Psalms written in Hebrew letters. The ideas laid out in his essay "Jerusalem: On Religious Power and Judaism," such as the need to separate the state from religion, were ahead of their time. His work also paved the way for the "Haskalah," the Jewish Enlightenment movement whose protagonists would include David Friedländer, founder of the Jewish Free School *(Freyschule)*; Isaac Euchel, publisher of the first Hebrew journal, "Der Sammler" (The Collector); the poet Hartwig Wessely and the educator Herz Homberg. The ecumenical reform projects of the Haskalah ultimately contributed to the assimilation of the Jewish minority, and to the emergence of the German-Jewish "modernism" from which our contemporary ideals of pluralism derive.

During his lifetime, Moses the philosopher became caught up in two momentous public debates with Christian theologians. The first began in 1770, when the Swiss Calvinist Lavater challenged the Berliner to either refute Christianity or convert. This provocation put Mendelssohn in a difficult dilemma: the philosopher who drew a distinction between a universally valid moral law of reason and the revealed, ritual laws of Judaism, which, he argued, had developed historically and were valid only for Jews, was precariously dependent on the tolerance of Protestant rulers. Although many intellectuals took Moses' side, he himself became ill from the stress of the dispute, which was carried out in public. Towards the end of Moses' life, his intellectual hackles were raised once again, this time by the Lutheran Jacobi, who asserted in 1785 that the recently deceased philosopher Lessing had been a "Spinozist," i.e. a follower of Spinoza. Since this was generally taken to imply that Lessing had been an atheist, Moses felt duty bound to defend his late friend as well as himself against an unacceptable accusation:

"Thus do I return to the faith of my fathers which, as the word was first understood, consisted not in a belief in doctrines and opinions, but in a trust and confidence in the attributes of G-d. I place my full, unlimited confidence in the power of almighty G-d, and in His ability to give Man the power to recognize the truths

Vordenker einer pluralistischen Gesellschaft

Der „Weltweise" und Reformer wirkt in die Jüdische Gemeinschaft hinein. Deutsche Übersetzungen der Thora und der Psalmen erscheinen in hebräischer Schrift. In seinem Essay „Jerusalem. Über religiöse Macht und Judentum" ist er der eigenen Epoche mit Überlegungen zur Trennung von Staat und Glaubensgemeinschaft voraus. Bahnbrechend erweist er sich als Vordenker der jüdischen Aufklärungsbewegung Haskala und ihrer Protagonisten, zu denen David Friedländer, Gründer der Jüdischen Freyschule, Isaac Euchel, Herausgeber der ersten hebräischen Zeitschrift „Der Sammler", der Dichter Hartwig Wessely und der Pädagoge Herz Homberg zählen. Die sich interreligiös öffnenden Reformprojekte der Haskala tragen bei zur Integration der Minderheit: zur Entstehung jener deutsch-jüdischen Moderne, aus deren Erfahrungen sich die Ideale unserer pluralistischen Gegenwart ableiten.

Folgenreiche Angriffe auf den Philosophen Moses führen zu seinen Lebzeiten zwei Theologen. Der Schweizer Calvinist Lavater legt dem Berliner nahe, das Christentum zu widerlegen oder zu konvertieren (1770). Für den unter evangelischen Regenten gefährdet lebenden Mendelssohn, der zwischen dem universalen ethischen Gesetz der Vernunft und dem (nur für Juden gültigen) offenbarten Ritualgesetz einer geschichtlich gewachsenen Religion unterscheidet, wird die Provokation zur Falle. Viele Intellektuelle stellen sich auf seine Seite, er selbst erkrankt aufgrund des öffentlich verhandelten Konfliktes. Am Ende seines Lebens ist es dann der Lutheraner Jacobi, welcher Mendelssohn mit der Behauptung, der verstorbene Lessing sei „Spinozist" gewesen, zu erregter Verteidigung provoziert (1785). Den Atheismus-Vorwurf, wie Jacobis Aussage verstanden wurde, mochte er für den Freund und sich selbst nicht hinnehmen:

„So kehre auch ich zum Glauben meiner Väter zurück, welcher nach der ersten ursprünglichen Bedeutung des Wortes, nicht in Glauben an Lehre und Meinung, sondern in Vertrauen und Zuversicht auf die Eigenschaften Gottes bestehet. Ich setze das volle, uneingeschränkte Vertrauen in die Allmacht Gottes, dass sie dem Menschen die Kräfte habe verleihen können, die Wahrheiten, auf welche sich seine Glückseligkeit gründet, zu erkennen, und hege die kindliche Zuversicht zu seiner Allbarmherzig-

„Die fünf Bücher Mose, zum Gebrauch der jüdischdeutschen Nation nach der Uebersetzung des Herrn Moses Mendelssohn". Erstes Buch, Berlin und Stettin 1780, bei Friedrich Nicolai. „Zum Nutzen der Kinder, mit denen mich Gott begnadete" hatte der „Luther der deutschen Juden" das Übersetzungswerk in hebräischer Schrift 1774 begonnen. Die Genesis erscheint auf Wunsch nichtjüdischer Gelehrter auch in deutscher Schrift.

"The Pentateuch as Translated by Mr. Moses Mendelssohn for the Use of the Jewish Nation." Book I, Berlin and Stettin 1780, published by Friedrich Nicolai. The "Luther of the German Jews" had begun working on his German translation, written in Hebrew letters, in 1774 "for the sake of the children with whom God has blessed me." At the request of non-Jewish scholars, the "Book of Genesis" was also published in the German alphabet.

BENED v. 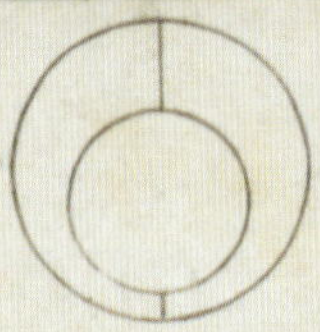 SPINOZA

Opp Posth. p. 469.

Ueber

die Lehre des Spinoza in Briefen an den Herrn Moses Mendelssohn.

Neue vermehrte Ausgabe.

Δος μοι πȣ ϛω.

Breslau, bey Gottl. Löwe,
1789.

upon which his blessedness rests, and, I cherish a childlike confidence that, in his infinite mercy, He wished to grant me these powers. Strengthened by this unwavering faith, I look for instruction and persuasion wherever I can find them. ... I have faith that I have found them, and believe that anyone who searches with his eyes open can find them, too." ("To the Friends of Lessing")

keit, dass sie mir diese Kräfte habe verleihen wollen. Von diesem unwankenden Glauben gestärkt, suche ich Belehrung und Überzeugung, wo ich sie finde. ... Ich glaube sie gefunden zu haben, und glaube, dass jeder sie finden könne, der mit offenen Augen sucht." („An die Freunde Lessings").

,Ueber die Lehre des Spinoza in den Briefen an den Herrn Moses Mendelssohn".
Neue vermehrte Ausgabe, Breslau, bey Gottl. Loewe, 1789.
Friedrich Heinrich Jacobis Schrift, erstmals erschienen 1785, konfrontierte die Öffentlichkeit und Mendelssohn mit dem angeblichen Atheismus des „Spinozisten" Lessing.
Rechts das Freundespaar Lessing und Mendelssohn, links Baruch Spinoza (1632 – 1677).

"On the Doctrine of Spinoza in the Letters to Mr. Moses Mendelssohn."
Newly expanded edition, published in Breslau by Gottl. Loewe in 1789.
Friedrich Heinrich Jacobi's book, first published in 1785, confronted the public – and Mendelssohn – with the accusation that Lessing was a "Spinozist."
Right: the friends Lessing and Mendelssohn; left: Baruch Spinoza (1632 – 1677).

Die Psalmen. Übersetzung von Moses Mendelssohn. Berlin 1783.
"The Psalms." Translated by Moses Mendelssohn. Berlin 1783.

Die
Psalmen.

Uebersetzt
von
Moses Mendelssohn.

Mit allergnädigsten Freyheiten.

Berlin,
bey Friedrich Maurer, 1783.

David Friedländer (1750 – 1834),
Fabrikant und Reformer.
Radierung (1789) von Daniel Berger nach Ridel.

David Friedländer (1750 – 1834).
Industrialist and Reformer.
Etching (1789) by Daniel Berger after Ridel.

Johann Caspar Lavater (1741 – 1801).
Öl auf Leinwand (1785) von Alexander Speisegger.

Johann Caspar Lavater (1741 – 1801).
Oil on canvas (1785) by Alexander Speisegger.

Friedrich Heinrich Jacobi
(1743 – 1819).
Öl auf Leinwand (1780)
von Johann Friedrich Eich.

Friedrich Heinrich Jacobi
(1743 – 1819).
Oil on canvas (1780)
by Johann Friedrich Eich.

Naftali Herz Homberg (1749 – 1841),
Hauslehrer bei Moses Mendelssohn und Kommentator seiner „Pentateuch"-Übersetzung, später Gründer und Oberaufseher von mehr als 100 deutsch-jüdischen Schulen in Galizien.

Naftali Herz Homberg (1749 – 1841).
He worked as home tutor in the Mendelssohn household and as commentator of Moses' "Pentateuch" translation; later, he became the founder and chief overseer of more than 100 German-Jewish schools in Galicia.

Exlibris Isaac Euchels (1756 – 1804), des Protagonisten der Haskala-Bewegung. Der Publizist begründete u.a. mit Joseph Mendelssohn die reformorientierte Gesellschaft der Freunde und schrieb eine hebräische, weit verbreitete Biographie Moses Mendelssohns.
Stich von C. Kampe, nach Benedikt Heinrich Bendix.

Ex libris Isaac Euchel (1756 – 1804), author and key protagonist of the Haskalah movement. Amongst other things, he founded the reform-oriented "Society of Friends" together with Joseph Mendelssohn and wrote a popular, Hebrew-language biography of Moses Mendelssohn.
Engraving by C. Kampe after Benedikt Heinrich Bendix.

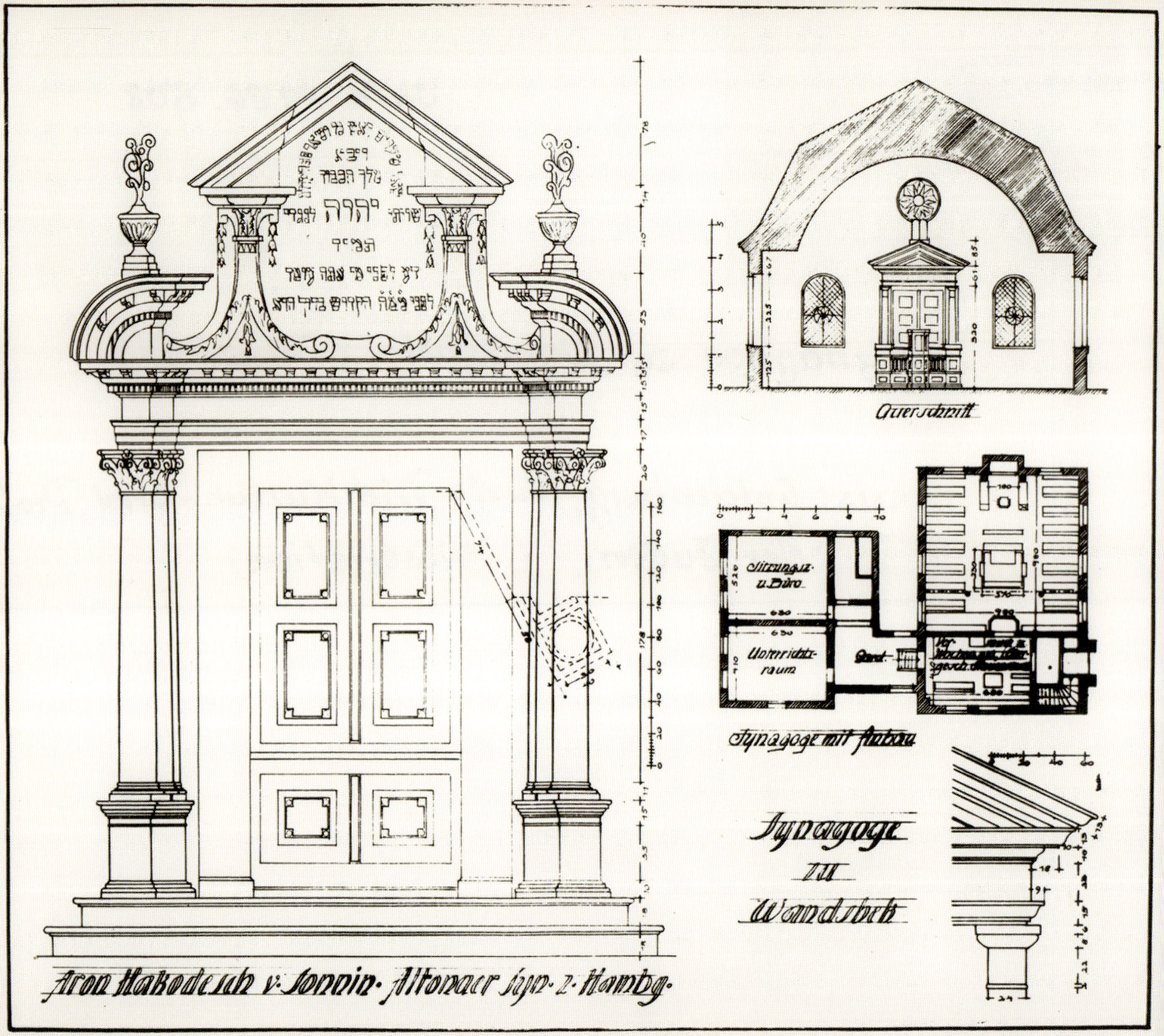
Querschnitt
Sitzungsz. u. Büro
Unterrichtsraum
Synagoge mit Anbau
Synagoge zu Wandsbek
Aron Hakodesch v. Sonnin. Altonaer Syn. z. Hambg.

Moses of the German Jews

The old Jewish saying "from Moses to Moses, there was none like Moses," intended to praise both the lawgiver on Mt. Sinai as well as the philosopher Maimonides, was expanded by Moses' Jewish admirers to also include Mendelssohn, "the Moses of the German Jews." Nonetheless, the image of a deeply religious Mausche – one who corresponded with famous rabbis of his day, advised Jewish congregations, and translated traditional Hebrew texts for contemporary readers – would eventually be supplanted in the eyes of posterity by that of the secular Socrates.

Joseph, Moses' oldest son, became known as a pillar of the Jewish community. The deed recording the sale of his house lists Tabernacle boards, for example, indicating that the Feast of Tabernacles was religious practice in his household. Although Moses' son Alexander belonged to the assembly of representatives of the Jewish congregation, he had his children baptized as Christians. Moses' second daughter Recha remained Jewish, while her ex-husband converted. Recha's daughter Betty became a Christian (according to unconfirmed reports), but then returned to the fold of the synagogue before marrying a brother of the composer Meyerbeer.

If only due to their famous ancestor, the majority Gentile community would continue to regard Moses' descendants as Jewish. On the other hand, Orthodox Jewish opponents of Moses Mendelssohn would continue to question his piety generations later, blaming him for having opened the door for the later "apostasy" of many Jews who preferred to assimilate.

Moses' oldest daughter Brendel (who later called herself "Dorothea") made an impetuous and stormy break both with her first husband and with Judaism. She then converted a second time from the Protestant to the Catholic Church (1808), which fulfilled her romantic longing for a mystical world order. Turning her back on the Enlightenment, she would nonetheless add "née Mendelssohn" to her signature. She would repeat anti-Jewish prejudices, while at the same time flirting with her "oriental" origins. Her later conciliatory attitude towards relatives whose faith differed from her own was motivated at least in part by her spiritual convictions.

Der Moses der deutschen Juden

Den Spruch „Von Moses bis Moses war keiner wie Moses", der den Gesetzgeber vom Sinai und Maimonides rühmt, erweitern jüdische Verehrer auf „den Moses der deutschen Juden". Doch für die Nachgeborenen wird dessen Bild als Sokrates den gesetzestreuen Mausche – der mit berühmten Rabbinern korrespondierte, jüdische Gemeinden beriet, Traditionstexte ins Heute übertrug – verdrängen.

Sein ältester Sohn Joseph unterstützt die jüdische Gemeinde. Er führt beim Verkauf seines Hauses Laubhüttenbretter auf: ein Hinweis auf religiöse Praxis. Sohn Alexander gehört zur Repräsentantenversammlung der Gemeinde, seine Kinder läßt er taufen. Moses zweitälteste Tochter Recha bleibt Jüdin, während ihr Ex-Mann konvertiert. Rechas Tochter Betty war (nach unbelegten Berichten) Christin geworden, sie kehrt vor ihrer Heirat mit einem Bruder des Komponisten Meyerbeer zur Synagoge zurück.

Aus der Perspektive der Mehrheitsgesellschaft werden Nachfahren des Moses, schon wegen des Ahnherrn, als jüdisch angesehen. Aus der Sicht jüdisch-orthodoxer Gegner wird dagegen, Generationen später, Mendelssohns Frömmigkeit angezweifelt: Man macht ihn als Initiator der Assimilation für abtrünnige Nachkommen verantwortlich.

Seine Älteste Brendel / Dorothea bricht stürmend, drängend aus ihrer Ehe, dem Judentum aus; ihre zweite Konversion, von der evangelischen zur katholischen Kirche (1808), entspringt romantischer Sinnsuche nach einer mystischen Weltordnung. Von der Aufklärung wendet sie sich ab, fügt jedoch beim Unterschreiben „geb. Mendelssohn" ihrem Namen hinzu; antijüdische Vorurteile reproduziert sie, kokettiert aber mit ihrer „orientalischen" Herkunft. Ihre später versöhnliche Haltung gegenüber andersgläubigen Verwandten ist auch spirituell motiviert.

Der mittlere Sohn Abraham zögert aus verwandschaftlichen Rücksichten die Entscheidung hinaus, ob die Zukunft seiner Kinder durch Emigration oder Konversion zu sichern sei. Deren Taufe (1816) soll die jüdische Großmutter zunächst nicht erfahren. Die Eltern vollziehen den Übertritt 1822, begleitet durch einen toleranten, kulturpolitisch profilierten Prediger, in Frankfurt

Synagogen der Dreigemeinde Altona – Hamburg – Wandsbeck. Deren umstrittener Rabbiner Jonathan Eybeschütz wurde vom Schwiegervater Moses Mendelssohns, Abraham Gugenheim, unterstützt.

The synagogues of the tripartite congregation Altona – Hamburg – Wandsbeck. Their controversial rabbi Jonathan Eybeschütz enjoyed the support of Moses Mendelssohn's father-in-law, Abraham Gugenheim.

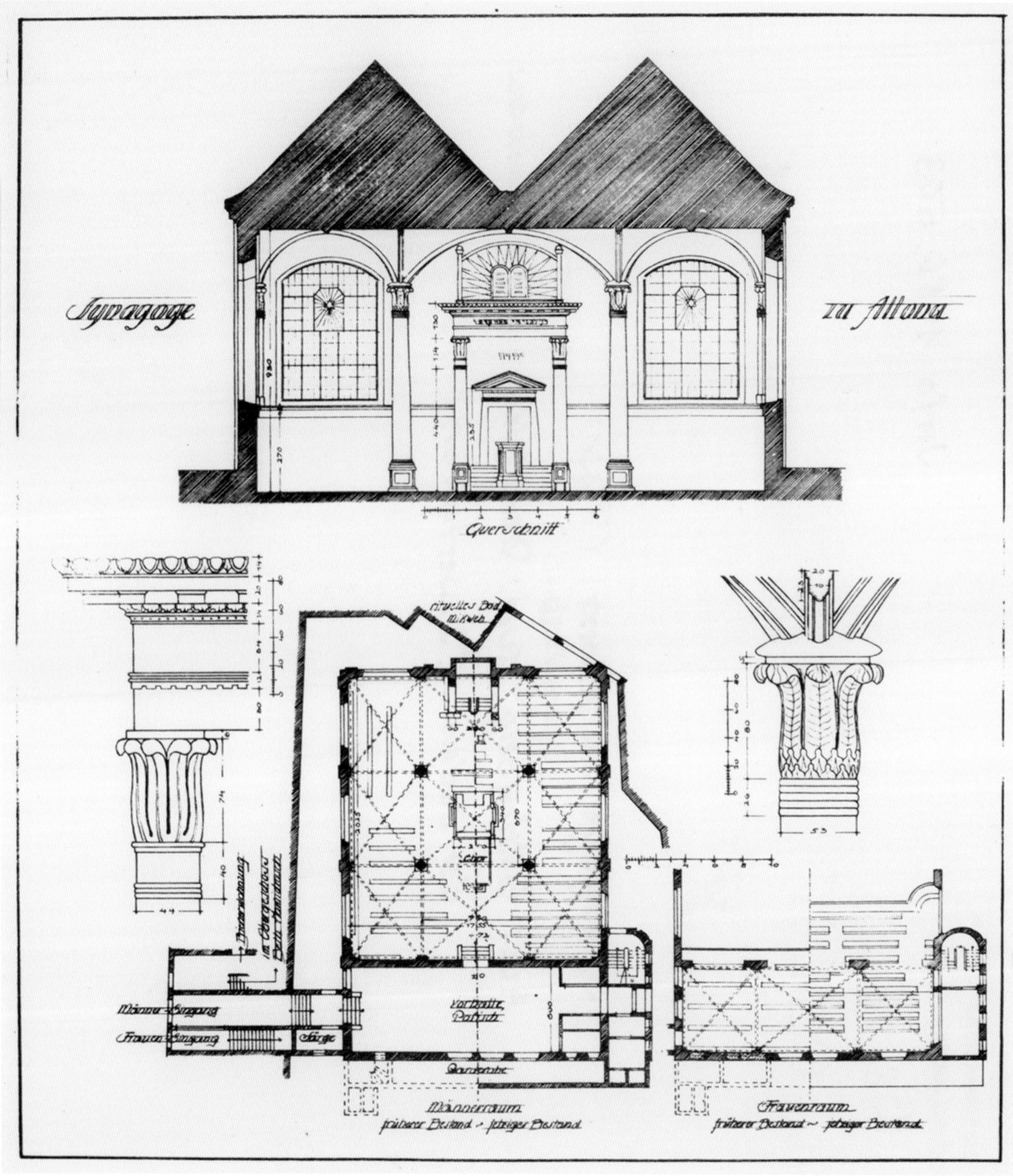
Synagoge
zu Altona
Querschnitt
rituelles Bad
Männer-Eingang
Frauen-Eingang
Särge
Chor
Garderobe
Männerraum
früherer Bestand ~ jetziger Bestand
Frauenraum
früherer Bestand ~ jetziger Bestand

Moses' middle son Abraham decided to bow to family sensibilities and thus postponed a decision on whether his children's future should be secured through conversion or emigration. When their baptism did finally take place (1816), it was initially kept secret from their Jewish grandmother. The parents followed suit and converted in Frankfurt am Main in 1822, assisted by a tolerant, culturally prominent preacher. The converts' declared intention was that "nothing should change with us as far as the Enlightenment is concerned." Nonetheless, Abraham harbored unfavorable views of Judaism and tried to discard his father's name, but was kept from doing so by his children.

am Main: mit der Intention, „daß sich bei uns hinsichtlich der Aufklärung nichts ändert". Antijüdische Ressentiments finden sich trotzdem bei Abraham. Den Namen des Vaters will er ablegen, was seine Kinder verhindern.

Mit dem berühmten Kabbalisten Jonathan Eybeschütz (1690 – 1767) korrespondierte Mendelssohn ebenso wie mit dessen Gegner Jacob Emden.

Mendelssohn corresponded with the famous Kabbalist Jonathan Eybeschütz (1690 – 1767), and also with Eybeschütz's opponent, Jacob Emden.

Die 1714 eingeweihte Berliner Synagoge in der Heidereutergasse (1821). Lavierte Tuschzeichnung von Leopold Ludwig Müller.

The Berlin Synagogue on Heidereutergasse in 1821 (consecrated in 1714). Aquatint by Leopold Ludwig Müller.

Fanny, Felix, Rebecka und Paul Mendelssohn im Jahr vor ihrer Taufe (1815).
Vier Miniaturen von August Grahl.
Fotografien von Loescher & Petsch, Berlin (1884).

Fanny, Felix, Rebecka and Paul Mendelssohn in 1815, the year before their baptism.
Four miniatures by August Grahl.
Photos by Loescher & Petsch, Berlin (1884).

Denkmal des aufgeklärten Predigers, Publizisten und Kulturpolitikers Anton Kirchner (1799 – 1834), bei dem Abraham und Lea Mendelssohn 1822 in Frankfurt am Main konvertierten.

Monument to the Enlightenment preacher, author and cultural luminary Anton Kirchner (1799 – 1834), who officiated at the conversion of Abraham and Lea Mendelssohn 1822 in Frankfurt am Main.

Veni Domine
Con moto
8 Voci
Organo
Ve - ni Do - mi ne! Ve - ni!
Veni Do - mine! et
noli tarda re et noli tarda re et no - li tar da
no - li tar da re et no - li tar dare et no - li tar da
cres
re
plebi tu - ae
Solo
re laxa facinora plebi tu ae re laxa facinora plebi tu ae et

The „Mendelssohn Madonna“

Moses' youngest son Nathan became a devout Protestant in 1809, despite the fact that his mother was still alive. He was able to reconcile this with his membership in Free Masonry, which testified to his Enlightenment ideals. Though also baptized a Protestant, Nathan's "prodigal son" Arnold would become a socialist revolutionary, and later an emergency medical worker among the Arabs in the Levant. He would eventually convert to Catholicism in order to obtain funding for a hospital foundation in Jerusalem but, as he wrote to his father, this was merely an expedient that in no way altered his basic convictions.

Dorothea's sons Philip and Jonas (later called "Johannes") were baptized as young men in Vienna's St. Stephen's Cathedral. The Catholic missionary zeal later felt by Philipp, a talented painter, is borne out in his triptych "Christianity Introduces the Arts to Germany." Meanwhile, his cousins Georg Benjamin and Alexander Mendelssohn – one Protestant, the other Jewish – would go on to jointly sponsor social projects associated with their different denominations. At their behest, the Arme-Leute-Kirche (Poor Folks' Church) in Horchheim near Coblenz, where their family owned a winery, was decorated with a copy of Raphael's Sistine Madonna, which became known as the "Mendelssohn Madonna."

Moses Mendelssohn's grandchildren Fanny Hensel and Felix Mendelssohn Bartholdy, as well as Arnold Mendelssohn Jr. (generation IV) were baptized as infants and saw themselves as Christians. Fanny and Felix were proud of the famous grandfather and selected Protestant, Catholic as well as Old Testament themes for their sacred music. When Felix began a composition with the abbreviation "L(ass) e(s) G(elingen) G(ott)" (God grant me a good result), he did so not merely to copy Bach's example, but out of genuine conviction. His nephew Arnold Mendelssohn (b. 1855) served as church cantor in Protestant congregations and gained wide recognition as a composer of Protestant sacred music. In his personal philosophical notes, he actually professes sympathy for the Jewish pantheist Spinoza, whom his ancestor Moses had regarded as an atheist.

Die „Madonna von Mendelssohn“

Der jüngste Moses-Sohn Nathan wird, noch zu Lebzeiten seiner Mutter, ein gläubiger Protestant (1809). Seine Freimaurer-Mitgliedschaft, ein Bekenntnis zu Aufklärungsidealen, vereinbart er damit. Nathans verlorener Sohn Arnold wandelt sich, evangelisch getauft, vom sozialistischen Revolutionär zum medizinischen Nothelfer unter Arabern. Seine katholische Konversion in Jerusalem dient der Finanzierung einer Krankenhausgründung; der politische Schritt ändere nichts an seiner Überzeugung, schreibt er dem Vater.

Dorotheas Söhne Philipp und Jonas/Johannes waren als junge Männer im Stephansdom getauft worden. Das Sendungsbewußtsein des Katholiken Philipp zeigt sich in seinem Triptychon „Die Einführung der Künste durch das Christentum in Deutschland“. Dagegen fördern seine Cousins Georg Benjamin und Alexander Mendelssohn – evangelisch der eine, jüdisch der andere – Sozialprojekte unterschiedlicher konfessioneller Anbindung gemeinsam. Die Arme-Leute-Kirche in Horchheim bei Koblenz, wo ihre Familie ein Weingut besitzt, wird mit einer Raffael-Kopie geschmückt, genannt „Madonna von Mendelssohn“.

Die Moses-Enkel Fanny Hensel und Felix Mendelssohn Bartholdy sowie Arnold Mendelssohn d.J. (IV. Generation) waren als Kinder getauft worden; sie verstehen sich als Christen. Fanny und Felix sind stolz auf den berühmten Großvater. Sie wählen kirchenmusikalische Stoffe mit protestantischen, katholischen, öfter mit alttestamentlichen Akzenten. Wenn Felix zu Beginn einer Komposition das Kürzel „L(aß) e(s) G(elingen) G(ott)“ notiert, ist das mehr als eine bei Bach abgeschaute Floskel. Sein Neffe Arnold Mendelssohn (geb. 1855) wirkt als Kantor in evangelischen Gemeinden; als Komponist evangelischer Sakralmusik hat er weitreichenden Erfolg. In philosophischen Notizen bekennt er Sympathie für den jüdischen Pantheisten Spinoza, der seinem Urahn Moses als Atheist galt.

Felix Mendelssohn Bartholdy: „Veni Domine“. Komponiert am 31. Dezember 1830 „für die Stimmen der Nonnen auf St. Trinita dei Monti“ in Rom.

Felix Mendelssohn Bartholdy: "Veni Domine." Composed on December 31, 1830 "for the voices of the nuns at St. Trinita dei Monti" in Rome.

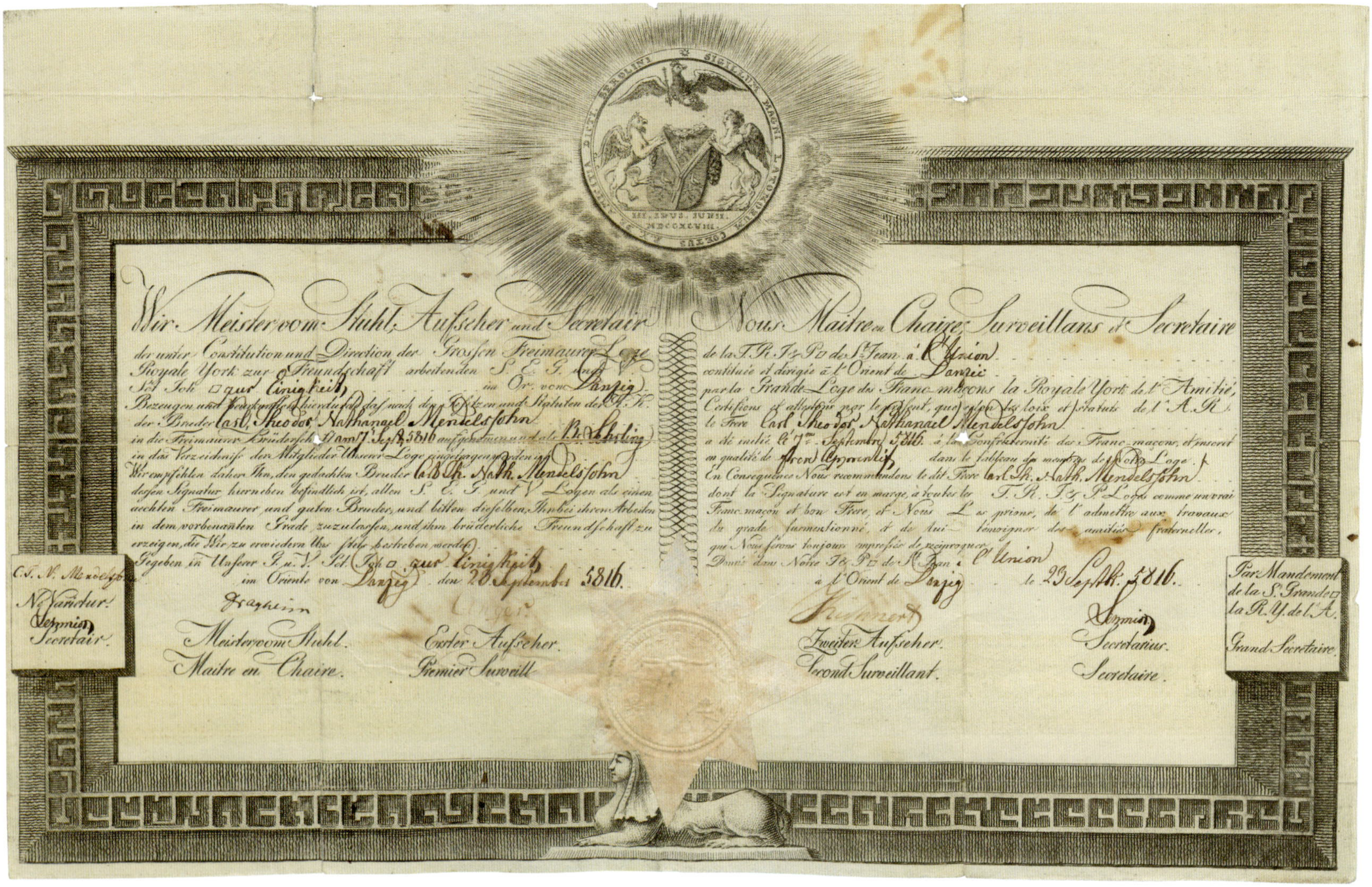

Nathan Mendelssohn: Urkunde seines Eintritts in die Freimaurerloge zu Danzig, 1816 (Anno Lucis 5816).

Nathan Mendelssohn: official record of his acceptance into the Masonic Lodge of Danzig, 1816 (Anno Lucis 5816).

Philipp Veit: Zeichnung der Taufe seines Bruders Jonas (Johannes) durch den päpstlichen Nuntius im Wiener Stephansdom am 26. Juli 1810. Links Friedrich, rechts Dorothea Schlegel.

Philipp Veit: drawing of the baptism of his brother Jonas (Johannes) by the Papal Nuntius in Vienna's St. Stephen's Cathedral on July 26, 1810. Left: Friedrich, right: Dorothea Schlegel.

Das Taufgeschirr für 27 Nachkommen Robert und Franz von Mendelssohns, von Emma Enole Clara Josepha (22. Januar 1890) bis zu Angelica Marie (29. Juni 1939). Auf dem Boden der Schale befindet sich das Wappen der Familie, der Kranich mit dem Stein.

The christening bowl and mug used for no less than 27 of Robert and Franz von Mendelssohn's descendants, from Emma Enole Clara Josepha (January 22, 1890) to Angelica Marie (June 29, 1939). The family's crest, the crane holding the pebble, can be seen on the bottom of the bowl.

„Die Madonna von Mendelssohn".
Kopie der „Sixtinischen Madonna" in Dresden, gestiftet für die Katholische Pfarrkirche St. Maximin in Koblenz-Horchheim.

„The Mendelssohn Madonna."
A copy of the "Sixtine Madonna" in Dresden, donated to the Catholic parish church of St. Maximin in Coblenz-Horchheim.

dieselben auch darum nicht lieber sind, und ein reinstoffs[?] Gewand kleiden, als der übermüthige Rabelais es zu thun pflegte, wissen daß die praktische Keuschheit der Frauen christlicher Länder im umgekehrten Verhältniß zu ihrer theoretischen Verehrung der heiligen Jungfrau zu stehen pflegt, wenn ich die Formel eines physikalischen Gesetzes auf ein geistiges oder sittliches Verhältniß anwenden darf.

Ich bin zu wenig Theolog, um Dir den Ursprung des griechischen Schisma's, der auf einer von der römischen abweichenden Lehre über die Procession des heiligen Geistes vom Vater und dem Sohne beruht, auseinanderzusetzen, glaubst Du aber, daß es diese dogmatische Differenz ist, welche die Griechen und Russen von der römischen Kirche so streng trennt und sie ihr feindlicher macht, als selbst die englische Hochkirche, die obgleich sie sich für eine fundamentale Reformation hielt [illegible]

versehen kannst,
Schisma geben würde, (tout comme chez nous, die Perser hassen die Türken, Araber und Afghanen, und werden von diesen mehr gehaßt, als sie alle die Christen oder Juden hassen, doch wirst Du schwerlich unter Hunderten einen finden, der wissen [illegible] warum sie sich religiös hassen und verfolgen, da sie alle Muselmänner sind. Aber so lächerlich und kleinlich [illegible] Ursprung des Streites, die Differenz des Dogmas ist, so [illegible] und wichtig sind gewisse Verschiedenheiten in der Moral [illegible] Sekten und deren praktischen Einfluß auf den Charakter und die staatliche Existenz dieser Völker.

~~10 Brief.~~

Ende December.

Als Mohammed, der Prophet der Moslim, nicht mit seinen treuen und späteren Nachfolgern, Abu-Bekr, Omar, Osman [illegible]

d. h. ohne die Prätension einen vorgefaßten kleinen[?] strenge logisch zu verfolgen, und ohne etwas Vollständiges, ein sogenanntes letztes Wort ~~liefern zu wollen~~ zu versprechen, ganz ~~wissenswürdige Dinge mittheilen kann.~~

Ich bitte um die Anonymität, weil wenn ich einmal schreiben soll und will, ich meine Meinung zu schreiben, und dabei weder die Regierung der ich diene, noch irgend eine andere zu schonen gedenke, d. h. ich will die Dinge sagen wie ich sie sehe, ohne über die Folgen die meine Ansichten für mich [persönlich] haben könnten, verantwortlich sein zu müssen. Finde eine Zeitung sich, die unter diesen Bedingungen meine Mittheilungen in ihrem Feuilleton aufnehmen will, ich glaube dies wird Dir um so leichter sein, als meines Wissens bei uns zu Hause die Namensunterschrift noch nicht die conditio sine qua non ist, wie in der seligen französischen Republik und dem gegenwärtigen dito Kaiserreich, und ich über oder gegen die Regierung, unter deren schützenden Flügeln meine Briefe hoffentlich gedruckt ~~werden~~ [erscheinen], durchaus nichts zu sagen haben werde.

[Um ~~nach dieser allgemeinen captatio benevolentiae auf~~ sonnigeschicher[?] Weise mitten in die Sache hinein zu springen glaube ich nicht besser verfahren zu können, als wenn ich die ~~[illegible]~~ Zustände Jerusalems eine wenig charakterisiren, ~~obgleich ich mich hierin hinter meinem Wissen und Können zurückbleiben müssen werde~~, weil die Personen alle leben und in voller Thätigkeit begriffen sind, und die Zustände von so brennendem Interesse sind, daß ich ohne Indiskretion nur die allgemeinsten Umrisse von ihrer Darstellung geben darf.

Ihr andern Norddeutschen, mögt Ihr nun Protestanten ~~oder Katholiken~~ sein, Ihr seid zu sehr Norddeutsche, Eure Gefühle sind zu sehr von der, wie Hegel sagte, grau in grau malenden Philosophie entfärbt, mit andern Worten, Ihr seid zu ~~sehr~~ „civilisirt", um Euch einen Begriff davon machen zu können, was Religion und religiöse Interessen im Orient sind. Ihr werdet schwerlich begriffen haben, wie die Frage der „heiligen Stätten" zwei Staaten, wie Frankreich und Rußland hat in Bewegung setzen können ~~Krieg vor dieser selben Frage unter einer anderen Form die ganze europäische Welt in Brand~~ setzt

(Ihr [illegible] auch [illegible] im Orient [illegible] Ausbrüchen [illegible])

zu stecken, droht, Ihr werdet es vielleicht affektirt finden, wenn ich sogar wenige nur mit Rücksicht von diesen Dingen zu sprechen wage. Ihr müßt schon zu meiner Entschuldigung dienen lassen, daß meine Briefe nicht wie jene Aufsätze von dem seligen Professor Gans „Rückblicke auf Personen und Zustände" sind, und daß ich gestern einen Brief aus Jerusalem erhalten habe, der mir mittheilt daß dort der Bürgerkrieg ausgebrochen ist, daß man in St. Johann in der Wüste, einem anderthalb Stunden von der Stadt gelegenen Dorf und Kloster, in einem Kampf zwischen Griechen und Lateinern zwanzig Personen getödtet und die doppelte Anzahl verwundet hat, daß Abu Gosch (der Vater des Letztern) ein bekannter arabischer Scheich einen vergeblichen[?] Krieg drei Stunden weit von Jerusalem gegen einen andern führt, daß alle Dörfer in der Umgebung Jerusalems in vollem Aufstand sind, daß sogar gegen zehn Schüsse gegen den Kanzler des französischen Consulats ~~gefallen sind, jedoch zum Glück keiner getroffen hat.~~

Jerusalem ist heut zu Tage eine Stadt von etwa 22,000, etwas mehr oder weniger Einwohnern, von denen 9000 und etwas mehr Juden, 3 bis 4000 nicht unirte Griechen, 2 bis 3000 schismatische Armenier, 1 bis 2000 Katholiken oder Lateiner wie man hier sagt, denn unirte Griechen gibt es nur einige wenige, katholische Armenier und Maroniten aber gar keine in Jerusalem, etwa 1000 Christen anderer Sekten, worunter [aber] Europäer und Amerikaner, und der Rest Muselmänner sind. Die Dörfer in der Umgebung sind ebenfalls größtentheils von einer gemischten Bevölkerung bewohnt, in der jedoch bald die eine, bald die andere Sekte vorwaltet, und somit die andere ausschließt; so z. B. gibt es in Bethlehem keinen Juden und sehr wenige Muselmänner, in Kolonia[?], der Residenz Abu Gosch's keinen Juden und keinen Christen u. s. f.

Auch für die Muselmänner ist die Stadt eine heilige, und die Moschee Omar's, welche auf dem Platze des ehemaligen Tempels Salomo's steht, eine Thatsache die niemand mit Ausnahme einer oder der anderen protestantischen Sekte bezweifelt, da deutliche Reste jenes Tempels noch heut sichtbar sind, unter welcher aber auch noch Einige das wahre heilige Grab sehen soll, (die Protestanten glauben nämlich nicht an

Lessing's "Nathan" as a model for interfaith dialogue

In his "Levantine Letters," which he dispatched from the Crimean War while serving as a doctor in the Ottoman army, Arnold Mendelssohn Sr. expressed admiration for the humanity he had experienced among the Muslims. Inspired by the example of Moses Mendelssohn, the writer Lessing had created the character "Nathan the Wise" to exemplify the ideal of an enlightened, pluralistic society. But by the time the funeral of the last Jewish member of the family (Marianne Mendelssohn) was held in 1880, many of the attending relatives had to admit that they had never experienced a Jewish ceremony before. As time went on and anti-Semitic sentiments began to spread, many of Moses' descendants began to rediscover an interest in their own Jewish roots.

"To search for truth, to love beauty, to desire the good, and to do what is best" – this was the "calling of man" according to Moses Mendelssohn. This great ethical legacy was elaborated upon in the fifth generation of the family by philosopher Paul Hensel, also known as the "Socrates of Erlangen." A Neo-Kantian, Hensel's religious philosophy distinguished between art, which maps the infinite onto the finite, and religion, which orients earthly concerns towards the infinite (this in contrast to the union of art and religious contemplation favored by the Romantics.) The Göttingen professor Leonard Nelson (1882 - 1927), a great-grandson of Rebecka Mendelssohn Bartholdy, would for his part espouse a "Neo-Socratic" approach to the revitalization and practical application of philosophy, along with an ethics-based socialism. Willi Eichler, author of the German Social Democratic Party's (SPD) Godesberg Program (1959), was just one of the people influenced by these ideals. Nelson's International Socialist Combat League would later serve as a rallying point of resistance against the Hitler regime.

Lessings „Nathan" als Ideal des Dialogs

In „Levantischen Briefen", die der osmanische Militärarzt Arnold Mendelssohn d.Ä. aus dem Krimkrieg versandte, klang Respekt an für die bei Muslimen erfahrene Humanität. Offenheit zwischen Juden, Christen und Muslimen hatte Lessings „Nathan der Weise" als Ideal der aufgeklärten Gesellschaft hingestellt, inspiriert durch das Vorbild des Moses. Doch bei der Bestattung der damals letzten Jüdin der Familie, Marianne Mendelssohn (1880), erleben viele Verwandte erstmals eine jüdische Zeremonie. Während sich antisemitische Stimmungen verbreiten, entdecken Moses-Nachkommen ihr Interesse an den eigenen jüdischen Wurzeln.

„Nach Wahrheit forschen, Schönheit lieben, Gutes wollen, das Beste tun" hatte Mendelssohn als „Bestimmung des Menschen" bezeichnet. Dem ethischen Vermächtnis des Urahnen stellt sich in der fünften Generation der Philosoph Paul Hensel, genannt „Sokrates von Erlangen". Der Neukantianer unterscheidet in seiner Religionsphilosophie zwischen der Kunst, die im Endlichen das Unendliche abbildet, und der Religion, die Irdisches aufs Unendliche ausrichtet – im Gegensatz zur Vereinigung von Kunst und frommer Anschauung bei den Romantikern. Der Göttinger Professor Leonard Nelson (1882 – 1927) wiederum, ein Urenkel Rebecka Mendelssohn Bartholdys, vertritt einen „neosokratischen" Unterricht zur Neubelebung der Philosophie, die mit Praxis zu verbinden sei, sowie einen ethisch begründeten Sozialismus. Willi Eichler, Autor des Godesberger SPD-Programms (1959), wird durch ihn geprägt. In Nelsons Internationalem Sozialistischen Kampfbund formiert sich später Widerstand gegen das NS-Regime.

„Levantische Briefe" des osmanischen Militärarztes Arnold Mendelssohn aus dem Krimkrieg, veröffentlicht 1853/1854 in europäischen Zeitungen: Berichte vom Leben in der Vielvölkerstadt Jerusalem und von der Toleranz der Muslime.

"Levantine Letters" written by Arnold Mendelssohn during his service as doctor in the Ottoman army during the Crimean War, published in 1853/1854 in various European newspapers: Reports on Life in the Multinational City of Jerusalem and on the Tolerance of the Muslims.

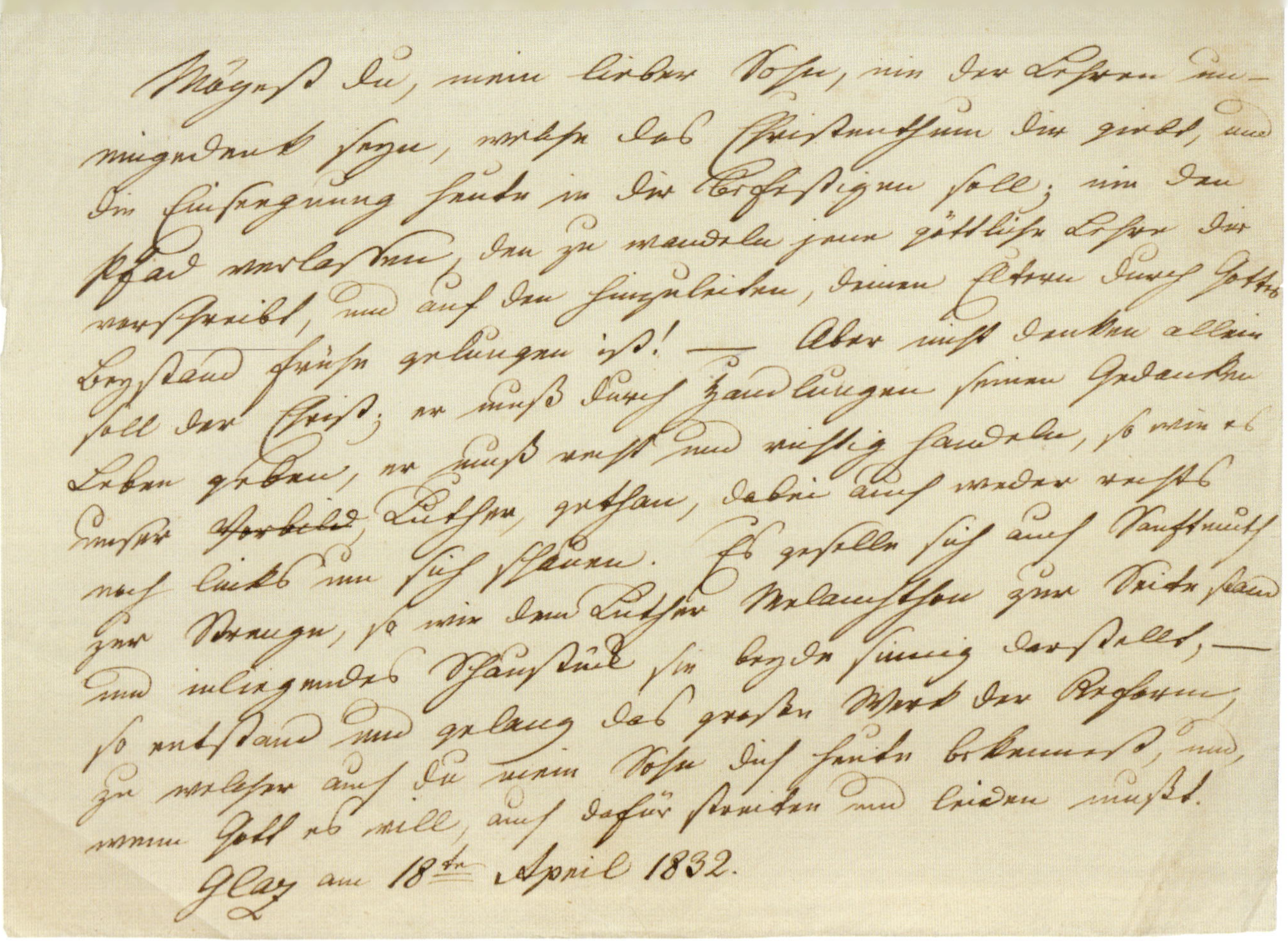

Mögest Du, mein lieber Sohn, nie der Lehren un-
eingedenk seyn, welche das Christenthum Dir giebt, und
die Einsegnung heute in Dir befestigen soll; nie den
Pfad verlassen, den zu wandeln jene göttliche Lehre Dir
vorschreibt, und auf den hinzuleiten, deinen Eltern durch Gottes
Beystand hoffentlich gelungen ist! — Aber nicht denken allein
soll der Christ; er muß durch Handlungen seinen Gedanken
Leben geben, er muß recht und richtig handeln, so wie es
unser ~~Vorbild~~ Luther gethan, dabei auch wieder recht
noch [illegible] um sich schauen. So gesellte sich auch Sanftmuth
zur Strenge, so wie dem Luther Melanchthon zur Seite stand
und [illegible] Schauspiel für beyde [illegible] darstellt, —
so entstand und gelang das große Werk der Reform,
zu welcher auch Du mein Sohn Dich heute bekennest, und,
wenn Gott es will, auch dafür streiten und leiden mußt.
Glaz am 18ten April 1832.

Brief Nathan Mendelssohns zur Konfirmation seines Sohnes Arnold (1832).
„Mögest Du, mein lieber Sohn, nie der Lehren uneingedenk sein, welche das Christenthum dir giebt ... Aber nicht denken allein soll der Christ, er muß durch Handlungen seinen Gedanken Leben geben, er muß recht und richtig handeln, so wie es unser Luther gethan ...“ So sei das große Werk der Reform entstanden, „zu welcher auch Du mein Sohn Dich heute bekennest, und, wenn Gott es will, auch dafür streiten und leiden mußt.“

Letter by Nathan Mendelssohn on the confirmation of his son Arnold (1832).
“Mayest thou, my beloved son, never be unmindful of the teachings which Christianity has imparted to you... But a Christian must not only think; he must infuse his thoughts with life through his actions, he must be just and upright in his dealings, just as our Luther was...” This, Nathan explained, was how the great work of the Reformation was accomplished, “to which you, my son, now also give credence and, if God wills it, for which you, too, will have to struggle and suffer.”

Die Gräber von Franz und Else Oppenheim auf dem Friedhof am Wannsee. Kreuz und Davidstern befinden sich auf der Friedhofsmauer.

The graves of Franz and Else Oppenheim in the Friedhof am Wannsee. The cemetery wall is adorned with both the Cross and the Star of David.

„Reisescizzen“ (1918) von Hugo Wach, einem Enkel von Felix Mendelssohn Bartholdy: Moschee in Cairo.

“Travel Sketches” (1918) by Hugo Wach, a grandson of Felix Mendelssohn Bartholdy: Mosque in Cairo.

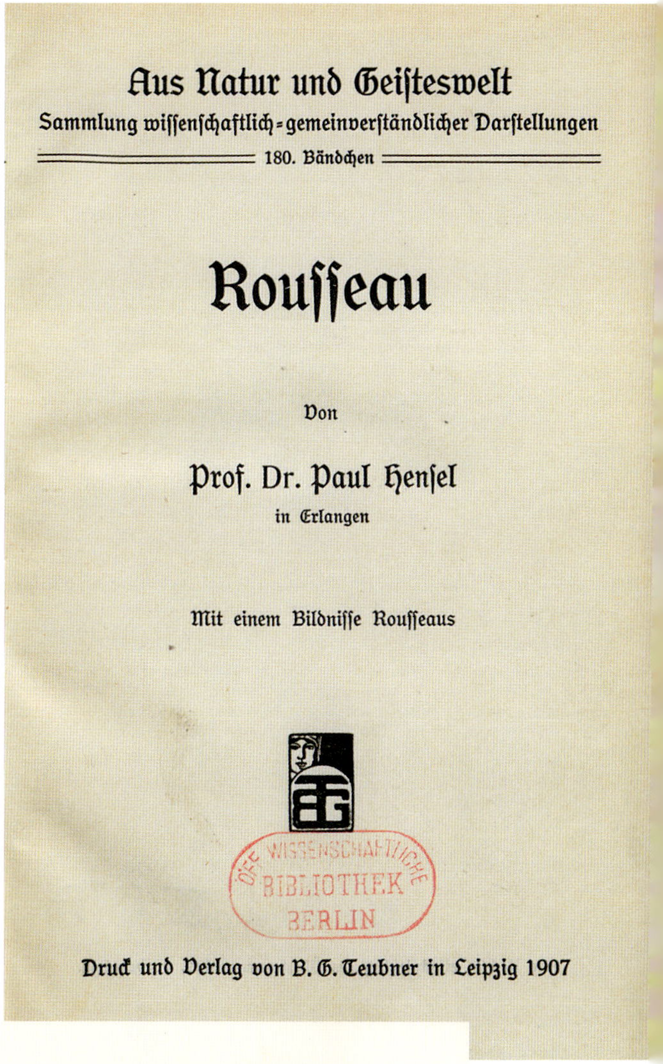

Aus Natur und Geisteswelt

Sammlung wissenschaftlich-gemeinverständlicher Darstellungen

180. Bändchen

Rousseau

Von

Prof. Dr. Paul Hensel

in Erlangen

Mit einem Bildnisse Rousseaus

Druck und Verlag von B. G. Teubner in Leipzig 1907

Paul Hensel: „Rousseau“. Leipzig 1907. Hier kreuzt der Ururenkel des kritischen Rousseau-Übersetzers Moses Mendelssohn die Wege seines Vorfahren.

Paul Hensel: “Rousseau.” Leipzig 1907. Hensel was following in the footsteps of his great-grandfather Moses Mendelssohn, who had translated and critically analyzed the works of Rousseau.

Der Philosoph Leonard Nelson, geb. 1882 in Berlin, gest. 1927 in Göttingen.

The philosopher Leonard Nelson, b. 1882 in Berlin, d. 1927 in Göttingen.

Paul Hensel (1860 – 1930). Porträtfoto in: „Kleine Schriften und Vorträge“, hrsg. zum 70. Geburtstag des Verfassers (Tübingen 1930).

Paul Hensel (1860 – 1930). Portrait photo in: “Kleine Schriften und Vorträge,” published on the occasion of the 70th birthday of the author (Tübingen 1930).

Faith from the bottom of the soul

During World War I, the international legal scholar Albrecht Mendelssohn Bartholdy summed up the issue of his ancestry with the following credo: "My ancestors include a long line of Jewish rabbis up to the Middle Ages, and an equally long line of priests, provosts, and martyrs of the French Reformed church up to the Edict of Nantes; they also comprise a series of German-Lutheran pastors as well as a fourth ancestral line of upstanding Austrian Catholics. I am sure many of us have a similar background. And yet I would aver that, even for those of us of mixed heritage, the faith of the fathers must serve as the foundation for our spiritual life, if we are to be good citizens of this world and our homeland." Today, as we enter the 21st century, the living descendants of Moses include atheists, Jews and Christians of various denominations, some of whom have also taken Muslim or Hindu marriage partners.

The notion that answers to questions of identity and truth could be found in the story of one's own origins was already expressed long ago by a reader of the 1786 edition of Moses' „Morgenstunden," who penned the following commentary in verse on the inside cover:

"Reaching the fork 'twixt heaven and hell
Mendelssohn set his sights on the Temple of Light
but Paradise had a Cerberus as well;
For up sprang Saints Peter, Calvin and Luther
who stood sentry at God's order
and lowered the boom to bar the border!
Together: Where are you going – whither, whither?
Mendelssohn: To the temple of light!
Together: Your papers, papers, papers!
St. Peter: Where did you get your papers, little man?
Calvin: in Geneva? Luther: in Wittenberg?
St. Peter: in Rome?
Mendelssohn: How do you mean? Together: Where was
your pass to heaven issued?
Calvin: in Geneva? Luther: in Wittenberg?
St. Peter: In Rome?
If not, you'll just have to hie yourself to hell, old boy!
Mendelssohn: My pass is old, you see, dated at the dawn
of time at headquarters in Mt. Sinai!
The turnpike creaked ajar and Moses went to heaven."

Der Glaube am Grund der Seele

Als persönliches Herkunfts-Credo formuliert während des Ersten Weltkriegs Albrecht Mendelssohn Bartholdy, der Völkerrechtler: „Unter meinen Vorfahren ist eine lange Reihe jüdischer Rabbiner bis ins Mittelalter hinauf, unter ihnen ist eine ebenso lange Reihe von Pfarrern und Vorstehern und Glaubensmärtyrern der französisch-reformierten Gemeinde bis unter das Edikt von Nantes, unter ihnen sind deutsch-evangelische Pfarrer aus der Reformationszeit und als vierte großelterliche Reihe gute katholische Österreicher. So wird es vielen von uns gehen. Und doch sage ich auch für uns Zusammengewürfelte, daß uns der Glaube der Väter den Grund zum Leben in unsere Seele legen muß, wenn wir gute Bürger dieser Welt und unserer Heimat werden sollen." Zu Beginn des 21. Jahrhunderts gibt es unter den Moses-Nachkommen Atheisten, Juden und Christen verschiedenster Konfessionen, manche verbunden mit muslimischen oder hinduistischen Ehepartnern.

Daß sich Antworten auf Identitäts- und Wahrheitsfragen in der eigenen Ursprungsgeschichte finden, hatte bereits das kommentierende Gedicht eines Lesers der Mendelssohnschen „Morgenstunden" nahegelegt, notiert auf dem Innenblatt seiner Ausgabe von 1786:

„Als Mendelssohn jüngst vor den Scheidewegen
Zum Himmel und zur Höll ankam
Und steil auf zum Visier den Sonnendohm sich nam
Um keinen Zerberus verlegen;
Sprang ihm von Kommandanten wegen
Sct. Peter, Luther und Calvin
Aus iren Schilderhäusergens entgegen
Und recta vor den Schlagbaum hin.
Tutti: Wohin? – Wohin? – Wohin? –
Mend. Zum Dohm!
Tutti: Den Pas! Den Pas! Den Pas!
Sct. Peter: Woher der Pas du kleiner Höckerschimmel?
Calvin: Von Genf? Luther: Von Wittenberg?
Sct. Peter: Von Rom?
Mend. Wi so? Tutti: Wo ist dein Pas datirt zum Himmel?
Calvin: Zu Genf? Luther: Zu Wittenberg? Sct. Peter: Zu Rom?
Sonst scher dich nur zum Teufel alter Schimmel!
Mend.: Mein Pas ist alt; datirt in aller Früh
Im Hauptquartier zu Sinai!
Der Schlagbaum knarrte auf und Moses ging gen Himmel."

„Christus und die Samariterin am Jakobsbrunnen". Relief nach Chodowiecki am Giebel der Französischen Friedrichstadtkirche.
Im Gespräch über das „Wasser des Lebens", das sich auch auf die Taufe bezieht, fällt der Satz Jesu: „Das Heil kommt von den Juden."
Gegenüber, im Haus Markgrafenstraße 48, wurden die Kinder Abraham Mendelssohns am 21. März 1816 getauft.

"Christ and the Samaritan Woman by Jacob's Well." Relief after Chodowiecki, on the frieze of the *Französische Friedrichstadtkirche* church.
While speaking of the "living water," which also refers to baptism, Christ says, "salvation is from the Jews."
Directly opposite the church, at Markgrafenstrasse 48, was the house in which the children of Mendelssohn were baptized on March 21, 1816.

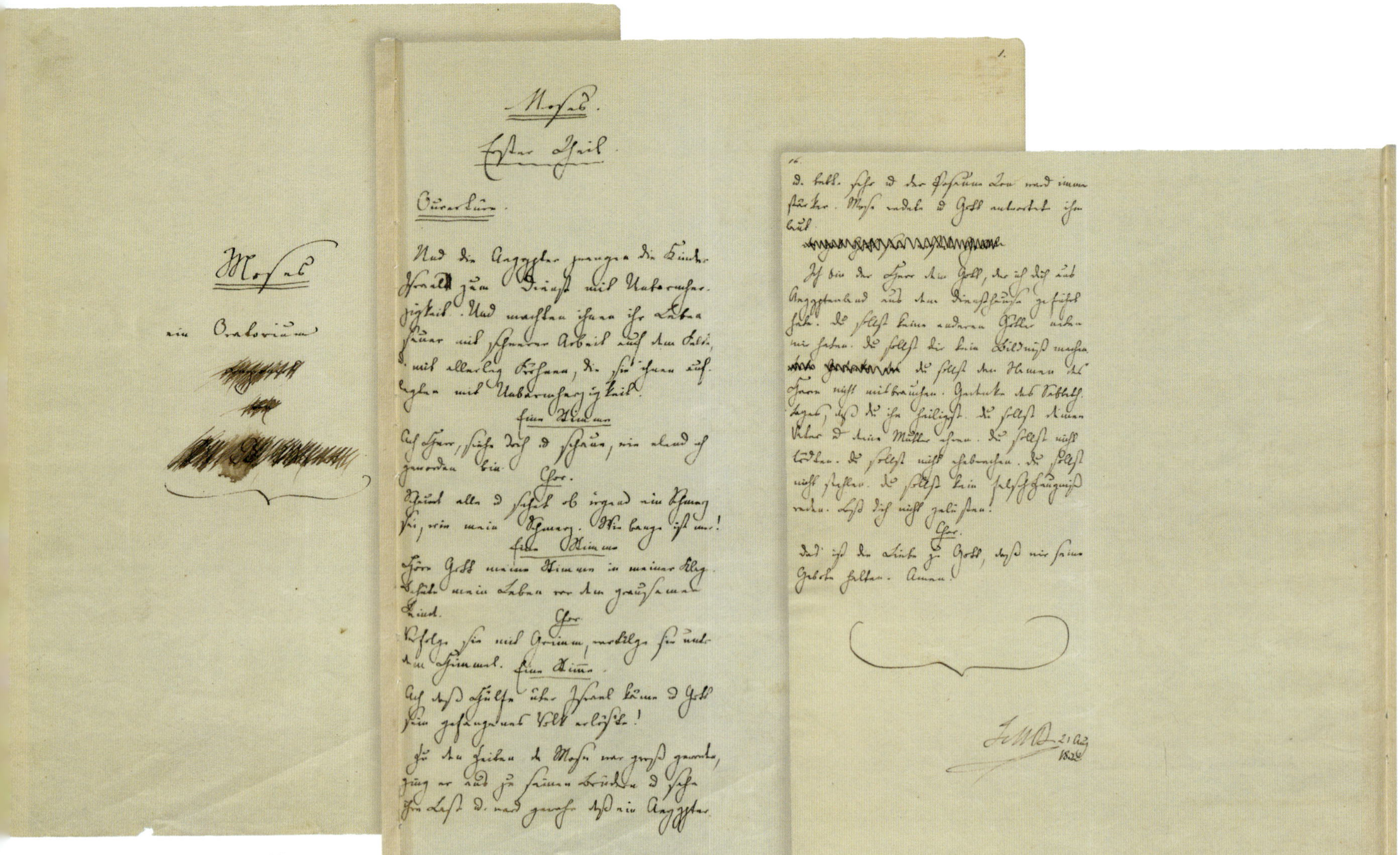

Felix Mendelssohn Bartholdy:
Libretto für das Moses-Oratorium von Adolph Bernhard Marx. Der Text endet mit der Aufforderung des neutestamentlichen Johannes-Briefes zur Gesetzeserfüllung in Liebe. Auf der Titelseite hat der Librettist den Namen des Komponisten durchgestrichen, die Freundschaft beider zerbrach an dem gemeinsamen Projekt.

Felix Mendelssohn Bartholdy: Libretto for the Moses Oratorium by Adolph Bernhard Marx. The text closes with a passage from the First Epistle of John on love as the fulfillment of God's law. On the title page, the librettist has crossed out the name of the composer: Sadly, the friendship between the two men came to grief over their collaboration on the project.

Eine evangelische Nachfahrin Fanny Hensels heiratet in Adelaide (Australien) einen Hindu: Stephanie Olsen und S.D. Kumar Darshan (2010).

A contemporary Mendelssohn wedding according to Hindu rites: Stephanie Olsen, a descendant of Fanny Hensel, ties the knot with S.D. Kumar Darshan in Adelaide, Australia (2010).

Das byzantinische Kreuz aus Fanny Hensels Musikzimmer, ein Souvenir von ihrer zweiten Italienreise (1845).

The Byzantine Cross from Fanny Hensel's music room, a souvenir from her second trip to Italy (1845).

„Auf Moses Mendelssohns Tod".
Kupferstich (o. J.) von Johann Christian Friedrich Räntz.

"Upon the Death of Moses Mendelssohn."
Engraving (undated) by Johann Christian Friedrich Räntz.

The Graves of Moses Mendelssohn's Descendants and the Cemeteries near Hallesches Tor

As successive generations of the Mendelssohns began to change their religious affiliation, this determined where they were buried. Thus, the graves of the original progenitors Moses and Fromet are located in Jewish cemeteries in Berlin-Mitte and in Altona (Hamburg), respectively, while their Jewish children and grandchildren are interred in Berlin's Schönhauser Allee graveyard. The grave of their daughter Henriette Maria Mendelssohn was located in the old Catholic burial ground behind Oranienburger Tor (today the garden of the Catholic Academy), while that of her brother Nathan, who converted to Protestantism, was in the graveyard of the congregation of Berlin's Sophienkirche.

As of 1835, most of the Protestant descendants and their spouses were buried in one of three cemeteries near the south-eastern gate to the city, the Hallesches Tor. Walking through this necropolis, one practically gets a tour of the prominent social circles of Berlin in the 19th and 20th centuries. In the Dreifaltigkeit I cemetery, we find the family plots of Lea and Abraham Mendelssohn Bartholdy and of their children Fanny Hensel, Felix Mendelssohn Bartholdy, and Paul Mendelssohn-Bartholdy. Also nearby are the resting places of some of their close friends: the renowned salon hostess Rahel Varnhargen von Ense and her husband Karl August; the theologian August Twesten, who assisted Joseph Mendelssohn's son Benjamin at his baptism; as well as the renowned gynecologist at the Charité hospital Adolf Gusserow, who was married to one of Joseph's granddaughters.

Cemetery I of the Jerusalems- und Neue Kirchengemeinde contains the family graves of Franz von Mendelssohn Jr. and Sr., and of Carl Westphal and his relatives. Carl Friedrich Fasch, the founder of the *Sing-Akademie*, is also buried here, along with the painter Ludwig Passini. Passini's wife Anna, who died in Rome, was originally laid to rest in the family plot of her parents Robert and Marie Warschauer (née Mendelssohn). Her grave had to be moved in the 1960s to make room for the expansion of Blücherstrasse, along with the graves of Otto Georg Oppenheim, his wife Margarethe (née Mendelssohn) and their son Hugo. Henriette Herz, another famous *salonière*, is buried in Cemetery II of the Jerusalems- und Neue Kirchengemeinde. Jerusalem/Neue Kirche Cemetery III: Here, next to the chapel, housing this exhibition, we find the graves of Adelbert Delbrück, co-founder of Deutsche Bank, and of Sebastian Hensel, the residential developer. Also in this section are the family plots of the von Simsons, in-laws of the Mendelssohns. And a memorial

Gräber der Nachkommen Moses Mendelssohns und die Friedhöfe vor dem Halleschen Tor

Unterschiedliche Ruhestätten verweisen auf erste konfessionelle Trennungen. Die Stammeltern Moses und Fromet sind begraben auf jüdischen Friedhöfen, in Berlin-Mitte und in Altona, ihre jüdischen Kinder und Enkel an der Schönhauser Allee in Berlin. Das Grab der Tochter Henriette Maria Mendelssohn befand sich auf dem Alten Katholischen Friedhof hinter dem Oranienburger Tor (heute: Garten der Katholischen Akademie), das ihres reformiert getauften Bruders Nathan auf einem Friedhof der Sophien-Gemeinde.

Die meisten Gräber evangelischer Nachkommen und ihrer Partner liegen ab 1835 auf den Friedhöfen vor dem Halleschen Tor. Diese Totenstatt ist ein Dokument der bürgerlichen Netzwerke im Berlin des 19./20. Jahrhunderts. Auf Dreifaltigkeit I befinden sich Familiengräber Lea und Abraham Mendelssohn Bartholdys sowie ihrer Kinder Fanny Hensel, Felix Mendelssohn Bartholdy und Paul Mendelssohn-Bartholdy, außerdem Ruhestätten von Freunden: der Salonière Rahel und ihres Gatten Karl August Varnhargen von Ense; des Theologen August Twesten, der Joseph Mendelssohns Sohn Benjamin zur Taufe begleitet hatte, und des mit einer Josephs-Enkelin verheirateten, berühmten Charité-Gynäkologen Adolf Gusserow.

Auf dem Friedhof I der Jerusalems- und Neuen Kirchengemeinde findet man Familiengräber Franz von Mendelssohns, des Jüngeren und des Älteren, sowie der Familie Carl Westphal. Carl Friedrich Fasch, der Gründer der Sing-Akademie, ist hier ebenso begraben wie der Maler Ludwig Passini: Dessen in Rom verstorbene Ehefrau Anna war seinerzeit im Erbbegräbnis ihrer Eltern, Robert und Marie Warschauer geb. Mendelssohn, bestattet worden – eine Anlage, die in den 1960er Jahren dem Ausbau der Blücherstraße weichen mußte, wie die Grabstellen Otto Georg Oppenheims, seiner Frau Margarethe geb. Mendelssohn und des Sohnes Hugo. Auf dem Friedhof II der Jerusalems- und Neuen Kirchengemeinde erhielt Henriette Herz, die Salonière, ihre Ruhestätte; auf Jerusalem / Neue Kirche III – neben der ehemaligen Kapelle, in der sich diese Ausstellung befindet – Adelbert Delbrück, Mitbegründer der Deutschen Bank, der Sebastian Hensel als Wohnungsbau-Manager engagiert hatte. Zudem befinden sich hier Familiengräber der mit den Mendelssohns verschwägerten von Simsons. Für den 1918 gefallenen Bankier Ludwig Mendelssohn Bartholdy wurde nicht weit vom Grab seines Vaters Paul, des Agfa-Gründers, eine Gedenksäule errichtet.

column was erected in honor of the banker Ludwig Mendelssohn Bartholdy, who died in combat in 1918; it is not far from the grave of his father Paul, the founder of Agfa.

The graves of Moses' descendants can also be found at a number of other locations in and around Berlin: at the cemeteries Luisenfriedhof I, Waldfriedhof Olympiapark and those of Bornstedt and Wannsee; in the churchyard of the patronage church of Börnicke; and in the graveyard of the Dahlem Dorfkirche. The fact that the graves of later generations are scattered all over the world is a testimony to the family's emigration, and also due to a number of accidental deaths. Thus, Roland du Bois-Reymond, a scion of the 6th generation, rests near his father Alard in the town of Plön near the Baltic Sea, where both men drowned in 1922. Albrecht and Dora Mendelssohn Bartholdy, meanwhile, are buried in Clifton Hampdon near Oxford. Eleonora von Mendelssohn's urn is located in the Ferncliff Mausoleum of Hartsdale, New York, USA, while the ashes of Fritz Kempner, a grandson of Franz von Mendelssohn Jr. who passed away in 2013, were scattered in the Kennebec River near Woolwich, Maine.

In Berlin und Umgebung liegen Moses-Nachkommen außerdem auf dem Luisenfriedhof I, auf dem Waldfriedhof Olympiapark, auf den Friedhöfen Bornstedt und am Wannsee, bei der Patronatskirche Börnicke, auf dem Dorffriedhof Dahlem. Die weltweite Zerstreuung der Grabstätten späterer Generationen spiegelt auch Unglücksfälle und Emigrationsgeschichte. Roland du Bois-Reymond, ein Nachfahre der 6. Generation, ruht neben seinem Vater Alard bei Plön, wo beide 1922 in der Ostsee ertranken. Albrecht und Dora Mendelssohn Bartholdy sind in Clifton Hampdon bei Oxford begraben. Eleonora von Mendelssohns Urne steht im Ferncliff Mausoleum von Hartsdale (NY/USA); die Asche Fritz Kempners, des 2013 verstorbenen Enkels Franz von Mendelssohns d.J., wurde in den Kennebec bei Woolwich (Maine) gestreut.

LUDWIG
MENDELSSOHN BARTHOLDY
+1. JAN. 1878 IN BERLIN
+14. OKT. 1918 IN BOLOWSK
ELSE von SIMSON
CLARA von SIMSON
MARGARETHE SIMSON
JOHN SIMSON
CLARA von SIMSON
GEB. ECKHOFF
geb. 29. August 1879
gest. 5. Februar 1964
OTTO OPPENHEIM
Cecile Gilbert
Enole
Mendelssohn Bartholdy
geb. Oppenheim
geb. 1. Juli 1855
gest. 20. März 1939
Paul
Felix Abraham
Mendelssohn Bartholdy
geb. 18. Januar 1841
gest. 17. Februar 1880
Else
Mendelssohn Bartholdy
geb. Oppenheim
geb. 16. November 1844
gest. 20. August 1868
BEATE von SIMSON
AUGUST von SIMSON
Gute Menschen –
wenn etwas Gutes für die
Menschheit geschieht –
dann gedenkt freundlich in
Eurer Freude auch meiner.
Rahel Friedericke
Varnhagen von Ense
geb. Robert.
1771 zu Berlin.
Karl August
Varnhagen von Ense
geb. den 21. Februar 1785
zu Düsseldorf.
gest. den 10. Oktober 1858
zu Berlin.
FAMILIE
DELBRÜCK

Abraham Ernst Mendelssohn Bartholdy
geb den 11ten Decbr 1776
gest den 19ten Novbr 1835
Lea Felicia Pauline Mendelssohn Bartholdy geb Salomon
geb den 26ten März 1777
gest den 12ten Decbr 1842
JACOB LUDWIG FELIX MENDELSSOHN BARTHOLDY
GEBOREN ZU HAMBURG AM 3. FEB. 1809
AM 4. NOV. 1847
PAULINE LUISE
MENDELSSOHN
GEB. HEIN
Henriette verwittwete Hofräthin Herz,
geb. de Lemos,
geb. d. 5. Septbr. 1764, gest. d. 22. Octbr. 1847.
Familie Franz von Mendelssohn
Franz von Mendelssohn
Enole von Mendelssohn
Franz von Mendelssohn
von Mendelssohn
Robert von Mendelssohn
Professor Dr. med.
Carl Westphal
geb. 23. März 1833
gest. 27. Januar 1890
Clara Westphal
geb. Mendelssohn
geb. 24. Juli 1840
gest. 3. Oktober 1927
Professor Dr. med.
Alexander Westphal
geb. 18. Mai 1863
gest. 9. Januar 1941
Elisabeth Westphal

Wirtschaft und Politik – I
Business and Politics – I

The rare ability to find a happy balance between commercial and cultural endeavors is what makes the Mendelssohns so unique. Thus, the family patriarch Moses Mendelssohn saw free intellectual enquiry as his highest pursuit, yet also derived income – and the right to reside in Berlin – from his activities in the textile trade. Instead of marrying a rabbi's daughter who had been proposed to him, he fell in love and tied the knot with the daughter of a merchant. One of the great-great-grandfathers of his wife Fromet Gugenheim was the Viennese court banker Samuel Oppenheimer, while her great-grandfather Lehmann Gomperz served as banker to the Great Elector of Brandenburg; Glückel von Hameln, a prominent Hamburg merchantwoman, was Fromet's great-great aunt. Moses Mendelssohn transacted his first private business deal – i.e. outside of his employment in a silk-making workshop – in 1765 when, together with Fromet, he granted his landlord a loan of 4,000 Reichsthaler as a mortgage lien on the residential building at Spandauer Strasse 68. Moses went on to execute private trading transactions; this would become the point of departure for the bank founded by his sons. Moses' eldest son Joseph began doing business at the same address in 1795.

His first business partner was a son of the silk manufacturer David Friedländer, who had been Moses' business associate and intellectual ally. In 1799, the two opened the Mendelssohn & Friedländer offices at Burgstrasse 25, a building belonging to the Itzig family. Joseph founded his next company, J. & A. Mendelssohn, together with his brother Abraham, who had returned home from a stint with the Fould banking house in Paris. Starting in 1804, this new firm was located in the Ephraim Palais at Poststrasse 16; in 1815, it was moved to Jägerstrasse 51, near the Gendarmenmarkt square. In the beginning, the company still derived most of its turnover from merchandise trading, as well as some insurance brokerage.

The opportunity to expand came with the outbreak of the Napoleonic Wars. The Mendelssohn bank was moved from occupied Berlin to the bustling port of Hamburg, a decision that paid off handsomely – until the customs inspectors deployed by the French occupation authorities forced the two banking brothers to

Die glückliche Verbindung von Ökonomie und Kultur ist das Besondere an der Familie Mendelssohn. Stammvater Moses zieht das freie Denken allen Leidenschaften vor, verdankt aber dem Textilhandel Einkommen und Aufenthaltsstatus. Statt einer Rabbinertochter, die ihm angetragen wird, entscheidet er sich für die Liebe zu einer Kaufmannstochter. Ein Ururgroßvater seiner Frau Fromet Gugenheim ist der Wiener Hofbankier Samuel Oppenheimer; ihr Urgroßvater Lehmann Gomperz war Bankier des Großen Kurfürsten; die Hamburger Kauffrau Glückel von Hameln ist ihre Urgroßtante. Das erste belegte Privatgeschäft Mendelssohns, abseits seines Angestellten-Jobs in der Seidenmanufaktur, schließen Fromet und Moses 1765 gemeinsam ab. Ihrer Vermieterin geben sie einen Kredit von 4000 Reichsthalern als Hypothek auf das Wohnhaus Spandauer Straße 68. Aus privaten Handelsgeschäften, die Mendelssohn abwickelt, entsteht hier ein Ausgangspunkt für die Bank seiner Söhne. Die Handlung seines Ältesten startet 1795 unter derselben Adresse.

Ein Sohn des Seidenfabrikanten David Friedländer, der Moses' Geschäfts- und Gesinnungspartner gewesen war, ist Josephs erster Kompagnon: Mendelssohn & Friedländer nehmen 1799 ihr Büro bei den Itzigs, Burgstraße 25. Die nächste Sozietät J. & A. Mendelssohn, gegründet mit dem vom Pariser Bankhaus Fould zurückgekehrten Bruder Abraham, residiert ab 1804 im Ephraim-Palais, Poststraße 16; ab 1815 unter der Adresse Jägerstraße 51, nahe dem Gendarmenmarkt. Zunächst machen noch Waren-, aber auch Versicherungsgeschäfte einen Teil des Umsatzes aus.

Mit den Napoleonischen Kriegen entstehen Expansions-Chancen. Der Umzug aus dem gebeutelten Berlin in die Hafenstadt Hamburg lohnt sich – bis dort die Zollfahndung der französischen Besatzer die Bankiersbrüder samt ihren Familien zur Heimkehr zwingt. Der Transfer preußischer Reparationszahlungen nach Paris, die nach Napoleons Niederlage (1815) eingeforderten Reparationen sowie die monetäre Versorgung preußischer Truppen im besiegten Frankreich verschaffen dem Geldinstitut große Gewinne. In der Jägerstraße, wo die Mendelssohns bis zum Jahrhundertende fünf Gebäude kaufen oder bauen, als Wohnung und Kontor nutzen werden, liegt ihr Hauptquartier zwischen zwei Staatsbanken: der Königlichen Giro- und Lehnbank an der

Relief zu „Handel und Verkehr" aus der Schadow-Schule, 1802 von Joseph Mendelssohn der neuen Berliner Börse gestiftet, nach Abriß des Hauses 1893 „zurück"gebracht ins neue Bankgebäude Jägerstraße 49/50 (heute: Deutsches Apothekerhaus).

"Trade & Transport:" A relief from the school of sculptor Johann Gottfried Schadow, donated to the Berlin Stock Exchange in 1802 by Joseph Mendelssohn; after the building was torn down in 1893, the work was "brought home" to the new bank building at Jägerstrasse 49/50 (today: Deutsches Apothekerhaus).

pull up stakes and return home with their families. However, the bank would go on to reap huge profits by handling the transfer of Prussian reparation payments to Paris and, after Napoleon's defeat in 1815, of French reparations to Prussia. Keeping the Prussian occupation forces in France supplied with liquid funds proved to be another lucrative line of business. The headquarters of the Mendelssohn bank was moved to Jägerstrasse, a strategic location between two important state banks: the Königliche Giro- und Lehnbank (Royal Current Accounts & Loan Bank) on the corner of Oberwall and Jägerstrasse, and the Preussische Seehandlung (Prussian Maritime Trade Society) on the Gendarmenmarkt. By end of the nineteenth century, the Mendelssohns would acquire, build and use no less than five buildings on Jägerstrasse, as residences or as business premises.

Ecke Oberwall /Jägerstraße und der Preußischen Seehandlung am Gendarmenmarkt.

Relief zu „Handel und Verkehr" aus der Schadow-Schule, 1802 von Joseph Mendelssohn der neuen Berliner Börse gestiftet, nach Abriß des Hauses 1893 „zurück"gebracht ins neue Bankgebäude Jägerstraße 49/50 (heute: Deutsches Apothekerhaus).

"Trade & Transport:" A relief from the school of sculptor Johann Gottfried Schadow, donated to the Berlin Stock Exchange in 1802 by Joseph Mendelssohn; after the building was torn down in 1893, the work was "brought home" to the new bank building at Jägerstrasse 49/50 (today: Deutsches Apothekerhaus).

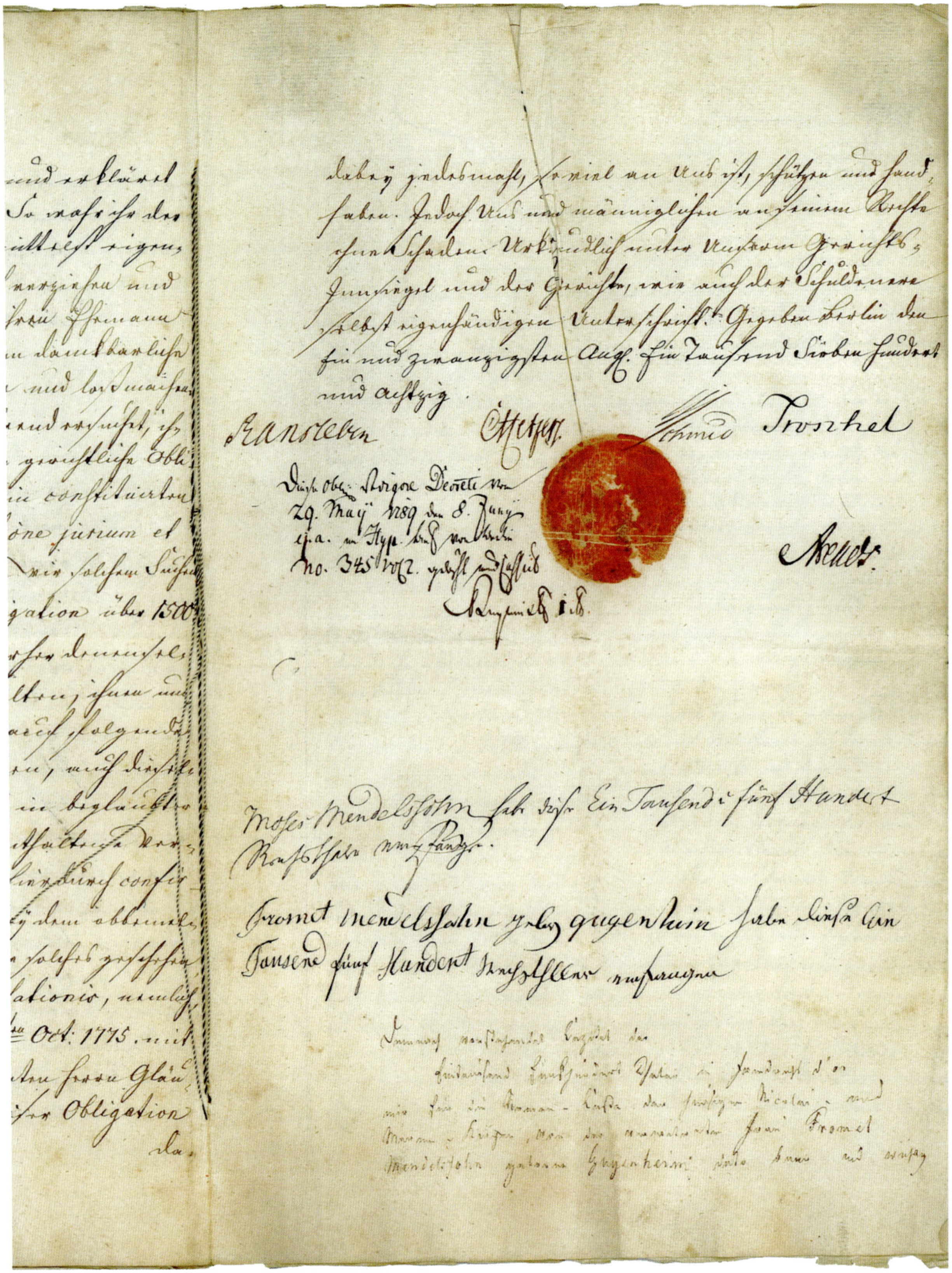

Kreditvertrag von Moses und Fromet Mendelssohn (1780).
Das Ehepaar leiht sich aus der vereinigten Armenkasse von St. Nikolai und St. Marien vom Schatzmeister Friederich Wilhelm Otto 1500 Thaler Friedrichsd'or „zu ihrem Handel". Beide haften einzeln für die Rückzahlung der ganzen Summe. Die Jahreszinsen betragen 4 Prozent, zahlbar vierteljährlich, der Kredit ist beidseitig halbjährlich kündbar. Als Sicherheit setzen beide ihre „Haab und Güter" ein. Fromet muß „So wahr ihr der wahre Gott Adonai helfen solle" sagen, um zu bekräftigen, daß sie auf eine die Ehefrauen schützende Klausel verzichte.

Loan agreement concluded by Moses and Fromet Mendelssohn (1780).
The couple took out a loan in the amount of 1,500 Friedrichs d'or "for use in their business" from the Vereinigte Armenkasse (Consolidated Charitable Relief Fund) of the parishes of St. Nikolai and St. Marien, as represented by its Treasurer Friederich Wilhelm Otto. Each of them was individually liable for repayment of the entire sum; annual interest amounted to 4 percent, payable quarterly. Either party to the loan agreement had the right to terminate it with six-months' notice. As collateral, both borrowers pledged their "goods and chattels." Fromet had to swear the oath "so help me the true God Adonai" in order to confirm her waiver of a clause that protected wives from debt liability.

Bankgründer Joseph Mendelssohn (1770 – 1848).
Heliogravüre eines Pastells von Friedrich Randel.

Bank founder Joseph Mendelssohn (1770 – 1848).
Photogravure of a pastel painting by Friedrich Randel.

Abraham Mendelssohn Bartholdy.
Zeichnung (o.J.) von Wilhelm Hensel.

Abraham Mendelssohn Bartholdy.
Drawing (undated) by Wilhelm Hensel.

Die Häuser der Mendelssohn-Bank, Jägerstraße 49 – 53 (um 1920).

The buildings of the Mendelssohn bank at Jägerstrasse 49 – 53 (c. 1920).

Der Erweiterungsbau der Börse in Berlin. Originalzeichnung von Robert Geißler.

Mendelssohn & Co. grows into the biggest German private bank

Joseph Mendelssohn, who enjoyed wide-spread respect as a confident market strategist, was also co-founder and acting Chairman of the Berlin mercantile corporation known as the Berliner Kaufmannschaft. In order to help clear payment traffic, he set up the Berliner Cassen-Verein as a clearinghouse which, after his death, would adapt the Mendelssohn emblem: the crane clutching the pebble. Having invested profitably in railroad construction in Eastern Europe and the Far East, and having secured the status of royal bankers to the Russian Czar, Mendelssohn & Co., gradually evolved into the biggest private banking house in Germany. Besides Berlin and Russia, Hamburg also continued to be a focal point: this is where a bank bearing the name of Paul Mendelssohn-Bartholdy continued to operate until 1888, and where the Mendelssohn financiers from Berlin participated in the founding of Commerzbank. Branch offices had by then also been opened in Paris and Amsterdam.

The later descendants of Moses, the penniless Talmudic scholar from Dessau, were raised to the ranks of the nobility and ascended into the inner circles of power in Germany, serving as financial advisors to Bismarck and later to Emperor William II – a role for which they were sometimes unflatteringly referred to as Kaiserjuden (the Kaiser's Court Jews). Ernst von Mendelssohn-Bartholdy and Franz von Mendelssohn Jr. were also sitting members of the Preussisches Herrenhaus (Prussian House of Lords), which met at Leipziger Strasse 3, the former site of the Mendelssohn-Bartholdy Palais. In recognition for their service to the Czar, five members of the banking family were awarded the Order of St. Anne, the Order of St. Stanislaus, and the Order of the White Eagle. Additional honors were conferred by Italy, Denmark, Spain, Portugal, and Serbia. Ernst von Mendelssohn-Bartholdy, who ranked as Berlin's richest citizen in 1908 (2.9 million marks in taxable income, 43 million marks in assets), became Danish Consul General, while his nephew Robert and his brother Franz von Mendelssohn Jr. fulfilled the same diplomatic function for Sweden and Belgium, respectively.

Major setback for Mendelssohn & Co.: the overthrow of the Czar in 1917, which resulted in huge losses. The negotiations with the Soviet regime regarding cooperation and compensation proved fruitless.

As a conservative captain of industry, Franz von Mendelssohn Jr. used his influence with other business leaders to solicit support

Mendelssohn & Comp. expandiert zur größten deutschen Privatbank

Joseph Mendelssohn, der als vorsichtiger, souveräner Marktstratege weithin Anerkennung genießt, hat die Berliner Kaufmannschaft mitbegründet und ihr vorgestanden; er entwickelt zur Abwicklung des Zahlungsverkehrs den Berliner Cassen-Verein, der nach seinem Tod das Mendelssohn-Emblem übernimmt – den Kranich mit dem Stein. Mit Beteiligungen am osteuropäischen und orientalischen Eisenbahnbau sowie als Hausbankiers des Zarenhofs steigen Mendelssohn & Comp. zur größten deutschen Privatbank auf. Ein Bankhaus Paul Mendelssohn-Bartholdy existiert bis 1888 in Hamburg, wo die Berliner an der Gründung der Commerzbank beteiligt sind. Zwischenzeitlich betreiben sie Niederlassungen in Paris und Amsterdam.

Als Finanzberater Bismarcks, als geschmähte „Kaiserjuden" von Wilhelm II., avancieren nobilitierte Nachkommen des brotlosen Dessauer Talmudschülers Moses in das Zentrum deutscher Macht. Ernst von Mendelssohn-Bartholdy und Franz von Mendelssohn d.J. sind Mitglieder des Preußischen Herrenhauses an der Leipziger Straße 3; wo sich vormals das Palais der Mendelssohn Bartholdys befand. Fünf Bankiers der Familie werden mit den russischen St. Annen-, St. Stanislaw- und Weißer-Adler-Orden dekoriert; weitere Ehrungen kommen aus Italien, Dänemark, Spanien, Portugal, Serbien. Ernst von Mendelssohn-Bartholdy, der 1908 (2,9 Millionen versteuertes Einkommen, 43 Millionen Mark Vermögen) reichste Berliner, wird dänischer, sein Neffe Robert schwedischer, dessen Bruder Franz von Mendelssohn d.J. belgischer Generalkonsul.

Beim Sturz des Zaren (1917) müssen Mendelssohn & Co. erhebliche Verluste hinnehmen. Verhandlungen mit der Sowjet-Regierung über Kooperation und Kompensation enden ergebnislos.

Der konservative Wirtschaftsführer Franz von Mendelssohn d.J. setzt sich im Kreis anderer Unternehmer für die ungefestigte Weimarer Republik ein. Seine Arbeitnehmerleistungen gelten als einzigartig: Wer bei Mendelssohn eingestellt wird, so heißt es, habe ausgesorgt.

Weniger glänzend agieren Moses-Nachfahren als Unternehmer jenseits des Geldmarktes: Die Versuche des Mechanicus Nathan Mendelssohn, sich in der Rüstung oder im Bergbau zu etablieren, schlagen fehl, ebenso Sebastian Hensels Manager-Einsätze als Direktor des nach der Gründung abgebrannten Luxushotels „Kaiserhof" oder beim Markthallen- und im Wohnungsbau. Eine

Die Börse an der Burgstraße, erbaut 1859 – 1864
von Friedrich Hitzig auf dem Terrain des Palais Itzig seiner Vorfahren.

The stock exchange on Burgstrasse, built between 1859 – 1864
by Friedrich Hitzig on the site of the former Palais Itzig owned by his forefathers.

Junkers
Luftbild

for the shaky Weimar Republic. The benefits he provided to his employees were one-of-a-kind: If you had a job with Mendelssohn, so the saying went, your future was secure.

The entrepreneurial undertakings of Moses' descendants outside of the financial markets proved less successful, however. Thus, Nathan Mendelssohn, a mechanic by trade, was unable to establish himself in the armaments and mining industry. Similarly ill-fated were Sebastian Hensel's stints as managing director of the hotel Kaiserhof (which had burned down shortly after its grand opening), or as a developer of market halls and apartment buildings. One remarkable success, however, was the establishment of an aniline factory in Berlin's Rummelsburg district by Paul Mendelssohn Bartholdy, a chemist. Known as Agfa, the company he founded would later merge with other enterprises into the world's largest chemicals conglomerate at the time, I.G. Farben.

Erfolgsstory wird dagegen der Aufbau einer Anilinfabrik in Rummelsburg durch den Chemiker Paul Mendelssohn Bartholdy: Seine Gründung Agfa fusioniert mit anderen Chemiewerken zum weltgrößten Konzern I.G. Farben.

Luftbild der Agfa Farbenfabrik Wolfen, Kreis Bitterfeld (um 1920).
Aerial photograph of Agfa Farbenfabrik Wolfen in the county of Bitterfeld (c. 1920).

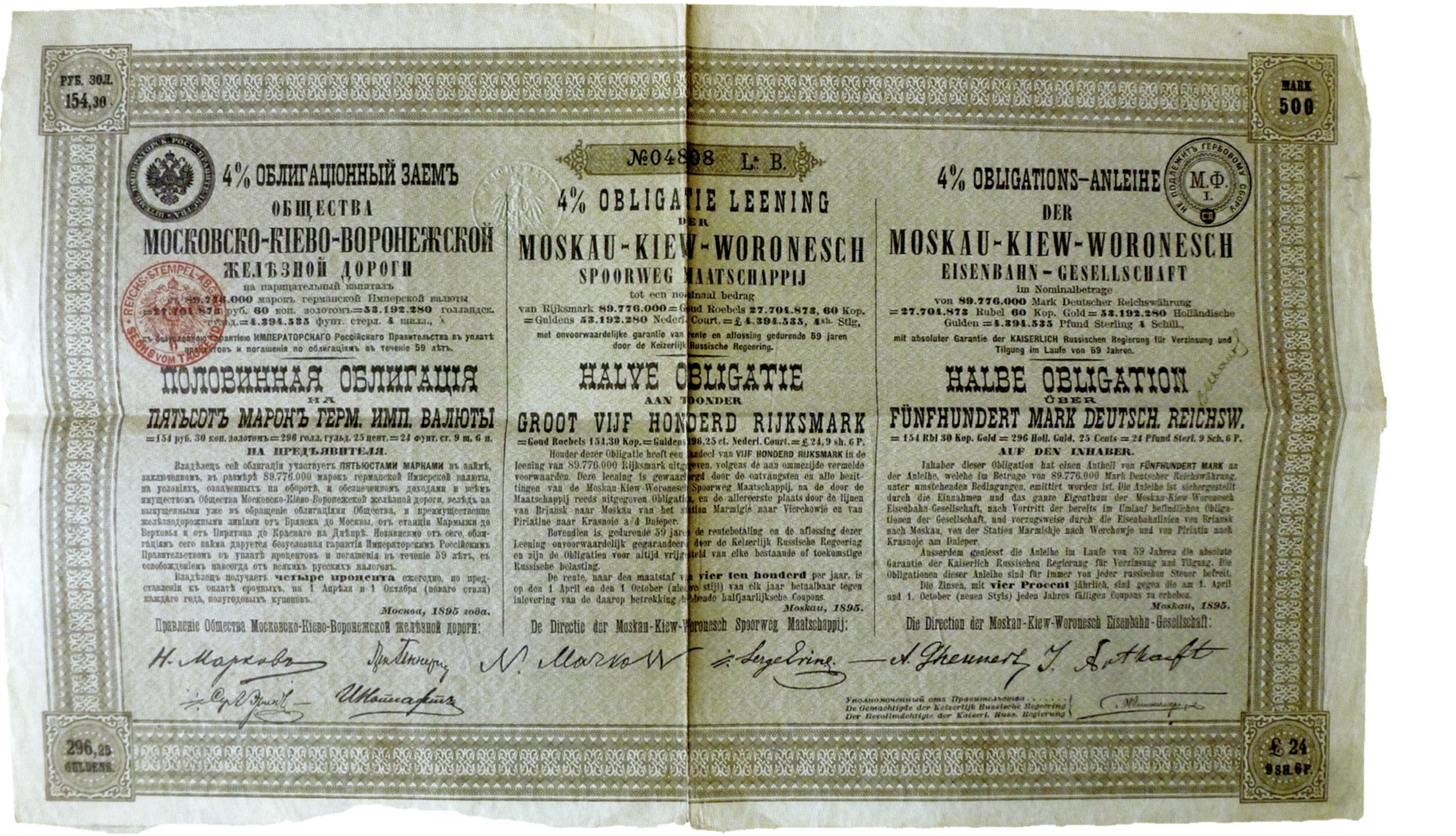

РУБ. ЗОЛ. 154,30

MARK 500

№04898 L: B.

4% ОБЛИГАЦІОННЫЙ ЗАЕМЪ ОБЩЕСТВА МОСКОВСКО-КІЕВО-ВОРОНЕЖСКОЙ ЖЕЛѢЗНОЙ ДОРОГИ

ПОЛОВИННАЯ ОБЛИГАЦІЯ НА ПЯТЬСОТЪ МАРОКЪ ГЕРМ. ИМП. ВАЛЮТЫ

НА ПРЕДЪЯВИТЕЛЯ.

Москва, 1895 года.

Правленіе Общества Московско-Кіево-Воронежской желѣзной дороги:

4% OBLIGATIE LEENING DER MOSKAU-KIEW-WORONESCH SPOORWEG MAATSCHAPPIJ

HALVE OBLIGATIE AAN TOONDER GROOT VIJF HONDERD RIJKSMARK

Moskau, 1895.

De Directie der Moskau-Kiew-Woronesch Spoorweg Maatschappij:

4% OBLIGATIONS-ANLEIHE DER MOSKAU-KIEW-WORONESCH EISENBAHN-GESELLSCHAFT

im Nominalbetrage von 89.776.000 Mark Deutscher Reichswährung = 27.704.873 Rubel 60 Kop. Gold = 53.192.280 Holländische Gulden = 4.394.535 Pfund Sterling 4 Schill.,

mit absoluter Garantie der KAISERLICH Russischen Regierung für Verzinsung und Tilgung im Laufe von 59 Jahren.

HALBE OBLIGATION ÜBER FÜNFHUNDERT MARK DEUTSCH. REICHSW.

= 154 Rbl 30 Kop. Gold = 296 Holl. Guld. 25 Cents = 24 Pfund Sterl. 9 Sch. 6 P.

AUF DEN INHABER.

Inhaber dieser Obligation hat einen Antheil von FÜNFHUNDERT MARK an der Anleihe, welche im Betrage von 89.776.000 Mark Deutscher Reichswährung, unter umstehenden Bedingungen, emittirt worden ist. Die Anleihe ist sichergestellt durch die Einnahmen und das ganze Eigenthum der Moskau-Kiew-Woronesch Eisenbahn-Gesellschaft, nach Vortritt der bereits im Umlauf befindlichen Obligationen der Gesellschaft, und vorzugsweise durch die Eisenbahnlinien von Briansk nach Moskau, von der Station Marmishje nach Werchowje und von Piriatin nach Krasnoje am Dnieper.

Ausserdem geniesst die Anleihe im Laufe von 59 Jahren die absolute Garantie der Kaiserlich Russischen Regierung für Verzinsung und Tilgung. Die Obligationen dieser Anleihe sind für immer von jeder russischen Steuer befreit.

Die Zinsen, mit **vier Procent** jährlich, sind gegen die am 1. April und 1. October (neuen Styls) jeden Jahres fälligen Coupons zu erheben.

Moskau, 1895.

Die Direction der Moskau-Kiew-Woronesch Eisenbahn-Gesellschaft:

Уполномоченный отъ Правительства
De Gemachtigde der Keizerlijk Russische Regeering
Der Bevollmächtigte der Kaiserl. Russ. Regierung

296,25 GULDENS

£ 24 9 SH. 6 P.

Obligation (Schuldverschreibung) der Moskau-Kiew-Woronesch-Eisenbahn-Gesellschaft von 1895, eingeführt an der Börse durch Mendelssohn & Co., die auf der Rückseite als erste von acht Auslandsadressen zur Auszahlung von Zinsen und Kapital verzeichnet sind.

Debt instrument (bond) of the Moscow-Kiev-Voronezh Railroad Company of 1895, for the public issuance of which Mendelssohn & Co. served as underwriter; the bank is set out on the back of the certificate as the first of eight addresses abroad from which to obtain the disbursement of interest and principal.

Wappen Franz (von) Mendelssohns d. Ä, Darstellung im Adelsbrief vom 5. Mai 1888.

Crest of Franz (von) Mendelssohn I, as shown in the patent of nobility dated May 5, 1888.

Foto des 1837 bis 1888 bestehenden Hamburger Bankhauses Paul Mendelssohn-Bartholdy, Dammtorstraße 32.

Photo of the Paul Mendelssohn-Bartholdy bank in Hamburg, which did business from 1837 until 1888 and was located at Dammtorstrasse 32.

Die Franz von Mendelssohn-Medaille der Industrie- und Handelskammer und der Handwerkskammer Berlin, seit 2005 verliehen an sozial engagierte Mittelstandsfirmen.

The Franz von Mendelssohn medal of the Berlin Chamber of Commerce & Industry and of the Berlin Chamber of Skilled Crafts. Since 2005, it has been awarded to midsized companies active in social projects.

Eduard von Simson eröffnet eine Sitzung des Norddeutschen Reichstages im Preußischen Herrenhaus in der Leipziger Straße 3, dem ehemaligen Palais der Mendelssohn Bartholdys. Holzstich (um 1867).

Eduard von Simson opening a session of the North-German Reichstag in the Preussischen Herrenhaus (House of Lords) at Leipziger Strasse 3, the site of the former Mendelssohn Bartholdy Palais. Wood engraving (c. 1867).

DÉCLARATION
DES DROITS DE L'HOMME
ET DU CITOYEN,
Décretés par l'Assemblée Nationale dans les séances des 20, 21
23, 24 et 26 août 1789, acceptés par le Roi
PRÉAMBULE
LES représantans du peuple François, constitués en assemblée nationale, considérant que l'ignorance, l'oubli ou le mépris des droits de l'homme sont les seules causes des malheurs publics et de la corruption des gouvernemens ont résolu d'exposer, dans une déclaration solemnelle, les droits naturels, inaliénables et sacrés de l'homme: afin que cette déclaration constamment présente a tous les membres du corps social, leur rappelle sans cesse leurs droits et leurs devoirs; afin que les actes du pouvoir legislatif et ceux du pouvoir exécutif, pouvant être a chaque instant comparés avec le but de toute institution politique, en soient plus respectés; afin que les reclamations des citoyens, fondées désormais sur des principes simples et incontestables, tournent toujours au maintien de la constitution et du bonheur de tous.
EN conséquence, l'assemblée nationale reconnoit et déclare, en presence et sous les auspices de l'Etre suprême les droits suivans de l'homme et du citoyen.
ARTICLE PREMIER.
LES hommes naissent et demeurent libres et égaux en droits; les distinctions sociales ne peuvent être fondées que sur l'utilité commune.
II.
LE but de toute association politique est la conservation des droits naturels et inprescriptibles de l'homme; ces droits sont la liberté, la propriete, la sureté, et la résistance à l'oppression.
III.
LE principe de toute souveraineté réside essentiellement dans la nation, nul corps, nul individu ne peut exercer d'autorité qui n'en émane expressément.
IV.
LA liberté consiste a pouvoir faire tout ce qui ne nuit pas à autrui Ainsi, l'exercice des droits naturels de chaque homme, n'a de bornes que celles qui assurent aux autres membres de la société la jouissance de ces mêmes droits; ces bornes ne peuvent être déterminées que par la loi
V.
LA loi n'a le droit de défendre que les actions nuisibles a la société, Tout ce qui n'est pas défendu par la loi ne peut être empéché, et nul ne peut être contraint à faire ce qu'elle n'ordonne pas.
VI.
LA loi est l'expression de la volonté générale; tous les citoyens ont droit de concourir personnellement, ou par leurs représentans, à sa formation; elle doit être la même pour tous, soit qu'elle protege, soit qu'elle punisse, Tous les citoyens étant égaux a ses yeux, sont également admissibles a toutes dignités, places et emplois publics, selon leur capacité, et sans autres distinction que celles de leurs vertus et de leurs talens
VII.
NUL homme ne peut être accusé, arreté, ni détenu que dans les cas déterminés par la loi, et selon les formes qu'elle a prescrites, ceux qui sollicitent, expédient, exécutent ou font exécuter des ordres arbitraires, doivent être punis; mais tout citoyen appelé ou saisi en vertu de la loi, doit obéir a l'instant, il se rend coupable par la résistance.
VIII.
LA loi ne doit établir que des peines strictement et évidemment nécessaire, et nul ne peut être puni qu'en vertu d'une loi établie et promulguée antérierement au délit, et légalement appliquée.
IX.
TOUT homme étant présumé innocent jusqu'à ce qu'il ait été déclaré coupable, s'il est jugé indispensable de l'arrêter, toute rigueur qui ne serait pas nécessaire pour s'assurer de sa personne doit être sévérement réprimée par la loi.
X.
NUL ne doit être inquiété pour ses opinions, mêmes religieuses pourvu que leur manifestation ne trouble pas l'ordre public établi par la loi.
XI.
LA libre communication des pensées et des opinions est un des droits les plus precieux de l'homme; tout citoyen peut dont parler écrire, imprimer librement: sauf à répondre de l'abus de cette liberté dans les cas déterminés par la loi.
XII.
LA garantie des droits de l'homme et du citoyen nécessite une force publique; cette force est donc instituée pour l'avantage de tous, et non pour l'utilité particuliere de ceux a qui elle est confiée.
XIII.
POUR l'entretien de la force publique, et pour les dépenses d'administration, une contribution commune est indispensable; elle doit être également répartie entre les citoyens en raison de leurs facultées
XIV.
LES citoyens ont le droit de constater par eux même ou par leurs représentans, la nécessité de la contribution publique, de la consentir librement, d'en suivre l'emploi, et d'en déterminer la quotité, l'assiette, le recouvrement et la durée.
XV.
LA société a le droit de demander compte a tout agent public de son administration.
XVI.
TOUTE société, dans laquelle la garantie des droits n'est pas assurée, ni les séparation des pouvoirs déterminée, n'a point de constitution
XVII.
LES propriétés étant un droit inviolable et sacré, nul ne peut en être privé, si ce n'est lorsque la nécessité publique, légalement constatée, l'exige évidemment, et sous la condition d'une juste et préalable indemnité.
AUX REPRESENTANS DU PEUPLE FRANCOIS

The "civil improvement of the Jews"

Moses Mendelssohn's generation, which had been subjected to ongoing discrimination, always had an ambivalent relationship with the political elite. Thus, Frederick II had the famous "Socrates of Berlin" invited to his court at Potsdam, yet failed to personally receive him there. And while the monarch gave positive recognition to Moses' activities as a silk trader, he refused to validate him as a philosopher by granting him membership in the Royal Academy of Sciences, or by granting the Mendelssohn family a permanent right of residency; they would eventually receive that right from Frederick's successor, Frederick William II. Moses, for his part, was not above writing verses of fulsome praise for the royal court on behalf of the Jewish community, but did not shy away from cheekily critiquing Frederick's poetry in his literary reviews. Moses was able to persuade his friend Christian Konrad Wilhelm Dohm, a member of the Prussian War Council, to put forward progressive reforms. Dohm's book "On the Civil Improvement of the Jews" (1791) set off lively debates in France and other West European countries. One of its attentive readers was Count Mirabeau, who spent time in Berlin shortly after Mendelssohn's death and who published a book about the great man. During the French Revolution, Mirabeau introduced and implemented many ideas in the National Assembly as it debated the issue of human rights that he had garnered during his stay in Berlin.

The Emancipation Edict of 1812, proclaimed in the midst of Germany's Wars of Liberation against Napoleon, finally offered Jews a path to citizenship. A community that had thus far been excluded was now given the chance to belong, but was also expected to make its contribution to the war effort. In March 1813, after Frederick William III had called the German people to arms, Joseph and Abraham Mendelssohn nonetheless concluded a deal for 40,000 muskets with Austria, which was still allied with Napoleon at the time. On the other hand, the call to enlist was loyally followed by Moses' son Nathan and by his nephews Philipp Veit and Benjamin Mendelssohn, as well as by Wilhelm Hensel (who was later to wed Fanny Mendelssohn Bartholdy). Abraham Mendelssohn, together with Rahel Levin, did his part by working at military hospitals in Prague, while also equipping volunteers in Berlin. His hopes for integration were dashed, however, by the conservative political climate that set in after the Congress of Vienna in 1815. Abraham decided to convert to Christianity along with his family; freshly baptized, he assumed the honorary office of an unremunerated City Council Member for Charitable Works.

Die „bürgerliche Verbesserung der Juden"

Kontakte zur politischen Macht waren für Moses' diskriminierte Generation immer zwiespältig gewesen. Friedrich II. ließ den Gelehrten nach Potsdam rufen, wo er nicht empfangen wurde. Dem Seidenhändler zollt der König Anerkennung; dem Philosophen verwehrt er die Akademie der Wissenschaften, der Familie sicheres Bleiberecht, das sie erst durch seinen Nachfolger erhält. Mendelssohn schreibt im Gemeinde-Auftrag Huldigungsverse an den Hof, scheut sich aber nicht, die Dichtkunst des Monarchen in einer kühnen Rezension zu kritisieren. Den befreundeten Kriegsrat Christian Konrad Wilhelm Dohm inspiriert er zu Reformprojekten. Dohms Buch „Über die bürgerliche Verbesserung der Juden" (1781) beeinflußt Diskurse in Frankreich und anderen Ländern Westeuropas, auch den Grafen Mirabeau, der sich kurz nach Mendelssohns Tod in Berlin aufhält und eine Schrift über diesen veröffentlicht. In der Menschenrechtsdebatte der französischen Nationalversammlung wird Mirabeau Berliner Ideen einbringen und umsetzen.

Das Emanzipationsedikt von 1812, mit dem Juden die Staatsbürgerschaft angeboten wird, schafft angesichts der Befreiungskriege eine neue Situation: Bislang Diskriminierte dürfen nun dazugehören, ihren Beitrag leisten. Nach dem Volkskriegsaufruf von Friedrich Wilhelm III. im März 1813 wickeln Joseph und Abraham Mendelssohn mit Österreich, Napoleons Noch-Verbündetem, ein Geschäft über 40000 Flinten ab, die nach Preußen geliefert werden. Moses' Sohn Nathan sowie seine Enkel Philipp Veit und Benjamin Mendelssohn und Wilhelm Hensel, der spätere Ehemann Fanny Mendelssohn Bartholdys, melden sich zum Militär. Abraham Mendelssohn engagiert sich mit Rahel Levin in Prager Lazaretten, in Berlin rüstet er Freiwillige aus. Die Restaurationspolitik nach dem Wiener Kongreß macht jedoch ab 1815 seine Integrationshoffnungen zunichte. Abrahams Familie wird konvertieren. Er selbst übernimmt nach seiner Taufe das Ehrenamt eines unbesoldeten Stadtrats für Armenpflege.

„Die Erklärung der Menschenrechte", von der französischen Nationalversammlung im August 1789 verkündet. Ölgemälde auf Holz (um 1790) von Jean Jacques François Lebarbier.

"The Declaration of the Rights of Man," proclaimed by the French National Assembly in August 1789. Oil painting on wood (c. 1790) by Jean Jacques François Lebarbier.

Christian Konrad Wilhelm von Dohm (1751 – 1820). Jurist, Diplomat und politischer Schriftsteller. Öl auf Leinwand (1795) von Karl Christian Kehrer.

Christian Konrad Wilhelm von Dohm (1751 – 1820), legal scholar, diplomat and political writer. Oil on canvas (1795) by Karl Christian Kehrer.

Unter den Linden. Am Horizont: die Quadriga auf dem Brandenburger Tor. Mitglied der Königlichen Akademie der Wissenschaften (am rechten Bildrand) ist Moses Mendelssohn nicht geworden, da Friedrich II. seine Zustimmung nicht gab. Hier, auf dem Forum Fridericianum, neben der Oper, scheiterte 1786 die Errichtung eines vom König erlaubten Gelehrtendenkmals, das Mendelssohn mit Kollegen würdigen sollte, an der Finanzierung durch die Bürger. Als 1840 Unter den Linden das Reiterdenkmal Friedrichs II. errichtet wurde, verweigerte Friedrich Wilhelm III. die Abbildung Mendelssohns am Postament des Denkmals.

Unter den Linden Boulevard. On the horizon: the quadriga (4-horse-chariot) atop the Brandenburg Gate. Moses Mendelssohn never became a member of the Royal Academy of Sciences (right-hand margin) because Frederick II withheld his approval. The site shown here (the Forum Fridericianum, next to the opera) was to be the site of a monument commemorating Moses and other eminent scholars, but the plan had to be scrapped in 1786 due to insufficient funding by the citizenry. In 1840, when the mounted statue of Frederick II was erected on Unter den Linden, King Frederick William III refused to allow Mendelssohn to be pictured on the monument's pedestal.

Honoré Gabriel de Riquite, Comte de Mirabeau,
1791 Präsident der französischen Nationalversammlung.
Gemälde von Joseph Boze (1789).

Honoré Gabriel de Riquite, Comte de Mirabeau,
President of the French National Assembly in 1791.
Painting by Joseph Boze (1789).

Porzellanaffe aus dem Besitz der Familie Mendelssohn.
Fotografie von 1929.
20 Porzellan-Ladenhüter dieser Art sollen sich laut Sebastian Hensel in der Familie befunden haben. Der Ramsch mußte im Rahmen einer diskrimierenden Sonderabgabe von Juden anläßlich genehmigungspflichtiger Ereignisse erworben werden.

Porcelain monkey owned by the Mendelssohn family.
Photo from 1929.
According to Sebastian Hensel, the family owned about 20 of these kitschy objects, which Jews were obligated by law to purchase; this served as a discriminatory special tax levied in connection with certain permits.

Bürger als Freiheitskämpfer.

Umzug des Königs u. Anerkennung d. National-Farben.

Studenten als Freiheitskämpfer.

Einzug der befreiten Polen.

Königs Wache v. Bürger, Studenten, Künstler.

Versöhnung zwischen Bürger u. Militair.

Pflege d. Verwundeten im Königl: Schlosse.

Barrikaden Vertheidigung.

Barrikaden Bau.

Berlin den 23/5 48

Liebe Ottilie

Ich schreibe heut an dich und die Kinder. Der Brief ist für dich, die Randzeichnungen für Jean bestimmt, ob ich dir eine Farbe von den nächsten Bilder-Tibel.

Der für uns so wichtige 22te Mai ist nun vorüber und leider — sind wir noch um Nichts gebessert! Die Sitzung des Constituante-Hauses begann gestern um ½ 10 Uhr und nach den üblichen Formalitäten, entwickelte Arnolds Stellvertreter, der Schultendorn, in einer schönen Rede, die Gründe, warum das Volk zu ... sei. Diese Rede wird für ein Meisterstück von ... gehalten. Sie ... auf die ... Seite der ..., ...

Lith. Atelier v. F. E. Feller Berlin Friedrichs Str. 62.

Wirtschaft und Politik – IV
Business and Politics – IV

Joining in the patriotism of mainstream society

During the revolution of 1848 the third generation of the family developed political views. Georg Benjamin Mendelssohn, a professor of geography at Bonn, fell out with his liberal colleagues by holding firm to his support for an anachronistic system of government in which power was exercised by the estates. Philipp Veit, meanwhile, painted the huge figure of Germania as a symbol of freedom for the Paulskirche Parliament, yet clung to his belief that the crisis could be solved under the leadership of Catholic Austria. Wilhelm Hensel went so far as to lead a bodyguard of artists to protect the king, while his wife Fanny, who died in 1847, complained loudly about the "hypocrisy and mendaciousness of everything the government does." Her sister Rebecka, wife of the mathematician Gustav Dirichlet, was even on hand to help spring the revolutionary Gottfried Kinkel out of Spandau Prison. Wilhelm Mendelssohn, a machine operator, voiced his anger over the fact that the bourgeoisie was striving for privileges at the expense of the working class; but despite participating in democratic demonstrations along with his father, he would ultimately remain loyal to the king. His brother Arnold Mendelssohn, the rebellious physician to the poor, continued to promote the idea of organizing society along socialist lines even while incarcerated.

Germany's victory in the Franco-Prussian War (1871) – prelude to the unification under the "Reich" – unleashed a euphoria that affected the family's fourth generation. Thus, the chemist Paul Mendelssohn Bartholdy, his brothers-in-law Hugo Oppenheim and the painter Ludwig Passini participated in the Prussian campaign against France. Their homecoming was painted by Rudolf Henneberg in a mural commissioned by the banking family Warschauer, affiliated to the Mendelssohns through business and marriage: Moses and his descendants in front of a medieval backdrop representing an idealized vision of Germano-Christian society. World War I again triggered patriotic assent. Church composer Arnold Mendelssohn writes soldiers' ballads, while the Agfa factories delivered war material. Ludwig Mendelssohn Bartholdy, a son of the Agfa founder, was killed on the Eastern Front in 1918; he had been trying to settle an ethnic dispute among allied soldiers. By that time, twelve other of Moses' descendants had already fallen in the field.

Im patriotischen Einklang mit der Mehrheitsgesellschaft

Während der 1848er Revolution politisiert sich die dritte Generation. Georg Benjamin Mendelssohn, der von liberalen Kollegen gemobbte Bonner Geographie-Professor, plädiert für einen anachronistischen Ständestaat. Philipp Veit malt zwar die Riesen-Germania für das Paulskirchen-Parlament, glaubt aber an eine katholisch-österreichische Lösung für Deutschland. Wilhelm Hensel führt ein Künstler-Korps zum Schutz des Königs; seine Frau Fanny, gestorben 1847, hatte sich oft über „Heuchelei und Lügenhaftigkeit in allen Schritten der Regierung" empört. Fannys Schwester Rebecka, die Ehefrau des Mathematikers Gustav Dirichlet, hilft bei der Befreiung des Revolutionärs Gottfried Kinkel aus Spandauer Festungshaft. Der Maschinist Wilhelm Mendelssohn ärgert sich, daß das Bürgertum auf Kosten der Arbeiter Privilegien anstrebt; mit seinem Vater besucht er demokratische Kundgebungen, bleibt aber königstreu. Sein Bruder Arnold Mendelssohn, der rebellische Armenarzt, propagiert noch aus dem Gefängnis sozialistische Wirtschaftsmodelle.

Von der Euphorie des Krieges, der 1871 zur Reichsgründung führt, wird die vierte Generation angesteckt. Der Chemiker Paul Mendelssohn Bartholdy, die mit ihm verschwägerten Hugo Oppenheim und der Maler Ludwig Passini nehmen am Feldzug gegen Frankreich teil. Ihre Heimkehr hält Rudolf Henneberg auf einem Wandgemälde für die Warschauer-Bankiers fest, mit denen die Mendelssohns durch Heirat und Geschäft verbunden sind: Moses und Kindeskinder vor der mittelalterlichen Kulisse einer germanisch-christlichen Gesellschaftsvision. Auch während des Ersten Weltkriegs wird in der Familie patriotischer Einklang mit der Mehrheitsbegeisterung überwiegen: Der Kirchenkomponist Arnold Mendelssohn schreibt Soldatenlieder, die Agfa liefert Rüstungsprodukte. Ludwig Mendelssohn Bartholdy, ein Sohn des Agfa-Gründers, stirbt 1918 nach dem Waffenstillstand an der Ostfront, beim Schlichten eines ethnischen Streites unter Verbündeten. Zwölf weitere Moses-Nachkommen sind zuvor gefallen.

Berlin 12. Mai 1848: Illustrierter Brief des Maschinisten Wilhelm Mendelssohn (1821 – 1866) an seine Schwester Ottilie Kummer (1819 – 1848) über die erfolglose Kassations-Verhandlung in der Sache seines zu Zuchthaus verurteilten Bruders Arnold.
Wilhelm hatte 260 Kölner Bürger-Unterschriften gesammelt, die das Gnadengesuch Alexander von Humboldts unterstützen sollten. „Ich werde mich von nun an wieder um meine Mechanik kümmern, von Weltläufen habe ich für die ersten 4 Wochen genug."

Berlin, May 12, 1848: Illustrated letter from the machinist Wilhelm Mendelssohn (1821 – 1866) to his sister Ottilie Kummer (1819 – 1848) in which he discusses the unsuccessful legal appeal of his brother Arnold's prison sentence.
Wilhelm had collected the signatures of 260 citizens of Cologne in support of a petition for clemency in the name of Alexander von Humboldt. "I'll now get back to my work as a mechanic," he writes, "for I've had enough of worldly affairs for at least the next 4 weeks."

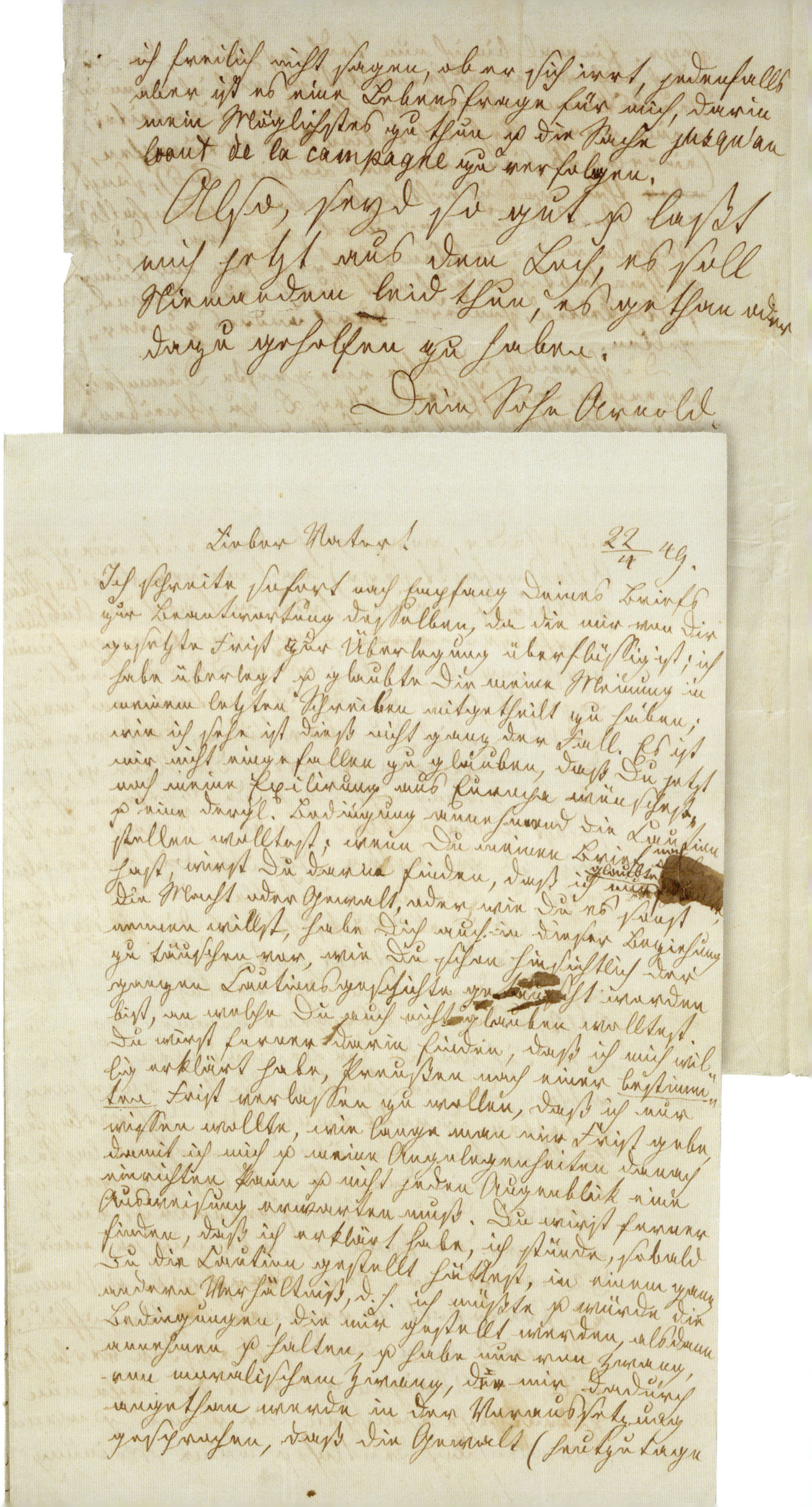

ich freilich nicht sagen, aber sich irrt, jedenfalls aber ist es eine Lebensfrage für mich, darin mein Möglichstes zu thun & die Sache jusqu'au bout de la campagne zu verfolgen.

Also, seid so gut & laßt mich jetzt aus dem Loch, es soll Niemandem leid thun, es gethan oder dazu geholfen zu haben.

Dein Sohn Arnold

Lieber Vater! 22/4 49.

Ich schreibe sofort nach Empfang Deines Briefs zur Beantwortung desselben, da die mir von Dir gesetzte Frist zur Überlegung überflüssig ist; ich habe überlegt ...

Arnold Mendelssohn:
Brief aus dem Gefängnis (22. April 1849).
Wegen Diebstahls zugunsten einer Mandantin seines Freundes Ferdinand Lassalle ist der Sozialist Arnold Mendelssohn zu einer harten Haftverstrafe verurteilt worden. In einem Vierzehn-Seiten-Brief an seinen Vater Nathan schildert er die eigene Entwicklung zum Revolutionär und Überlegungen für eine soziale Wirtschaftsordnung.
„Also, seid so gut und laßt mich jetzt aus dem Loch, es soll niemandem leid tun, es getan oder dazu geholfen zu haben."

Arnold Mendelssohn:
letter from prison (April 22, 1849).
Charged with theft on behalf of a client of his friend Ferdinand Lassalle, the socialist activist Arnold Mendelssohn was given a harsh prison sentence. In a fourteen-page letter to his father Nathan, he describes his own evolution into a revolutionary as well as his ideas for organizing society along socialist lines.
"And so, please be so kind as to get me out of this hole now; I promise no one will regret having done so or having helped it to happen!"

Rudolf Hennebergs Wandgemälde für die Mendelssohn-Nachkommen in der Villa Warschauer am Charlottenburger Knie (1872) zeigen Personen aus der Verwandschaft: heimkehrende Krieger und Mädchen in einem allegorischen Brautzug. Ein alter Mann mit Krücken am Bildrand stellt der familiären Überlieferung nach den Urahn Moses dar.

Mural by Rudolf Henneberg (1872) commissioned by the Mendelssohn descendants for the villa of the Warschauer family in the Charlottenburg Knie district. Shown are various relatives as homecoming soldiers or as girls in an allegorical wedding procession. According to family lore, the old man on crutches at the margin of the painting represents the ancestral patriarch Moses Mendelssohn.

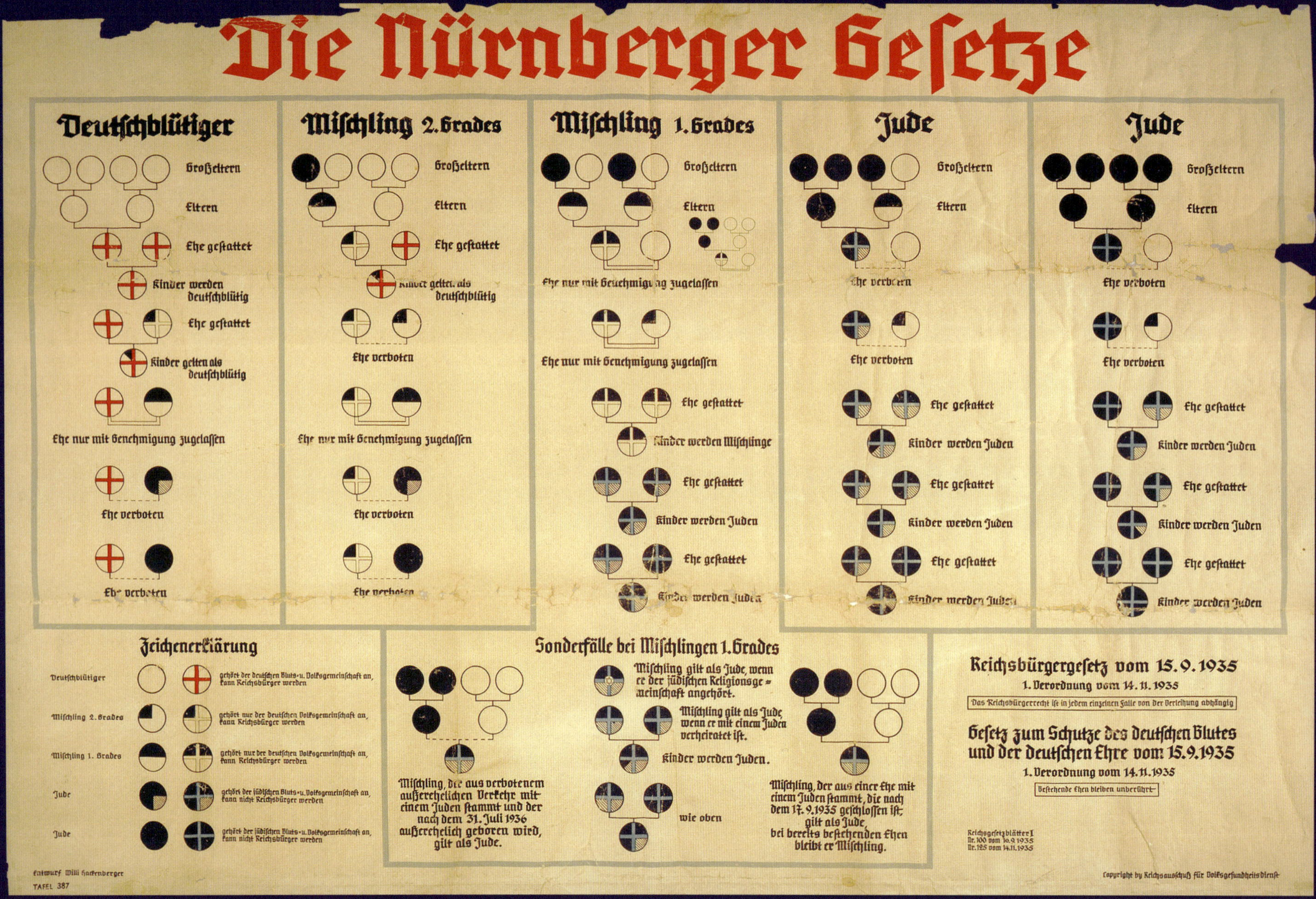

Die Nürnberger Gesetze
Deutschblütiger
Großeltern
Eltern
Ehe gestattet
Kinder werden deutschblütig
Ehe gestattet
Kinder gelten als deutschblütig
Ehe nur mit Genehmigung zugelassen
Ehe verboten
Ehe verboten
Mischling 2. Grades
Großeltern
Eltern
Ehe gestattet
Kinder gelten als deutschblütig
Ehe verboten
Ehe nur mit Genehmigung zugelassen
Ehe verboten
Ehe verboten
Mischling 1. Grades
Großeltern
Eltern
Ehe nur mit Genehmigung zugelassen
Ehe nur mit Genehmigung zugelassen
Ehe gestattet
Kinder werden Mischlinge
Ehe gestattet
Kinder werden Juden
Ehe gestattet
Kinder werden Juden
Jude
Großeltern
Eltern
Ehe verboten
Ehe verboten
Ehe gestattet
Kinder werden Juden
Ehe gestattet
Kinder werden Juden
Ehe gestattet
Kinder werden Juden
Jude
Großeltern
Eltern
Ehe verboten
Ehe verboten
Ehe gestattet
Kinder werden Juden
Ehe gestattet
Kinder werden Juden
Ehe gestattet
Kinder werden Juden
Zeichenerklärung
Deutschblütiger
gehört der deutschen Bluts- u. Volksgemeinschaft an, kann Reichsbürger werden
Mischling 2. Grades
gehört nur der deutschen Volksgemeinschaft an, kann Reichsbürger werden
Mischling 1. Grades
gehört nur der deutschen Volksgemeinschaft an, kann Reichsbürger werden
Jude
gehört der jüdischen Bluts- u. Volksgemeinschaft an, kann nicht Reichsbürger werden
Jude
gehört der jüdischen Bluts- u. Volksgemeinschaft an, kann nicht Reichsbürger werden
Sonderfälle bei Mischlingen 1. Grades
Mischling, der aus verbotenem außerehelichen Verkehr mit einem Juden stammt und der nach dem 31. Juli 1936 außerehelich geboren wird, gilt als Jude.
Mischling gilt als Jude, wenn er der jüdischen Religionsgemeinschaft angehört.
Mischling gilt als Jude, wenn er mit einem Juden verheiratet ist.
Kinder werden Juden.
wie oben
Mischling, der aus einer Ehe mit einem Juden stammt, die nach dem 17.9.1935 geschlossen ist; gilt als Jude, bei bereits bestehenden Ehen bleibt er Mischling.
Reichsbürgergesetz vom 15.9.1935
1. Verordnung vom 14.11.1935
Das Reichsbürgerrecht ist in jedem einzelnen Falle von der Verleihung abhängig
Gesetz zum Schutze des deutschen Blutes und der deutschen Ehre vom 15.9.1935
1. Verordnung vom 14.11.1935
Bestehende Ehen bleiben unberührt
Reichsgesetzblätter I
Nr. 100 vom 16.9.1935
Nr. 125 vom 14.11.1935
Entwurf Willi Hackenberger
TAFEL 387
Copyright by Reichsausschuß für Volksgesundheitsdienst

Holding on to illusions at the outset of the Third Reich

Albrecht Mendelssohn Bartholdy's attempts to carve out a patriotic yet sensible position would take an altogether different path. In 1916, the legal scholar helped to found the Deutsche Gesellschaft für Völkerrecht (German Society for International Law), while also caring for wounded prisoners of war. He joined the academic circle known as the Heidelberger Vereinigung, which criticized Germany's expansionist course, and gradually developed from a civil rights advocate to a political scientist. As a member of the professorial delegation designated to participate in the official handover of the Versailles Peace Treaty, he added his voice to protests against Article 231, which placed sole guilt for the war on Germany. He would go on to author numerous publications on foreign policy, to found the "Mendelssohn Institute for Foreign Policy" in Hamburg, and to serve at the World Court in Den Haag and at the League of nations. All these activities had a common goal: to improve understanding between the Germans, untutored in the ways of representative democracy, and the other nations of the world. Hearing of Hitler's accession to power in 1933 while on a speaking tour in Chicago, Albrecht at first refused to believe reports of Nazi terror. For a time, he deluded himself that he was safe, just like many of his relatives, who clung to the illusion that they would be spared – thanks either to their conversion, valorous army service, high social standing, and/or self-image as loyal Germans. Albrecht would soon be forced to emigrate – just like other relatives (to England, Switzerland, Palestine, and North/South America). Following the adoption of the Nuremberg Race Laws, some tried to play down or hide their Jewish origins by producing faked baptismal certificates, or by dropping the tell-tale Mendelssohn family name and going undercover altogether.

While the fortunes of the Mendelssohn bank began to decline rapidly, the renown associated with the family name remained high. Thus, the Nazis would have loved to carry on the brand with Aryan partners following the deaths of Franz von Mendelssohn Jr. and Paul von Mendelssohn-Bartholdy (1935). At the same time, Mendelssohn & Co., which had invested in a Baltic shale-oil plant, was pressured by the German navy to support rearmament by helping to secure oil-delivery contracts from the Estonians. Instead of agreeing to "aryanize" the banking firm, senior director Rudolf Loeb (the first non-Mendelssohn to occupy the post) and his partner Paul Kempner ultimately decided to liquidate everything in 1938. Deutsche Bank, under its Board member Hermann J. Abs, took over all active operations.

Illusionen beim Beginn des „Dritten Reiches"

Albrecht Mendelssohn Bartholdys patriotische Positionssuche verläuft anders. Der Jurist ist 1916 beteiligt an der Gründung der Deutschen Gesellschaft für Völkerrecht. Er betreut verwundete Kriegsgefangene, stößt zu der akademischen „Heidelberger Vereinigung", die den deutschen Expansionsdrang kritisiert. Wandelt sich vom Zivilrechtler zum politischen Wissenschaftler. Als Mitglied der Professorendelegation, die den Versailler Friedensvertrag mit in Empfang nehmen soll, protestiert auch er gegen den Kriegsschuld-Artikel 231. Mit Publikationen zur Außenpolitik, seinem „Mendelssohn-Institut" genannten „Institut für Auswärtige Politik" in Hamburg und seinen Ämtern in Den Haag und beim Völkerbund versucht er, die Verständigung zwischen den ungelernten deutschen Republikanern und anderen Nationen zu fördern. Als er 1933 auf Vortragsreise in Chicago von Hitlers Machtübernahme hört, bezweifelt er Meldungen über ersten Nazi-Terror. Viele Verwandte, die wie er bald (nach England, in die Schweiz, nach Palästina, Nord- und Südamerika) emigrieren sollen, machen sich zunächst wegen ihrer Taufe, wegen ihrer Frontkämpfer-Verdienste, auf Grund ihrer arrivierten Stellung oder ihres Selbstverständnisses als Deutsche Illusionen. Nach dem Erlaß der Nürnberger Rassengesetze versuchen einige, die jüdische Abstammung durch fingierte Taufurkunden abzuschwächen oder durch das Ablegen des Mendelssohn-Namens an Unauffälligkeit zu gewinnen.

Das Geschäft der Mendelssohn-Bank geht zurück, doch deren Renommé ist so groß, daß nach dem Tod Franz von Mendelssohns d.J. und Paul von Mendelssohn-Bartholdys (1935) Nationalsozialisten den Markennamen gern mit arischen Partnern fortgeführt hätten. Zugleich werden Mendelssohn & Co., die an einer baltischen Schieferöl-Fabrik beteiligt sind, von der Kriegsmarine zur Unterstützung der Aufrüstung gedrängt: Sie sollen bei Lieferverträgen mit den Esten behilflich sein. Statt einer Arisierung zuzustimmen, entscheidet sich der (erste nichtverwandte) Seniorchef Rudolf Löb mit dem Sozius Paul Kempner 1938 schließlich für eine Liquidation des Geldinstituts. Die Deutsche Bank mit ihrem Vorstandsmitglied Hermann J. Abs übernimmt die Aktiva des Unternehmens.

Bildtafel zu den Nürnberger Rassengesetzen. Das am 15. September 1935 „zum Schutze des deutschen Blutes und der deutschen Ehre" erlassene Gesetz verbot die Eheschließung und außerehelichen Geschlechtsverkehr zwischen Juden und „Ariern".

Chart illustrating the Nuremberg race laws, which were proclaimed on September 15, 1935 "to protect German bloodlines and German honor" and which forbade weddings or extra-marital intercourse between Jews and "Aryans."

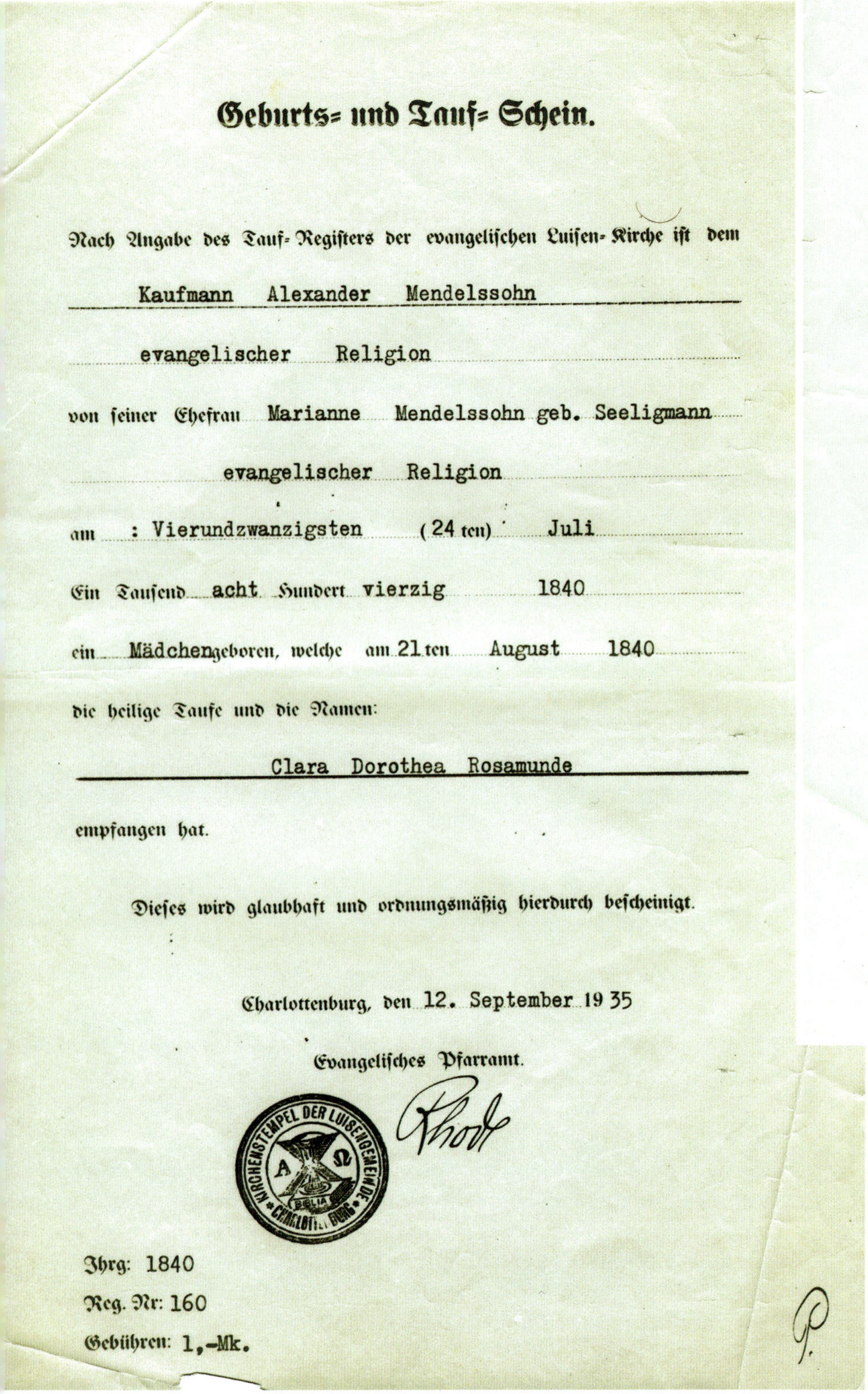

Geburts= und Tauf= Schein.

Nach Angabe des Tauf=Registers der evangelischen Luisen=Kirche ist dem

Kaufmann Alexander Mendelssohn

evangelischer Religion

von seiner Ehefrau Marianne Mendelssohn geb. Seeligmann

evangelischer Religion

am : Vierundzwanzigsten (24 ten) Juli

Ein Tausend acht Hundert vierzig 1840

ein Mädchen geboren, welche am 21 ten August 1840

die heilige Taufe und die Namen:

Clara Dorothea Rosamunde

empfangen hat.

Dieses wird glaubhaft und ordnungsmäßig hierdurch bescheinigt.

Charlottenburg, den 12. September 1935

Evangelisches Pfarramt.

KIRCHENSTEMPEL DER LUISENGEMEINDE CHARLOTTENBURG

Rhode

Jhrg: 1840

Reg. Nr: 160

Gebühren: 1,-Mk.

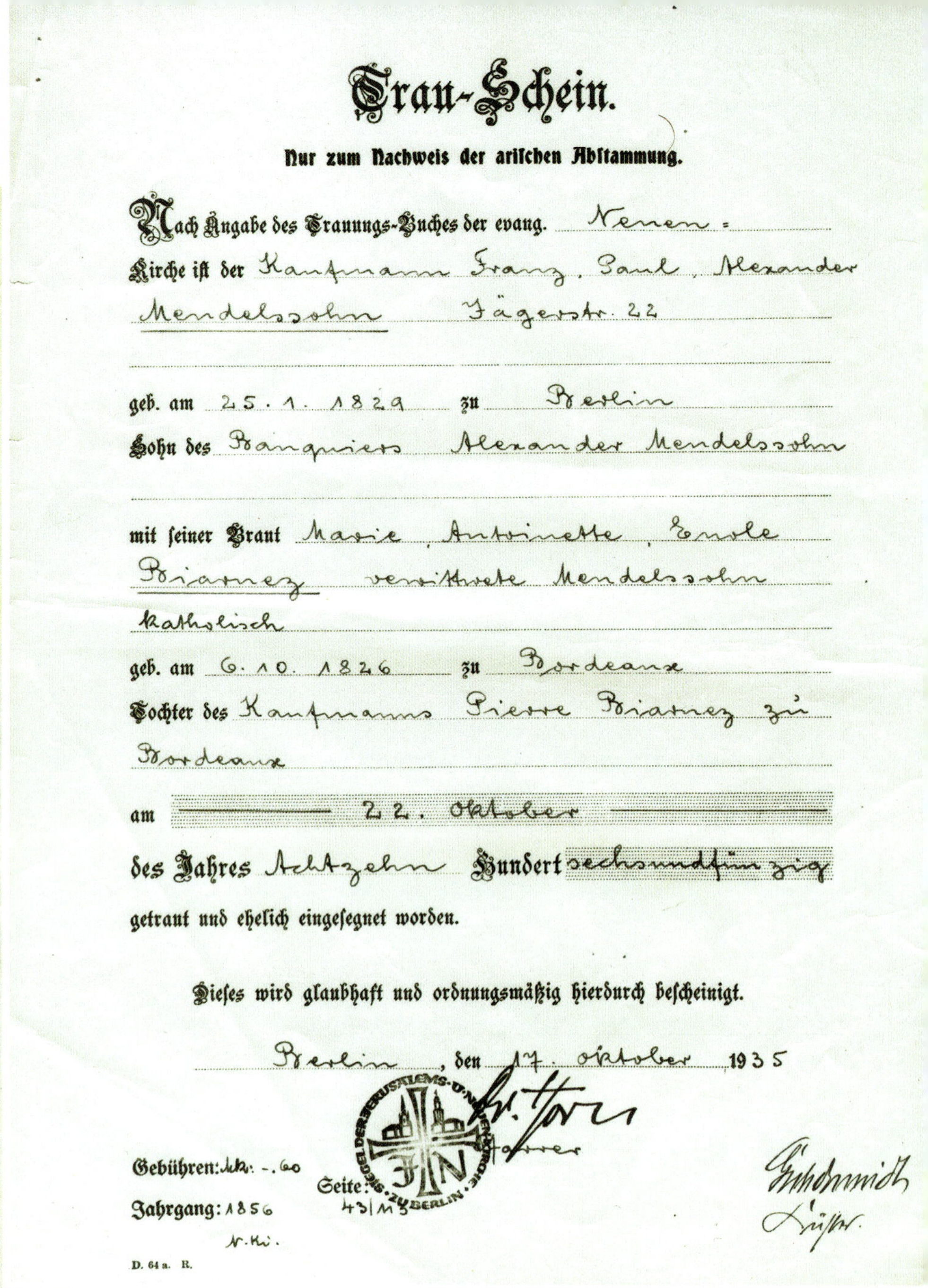

Trau-Schein.

Nur zum Nachweis der arischen Abstammung.

Nach Angabe des Trauungs-Buches der evang. Neuen Kirche ist der Kaufmann Franz Paul Alexander Mendelssohn Jägerstr. 22

geb. am 25.1.1829 zu Berlin

Sohn des Banquiers Alexander Mendelssohn

mit seiner Braut Marie Antoinette Enole Biarnez verwittwete Mendelssohn katholisch

geb. am 6.10.1826 zu Bordeaux

Tochter des Kaufmanns Pierre Biarnez zu Bordeaux

am 22. Oktober

des Jahres Achtzehn Hundert sechsundfünfzig

getraut und ehelich eingesegnet worden.

Dieses wird glaubhaft und ordnungsmäßig hierdurch bescheinigt.

Berlin, den 17. oktober 1935

Pfarrer

Gebühren: Mk. -.60

Seite: 43/113

Jahrgang: 1856

Schmidt

Küster

D. 64 a. R.

Dokumente zur Erstellung der Ahnennachweise nach dem Erlass der Nürnberger Rassengesetze: Geburts- und Tauf-Schein für Clara Mendelssohn (später verh. Westphal) mit gefälschter Taufbescheinigung Alexander Mendelssohns, ausgestellt am 12. September 1935. Der Trau-Schein „zum Nachweis der arischen Abstammung“ (ausgestellt am 17.10.1935) für Alexanders Sohn Franz Mendelssohn d.Ä., geb. 1829, erwähnt dessen Taufe nicht, nur die katholische Konfession seiner Frau Enole.

Documents used to provide proof of ancestry as required under the Nuremberg race laws: certificates of birth and baptism for Clara Mendelssohn (after her marriage, Clara Westphal), along with a forged baptismal certificate for Alexander Mendelssohn, issued on September 12, 1935. The wedding certificate “to prove Aryan ancestry” (issued on October 17, 1935) for Alexander’s son Franz Mendelssohn Sr, born in 1829, does not mention his baptism, only the Catholic affiliation of his wife Enole.

Rudolf Löb (1877 – 1966) war 1896 als kaufmännischer Angestellter bei Mendelssohn & Co. eingetreten, ab 1935 war er der Seniorchef, führte zuletzt die Liquidationsverhandlungen mit der Deutschen Bank. Er emigrierte 1939. Aufnahme von 1925.

Rudolf Loeb (1877 – 1966), who joined Mendelssohn & Co. as a clerk in 1896, became senior partner in 1935; his final task before emigrating in 1939 was to oversee the liquidation negotiations with Deutsche Bank. Photo from 1925.

Das Stammhaus der Mendelssohn-Bank, Jägerstraße 51, als Abteilung des Reichsfinanzministeriums (um 1942).

The original head office of the Mendelssohn bank, Jägerstrasse 51, when it was in use as a department of the Reich Finance Ministry (c. 1942).

Paul Kempner (1889 – 1956), Teilhaber der Mendelssohn-Bank und Schwiegersohn Franz von Mendelssohns II (1935), führte nach dessen Tod gemeinsam mit Rudolf Loeb bis zu seiner Emigration (1938) die Geschäfte von Mendelssohn & Co. Aufnahme von 1930.

Paul Kempner (1889 – 1956), partner in the Mendelssohn bank and son-in-law of Franz von Mendelssohn II (1935). After Franz' death, Paul Kempner assumed responsibility for the operations of Mendelssohn & Co. together with Rudolf Loeb, but eventually emigrated in 1938. Photo from 1930.

Surviving under assumed names, in the Wehrmacht, and as refugees

And so the descendants of Moses Mendelssohn were robbed and driven to flee or go undercover, or even to commit suicide. Some, like the Potsdam-based Franz Mendelssohn, a naval engineer working for the government, belonged to the technocratic elite and thus enjoyed protection, at least for a time. No less than 35 descendants or their spouses survived the war as soldiers. Some of them did so by serving in the Wehrmacht, while 20 lost their lives on the front fighting for Hitler. When Erich Schwarz, a highly decorated member of Cavalry Battalion 15 (and a descendant of Nathan Mendelssohn) returned from the Soviet Union, he found that his father, Heinrich, after being classified a "half jew," had taken his own life. The editor and author Anna-Luise Jones, daughter of painter Josef Block and Moses descendant Else Oppenheim, took on risky courier missions to Prague as a member of the Social Democratic Party. The theologian Paul Leo, a great-grandson of Fanny Hensel, worked on behalf of baptized and unbaptized Jews within the Protestant Church of Hanover. After being forced into retirement, he worked illegally as a teacher in the Confessional Church (Bekennende Kirche). During the Kristallnacht pogrom of 1938, he was interned at the Buchenwald concentration camp. Upon his release, he emigrated to the United States.

Marie-Louise Hensel conceived a plan to rescue Jews of Marburg by spiriting them across the Swiss border but failed in the attempt. Many of the relatives had little sympathy for the deed, since it resulted in a deportation order for her mother-in-law Gertrud Hensel – a typical example of how the Nazi regime was able to play those it persecuted one against the other. In his 1944 poem "The Final Epiphany," Marie-Louise's brother-in-law Werner Bergengruen envisioned the moral predicament of the individual in the face of the Nazi tyranny as a rendering of accounts on Judgment Day. The poem would be read out loud at the start of the Eichmann trial in Jerusalem in 1962:

I took this country to my heart
I sent messenger after messenger
I came in so many guises
Not once did you recognize me.

Überleben unter anderem Namen, in der Wehrmacht, auf der Flucht

Nachkommen Moses Mendelssohns werden beraubt, in die Flucht, zum Abtauchen, in den Selbstmord getrieben. Andere wie der Potsdamer Marinebaurat Franz Mendelssohn gehören zur Funktionselite, was ihnen zeitweise Schutz garantiert. 35 Nachkommen oder deren Ehepartner überleben in der Wehrmacht den Krieg, 20 sterben als Soldaten Hitlers an der Front. Als Erich Schwarz, ein hochdekorierter Held des Reiterbataillons 15 und Nachkomme Nathan Mendelssohns, aus der UdSSR heimkehrt, hat sich sein Vater Heinrich, der als „nichtarischer Mischling" gilt, das Leben genommen. Die Lektorin und Autorin Anna-Luise Jones, Tochter des Malers Josef Block und der Moses-Nachfahrin Else Oppenheim, übernimmt als SPD-Mitglied riskante Kurierdienste nach Prag. Der Theologe Paul Leo, ein Urenkel Fanny Hensels, setzt sich in der Hannoverschen Landeskirche für getaufte und ungetaufte Juden ein, wirkt zwangspensioniert als illegaler Dozent der Bekennenden Kirche. Während der Novemberpogrome 1938 wird er ins KZ Buchenwald eingeliefert, emigriert nach der Entlassung in die USA.

Beim Scheitern des Rettungsversuches der Marie-Louise Hensel, die Marburger Juden über die Schweizer Grenze bringen wollte, zeigt sich, wie das Regime Verfolgte gegeneinander ausspielt: Unter Verwandten findet diese Tat, mit der ein Deportationsbescheid für Marie-Louises Schwiegermutter Gertrud Hensel ausgelöst wurde, nur bedingt Verständnis. Ihr Schwager Werner Bergengruen hat in seinem Gedicht „Die letzte Epiphanie" (1944), das 1962 zu Beginn des Jerusalemer Eichmann-Prozesses verlesen werden soll, die moralischen Herausforderungen des Einzelnen unter der NS-Herrschaft zum Weltgerichts-Szenario verdichtet:

Ich hatte dies Land in mein Herz genommen,
ich habe ihm Boten um Boten gesandt.
In vielen Gestalten bin ich gekommen.
Ihr aber habt mich in keiner erkannt.

Ich klopfte bei Nacht, ein bleicher Hebräer,
ein Flüchtling, gejagt, mit zerrissenen Schuh'n.
Ihr riefet dem Schergen, ihr winktet dem Späher
und meintet noch, Gott einen Dienst zu tun.

Die Hakenkreuzfahne weht beim Appell eines „Kraft durch Freude"-Lagers über dem von Franz von Mendelssohn d.J. erbauten Sommersitz der Familie im österreichischen Rindbach (Salzburger Land). Das Anwesen war von den NS-Behörden beschlagnahmt worden.

The swastika flag flies above the roll-call at a "Kraft durch Freude" camp (Strength through Joy) at the former Mendelssohn summer retreat in Rindbach (near Salzburg, Austria). Built for his family by Franz von Mendelssohn Jr., the property was confiscated by the Nazis.

Wendet zur Klarheit
euch, liebende Flammen!
Die sich verdammen,
heile die Wahrheit.
Faust II.

Achensee, Juni/Juli 1944

Dies irae

I. Die Lüge

Wo ist das Volk, das dies schadlos an seiner Seele ertrüge?
Jahr und Jahr war unsre tägliche Nahrung die Lüge.
Festlich luden sie an, bekränzten Maschinen und Pflüge,
sprachen von Freiheit und Brot, und alles, alles war Lüge.
Borgten von heldischer Vorzeit aufrauschende Adlerflüge,
rühmten in Vätern sich selbst, und alles, alles war Lüge.
Durch die Straßen marschierten die endlosen Fahnenzüge,
Glocken dröhnten dazu, und alles, alles war Lüge.
Nicht nach anderm Gesetz bemaßen sie Lobspruch und Rüge,
Leben riefen sie an, und alles, alles war Lüge.
Dürres sollte erblühn! Sie wußten sich keine Genüge
in der Verheißung des Heils, und alles, alles war Lüge.
Noch das Blut an den Händen, umflorten sie Aschenkrüge,
sangen der Toten Ruhm, und alles, alles war Lüge.
Lüge atmeten wir. Bis ins innerste Herzgefüge
sickerte, Tropfen für Tropfen, der giftige Nebel der Lüge.
Und wir schrien zur Hölle, gewürgt, erstickt von der Lüge,
daß im Strahl der Vernichtung die Wahrheit herniederschlüge.

II. Die letzte Epiphanie

Ich hatte dies Land in mein Herz genommen,
Ich habe ihm Boten um Boten gesandt.
In vielen Gestalten bin ich gekommen.
Ihr aber habt mich in keiner erkannt.

Ich klopfte bei Nacht, ein bleicher Hebräer,
ein Flüchtling, gejagt, mit zerrissenen Schuhn.
Ihr riefet dem Schergen, ihr winktet dem Späher
und meintet noch Gott einen Dienst zu tun.

Ich kam als zitternde geistgeschwächte
Greisin mit stummem Angstgeschrei.
Ihr aber spracht vom Zukunftsgeschlechte
und nur meine Asche gabt ihr frei.

Verwaister Knabe auf östlichen Flächen,
ich fiel euch zu Füßen und flehte um Brot.
Ihr aber scheutet ein künftiges Rächen,
ihr zucktet die Achseln und gabt mir den Tod.

Ich kam als Gefangner, als Tagelöhner,
verschleppt und verkauft, von der Peitsche gefetzt.
Ihr wandtet den Blick von dem struppigen Fröner.
Nun komm ich als Richter. Erkennt ihr mich
jetzt?

III. Fall nieder, Feuer

Das Brot wird bitter sein. Ihr gabt die Lüge
bereits der Aussaat als Geleitwort mit.
Am Brunnen füllen sich die Tränenkrüge.
Die Diele dorrt vom hingestampften Schritt.

Des Frevels Äußerstes habt ihr vollendet.
Maßlose, grifft ihr nach der Schöpfung ganz.
Der Elemente Unschuld ist geschändet.
Der Wald gab Laub zum lügnerischen Kranz.

Der Wind hat euren Wimpeln dienen müssen
und falschem Glanz das lautere Metall.
Ihr triebt das Schweigen von Geklüft und Flüssen,
die Luft bewahrt der blinden Worte Schall.

Dem Widergott zu Tor und Tempelstufen,
zu Kerkermauern brachet ihr das Gestein.
Ihr habt das Feuer tausendfach gerufen –
Fall nieder, Feuer! Brenne du uns rein.

IV. An Dante

Du des Jüngsten Richters Diener,
übermenschlich von Gesichten,
kehre wieder, Florentiner!
Eins noch bleibt dir zu verrichten.

At night I knocked on your door, a white-faced Jew
A refugee, hunted down, in torn shoes.
You called the authorities, tipped off the spies
And thought, well done, all in the service of God.

I came as an old lady, trembling, weak
In my mind, screaming in fear.
You spoke of the future generations
And only my ashes were set free.

An orphan boy from the eastern plains
I fell at your feet, begging for bread.
But you feared the future repercussions
Shrugged your shoulders and murdered me.

I came as a prisoner, as a forced laborer
Displaced, sold, torn to bits with the whip.
You turned your eyes from the disheveled slave.
Now I come as judge. Now do you recognize me?

Ich kam als zitternde, geistesgeschwächte
Greisin mit stummem Angstgeschrei.
Ihr aber spracht vom Zukunftsgeschlechte
und nur meine Asche gabt ihr frei.

Verwaister Knabe auf östlichen Flächen,
ich fiel euch zu Füßen und flehte um Brot.
Ihr aber scheutet ein künftiges Rächen,
ihr zucktet die Achseln und gabt mir den Tod.

Ich kam, ein Gefangener, als Tagelöhner,
verschleppt und verkauft, von der Peitsche zerfetzt.
Ihr wandtet den Blick von dem struppigen Fröner.
Nun komm ich als Richter. Erkennt ihr mich jetzt?

Werner Bergengruen: „Die letzte Epiphanie“ (1944). Manuskript.
Werner Bergengruen: “The Last Epiphany” (1944). Manuscript.

Anna-Luise Block, gesch. Hauser (später verh. Jones).
Porträt von Josef Block (1931).

Anna-Luise Block (previously Anna-Luise Hauser from a divorced marriage, later Anna-Luise Jones).
Portrait by Josef Block (1931).

Der Theologe Paul Leo,
geb. 1893 in Göttingen,
gest. in Dubuque 1958.

The theologian Paul Leo,
b. 1893 in Göttingen,
d. in Dubuque 1958.

Ingenieur Heinrich Schwarz (1882 – 1945),
Urenkel Nathan Mendelssohns und „Vierteljude".

Heinrich Schwarz (1882 – 1945),
Nathan Mendelssohn's great-grandson,
classified as "quarter-Jew."

Sein Sohn Erich (1921 – 2005)
auf Heimaturlaub in Hösel (1942).

His son Erich (1921 – 2005)
home from Russia (1942).

Fritz Kempner (1921 – 2013),
ein emigrierter Enkel Franz von Mendelssohns d.J., als GI im befreiten Paris.

Fritz Kempner (1921 – 2013).
This grandson of Franz von Mendelssohn the Younger had managed to emigrate. He is shown as a GI in Paris following the city's liberation.

How Thought and Experience Change: Many Images, One Family

According to Moses Mendelssohn, "the love of beauty is part of the calling of man." Along the front wall of the exhibition space, around the altar block of the former chapel, hang reproductions of works painted by various Mendelssohn descendants or by artists who married into the family. The fact that religious iconography has pride of place in this collection is due in part to the strong Catholic convictions of Johannes and Philipp Veit, members of the so-called "Nazarene" school of painting. Yet religious themes were also important to Wilhelm Hensel, a Protestant artist who drew inspiration from the Old Testament, as well as to Josef Block, who though Jewish also painted Christian motifs. In striving for a higher truth, these artists of the 19th and 20th centuries, transcending many boundaries, have found their common ground.

Wie Denken und Sehen sich verändern: Bilder aus der Familie

„Schönheit lieben" bezeichnet Moses Mendelssohn als eine „Bestimmung des Menschen". An der Frontwand des Ausstellungsraumes sind, rund um den Altarblock der ehemaligen Kapelle, Reproduktionen versammelt: Kunstwerke von Mendelssohn-Nachfahren oder von Künstlern, die durch Heirat zur Familie gehören. Die starke Präsenz religiöser Ikonographie in dieser Auswahl entsteht nicht nur aus dem katholischen Sendungsbewusstsein der Nazarener-Maler Johannes und Philipp Veit. Den Protestanten Wilhelm Hensel inspirieren auch alttestamentliche, den Juden Josef Block auch christliche Motive. Im Drang, einer tieferen Wirklichkeit nahe zu kommen, begegnen sich Grenzüberschreiter des 19. und 20. Jahrhunderts.

Wohnräume der Familie Sebastian Hensel in Berlin-Westend.
Living rooms of Sebastian Hensel and family in Berlin-Westend.

Wilhelm Hensel (1794 – 1861). „Miriam's Song of Praise". Öl auf Leinwand (1836). Das Gemälde zeigt den Siegesgesang der Prophetin Miriam über Pharaos untergegangene Armee beim Exodus der Israeliten; im Hintergrund Moses und Aaron, am Horizont die Pyramiden. Hensel schenkte das Werk während seiner zweiten Englandreise der jungen Queen Victoria und erhielt im Gegenzug einen Diamant- und Smaragd-Ring. „Die Königin hat ihn mir für Mirjam gegeben und da Du Mirjam bist, geb' ich ihn Dir. Und als Mirjam wirst Du im Buckingham-Palast wohnen und als Mirjam wirst Du in Kupfer gestochen werden, wie mir Prinz Albert fest versprochen hat" (Brief an Fanny Hensel, 29. August 1843).

Wilhelm Hensel (1794 – 1861). "Miriam's Song of Praise." Oil on canvas (1836). The painting depicts the Prophetess Miriam singing her victory song after the Pharaoh's army is drowned during the Exodus of the Israelites; in the background we see the Prophet Moses and the Priest Aaron, with the Pyramids in the background. During his second trip to England, Hensel presented the work as a gift to the young Queen Victoria, who gave him a diamond and emerald ring in return: "The Queen has given it to me for Mirjam, and since you are Mirjam, I give it to you. And as Mirjam you will live in Buckingham Palace and as Mirjam you will be engraved, so Prince Albert has told me." (Letter to Fanny Hensel, August 29, 1843).

Wilhelm Hensel (1794 – 1861). „Sie ist gerichtet! – Ist gerettet!" Aus: „Scenen aus Goethes Faust in acht lithographierten Blättern nach den Angaben des Fürsten Radziwill zu seinen Compositionen des Faust" (1835). Druck: Friedrich Jentzen.

Wilhelm Hensel (1794 – 1861). "She is judged! – and saved!" From: "Scenes from Goethe's 'Faust' in Eight Lithographed Sheets in Accordance with Duke Radziwill's Descriptions of his Musical Settings of Faust" (1835). Printer: Friedrich Jentzen.

Johannes [Jonas] Veit (1790 – 1854). „Christus am Ölberg". Öl auf Leinwand.

Johannes [Jonas] Veit (1790 – 1854). "Christ on the Mount of Olives." Oil on canvas.

Philipp Veit (1793 – 1877). „Die Religion“. Öl auf Leinwand (1819).
Philipp Veit (1793 – 1877). “Religion.” Oil on canvas (1819).

Philipp Veit (1793 – 1877). „Himmelfahrt Mariens“. Ölskizze (1843/1847).
Philipp Veit (1793 – 1877). “The Ascension of Mary.” Oil sketch (1843/1847).

Philipp Veit (1793 – 1877). „Die sieben fetten Jahre“. Wandgemälde aus der Casa Bartholdy / Palazzo Zuccari in Rom (1817) zur biblischen Erzählung von einer Traumdeutung Josephs am Hof des Pharao. Die Fresken der Nazarener wurden 1886/1887 nach Berlin überführt.

Philipp Veit (1793 – 1877). “The Seven Years of Plenty.” Wall fresco from the Casa Bartholdy / Palazzo Zuccari in Rome (1817) depicting the Biblical tale of Joseph’s interpretation of a dream at the Pharaoh’s court. The frescos of the Nazarene painters were transferred to Berlin in 1886/1887.

Sebastian Hensel (1830 – 1898). Groteske an der Fassade von Notre Dame, Paris. Aquarell für „Zugvögel. Ein Märchen“ (1897).

Sebastian Hensel (1830 – 1898). Grotesque on the Façade of Notre Dame in Paris. Water color for “Birds of Passage: a Fable” (1897).

Philipp Veit (1793 – 1877). „Germania“. Aus dem Triptychon: „Einführung der Künste in Deutschland durch das Christentum“ (1834-1836). Das Fresko wurde 1877 abgenommen und auf Leinwand übertragen.

Philipp Veit (1793 – 1877). “Germania.” From the triptych: “Christianity Brings the Arts to Germany” (1834 – 1836). The fresco was removed in 1877 and transferred onto canvas.

Wilhelm Hensel (1794 – 1861). „Orientalische Badeszene“. Öl auf Papier. Eine der ersten Arbeiten Hensels als Kunstschüler (um 1812).

Wilhelm Hensel (1794 – 1861). “Oriental Bathing Scene.” Oil on paper. One of Hensel’s first works as an art student (c. 1812).

Josef Block (1863 – 1943). „Grablegung“. Öl auf Leinwand. Aus: „Die Kunst für Alle“ (1909/1910).

Josef Block (1863 – 1943). “The Entombment of Christ.” Oil on canvas. From: “Die Kunst für Alle” (1909/1910).

Vita Petersen (1915 – 2011). „The Dominant Green“.
Pastell auf Papier (2010).

Vita Petersen (1915 – 2011). “The Dominant Green.”
Pastel on paper (2010).

Vita Petersen (1915 – 2011). „The Red Curtain“.
Pastell auf Papier (2010).

Vita Petersen (1915 – 2011). “The Red Curtain.”
Pastel on paper (2010).

Josef Block (1863 – 1943). „Der Gekreuzigte“. Öl auf Leinwand (1940). Das letzte zu Hause geschaffene Werk des Malers vor seinem Aufenthalt im Jüdischen Krankenhaus, wo er am 20. Dezember 1943 starb.

Josef Block (1863 – 1943). “The Crucified One.” Oil on canvas (1940). The final work of the painter, which he completed at home before going into hospital at the *Jüdisches Krankenhaus*, where he died on December 20, 1943.

The essence of the fine arts, according to Moses Mendelssohn, can be found "in their sensory expression of perfection." Beauty, according to the Enlightenment philosopher, is "the sovereign queen and ruler over all our sentiments, the basis for all our natural impulses, and the animating spirit that turns our speculative knowledge of truth into sentiment, firing us up with a resolution to action." Thus, the artist is entitled to freely "distill [Beauty] in higher concentrations, so that she may move us all the more" (1756). Later, arguing as aesthetician and psychologist, Moses would try to reconcile what he saw as the moral purpose of art – to give expression to rational knowledge – with his theory that art also played an autonomous role in the "game of illusion."

Moses' oldest grandson, the painter Johannes (Jonas) Veit, strove to express the beliefs of his Christian faith on canvas. His role models in this regard were Giovanni Bellini and his friend Friedrich Overbeck, a fellow member of the devoutly Catholic circle of German painters known as the "Nazarenes." The surviving works of Jonas Veit include his altar panel "Christ on the Mt. of Olives" as well as his portraits of his parents and of Henriette Herz. Veit lent financial support to the construction of St. Hedwig's Hospital, and his "Adoration of the Shepherds" adorned the altar of St. Hedwig's church, Berlin's Catholic cathedral. The following, written about the altarpiece by a critic in 1819, could well apply to the work of many of the Nazarene painters: "These figures exude such devotion and pious simplicity, such purpose and dignity in their gestures and attitudes, such a natural beauty in their heads, hands and clothing, such a stillness in the most reverent expectation of the moment, and such a divine serenity round about them... Here, we see poured forth the treasure trove of a loving spirit seeking after the truth." Another member of the Nazarenes was Jonas' brother, Philipp Veit. He, too, believed that true art does not emulate fallen nature but rather reveals its original beauty, and must serve a historical objective, namely the "restoration of the divine image" (Friedrich Schlegel). While the style of the other Nazarene painters became static, Philip never ceased being a seeker, an explorer – as his portraits and self-portraits show. Still, as Director of the Städelsche Kunstinstitut in Frankfurt, he refused to compromise with liberal cultural notions, resigning from the post in 1843. His works include the allegory "The Triumph of Religion" (1817/1818), which hangs in the Vatican, and frescoes of Paradise inspired by Dante's "Divine Comedy" (1818 – 1824).

„In dem sinnlichen Ausdruck der Vollkommenheit" besteht nach Moses Mendelssohn das Wesen der schönen Künste. „Eigenmächtige Beherrscherin aller unserer Empfindungen, der Grund von allen unsern natürlichen Trieben, und der beseelende Geist, der die speculative Erkenntniß der Wahrheit in Empfindung verwandelt, und zu thätiger Entschließung anfeuert", sei die Schönheit. Deshalb stehe es dem Künstler frei, sie „zu concentriren, damit sie uns stärker rühre" (1756). Später sucht der Ästhetiker und Psychologe Moses die moralische Aufgabe der Kunst als Darstellerin vernünftiger Erkenntnisse und eine Theorie von ihrer Autonomie im „Spiel der Illusion" zu verbinden.

Der erste Enkel des Aufklärers, Johannes (Jonas) Veit, entwickelt sich als Katholik – beeindruckt durch Gemälde Bellinis und den Nazarener-Freund Overbeck – zum Maler imaginierter Glaubenswirklichkeit. Erhalten sind sein Altarbild „Christus am Ölberg" sowie Porträts seiner Eltern und der Henriette Herz. Veit unterstützt den Bau des St. Hedwig-Krankenhauses, in Berlins katholischer Kathedrale befand sich sein Altarbild „Anbetung der Hirten": „Es ist in diesen Gestalten eine solche treue, fromme Einfalt, Sinnigkeit, und Würde in Geberde und Haltung; eine solche reine natürliche Schönheit in den Köpfen, in den Händen und Gewändern, eine Stille in der ehrfurchtsvollen Erwartung des Augenblicks, ein so wahrhaftiger Friede Gottes rings umher verbreitet ... Hier offenbart sich der ganze Reichtum eines liebenden, die Wahrheit suchenden Gemüths" – so ein Rezensent Anno 1819. Auch für seinen Bruder Philipp steht wahre Kunst, welche die zerstörte Natur nicht nachahmt, sondern deren Ursprungs-Schönheit offenlegt, im Dienst eines geschichtlichen Zieles: der „Wiederherstellung des göttlichen Ebenbildes" (Friedrich Schlegel). Während der Stil anderer Nazarener erstarrt, bleibt Philipp – wie Porträts und Selbstbildnisse zeigen – der Suchende. Doch als Direktor des Städelschen Kunstinstitutes in Frankfurt verweigert er Kompromisse mit liberalen Kulturkonzepten, gibt das Amt 1843 auf. Zu seinen Werken zählen die Allegorie „Triumph der Religion" (1817/1818) und Paradies-Fresken nach Dantes „Göttlicher Komödie" (1818 – 1824).

Philipp Veit: „Einführung der Künste in Deutschland durch das Christentum" (1834 – 1836). Mittelteil des Triptychons.
Philipp Veit: "Christianity Introduces the Arts to Germany" (1834 – 1836). Middle panel of the triptych.

Johannes Veit: Brief vom 11. Februar 1851 aus Frankfurt an Eduard Bendemann (1811 – 1889), Dozent an der Hochschule für Bildende Künste in Dresden. Veit empfiehlt seinem Malerkollegen Bendemann sowie „allen, die Apostel und sonstige Bartinhaber brauchen“, den Überbringer des Schreibens als „Kopfmodell“.

Johannes Veit: letter written February 11, 1851 in Frankfurt to Eduard Bendemann (1811 – 1889), professor at the Academy of the Visual Arts in Dresden. Veit recommends the bearer of the letter as an ideal “head model” as well as for “anyone in need of an apostle or other bearded type.”

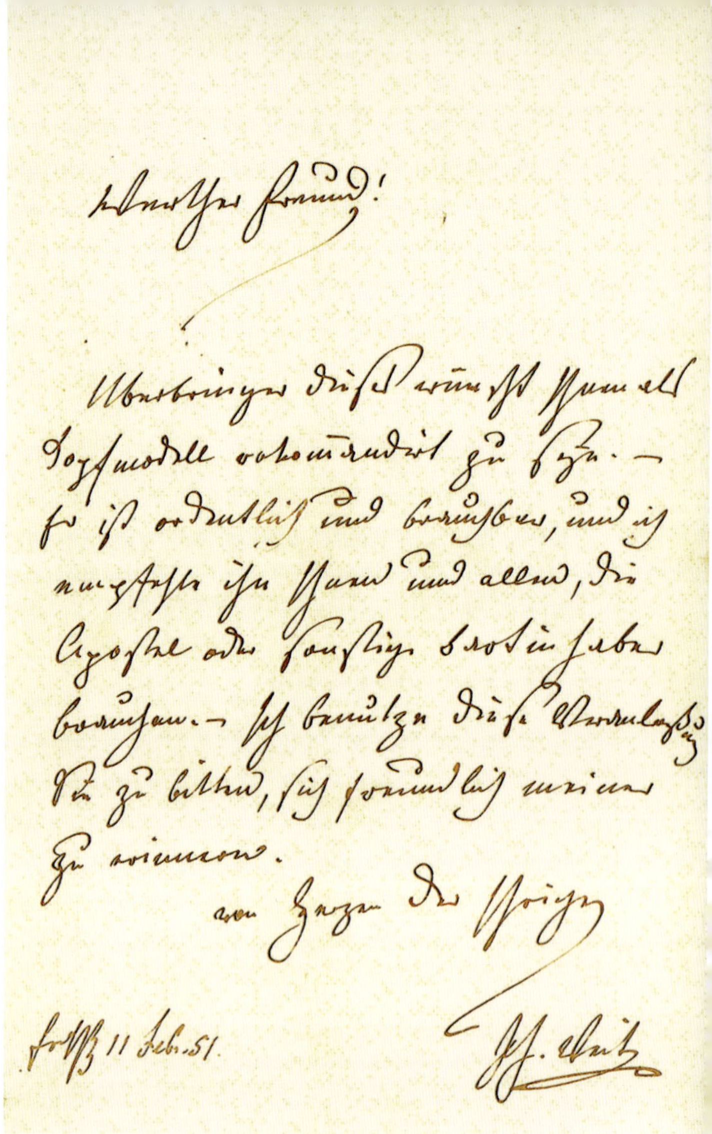

Werther Freund!

Überbringer dieses wünscht Ihnen als Kopfmodell recommandirt zu sein – er ist ordentlich und brauchbar, und ich empfehle ihn Ihnen und allen, die Apostel oder sonstige Bartinhaber brauchen. – Ich benutze diese Veranlassung Sie zu bitten, sich freundlich meiner zu erinnern.

von Herzen der Ihrige

Frankfurt 11 Febr. 51. J. Veit

Philipp Veit: „Johannes Veit und Johann Friedrich Overbeck“. Fotografie des 1931 im Münchner Glaspalast verbrannten Ölgemäldes (1816 (1810 oder 1820).

Philipp Veit: “Johannes Veit and Johann Friedrich Overbeck.” Photograph of the oil panting (1816 (1810 or 1820) destroyed by fire in the Munich Glaspalast in 1931.

Johannes Veit: „Bildnis der Henriette Herz“. Vermutlich entstand das Gemälde bei dem Aufenthalt der ehemaligen Berliner Salonière in Rom (1817 – 1819), kurz nach ihrer Konversion zur evangelisch-lutherischen Kirche. Begraben ist sie auf dem Friedhof II der Jerusalems- und Neuen Kirchengemeinde.

Johannes Veit: “Portrait of Henriette Herz.” The painting was presumably created while Henriette, formerly a Berlin salon hostess, was living in Rome (1817 – 1819), shortly after her conversion to the Evangelical-Lutheran church. She is buried in Cemetery II of the “Jerusalems- und Neue Kirchengemeinde.”

Philipp Veit: „Selbstbildnis im 80. Lebensjahre“.
Öl auf Leinwand (um 1873).

Philipp Veit: “Self-portrait at the age of 80.”
Oil on canvas (c. 1873).

In St. Hedwig befand sich die „Anbetung der Hirten“, das bekannteste Gemälde Johannes Veits. Seine konvertierte Tante Henriette Mendelssohn wohnte zeitweise „Hinter der Katholischen Kirche“.

St. Hedwig’s Church was the location of the “Adoration of the Shepherds,” Johannes Veit’s best-known painting. His aunt Henriette Mendelssohn, a convert, temporarily lived at the address “Behind the Catholic church.”

Wilhem Hensel, Ludwig Passini and Josef Block

Of the three painters who married into the Mendelssohn family, it was the preacher's son Wilhelm Hensel, who left the biggest mark. Having returned home from his scholarship-funded studies in Rome, he was appointed Court Painter by Frederick William III (1829). Once he had married Fanny, Hensel set up his studio near the garden salon of the residence on Leipziger Strasse, making the house feel even more like a temple to the muses. His magnum opus, "Christ before Pilate," was purchased by the King for the Berlin Garrison Church. When Fanny Hensel died, this master of romantic realism gave up painting altogether. His over 1,000 portrait drawings offer an invaluable window into his times.

In 1864, the popular Viennese genre painter Ludwig Passini married Anna Warschauer, a great-great-granddaughter of Moses Mendelssohn. After Anna's death in 1866, Passini went on to paint several portraits of the family. He lies buried on the cemetery near Hallesches Tor. In 1895, Josef Block married Else Oppenheim of the Joseph-Mendelssohn branch; the nuptials were held in the New Church on Gendarmenmarkt. A founder of the Munich Secession and later of the Berlin Secession, Block painted Biblical scenes, landscapes and portraits. Starting in 1933, he was forced to sell off parts of his collection, while his apartment in Tiergarten was expropriated to make way for Speer's Germania project. Before entering the Jewish Hospital, he was able to complete his painting "The Crucified One." He died in December 1943 and was buried in the Jewish Cemetery at Weissensee in the following year.

Part of the family's educational concept was the acquisition of artistic skills for their own sake. Thus, the drawings executed by Felix Mendelssohn Bartholdy sprang from a desire to pass on his life experiences. Felix' grandson, the architect Hugo Wach, would similarly record European and Oriental landscapes in pencil drawings around 1900, while his cousin Albrecht Mendelssohn Bartholdy would later publish these "Travel Sketches" with a grant from Agfa Director Franz Oppenheim. Felix' nephew Sebastian Hensel used his drawing aptitude for personal fairytale books. His "Nature Stories for Children" (1896) was illustrated by Lucy du Bois Reymond, a great-great-granddaughter of Daniel Chodowiecki and sister-in-law of Hensel's daughter Lili. Sebastian's daughter Cécile Leo, despite being extremely near-sighted, was able to create outstanding silhouette cut-outs, influenced by Paul Konewka and Jugendstil.

Wilhem Hensel, Ludwig Passini und Josef Block

Unter jenen drei Künstlern, die durch Heirat zu Mendelssohn-Verwandten werden, beeinflußt vor allem der Predigersohn Wilhelm Hensel die Familien-Entwicklung. Heimgekehrt aus seiner römischen Stipendiatszeit, ernennt ihn Friedrich Wilhelm III. zum Hofmaler (1829). Hensels Atelier, das er als Ehemann Fanny Mendelssohn Bartholdys an der Leipziger Straße neben dem Gartensaal einrichtet, verstärkt dort die Anmutung des Musentempels. Sein Opus magnum „Christus vor Pilatus" erwirbt der König für die Garnisonkirche. Nach Fanny Hensels Tod gibt der romantisierende Realist die Malerei auf; mit über 1000 Porträtzeichnungen wird er zum Dokumentaristen seiner Epoche.

Der gefragte Wiener Genremaler Ludwig Passini heiratet 1864 Anna Warschauer; die Ururenkelin des Moses stirbt anderthalb Jahre nach der Hochzeit in Rom. Passini, der die Verwandtschaft noch oft porträtiert hat, ist auf dem Friedhof vor dem Halleschen Tor begraben. Der Schlesier Josef Block heiratet 1895 in der Neuen Kirche am Gendarmenmarkt Else Oppenheim aus der Joseph-Mendelssohn-Linie. Block, ein Mitgründer der Münchner, später der Berliner Secession, malt biblische Szenen, Landschaften, Porträts. Ab 1933 muß er Teile seiner Sammlung verkaufen, seine Wohnung in Tiergarten wird für Speers Germania-Projekt beschlagnahmt. Vor seiner Einlieferung ins Jüdische Krankenhaus entsteht sein Bild „Der Gekreuzigte". Er stirbt im Dezember 1943, wird im darauffolgenden Jahr auf dem Jüdischen Friedhof Weißensee beerdigt.

Zum Bildungsideal der Familie gehört die zweckfreie Aneignung künstlerischer Fertigkeiten. Fürs Komponieren läßt sich Felix Mendelssohn Bartholdy vom Ernst der Renaissance-Kunst inspirieren. Seine Alltags- und Reise-Zeichnungen entspringen dem Drang, Erlebtes zu erzählen. So wird auch sein Enkel, der Architekt Hugo Wach, um 1900 europäische und orientalische Topographien mit dem Bleistift fixieren; Cousin Albrecht Mendelssohn Bartholdy ediert diese „Reise-Scizzen", finanziert durch den Agfa-Chef Franz Oppenheim. Felix' Neffe Sebastian Hensel nutzt sein Zeichentalent für private Märchenbücher. Seine 1896 publizierten „Naturgeschichten für Kinder" illustriert die Malerin Lucy du Bois Reymond, eine Ururenkelin Daniel Chodowieckis, Schwägerin der Hensel-Tochter Lili. Sebastians Tochter Cécile Leo wiederum beeindruckt, bei extremer Kurzsichtigkeit, als Scherenschnitt-Virtuosin, geprägt durch den Klassiker Paul Konewka und vom Jugendstil.

August Theodor Kaselowsky: „Wilhelm Hensel in der Campagna". Ölgemälde (1841).
August Theodor Kaselowsky: "Wilhelm Hensel in the Italian Campagna." Oil painting (1841).

Julius Helfft: „Ausschnitt von Fanny Hensels Musikzimmer." Gouache, 1849. Einige Gemälde an der Wand dieses Raumes im Gartentrakt Leipziger Straße 3 sind Werke von Wilhelm Hensel, dessen Atelier angrenzte.

Julius Helfft: "Partial View of Fanny Hensel's Music Room." Gouache, 1849. Some of the paintings hanging on the wall of this room along the garden tract of Leipziger Strasse 3 are by Wilhelm Hensel, whose atelier was right next door.

Ludwig Passini (1832 – 1903). Aufnahme von 1869.

Ludwig Passini (1832 – 1903). Image taken in 1869.

Scherenschnitt von Cécile Leo, geb. Hensel (1858 – 1928).

Silhouette cut-out by Cécile Leo, née Hensel (1858 – 1928).

Josef Block: „Selbstporträt“ (um 1940).
Josef Block: “Self-portrait” (c. 1940).

Atelier von Josef Block in Berlin.
Aus: „Berliner Leben, Zeitschrift für Schönheit und Kunst“ (1904).
Josef Block’s studio in Berlin.
From: ”Berliner Leben, Zeitschrift für Schönheit und Kunst“ (1904).

37

The great collectors

The first systematic collector among the art-loving Mendelssohns was Jacob Ludwig Salomon Bartholdy. In 1816, as Prussia's ambassador to the Papal States and Tuscany, he hired the Nazarenes (despite disagreeing with their ideals) to decorate a drawing room in Rome's Palazzo Zuccari near the Spanish Steps with frescos. Chosen by Jacob himself, the motifs included the Biblical story of Joseph as well as landscapes and allegories. Jacob would go on to advise King Frederick William III on the acquisition of entire collections, thereby paving the way for the Königliches Museum in Berlin, whose cornerstone was laid shortly after his death (1825). His collection of coins and cut stones – as well as thousands of additional objects from his estate – eventually found a home in Berlin's various museums of sculpture, antiquities and Egyptian art, often by way of his in-law Abraham Mendelssohn Bartholdy. His majolica collection ended up in the cabinet of arts and curios of Berlin's Royal Palace, pulled down by the Communists in 1950.

Paul von Mendelssohn-Bartholdy, son of the Director of Mendelssohn & Co., and Charlotte Reichenheim (married in 1902 / divorced in 1927) were well matched as art collectors. Paul mostly steered clear of the bank's day-to-day operations. In 1909, he had the architect Bruno Paul convert the old Börnicke Manor into his own "castle in the March of Brandenburg." In 1913/15, he built a three-wing palatial urban residence on the Alsenstrasse, near the Reichstag. Besides East Asian art, his collection comprised well-known works by Picasso and van Gogh. His wife Charlotte, meanwhile, brought a sharp instinct for quality that she may well have inherited: Her mother, the collector Margarete Reichenheim, had married AGFA head Franz Oppenheim in 1906 (or 1907). With its fashionable accessories, silver vessels and paintings – including the largest single holding of artwork by Cézanne – the Reichenheim-Oppenheim collection was considered one of the most valuable in Germany. The collections of both couples were eventually scattered through inheritance, divorce, emigration, and sales under duress. Restitution proceedings are ongoing. The palatial villa in the *Alsenviertel* neighborhood was subjected to a forced sale to make way for Albert Speer's Germania, while the Börnicke manor was expropriated by the Soviet occupation forces. The

Die großen Sammler

Erster systematisch ankaufender Kunstfreund in Mendelssohn-Kreisen ist Jacob Ludwig Salomon Bartholdy. Als Preußens Gesandter in Rom und der Toskana läßt er die Nazarener, deren fromme Ideen er nicht teilt, im Palazzo Zuccari an der Spanischen Treppe ab 1816 ein Gesellschaftszimmer ausmalen: Fresken eigener Themenwahl, zur biblischen Josephs-Geschichte, Landschaften, Allegorien. Er schlägt Friedrich Wilhelm III. den Erwerb ganzer Sammlungen vor, gilt als Wegbereiter des Königlichen Museums in Berlin, zu dem kurz nach seinem Tod (1825) der Grundstein gelegt wird. Münzen und geschnittene Steine aus seinem Besitz gelangen, wie über tausend weitere nachgelassene Stücke, teils über den Schwager Abraham Mendelssohn Bartholdy, in die Antiken-, die Ägyptische und in die Skulpturensammlung Berlins. Die Kunstkammer im Schloß erhält seine Majolika-Kollektion.

Paul von Mendelssohn-Bartholdy, Sohn des Seniorchefs von Mendelssohn & Comp., und Charlotte Reichenheim (Heirat 1902 / Scheidung 1927) ergänzen sich als Sammler. Ins operative Geschäft begibt sich der Bankier nicht; durch den Architekten Bruno Paul läßt er sich 1909 das Herrenhaus Börnicke zum „Schloß in der Mark" umbauen und 1913/15, nahe dem Reichstag an der Alsenstraße, ein dreiflügeliges Palais errichten. Zu seinen Sammlungen gehören neben Ostasiatika berühmte Picassos und van Goghs. Gattin Charlotte bringt aus ihrem Elternhaus Qualitätsinstinkt mit; ihre Mutter, die Sammlerin Margarete Reichenheim, heiratet 1906 (oder 1907) den Agfa-Chef Franz Oppenheim. Die Sammlung Reichenheim-Oppenheim gilt mit ihren Galanterien, Silbergefäßen, Gemälden – unter anderem der größte Bestand an Cézanne – als eine der wertvollsten Deutschlands. Die Schätze beider Paare werden durch Erbgänge, Scheidung, Emigration, Notverkäufe verstreut, Restitutionsverfahren dauern noch an. Das Palais im Alsenviertel fällt 1938 unter den Zwangsverkauf für die Germania-Pläne, Schloß Börnicke enteignen sowjetische Besatzer. Die durch Alfred Messel erbaute Oppenheim-Villa am Großen Wannsee beschlagnahmt der Sicherheitsdienst bereits 1937. In diesem Haus der Bilder war eine Enkelin zur Kunstbegeisterten geworden: Vita Petersen, die dann Karl Hofers Meisterklasse besuchte und sich als Emigrantin in New York mit Form, Farbe, Rhythmus zwischen

Spanische Treppe mit dem Palazzo Zuccari, der „Casa Bartholdy".
Zeichnung von Felix Mendelssohn Bartholdy (1831).

The Spanish Steps with the Palazzo Zuccari, the "Casa Bartholdy."
Drawing by Felix Mendelssohn Bartholdy (1831).

Vita Petersen 2011 in ihrem New Yorker Atelier.
Vita Petersen 2011 in her New York atelier.

Franz Oppenheim (1852 – 1929) und Margarete Oppenheim, geb. Eisner, verw. Reichenheim (1857 – 1935).
Franz Oppenheim (1852 – 1929) and Margarete Oppenheim, née Eisner, widowed Reichenheim (1857 – 1935).

Villa Oppenheim am Großen Wannsee, erbaut von Alfred Messel (1907/1908). Der Architekt hatte bereits für Paul und Charlotte von Mendelssohn-Bartholdy zu deren Hochzeit (1902) Schloß Hasenheide bei Börnicke entworfen.

Villa Oppenheim on *Grosser Wannsee* lake, built by Alfred Messel (1907/1908). The architect had already designed Schloss Hasenheide near Börnicke for Paul and Charlotte von Mendelssohn-Bartholdy, who were to move in after their wedding (1902).

Taf: II.

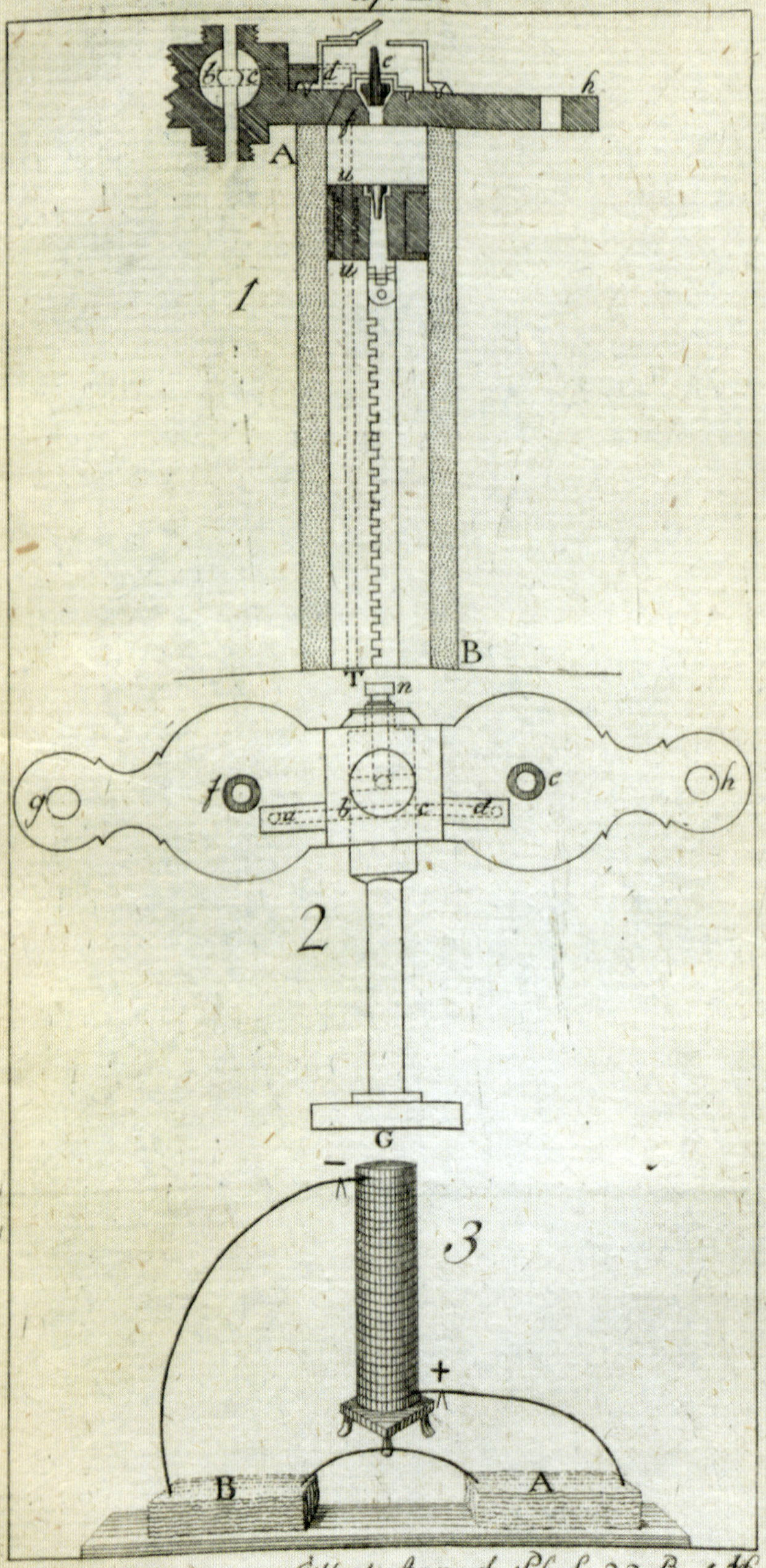

Gilberts Ann: d: Phyſ: 22 B: 1 H.

VI.

BESCHREIBUNG *einer verbeſſerten Einrichtung der Luftpumpe,*

von

N. Mendelssohn
in London.

Folgendes iſt der Brief an Nicholſon, geſchrieben zu London *Surry-Street*, *Black-Friars*, Februar 13, 1805, womit Herr Mendelsſohn die Beſchreibung begleitete, welche in Nicholſon's *Journal*, March 1805, pag. 201, eingerückt iſt. „Ich hatte den Vorſatz, da ich mich, als mathematiſcher Inſtrumentenmacher, niederlieſs, es mein Hauptbemühen ſeyn zu laſſen, die Inſtrumente ſo weit zu verbeſſern, als es die gegenwärtigen Fortſchritte in den Wiſſenſchaften, die Natur der Sache und meine geringe Geſchicklichkeit nur immer erlauben möchte. Ich begann mit Volta's electriſchem Feuerzeug und mit der Luftpumpe. Den Bau der letztern glaube ich ſehr vereinfacht zu haben, ſo daſs ſie nicht ſo leicht als bisher wandelbar werden kann, und doch ein ſehr groſses Exhauſtionsvermögen beſitzt. Sie ſteht, wie ich ſie hier beſchrieben und abgebildet habe, zu Ihrer Anſicht bereit, und ich würde mich glücklich ſchätzen, wenn dieſes phyſikaliſche Inſtrument Ihren Beifall fände. — — —“

Der

Scientists and mathematicians

Moses Mendelssohn had a wide range of intellectual passions, which also included mathematics. Thus, his descendants seem to have inherited an aptitude not just for the liberal arts, but for math and science as well. His son Nathan, the mechanic, built astronomical instruments for example. Nathan's oldest son Arnold embarked on a medical career and worked with Rudolf Virchow and Emile du Bois Reymond on a number of hopeful physiological research projects (e.g. "On Favus" (a fungal skin infection) in 1841). Sadly, Arnold's vocation would later be cut short by his imprisonment as a political subversive. The quaint notion that mathematical affinity "tends to be passed down from the father to the son-in-law" (Hans Freudenthal) is certainly borne out in Nathan's branch of the family: his daughter Ottilie was married to number theorist Eduard Kummer (proof of Fermat's Last Theorem for primary numbers), while Nathan's granddaughter Marie Kummer tied the knot with Hermann C. Amandus Schwarz (Cauchy-Schwarz inequality, Schwarz lemma, Schwarz reflection principle, Schwarz-Pick lemma). Mathematical aptitude can still be seen in the sixth generation, in the person of Nathan's great-great-grandson Roland Percival Sprague, who made contributions to game theory (Sprague-Grundy theorem) and recreational mathematics.

Another mathematician who married into the family was Gustav Lejeune Dirichlet, the husband of Rebecka Mendelssohn Bartholdy. Dirichlet succeeded the great Carl Friedrich Gauss in the higher mathematics chair at Göttingen University and gave his name to no less than 14 operations in the field of number theory. A prominent math wizard in the fifth generation was Marburg Professor Kurt Hensel (Hensel lemma and Hensel ring). His grandson is the British function theorist Walter Hayman (Hayman's alternative in Nevanlinna's value-distribution theory). Last but not least, Joseph's side of the family has also produced a 20th-century luminary in the sciences: Israeli astrophysicist Amos Yahil (seventh generation, born 1943).

Die Naturwissenschaftler

Der mathematisch ambitionierte Moses hat die Neigung zu Natur- und Geisteswissenschaften in seiner Familie angelegt. Sohn Nathan, der Mechanicus, fertigt astronomische Instrumente; dessen Ältester Arnold beginnt, vor seinem Absturz als Zuchthäusler, an der Seite von Rudolf Virchow und Emile du Bois Reymond hoffnungsvolle physiologische Forschungen als Mediziner („Über den Erbgrind", 1841). Daß Mathematik-Affinität sich „eher vom Vater auf den Schwiegersohn" vererbt (Hans Freudenthal), belegen in dieser Stammbaumlinie der Zahlentheoretiker Eduard Kummer (Beweis des Großen Fermatischen Satzes für Primzahlen) und Hermann C. Amandus Schwarz (Cauchy-Schwarz-Ungleichung, Schwarzsches Lemma, Lemma von Schwarz-Pick, Schwarzsches Spiegelungsprinzip): Kummer heiratet Nathans Tochter Ottilie, Schwarz Nathans Enkelin Marie Kummer. In der VI. Generation lebt bei Nathans Ururenkel Roland Percival Sprague (Satz von Sprague-Grundy) die Begabung des Ahnen mit Beiträgen zur Unterhaltungsmathematik auf.

Ebenfalls eingeheiratet – als Gatte der Rebecka Mendelssohn Bartholdy – ist der Gauß-Nachfolger in Göttingen Gustav Lejeune Dirichlet, dessen Namen 14 zahlentheoretische Verfahren tragen. In der V. Generation ragt der Marburger Professor Kurt Hensel (Henselsches Lemma, Henselscher Ring) heraus. Sein Enkel ist der preisgekrönte britische Funktionentheoretiker Walter Hayman (Haymansche Alternative in der Wertverteilungstheorie von Nevanlinna). Mit dem israelischen Astrophysiker Amos Yahil (VII. Generation, geb. 1943) profiliert sich im 20. Jahrhundert eine naturwissenschaftliche Koryphäe für die Josephs-Linie.

Nathan Mendelssohn: Illustration zur Beschreibung einer verbesserten Einrichtung der Luftpumpe. Gilberts „Annalen der Physik" (1806).

Nathan Mendelssohn: illustration of an improved configuration for an air pump. Gilbert's "Annalen der Physik" (1806).

Roland Percival Sprague (1894 –1967), beim Brettspiel. Der Enkel des Mathematikers Hermann Schwarz, Urenkel von Ernst Eduard Kummer, Ururururenkel Moses Mendelssohns, war ab 1955 Professor an der Pädagogischen Hochschule Berlin.

Roland Percival Sprague (1894 – 1967) playing a board game. The grandson of the mathematician Hermann Schwarz, great-grandson of Ernst Eduard Kummer, and great-great-great-grandson of Moses Mendelssohn, he became a professor at the Berlin's Pädagogische Hochschule in 1955.

Ernst Eduard Kummer (1810 – 1892).
Aufnahme von 1875.
Der Mathematiker heiratete in erster Ehe Ottilie Mendelssohn, eine Moses-Enkelin, und nach deren Tod Bertha Cauer, die Schwägerin des Maschinisten Wilhelm Mendelssohn.

Ernst Eduard Kummer (1810 – 1892).
Image taken in 1875.
The mathematician's first marriage was to Ottilie Mendelssohn, a granddaughter of Moses; after her death, he married Bertha Cauer, a sister-in-law of the machinist Wilhelm Mendelssohn.

Hermann Amandus Schwarz (1842 – 1921) war Professor in Halle und an der ETH Zürich, wirkte ab 1892 an der Berliner Akademie der Wissenschaften. 1868 heiratete er Marie Kummer, eine Enkelin Nathan Mendelssohns.

Hermann Amandus Schwarz (1842 – 1921) was a professor in Halle and at ETH Zurich who, in 1892, became a member of the Berlin Academy of Sciences. In 1868, he married Marie Kummer, a granddaughter of Nathan Mendelssohn.

Kurt Hensel 1915, im Jahr seiner Präsidentschaft für die Deutsche Mathematiker-Vereinigung.
Der 1861 geborene, zweite Sohn Sebastian Hensels starb 1941 emeritiert in Marburg, wo er 29 Jahre Ordinarius für Mathematik gewesen war.

Kurt Hensel in 1915, the year he served as president of the German Mathematical Society.
Born in 1861, this second son of Sebastian Hensel died in 1941 as an emeritus professor in Marburg, where he had taught mathematics for 29 years.

Amos Yahil erforschte um 1985 im Lick Observatory (San José, CA) die Dichte des Universums. Seine Analyse der Daten des Hubble-Teleskops führte zur Entdeckung der entferntesten Galaxien.

Around the year 1985, Amos Yahil set about investigating the density of the universe at Lick Observatory (San Jose, CA). His analysis of data from the Hubble Telescope led to the discovery of the furthest galaxies yet known.

Walter Hayman, geboren 1926 in Köln, kam 1938 ohne seine Eltern nach England. Mitglied der Royal Society (seit 1955), Professor für Reine Mathematik am Imperial College in London.

Walter Hayman, born in 1926 in Cologne, emigrated to England in 1938 without his parents. A member of the Royal Society (since 1955), he was a professor of pure mathematics at the Imperial College in London.

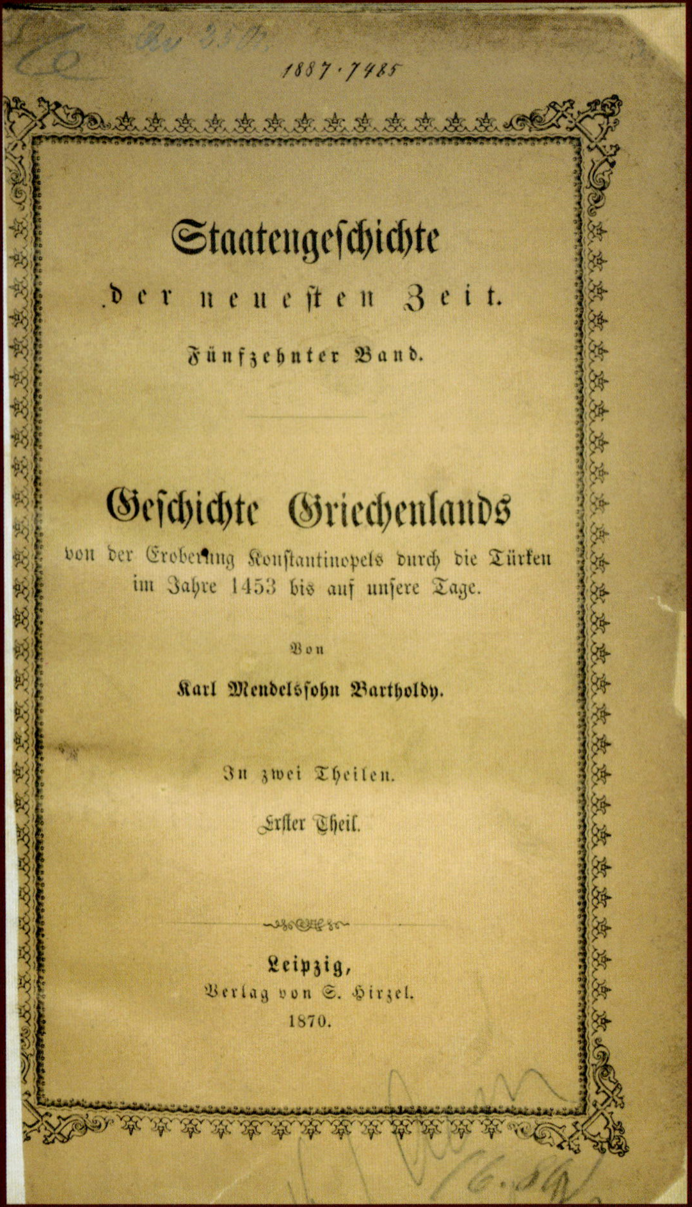
1887·7485
Staatengeschichte
der neuesten Zeit.
Fünfzehnter Band.
Geschichte Griechenlands
von der Eroberung Konstantinopels durch die Türken
im Jahre 1453 bis auf unsere Tage.
Von
Karl Mendelssohn Bartholdy.
In zwei Theilen.
Erster Theil.
Leipzig,
Verlag von S. Hirzel.
1870.

RECHT u. STAAT
IN GESCHICHTE UND
GEGENWART
80
ALBERT HENSEL
GRUNDRECHTE
UND POLITISCHE
WELTANSCHAUUNG
1931
J.C.B. MOHR (PAUL SIEBECK)
TÜBINGEN

Leni Yahil
Die Shoah
Überlebenskampf
und Vernichtung
der europäischen Juden

History from varying perspectives

Joseph Mendelssohn, who had to abandon his career as a liberal arts scholar, allowed his oldest son, Georg Benjamin Mendelssohn, to choose his own vocation. Georg decided to become a geography professor. However, the author of a historical geography entitled "Germanic Europe" (1835) was an isolated conservative in the academic circles of Bonn. His historian nephew Carl Mendelssohn Bartholdy, by contrast, harbored anti-Prussian sentiments and wrote biographical essays about personalities who exhibited shifting, ambivalent identities during the Wars of Liberation of the 18th and 19th centuries. He also produced a history of the Greek War of Independence which he researched on site in the Balkans and which later was to become a reference work. Resistance to authority can be seen as a recurring personal theme in Carl's writings.

The Haifa-based Israeli history professor Leni Yahil (sixth generation), whose father Ernst Westphal had been a judge in Potsdam, became caught up in a polemical exchange of letters with Hannah Arendt regarding the Jewish State and various ethical questions. Originally triggered by the Eichmann trial in 1961, the debate between the two scholars failed to bring about a reconciliation of views. In her *magnum opus* "The Holocaust: The Fate of European Jewry" (1987), Yahil recounted the Holocaust from a variety of differing points of view that included perpetrators as well as victims.

The tax-law expert Albert Hensel (sixth generation) carried out research on optimizing fiscal equalization among the German federal states. The author of various works on constitutional law ("Fundamental Rights and Political Ideology," 1931), he held the chair for public law at the University of Königsberg until his forced retirement in 1933. In 1981, the Albert-Hensel Prize was endowed, to be awarded for innovative contributions in the field of tax law.

Manuscripts and paintings, hospitals and scholarships

The history of the Mendelssohns as philanthropists begins with a donation given by Moses and his wife to their Synagogue:

Geschichte aus wechselseitigen Perspektiven

Joseph Mendelssohn, der auf die Geisteswissenschaftlerlaufbahn verzichten mußte, läßt seinem Ältesten die Wahl: Georg Benjamin Mendelssohn wird Geographieprofessor – und bleibt mit seiner geschichtlichen Erdkunde „Das germanische Europa“ (1835) ein isolierter Konservativer im akademischen Bonn. Sein antipreußisch gestimmter Historiker-Neffe Carl Mendelssohn Bartholdy bearbeitet in biographischen Essays über Grenzgänger in den Freiheitskriegen des 18./19. Jahrhunderts sowie in seinem auf dem Balkan recherchierten Standardwerk zum griechischen Unabhängigkeitskampf auch ein persönliches Thema: Widerstand gegen Autoritäten.

Die Geschichtsprofessorin in Haifa, Leni Yahil (VI. Generation), eine Tochter des Potsdamer Richters Ernst Westphal, hatte ab 1961 mit Hannah Arendt, ausgelöst durch den Eichmann-Prozeß, über den Staat Israel und Moralfragen kontrovers korrespondiert; der Briefwechsel endet unversöhnt. Yahil wird in ihrem Opus magnum „Die Shoah. Überlebenskampf und Vernichtung der europäischen Juden“ (1987) die Genozid-Geschichte aus wechselseitigen Perspektiven – der Täter, der Opfer – erzählen.

Der Steuerrechtler Albert Hensel (VI. Generation) betreibt Grundlagenforschung zum bundestaatlichen Finanzausgleich. In Königsberg war er bis zu seiner zwangsweisen Beurlaubung 1933 Ordinarius für Öffentliches Recht, publiziert hat er auch staatsrechtliche Werke („Grundrecht und politische Weltanschauung“, 1931). Seit 1981 würdigt ein Albert-Hensel-Preis innovative Forschungsbeiträge zum Steuerrecht.

Autographe und Gemälde, Krankenhäuser und Stipendien

Die Stiftungs-Chronik der Mendelssohns beginnt mit einer Spende der Stammeltern an ihre Synagoge: Fromets Brautkleid wird zum Toravorhang (1775/1776). Sara Levi, die Itzig-Tochter, schenkt Noten-Autographe an die Sing-Akademie, ebenso Abraham Mendelssohn, der Mann ihrer Nichte Lea. In der dritten Generation wird eine Siftung zur Unterstützung bedürftiger Angehöriger (1868) und ein Institut zur Versorgung pensionierter Hausangestellter gegründet. Konservative Mendelssohn-Bankiers machen

Karl Mendelssohn Bartholdy: „Geschichte Griechenlands.“ Erster Theil, Leipzig 1870.
Karl Mendelssohn Bartholdy: "A History of Greece." Part I, Leipzig 1870.

Albert Hensel: „Grundrechte und politische Weltanschauung.“ Tübingen 1931.
Albert Hensel: "Fundamental Rights and Political Ideology," Tübingen 1931.

Leni Yahil: „Die Shoah. Überlebenskampf und Vernichtung der europäischen Juden.“ Die deutsche Übersetzung erschien 1998, die hebräische Originalausgabe 1987 bei Schocken in Jerusalem.
Leni Yahil: "The Holocaust. The Fate of European Jewry." Originally published in Hebrew in 1987 by Schocken in Jerusalem, translated into German in 1998.

Fromet's wedding dress, which was made into a Torah curtain (1775/76). Sara Levi, daughter of the Itzigs, donated original music manuscripts to the *Sing-Akademie*, as did Abraham Mendelssohn, the husband of her niece Lea. In the third generation, the family's philanthropic projects included the endowment of a fund for needy relatives (1868) and an institute for retired domestic servants. Although politically conservative, the Mendelssohn bankers supported progressive cultural trends as patrons (in contrast to the Kaiser), as evidenced by their donation of the first Manet painting held by a German Museum ("In the Conservatory Garden," 1896). The heirs of Felix Mendelssohn Bartholdy donated his precious musical manuscripts to the Prussian government which, in return, agreed to endow the Mendelssohn-Preis (1878), Germany's first music prize for up-and-coming musicians. A particularly valuable collection of original musical manuscripts was presented to the Prussian Royal Library (1908) by the composer's nephew Ernst von Mendelssohn-Bartholdy, who also presented the Kaiser with the Villa Falconieri in Frascati, Italy, so that it could be used as a retreat for German artists. Felix' great-grandson Hugo von Mendelssohn Bartholdy laid the foundations for the Mendelssohn Archive by donating a large collection of papers to the Staatsbibliothek (State Library) (1964). Georg Benjamin and Alexander Mendelssohn provided the start-up funds for the Charlottenburg Hospital and the St. Josefs-Haus, a religious-order hospital in Horchheim near Coblenz (1865). The Mendelssohn manor house located in Horcheim was later donated to the Church as a residence for deaconesses (around 1900). In the 1920s, the family's bankers financed the publication of Felix Mendelssohn's collected works ("Mendelssohn-Gesamtausgabe"), as well as the Moses-Mendelssohn Foundation in Dessau for the promotion of the liberal arts.

als Stifter (gegen den Kaiser) progressive Kulturpolitik, wie die Schenkung des ersten Manet für ein Museum („Im Wintergarten“, 1896) zeigt. Erben Felix Mendelssohn Bartholdys überlassen dem Staat Autographen-Schätze, der dafür den ersten deutschen Musikpreis begründet (1878). Eine einmalig reiche Autographen-Schenkung erfolgt durch den Neffen des Komponisten, Ernst von Mendelssohn-Bartholdy, an die Königliche Bibliothek (1908). Felix' Urenkel Hugo von Mendelssohn Bartholdy wird mit der Übergabe eines Konvoluts für die Staatsbibliothek das Mendelssohn-Archiv begründen (1964). Georg Benjamin und Alexander Mendelssohn ermöglichen den Bau des Charlottenburger Krankenhauses und des Ordens-Hospitals St. Josefs-Haus in Horchheim bei Koblenz (1865); das dortige Mendelssohn-Gutshaus erhalten Diakonissen (um 1900). In den 1920er Jahren werden die Mendelssohn-Gesamtausgabe und die Dessauer Moses-Mendelssohn-Stiftung zur Förderung der Geisteswissenschaftlern von den Bankiers finanziert.

Edouard Manet: „Im Wintergarten“ (1879).
Edouard Manet: "In the Conservatory" (1879).

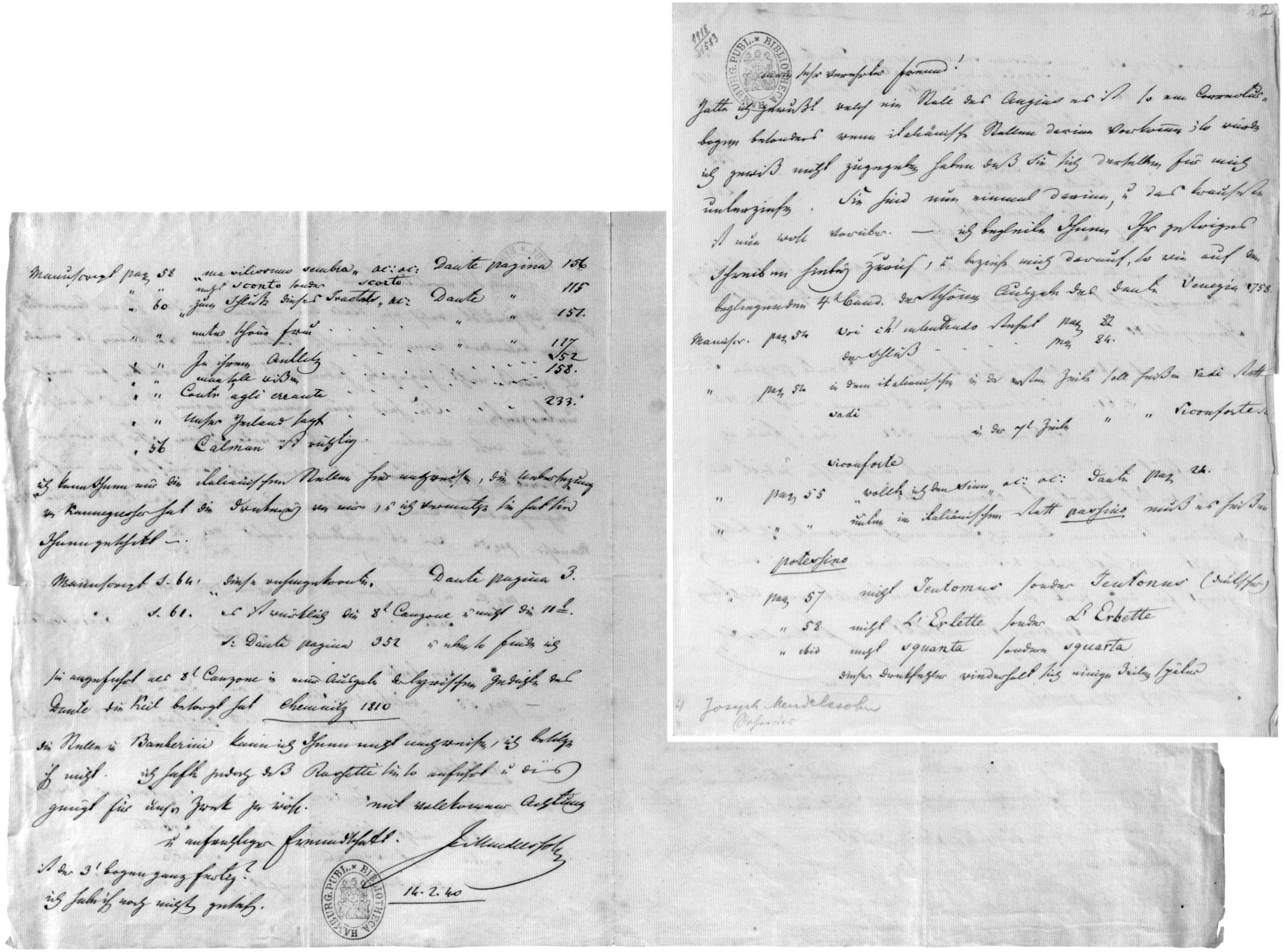

Korrekturen des Bankiers und Hobby-Gelehrten Joseph Mendelssohn für die Publikation seiner Schrift zur Dante-Interpretation. Der „Bericht über Rossetti's Ideen zu einer neuen Erläuterung des Dante und des Dichters seiner Zeit. In zwei Vorlesungen“ erschien 1840 anonym bei Alexander Duncker, Hamburg.

Corrections made by the banker and amateur scholar Joseph Mendelssohn for the publication of his work on Dante: “Report on Rossetti's Ideas on a New Interpretation of Dante and the Poets of his Age, in Two Lectures.” This was published anonymously in 1840 by Alexander Duncker in Hamburg.

Die Historikerin Leni Yahil, geb. Westphal (1912 – 2007), mit Familie 1961 in Jerusalem: der KZ-Überlebende und Diplomat Chaim Yahil, Amos (links) und Jonathan, der 1967 im Sechstagekrieg fiel.

The historian Leni Yahil, née Westphal (1912 – 2007), with her family in Jerusalem in 1961: the concentration-camp survivor and diplomat Chaim Yahil, along with Amos (left) and Jonathan, who fell in the Six-Day War in 1967.

Das von den Brüdern Alexander und Georg Benjamin Mendelssohn mitbegründete Städtische Krankenhaus Charlottenburg (um 1920).

The Hospital of the City of Charlottenburg (c. 1920). This was co-founded by the brothers Alexander and Georg Benjamin Mendelssohn.

The crane clutching the pebble

Joseph Mendelssohn, the family's first great philanthropists, presented the Berlin Stock Exchange with bas-reliefs from Johann Gottfried Schadow (1802). He also granted Alexander von Humboldt unlimited credit for his research. In 1839, Joseph introduced the family seal – the ever-watchful crane with the pebble. Besides launching or supporting various educational and pedagogical projects for the Jewish community, he sponsored the first popular theatre and the zoo, as well as a company for low-income housing and a discount bank extending affordable loans to the unemployed. In Horchheim, the vineyard owner subsidized his tenant farmers, financed the education of a talented piano maker and the construction of the local village school (1840/1846).

Laudatory poem for the 72nd birthday of Joseph Mendelssohn in Horchheim on August 15, 1842:

Lucky the one raised by his father as you were
to know both God and the tasks of Man.
Lucky the one whose father proved in practice
what others merely mouth with feeling.
For in the "Phaedon" blooms the soul's true rapture
for there immortal shines the sun,
Which, glowing in the doubter's breast,
brings forth heaven's rays and the heart's delight!

And to your gifted father's teachings
you have proved true throughout your life.
Drying our tears through counsel and deeds,
as a constant shelter and refuge for the poor.
Indeed, to spy out despised poverty
and not to wait till pleas grow to a clamor:
This was grasped and practiced by the eldest son
of the famous Mendelssohn!

So hail and welcome, noble grey head
to our Rhenish banks on this happy day!
We're moved with joy and nearly overcome,
with all the thanks our hearts can show.
So may God most richly bless you
along your path of life hereafter,
Until your evening star sinks low
and the angels beckon you to the Father!

Der Kranich mit dem Stein

Joseph Mendelssohn, der wegweisende Stiftungspatron, hatte der Berliner Börse Reliefs aus der Schadow-Schule spendiert (1802). Unbegrenzt kreditiert er Forschungsreisen Alexander von Humboldts. Das Familienemblem, den fürsorglichen Kranich mit dem Stein, hatte Joseph um 1839 als Siegel eingeführt. Er initiiert oder fördert Ausbildungs- und Erziehungsstiftungen der Jüdischen Gemeinde, das erste bürgerliche Theater, den Zoologischen Garten, eine Gesellschaft für sozialen Wohnungsbau, eine Diskontbank für billige Kredite zugunsten Arbeitsloser. In Horchheim unterstützt er als Weingutsherr seine Pächter durch Finanzspritzen, die Ausbildung eines begabten Klavierbauers und den Bau der Dorfschule (1840/1846).

Zum 72. Geburtstag Joseph Mendelssohns in Horchheim am 15. August 1842:

Glücklich! wen wie Dich der Vater lehrte,
Gott erkennen und des Menschen Pflicht:
Glücklich! dem der Vater selbst bewährte,
was pathetisch oft der Mund nur spricht.
In dem Phädon blüht der Seele Wonne,
denn unsterblich strahlt ja dort die Sonne,
Welche leuchtend in des Zweiflers Brust
zieht des Himmels Licht und seel'ge Lust!

Und des hochbegabten Vaters Lehren
hast bewährt Du treu im Leben fort.
Hier durch Rath und That getrocknet Zähren,
warst Du stets der Armen Schirm und Hort.
Ja verkannte Armuth auszuspähen,
nicht zu Warten auf das laute Flehen,
Das versteht und übt der ältste Sohn,
des berühmten Moses Mendelssohn!

Sey gegrüßt und uns am Rhein willkommen,
edler Greis am heut'gen Jubeltag!
Froh sind wir bewegt, und fast beklommen,
Was das Herz Dir dankbar zeigen mag.
Möge Gott fortan auf Deinen Wegen
Dich begnad'gen mit dem reichsten Segen,
Bis der Abendstern des Lebens sinkt,
und zum Vater Dir der Engel winkt!

Das Kuratorium der Moses Mendelssohn-Stiftung zur Förderung der Geisteswissenschaften 1930 vor dem Wörlitzer Schloß. Mit dem Dessauer Flugzeugbauer Hugo Junkers (3.v.l.), Robert von Mendelssohn d.J. (4.v.l.), rechts daneben Marie von Mendelssohn und der Philosoph Eduard Spranger, schräg hinter diesem Präsident Franz von Mendelssohn d.J. und der Architekt Walter Gropius, rechts davon der Schriftsteller Arnold Zweig (mit Fliege).

The Board of Trustees of the Moses Mendelssohn Foundation for the Promotion of the Liberal Arts, assembled before Wörlitz Palace in 1930. With the Dessau-based aircraft manufacturer Hugo Junkers (3rd from left), Robert von Mendelssohn Jr. (4th from left), to his right Marie von Mendelssohn and the philosopher Eduard Spranger, angled behind him Franz von Mendelssohn Jr. as President and the architect Walter Gropius, to his right Arnold Zweig (with bow tie).

Alexander von Humboldt (1769 – 1859). Die Kreditierung der Humboldt-Reisen ab 1799 und späterer Forschungen erfolgte durch Mendelssohn & Co., ebenso weitgehend eine finanzielle Buchführung für den Gelehrten. Als dem Mieter von Humboldt 1844 seine Wohnung Oranienburger Straße 67 gekündigt wurde, kaufte Joseph Mendelssohn spontan das Haus, um dem Freund mit der gewaltigen Bibliothek den Umzug zu ersparen.
Öl auf Leinwand (1806) von Friedrich Georg Weitsch.

Alexander von Humboldt (1769 – 1859). As of 1799, Humboldt's travels and subsequent research were financed by Mendelssohn & Co; the bank also kept most of his financial records. In 1844, after von Humboldt had lost the lease to his flat at Oranienburger Strasse 67, Joseph Mendelssohn decided on an impulse to buy the building, so as to spare his friend the effort of relocating along with his huge library.
Oil on canvas (1806) by Friedrich Georg Weitsch.

Postkarte aus Horchheim mit Ansichten des Mendelssohn-Gutshauses als Diakonissen-Heim (1910).

Post card from Horchheim with views of the Mendelssohn manor house, now in use as a residence for deaconesses (1910).

Der Kranich mit Stein als Briefsiegel der Familie Mendelssohn.

The crane clutching the pebble as a letter seal of the Mendelssohn family.

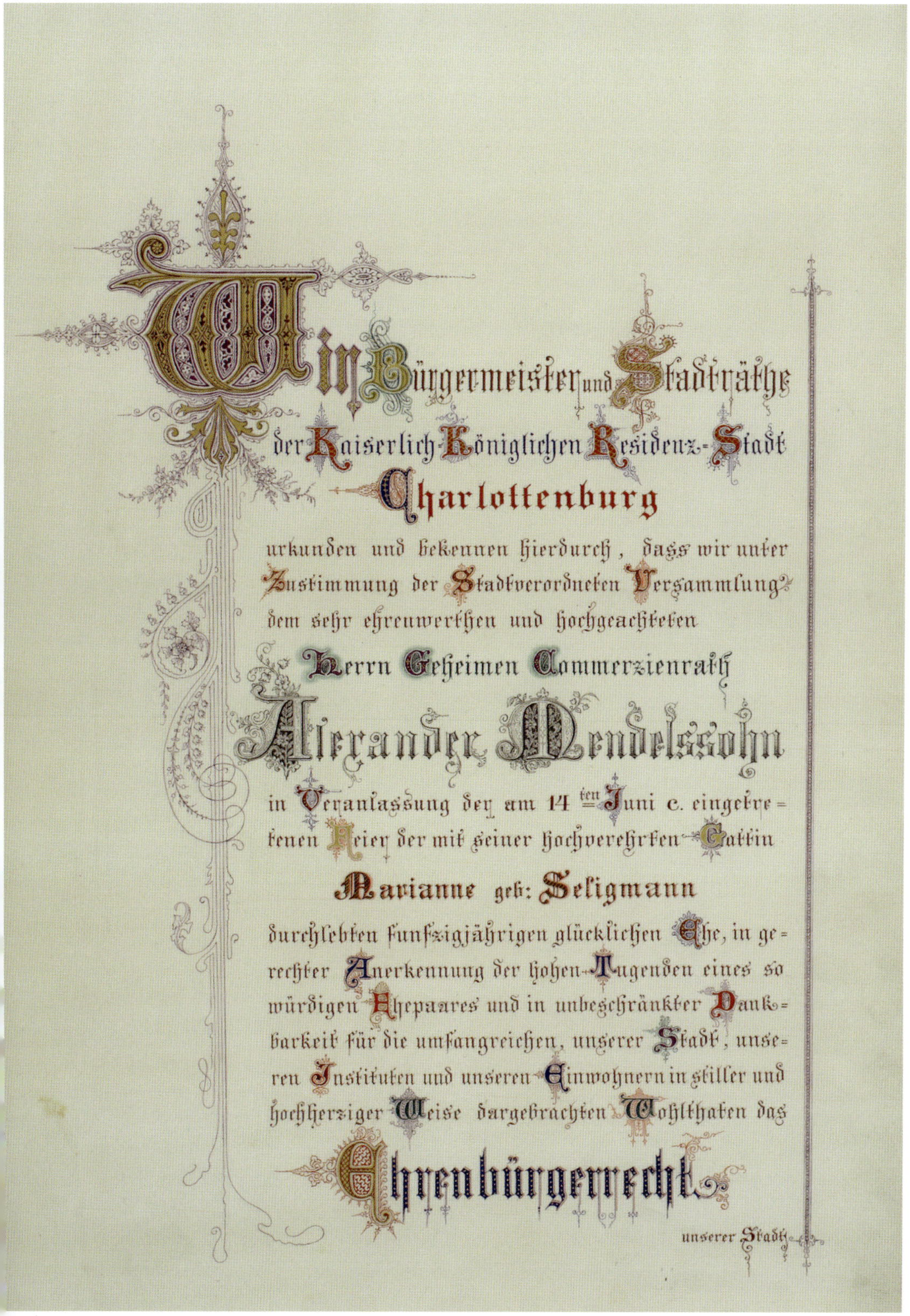

Wir Bürgermeister und Stadträthe
der Kaiserlich-Königlichen Residenz-Stadt
Charlottenburg
urkunden und bekennen hierdurch, dass wir unter Zustimmung der Stadtverordneten Versammlung dem sehr ehrenwerthen und hochgeachteten
Herrn Geheimen Commerzienrath
Alexander Mendelssohn
in Veranlassung der am 14ten Juni c. eingetretenen Feier der mit seiner hochverehrten Gattin
Marianne geb: Seligmann
durchlebten funfzigjährigen glücklichen Ehe, in gerechter Anerkennung der hohen Tugenden eines so würdigen Ehepaares und in unbeschränkter Dankbarkeit für die umfangreichen, unserer Stadt, unseren Instituten und unseren Einwohnern in stiller und hochherziger Weise dargebrachten Wohlthaten das
Ehrenbürgerrecht
unserer Stadt

Ehrenbürgerbrief der Stadt Charlottenburg für die Wohltäter Alexander und Marianne Mendelssohn anläßlich ihrer Goldenen Hochzeit (1871).

Letter from the City of Charlottenburg conferring honorary citizenship on the philanthropists Alexander and Marianne Mendelssohn, on the occasion of their golden wedding anniversary (1871).

Preserved for Posterity: A Symphony of Signals

By the music they composed and the texts they wrote, the descendants of Moses Mendelssohn have left us impressions and reflections of their world, stories about the times that, for them, were new. Drawing upon literally thousands of letters, compositions, notebooks, manuscripts, editions, autographs, and typescripts gleaned from private and public archives, this exhibition presents a collage of communication, news about life over the course of two centuries.

Was war und was bleibt: Sinfonie der Signale

Mit Noten und Texten haben Moses Mendelssohns Nachkommen Eindrücke und Reflexionen von ihrer Welt weitergegeben, Geschichten ihrer Neuen Zeit. Aus tausenden von Briefen und Kompositionen, von Notizen, Manuskripten und Editionen, von Autographen und Typoskripten, die in privaten und öffentlichen Archiven verwahrt werden, zeigt die Ausstellung eine Collage der Kommunikation, Mitteilungen über das Leben in zwei Jahrhunderten.

Fenster an der Südseite der Leipziger Thomaskirche: Johann Sebastian Bach (eingebaut nach 1889) und Felix Mendelssohn Bartholdy (eingebaut 1997).

Window on the south side of Leipzig's Thomaskirche: Johann Sebastian Bach (installed after 1889) and Felix Mendelssohn Bartholdy (installed 1997).

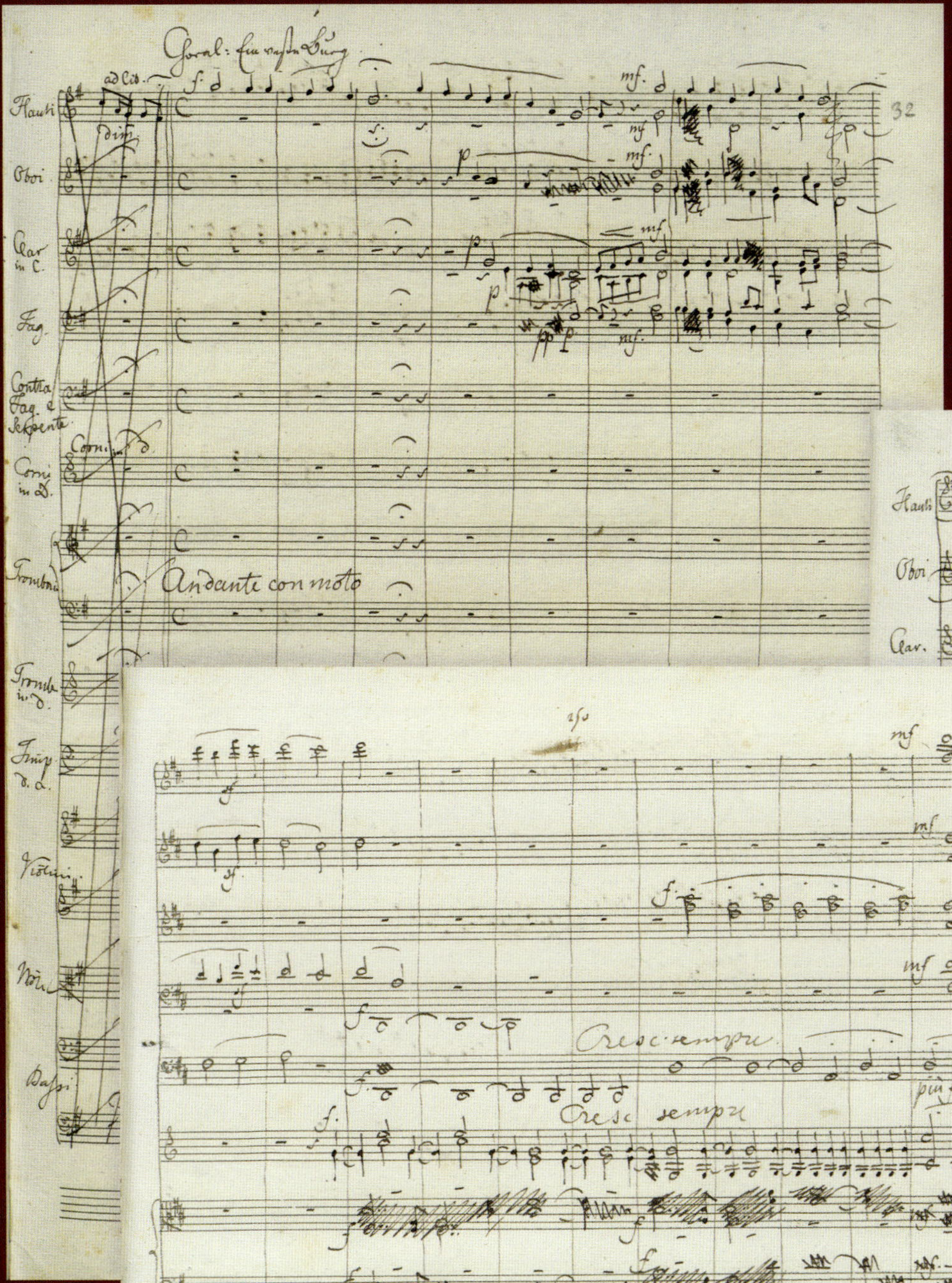

Felix Mendelssohn Bartholdy: „Reformations-Sinfonie“ (1830) zur 400-Jahrfeier der „Confessio Augustana“ von 1530.

Felix Mendelssohn Bartholdy: “Reformation Symphony” (1830) composed for the 400-year anniversary of the “Confessio Augustana” of 1530.

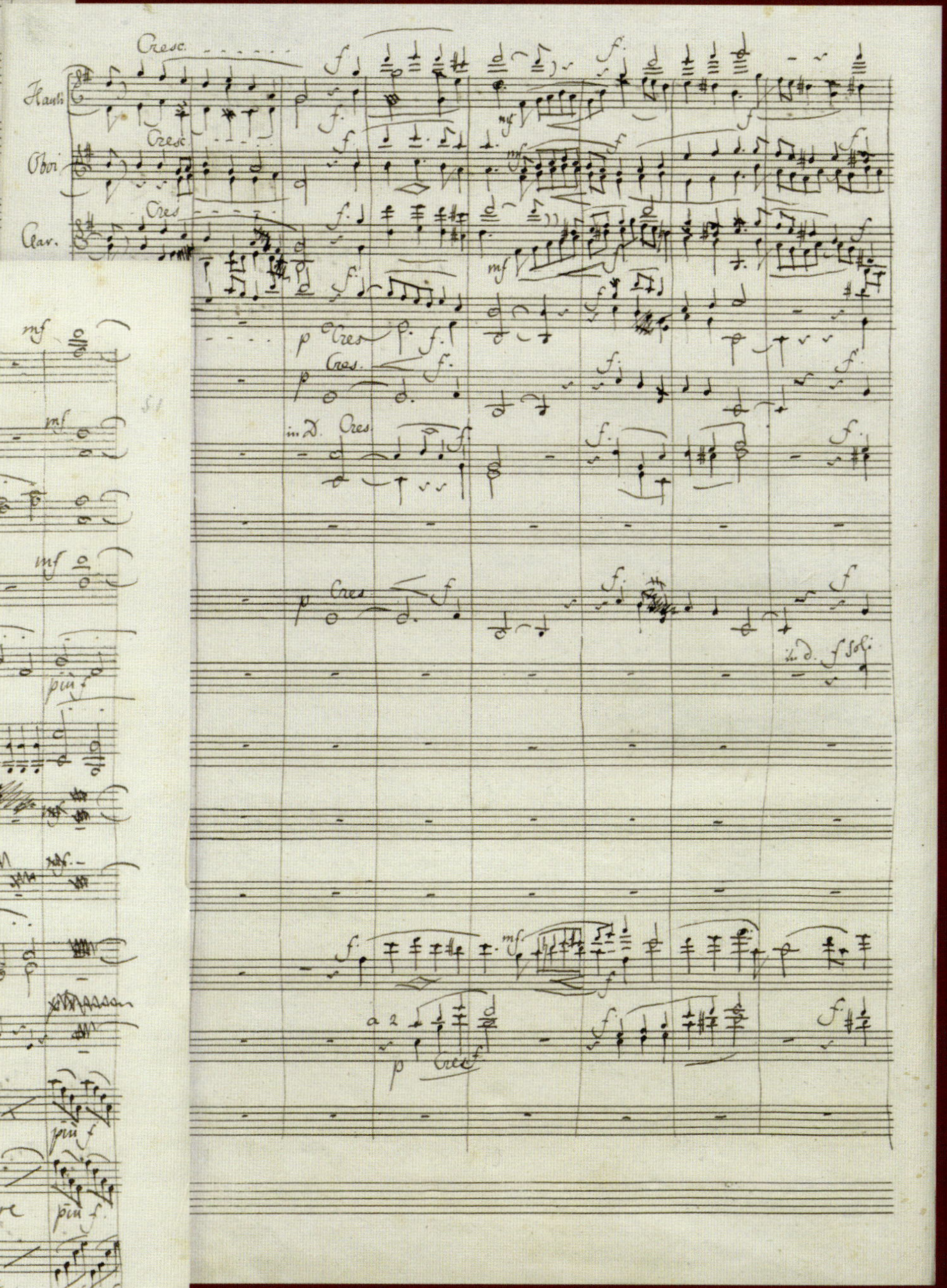

Fanny Hensel: Quartett Es-dur (1829 –1834). Inspiriert von einer unvollendeten Klaviersonate – und ihre Antwort auf op.12 des Bruders Felix.

Fanny Hensel: Quartet in E flat major (1829 – 1834). This work was inspired by an unfinished piano sonata – and her answer to her brother Felix' Opus 12.

„Meine Liebste", ein Text von Max Dauthendey, vertont von Albrecht Mendelssohn Bartholdy in seiner Hamburger Zeit (1931). Das Autograph gehört zu einer Liedersammlung Mendelssohn Bartholdys, die 2006 im Nachlaß seiner 1937 aus Deutschland emigrierten Mitarbeiterin Magdalena Schoch in Arlington (Virginia) aufgefunden wurde.

"My Most Beloved," a text by Max Dauthendey, set to music by Albrecht Mendelssohn Bartholdy during his Hamburg period (1931). The autograph belongs to a collection of *Lieder* by Mendelssohn Bartholdy that was discovered in Arlington, VA in 2006 among the estate of Magdalena Schoch, an associate of the composer who had emigrated to the United States in 1931.

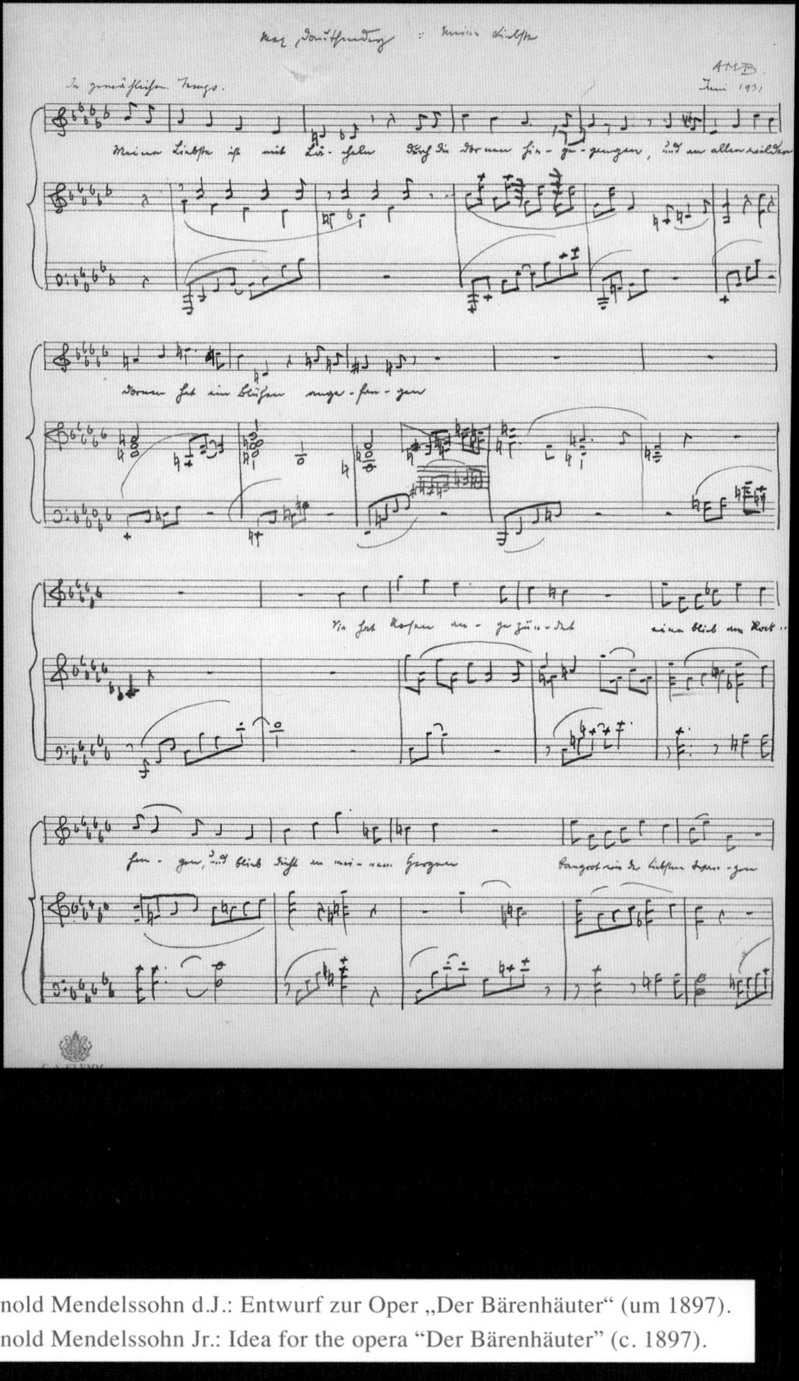

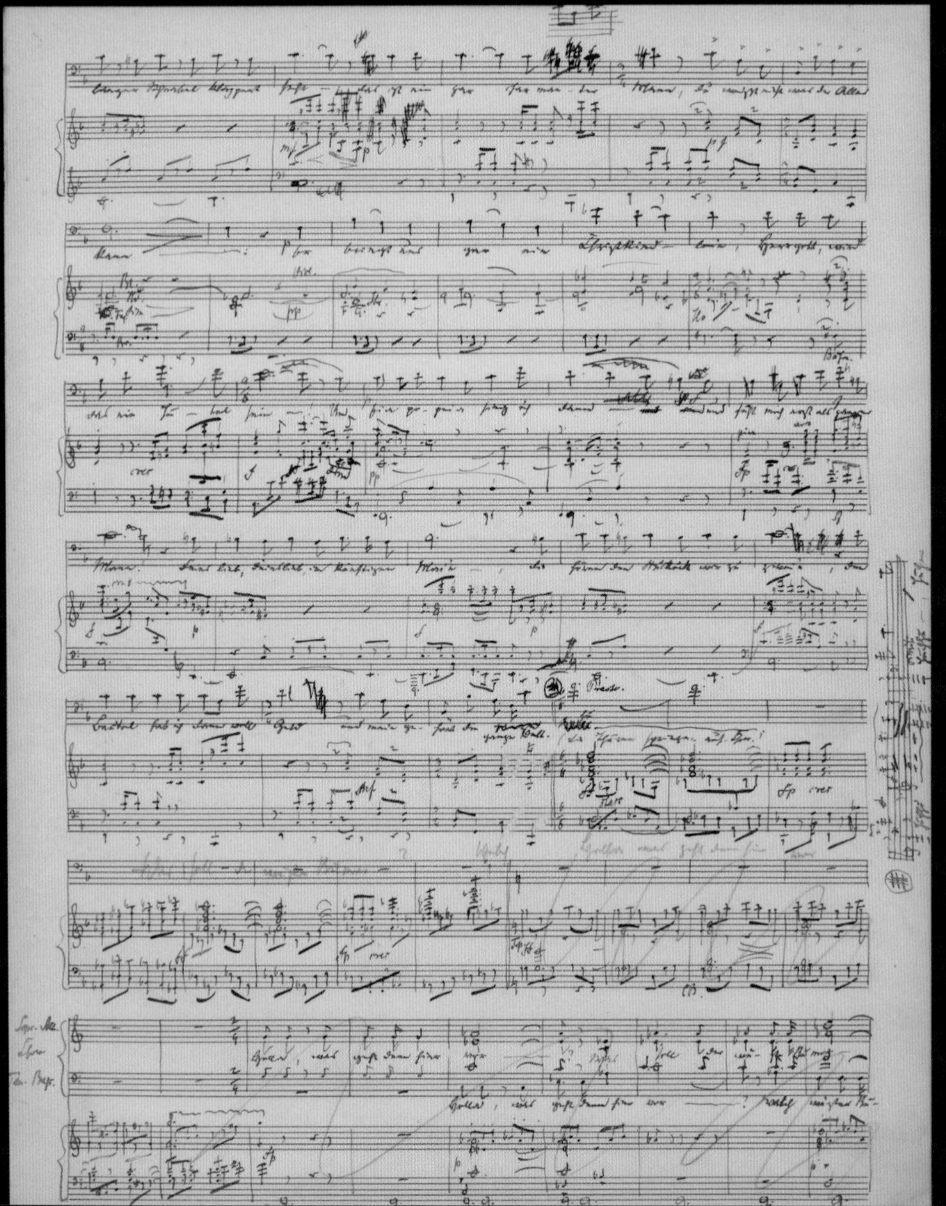

Arnold Mendelssohn d.J.: Entwurf zur Oper „Der Bärenhäuter" (um 1897).

Arnold Mendelssohn Jr.: Idea for the opera "Der Bärenhäuter" (c. 1897).

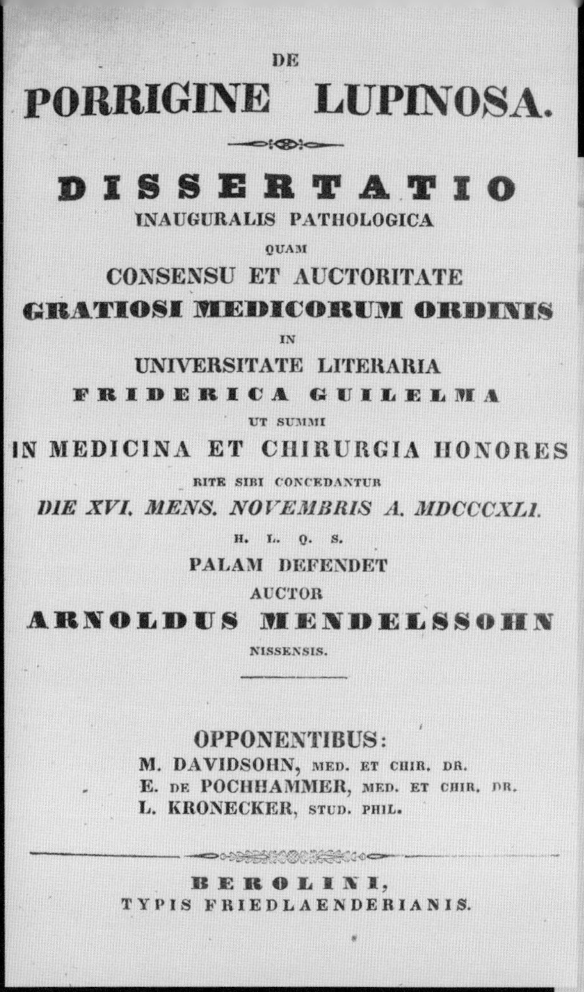

DE

PORRIGINE LUPINOSA.

DISSERTATIO
INAUGURALIS PATHOLOGICA
QUAM
CONSENSU ET AUCTORITATE
GRATIOSI MEDICORUM ORDINIS
IN
UNIVERSITATE LITERARIA
FRIDERICA GUILELMA
UT SUMMI
IN MEDICINA ET CHIRURGIA HONORES
RITE SIBI CONCEDANTUR
DIE XVI. MENS. NOVEMBRIS A. MDCCCXLI.
H. L. Q. S.
PALAM DEFENDET
AUCTOR
ARNOLDUS MENDELSSOHN
NISSENSIS.

OPPONENTIBUS:
M. DAVIDSOHN, MED. ET CHIR. DR.
E. DE POCHHAMMER, MED. ET CHIR. DR.
L. KRONECKER, STUD. PHIL.

BEROLINI,
TYPIS FRIEDLAENDERIANIS.

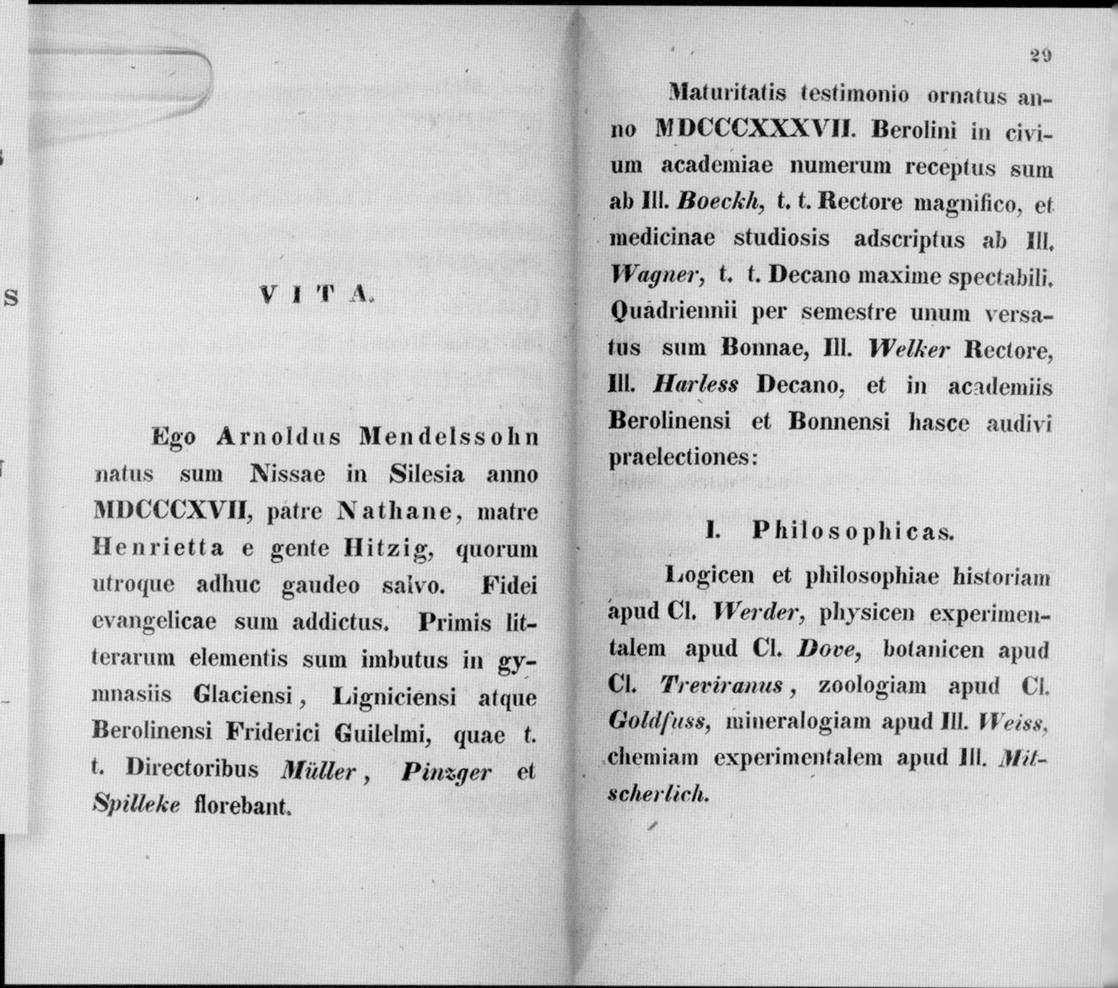

VITA.

Ego Arnoldus Mendelssohn natus sum Nissae in Silesia anno MDCCCXVII, patre Nathane, matre Henrietta e gente Hitzig, quorum utroque adhuc gaudeo salvo. Fidei evangelicae sum addictus. Primis litterarum elementis sum imbutus in gymnasiis Glaciensi, Ligniciensi atque Berolinensi Friderici Guilelmi, quae t. t. Directoribus *Müller*, *Pinzger* et *Spilleke* florebant.

29

Maturitatis testimonio ornatus anno MDCCCXXXVII. Berolini in civium academiae numerum receptus sum ab Ill. *Boeckh*, t. t. Rectore magnifico, et medicinae studiosis adscriptus ab Ill. *Wagner*, t. t. Decano maxime spectabili. Quadriennii per semestre unum versatus sum Bonnae, Ill. *Welker* Rectore, Ill. *Harless* Decano, et in academiis Berolinensi et Bonnensi hasce audivi praelectiones:

I. Philosophicas.

Logicen et philosophiae historiam apud Cl. *Werder*, physicen experimentalem apud Cl. *Dove*, botanicen apud Cl. *Treviranus*, zoologiam apud Cl. *Goldfuss*, mineralogiam apud Ill. *Weiss*, chemiam experimentalem apud Ill. *Mitscherlich*.

Arnold Mendelssohn d.Ä.: „De Porrigine Lupinosa" (Über den Erbgrind), 1841. Die Dissertation des späteren Armenarztes, Revolutionärs und Exulanten.

Arnold Mendelssohn the Elder: Medical dissertation, "De Porrigine Lupinosa" (On Favus), 1841. Arnold would later become a physician to the poor, a social revolutionary and, ultimately, an exile.

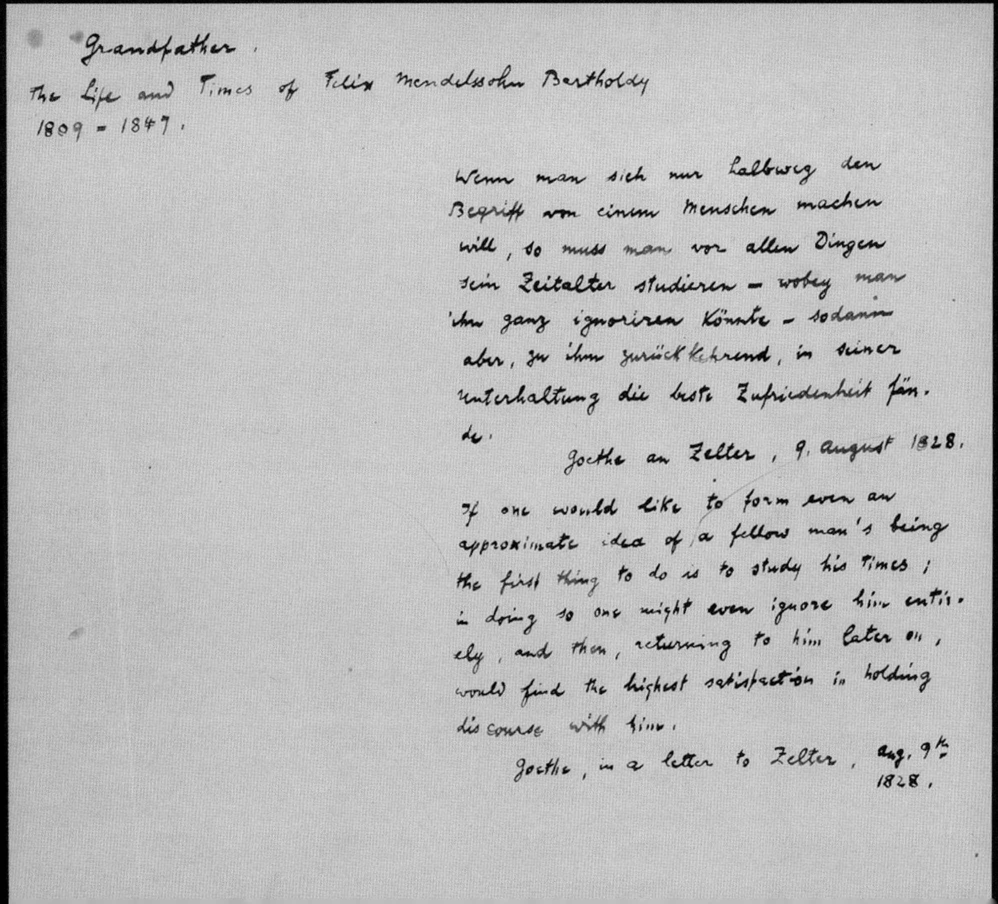

Grandfather.
The Life and Times of Felix Mendelssohn Bartholdy
1809 – 1847.

Wenn man sich nur halbweg den Begriff von einem Menschen machen will, so muss man vor allen Dingen sein Zeitalter studieren – wobey man ihn ganz ignoriren könnte – sodann aber, zu ihm zurückkehrend, in seiner Unterhaltung die beste Zufriedenheit finde.

Goethe an Zelter, 9. August 1828.

If one would like to form even an approximate idea of a fellow man's being the first thing to do is to study his times; in doing so one might even ignore him entirely, and then, returning to him later on, would find the highest satisfaction in holding discourse with him.

Goethe, in a letter to Zelter, Aug. 9th 1828.

Albrecht Mendelssohn Bartholdy: „Grandfather. The Life and Times of Felix Mendelssohn Bartholdy." Manuskriptseite zur Familiengeschichte, mit Goethe-Zitat.

Albrecht Mendelssohn Bartholdy: "Grandfather. The Life and Times of Felix Mendelssohn Bartholdy." The page of the family history manuscript containing the quote by Goethe.

Nathan Mendelssohn: Tagebuch aus den Befreiungskriegen (1813). Auf dem Weg nach Weimar, wo er Goethes „Götz von Berlichingen“ im Theater sieht, begegnet der Leutnant „höllischem Schneegestöber“, viele tote Pferde liegen am Weg (10.12.).

Nathan Mendelssohn: Diary from the Wars of Liberation (1813). On his way to Weimar, where he was to attend a theater performance of Goethe's "Götz von Berlichingen," the Lieutenant reports that he ran into a "hellish blizzard" with many dead horses on the road (December 10).

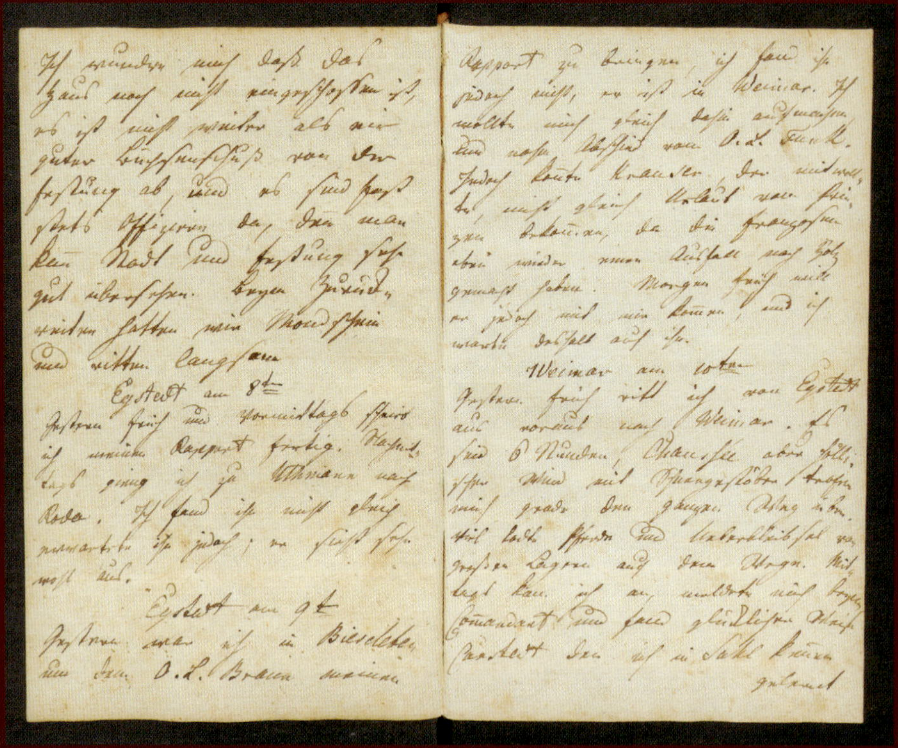

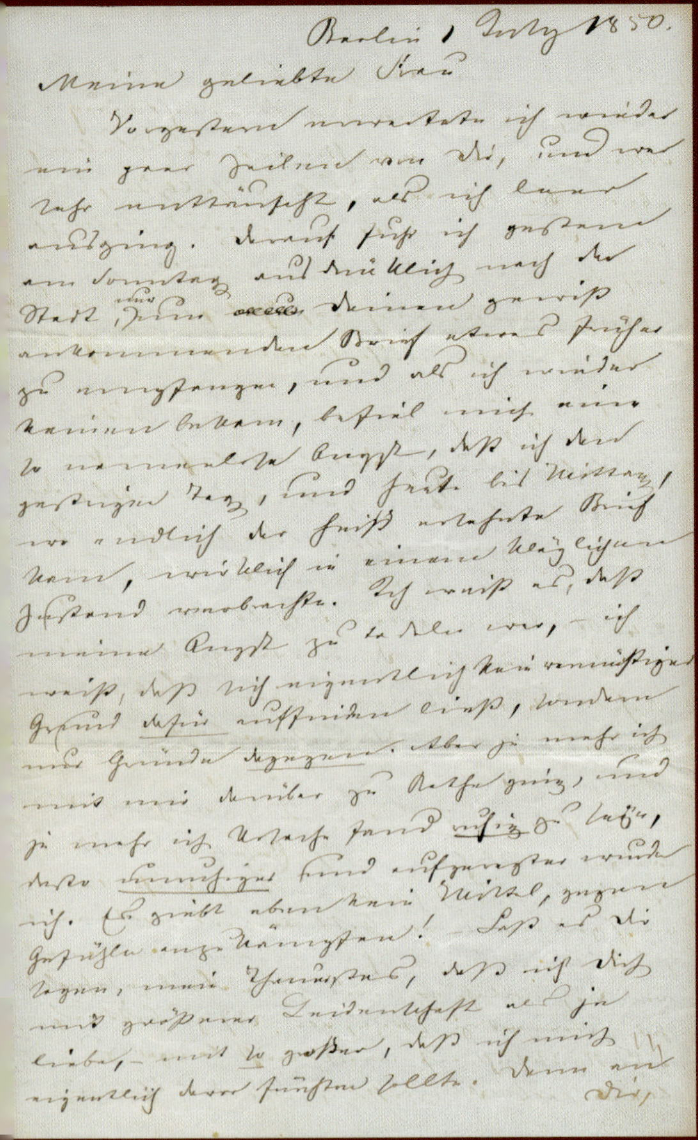

Paul Mendelssohn Bartholdy: „Dieser Brief sieht fast aus, wie ein Liebesbrief. Verzeih es.“ 15 Jahre nach seiner Eheschließung verfaßt der Bankier ein leidenschaftliches Schreiben an seine zur Kur verreiste Frau Albertine (1. Juli 1850). Seit ihrer Hochzeit haben beide den Tod der Eltern, mehrerer Geschwister, den Verlust eines neugeborenen Kinders miteinander durchgestanden. Der Tod ihrer Ältesten, Pauline, im Alter von 19 Jahren steht ihnen noch bevor.

Paul Mendelssohn Bartholdy: "This letter nearly seems to have turned out a love letter. Forgive me." Fifteen years after having married Albertine, the banker sent a passionate letter to his wife on July 1, 1850, when she was away taking the waters. In the years following their wedding, they went through the deaths of their parents and numerous siblings, as well as the loss of a newborn child. At this point, their daughter Pauline was still alive; she would die at the age of 19.

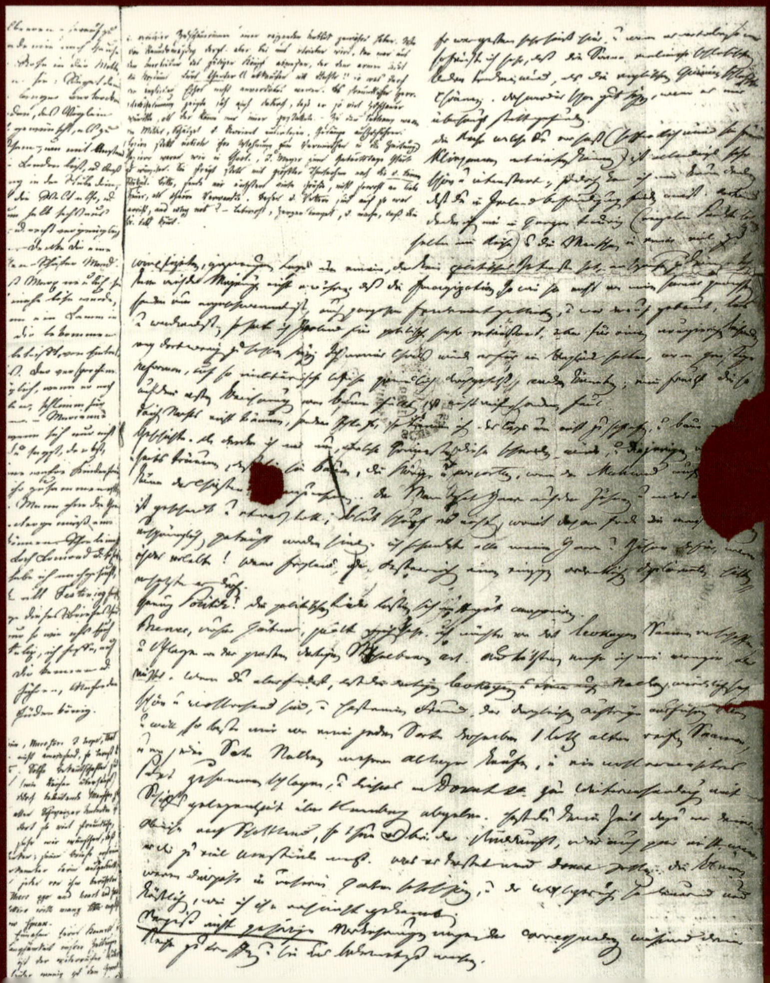

„Familienbrief“ der Mendelssohn Bartholdys über Klatsch, Reisepläne und Politik: an den Bruder und Sohn Felix in London, 13. Juli 1829. Fanny hat auf Seite 1 begonnen, gefolgt auf Seite 2 von Rebecka (links angeschnitten), von Mutter Lea mit winziger, von Vater Abraham mit ausladender Schrift.

Letter from all the members of the Mendelssohn Bartholdy family reporting the latest in gossip, travel plans, and political events to their brother and son Felix in London, dated July 13, 1829. Fanny started the letter on page 1, followed by Rebecka on page 2 (cut off on the left-hand side), and then by mother Lea's tiny handwriting and father Abraham's expansive cursive.

Franz von Mendelssohn d.J.: Konfirmationsaufsatz (um 1879). „ ... ich glaube an die unwandelbare, weltregierende Liebe in Gott ... Den Glauben an die Einheit Gottes haben die Juden zuerst besessen und ihn trotz aller Anfechtung der Polytheisten tapfer verteidigt und bewahrt."

Franz von Mendelssohn Jr.: Confirmation essay (c. 1879). " ... I believe in the immutable, all-governing love that is in God ... The Jews were the first to hold the faith in the unity of God, and they courageously defended and upheld it against all attacks by polytheists."

Glaubensbekenntnis von Franz Mendelssohn

I. Ich glaube an Gott den Vater, allmächtigen Schöpfer Himmels und der Erden, d. h. ich glaube an die unwandelbare, weltregierende Liebe in Gott.

Gott ist der verborgene, offenbare, der einige, der unendliche Gott. Er ist nicht zu ergründen, nicht zu erkennen. Kein Mensch wird jemals das Geheimnis seines Daseins aufdecken, denn es ist unmöglich, daß der enge Menschengeist das volle Verständnis des unendlichen Gottes gewinnt. Doch offenbart er sich meinem Verstande, der mich nötigt, einen letzten Urgrund für das Weltall anzunehmen, und meinem Herzen, das einen liebenden Vater im Himmel fordert, vor Allem aber erkenne ich ihn aus dem Leben Jesu Christi, in welchem er sich vollkommen offenbart. Den Glauben an die

Aus dem während des Eichmann-Prozesses begonnenen Briefwechsel zwischen Hannah Arendt und Leni Yahil, geb. Westphal.

From the correspondence, begun during the Eichmann Trial, between Hannah Arendt and Leni Yahil, née Westphal.

370 Riverside Drive New York 25 N.Y.

Jerusalem- Katamon, 21/3/63
4 Hamaapilim St.

Liebe Hannah Arendt,

die Verbindung zwischen uns ist abgerissen oder eingeschlafen - wie immer Sie es nennen wollen, und von mir aus hätte ich so nichts dazu getan, um sie wieder anzuknüpfen. Nun zwingen mich Ihre Artikel - fast möchte ich sagen: gegen besseres Wissen und Gewissen - doch eine Frage an Sie zu richten.

Ich las bisher nur 4 Artikel, der 5. kam noch nicht in meine Hand, aber das ist eine Frage von Tagen, und er wird ja kaum prinzipiell Neues bringen, mehr die Schlussfolgerungen aus all den vorigen. Ich will Ihnen hier nicht beschreiben, welchen Eindruck Ihre Angriffe und Darstellungen hier machen - das werden Sie - wenn es Ihnen nicht übermittelt wird - sich wohl selbst vorstellen können. Ich will Ihnen auch nicht meine Meinung, Analyse, allgemeine und persönliche Reaktion vorsetzen - ich weiss nicht, wie weit Sie daran interessiert sind und in einem Brief ist kaum dafür Raum. Ich will auch nicht auf Ihre Darstellung der skandinavischen Ereignisse im allgemeinen und der dänischen im besonderen eingehen - obwohl ich dazu manches zu sagen hätte.

Ich möchte, wie gesagt, eine Frage an Sie richten: was war, resp. ist, Ihre eigene innerste Absicht, die Sie mit ihnen verfolgen? Wem glauben Sie damit zu dienen: der historischen Wahrheit? Der Gerechtigkeit? Der Gegenwart oder der Zukunft des deutschen oder des jüdischen Volkes? Oder wollen Sie speziell von dem letzteren xxxx beweisen, dass es nicht wert ist oder geeignet ist als Volk unter den Völkern zu existieren? Ich frage Sie im Ernst, nicht polemisch, ich versteh es nicht.

Ich bin einer der wenigen Kommentatoren, der bei Ihnen mit einer guten Note, sozusagen, davonkommt. Womit ich das verdient habe, weiss ich nicht recht, schliesslich habe ich noch nichts Geschlossenes vorgelegt, und es dürfte Ihnen bekannt sein, dass meine Gesammteinstellung und grundsätzliche Haltung nicht unbedingt so verschieden ist von der derjenigen, die von Ihnen so hart angeprangert werden.

Es steht Ihnen natürlich frei, auf meine Frage zu antworten - oder nicht. Der ganze Problemkomplex ragt so weit aus dem persönlichen Bereich heraus, dass ich eine Nicht-Reaktion Ihrerseits nicht weiter persönlich auffassen würde.

Ich hoffe, dieser Brief wird Sie irgendwann in nicht zu ferner Zukunft erreichen. Ich habe ja keine Ahnung, ob Sie z.Zt. in N.Y. sind oder irgendwo anders.

Mit besten Grüssen

Jerusalem-Katamon, 30/4/63
4 Ha maapilim Street

So einfach, Hannah, wie Sie sich, umgeben von Schönheit und klassischer Harmonie, die Dinge machen wollen, sind sie leider nicht. Was das "Bocken" angeht - warum sollten Sie das tun? Bocken tun Kinder (und nicht selten auch sogenannte Erwachsene), die wissen, dass Sie im Unrecht sind, es aber nicht zugeben können oder wollen. Sie aber sind doch wohl nicht nur der Meinung, dass Sie recht haben, sondern auch, dass Sie das Recht haben, alles das zu sagen, was Sie da in Ihren Artikeln ausgesprochen haben.

Noch bevor ich Ihre Antwort erhielt, hatte ich beschlossen, die Diskussion in dem Raum auszutragen, in den sie gehört, nämlich dem öffentlichen. Inzwischen habe ich einen guten Teil des Artikels schon geschrieben. Es scheint sich schwer vermeiden zu lassen, dass er ziemlich umfangreich wird. Wer ihn mir drucken wird, weiss ich noch nicht, aber das wird sich finden.

Für das Streiten ist also gesorgt. Ob wir danach noch Freunde bleiben können, oder besser gesagt: wieder werden können, wird sich weisen . Ich glaube nicht, dass die Melodie, die ich "an meinen fünf intelligenten Fingern abklaviere", Ihren Ohren übermässig angenehmsein wird, jedenfalls ist das nicht meine Absicht.

Ich weiss nicht, ob Sie sich noch erinnern, dass ich Ihnen zu Ihrer ersten Abreise hier eines jener jemenitischen alten Stücke, eine Hand, schenkte. Sie schrieben mir damals:"....Ausserdem ist es natürlich genau die Hand, die mir das Land diesmal entgegenhielt und die ich manchmal nahm und manchmal wegschob und auf die Sie mich nun doch verpflichten wollen." Es dürfte Ihnen wohl klar sein, dass Sie diese Hand jetzt sehr heftig weggestossen haben. Ob Sie Ihnen, selbst wenn Sie daran einmal interessiert sein sollten, je wieder geboten werden wird, ist schwer abzusehen, z.Zt. jedenfalls kaum anzunehmen - trotz der Veröffentlichungen aus dem Artikel-Buch durch den "Haarez".

Soviel für heute. Das übrige werden Sie, hoffe ich, gedruckt lesen können, auch dort nicht alles, aber immerhin einen beträchtlichen Teil. Dass ich diese Entwicklung von allen Gesichtspunkten, allgemeinen wie persönlichen, tief bedaure, mögen Sie mir glauben. Und wenn schon sonst nichts, wird Sie vielleicht die Schärfe meiner Antwort davon überzeugen. Vielleicht entdecken Sie eines Tages, dass Sie zwar keine unausgesprochenen Absichten mit dieser Anklageschrift hatten aber unbewusste? Wie tief reicht Ihre Selbstkritik?

Bis auf weiteres.......

The musical side of the family saga begins with Moses Mendelssohn's piano studies under the tutelage of Johann Philipp Kirnberger, a Saxon composer, violinist and collector of Bach manuscripts. Moses' passion for music becomes evident in his aesthetic philosophy: "O divine art of music! Thou art the only one that surprises us with all sorts of delights! What a sweet confusion of perfection, sensuous rapture and beauty!" ("On Sentiment," 1755). Moses was interested in music mainly for its ability to reinforce man's rational moral sense, but also enjoyed singing psalms. Working together, Moses and Kirnberger conducted experiments on measuring the effects of sound. Kirnberger was also music tutor to Lea Salomon, a granddaughter of the Itzigs; Lea would later marry Abraham Mendelssohn and make "playing the well-tempered piano part of her household's constant routine" (Adolph Bernhard Marx). Just like his aunt Lea, a devotee of Bach, and many subsequent descendants, Abraham joined the Sing-Akademie, the world's first mixed choir, while still an adolescent. During his years of schooling in Paris, Abraham would also become a lover of opera.

His wife Lea gave their children Fanny and Felix their first music lessons on the piano, a task later assumed by renowned pianists and composers such as Franz Seraphikus Lauska, Marie Bigot, Ludwig Berger, Johann Nepomuk Hummel, and Ignaz Moscheles. The children's composition teacher was Sing-Akademie Director Carl Friedrich Zelter. The Sunday recitals of the child prodigies at the family residence became significant cultural and social events.

Fanny Hensel, née Mendelssohn, left behind over 450 works. More than half are Lieder for solo voice, followed by pieces for piano, organ, orchestra, and chamber ensembles, as well as cantatas and an oratorio. Fanny's ambitions were viewed skeptically by her father and by her brother Felix, who edited some of her early Lieder. Fanny's first work under her own name, "Ave Maria," was printed in England. This was followed by six albums of Lieder and piano pieces in 1846/1847. Particularly adept in smaller compositional formats, Fanny captivated audiences at the Sunday recitals held in the garden room of the Leipziger Strasse residence. Here, between 1825 and 1847, she performed together with professional and amateur musicians drawn from family and friends, presenting her own works, those of her brother and other contemporaries. Cantatas by Bach were a particular favorite.

Den Auftakt macht Johann Philipp Kirnberger, ein sächsischer Komponist und Geiger, der Bach-Noten sammelt und dem Ästhetiker Moses Klavierstunden gibt. „Göttliche Tonkunst! Du bist die einzige, die uns mit allen Arten von Vergnügen überrascht! Welch süße Verwirrung von Vollkommenheit, sinnlicher Lust und Schönheit!" hatte Mendelssohn schon 1755 gejubelt („Über die Empfindungen"). Ihn interessiert Musik als emotionale Verstärkung vernunftgeleiteter Moral, er singt aber auch Psalmen. Gemeinsam betreiben der Philosoph und der Musiktheoretiker Forschungen zur Berechnung klingender Effekte. Kirnberger unterrichtet ebenso die Itzig-Enkelin Lea Salomon, welche später als Ehefrau des Mendelssohn-Sprosses Abraham „das unausgesetzte Spiel des temperierten Klavieres ihrem Hause eingepflanzt" (Adolph Bernhard Marx) hat. Abraham wiederum war schon als Jugendlicher Mitglied der Sing-Akademie, des ersten gemischten Chores, wie Leas Tante, die Bach-Verehrerin Sara Levy, und in der Folge zahlreiche Mendelssohn-Verwandte. Er wird während seiner Pariser Ausbildungsjahre zum Opernfan.

Mutter Lea unterrichtet ihre Kinder Fanny und Felix am Klavier, später übernehmen renommierte Pianisten und Tonsetzer die Aufgabe: Franz Seraphikus Lauska, Marie Bigot, Ludwig Berger, Johann Nepomuk Hummel, Ignaz Moscheles. Der Sing-Akademie-Direktor Zelter gibt Kompositionsunterricht. Die Sonntagsmusiken der beiden Ausnahmebegabungen in der elterlichen Wohnung werden zum künstlerischen, gesellschaftlichen Ereignis.

Von Fanny Hensel, geb. Mendelssohn, sind über 450 Werke erhalten, mehr als die Hälfte Lieder für Solostimme, außerdem Stücke für Klavier und Orgel, Chor, Orchester, instrumentale Kammermusik, Kantaten, ein Oratorium. Der Vater und Felix stehen ihren Wünschen, als Komponistin publik zu werden, skeptisch gegenüber. Einige ihrer frühen Lieder ediert der Bruder; Fannys erste namentliche Publikation „Ave Maria" wird in England gedruckt. Sechs Hefte mit Liedern und Klavierstücken erscheinen 1846/1847. Erfahrungen macht sie mit der kleinen Form, ihr Forum sind die anspruchsvollen Sonntagsmusiken im Gartensaal an der Leipziger Straße. Hier führt sie zwischen 1825 und 1847, mit Profis und Amateuren aus Familie und Bekanntschaft, neben eigenen Werken, denen des Bruders und weiterer Zeitgenossen vor allem Bach-Kantaten auf.

Die Sing-Akademie am Festungsgraben. Zeichnung von Adolf Becker (1830).
In dem 1828 fertiggestellten Gebäude für den weltweit ersten gemischten Chor fand beim Naturforscherkongreß auch die Uraufführung der dafür komponierten „Humboldt-Kantate" von Felix Mendelssohn Bartholdy statt (1828) sowie dessen Wiederaufführung der Matthäus-Passion (1829).

The Sing-Akademie at the Festungsgraben. Drawing by Adolf Becker (1830).
The concert hall was completed in 1828 to house the world's first mixed chorus. This is also where Felix Mendelssohn Bartholdy premiered his "Humboldt Cantata" (specially composed for the Congress of Natural Scientists that met there), as well as his revival of Bach's St. Matthew's Passion (1829).

Johann Philipp Kirnberger (1721 – 1783), Musiktheoretiker.
Bildnis von Heinrich Eduard Winter.

Johann Philipp Kirnberger (1721 – 1783), music theorist.
Portrait by Heinrich Eduard Winter.

Sara Levy (1761 – 1854), Pianistin, Salonière und Großtante der Geschwister Mendelssohn Bartholdy. Lithographie von P. Rohrbach.

Sara Levy (1761 – 1854), pianist, salon hostess, and great-aunt of the Mendelssohn Bartholdy siblings. Lithograph by P. Rohrbach.

Felix Mendelssohn Bartholdy als Kind am Klavier.
Zeichnung von Wilhelm Hensel (um 1820).

Felix Mendelssohn Bartholdy at the piano as a child.
Drawing by Wilhelm Hensel (c. 1820).

Fanny Hensel: „Ave Maria." Vertonung des Textes von Walter Scott. Erste Publikation eines Werkes der Komponistin unter ihrem Namen (in der Londoner Musikzeitschrift „The Marmonicon", 1834).

Fanny Hensel: "Ave Maria." Musical setting of a text by Walter Scott. This was the first of Fanny's compositions published under her own name (in the London music journal "The Marmonicon," 1834).

Ludwig Berger (1777 – 1839), Komponist, Pianist, Klavierpädagoge. Zeichnung von Philipp Otto Runge.

Ludwig Berger (1777 – 1839), composer, pianist, piano teacher. Drawing by Philipp Otto Runge.

Reise-Album.
1839-1840.
Fanny
Wilhelm
Hensel.
Deutschland --- Italien.

Nach Süden.
Allegro molto vivace.

"A voice that seemed to come from her innermost depths"

Playing the role of hostess, director and pianist in front of 250 to 300 friends, artists, intellectuals, and other guests from Berlin society, Fanny rose to the task with her intelligence, wit, warm-heartedness, and keen critical standards; yet she chose to appear in public at the piano only three times in Berlin. A skilled interpreter of Beethoven, she initially progressed faster than her brother, who admiringly compared her to a charismatic piano virtuoso in Milan: "No longer able at times to fully express the sound, she began to sing along with a voice that seemed to come from her innermost depths – which frequently made me think of you, my dear Fanny, though you are of course far better than she is" (1831).

Felix Mendelssohn Bartholdy's caring and outgoing personality, his many travels and his rich education are reflected in the diversity of the compositions he was able to complete in his 38-year-life. They included symphonies written in his youth, chamber music, orchestral works, oratorios, a large collection of *Lieder*, as well as piano and organ pieces ranging from fugues to subtle miniatures ("Songs without Words"). 750 compositions in all, they form a microcosm of the mature Romantic style, artfully executed and imbued with Felix' own refined sensibility, while also acknowledging the masters who had come before. Working in every genre except opera, Felix left behind masterworks and perennial repertory favorites, such as the theater music for "A Mid-Summer Night's Dream," the Italian and Scottish Symphonies, the oratorio "Elias," the octet, string quartets, and Violin Concerto No. 2, or the choral favorite "Abschied vom Walde," based on a poem by Eichendorff. He probably inspired more vocal ensembles than anyone else; in 1855, for example, the Mendelssohn Bartholdy Montabaur Men's Choir was named after him, at the suggestion of the Dernbacher nuns who lived on the Mendelssohn estate in Horchheim. Felix traveled to England no less than ten times, where he was received by Queen Victoria and where his fame became even greater than in Germany. He was enormously influential as an interpreter of Bach and Handel, while also creating the role of the modern orchestra conductor as we know him today.

„Eine Stimme, die so recht aus dem Inneren kommt"

Für ein Publikum aus bis zu 250, ja 300 Freunden, Künstlern, Gelehrten und anderen Gästen der Berliner Gesellschaft ist die kluge, witzige, warmherzige und kritische Fanny Veranstalterin, Dirigentin, Pianistin; öffentlich jedoch in Berlin nur dreimal am Flügel zu hören. Als starke Beethoven-Interpretin war sie dem Bruder zunächst voraus. Er vergleicht die Schwester mit einer faszinierenden Klaviervirtuosin in Mailand: „Wenn sie zuweilen gar nicht mehr den Ton herausdrücken kann u. nun dazu zu singen anfängt, mit einer Stimme, die so recht aus dem tiefsten Inneren heraufkommt, so hat sie mich oft an Dich, o Fanny, erinnert, obwohl Du ihr freilich weit überlegen bist" (1831).

Felix Mendelssohn Bartholdys sozial engagierte, kommunikative Persönlichkeit, seine Reise- und Bildungserfahrungen spiegeln sich in der Vielfalt des mit 38 Jahren vollendeten Lebenswerkes. Von seinen Jugendsinfonien und der Kammermusik über Orchesterstücke und Oratorien bis zum reichen Lied-Œuvre, dem Orgel- und Klavierwerk der Fugen und subtilen Miniaturen („Lieder ohne Worte") entwickelt er seinen romantischen Kosmos, 750 Kompositionen, in souveräner Auseinandersetzung mit großen Vorgängern. Für jedes Genre, außer der Oper, hinterläßt er Meisterwerke und Spielplan-Hits: Theatermusik zum „Sommernachtstraum", seine Italienische und die Schottische Sinfonie, das Oratorium „Elias", sein Oktett, Streichquartette, das Violinkonzert Nr. 2 und Chor-Dauerbrenner wie die Eichendorff-Vertonung „Abschied vom Walde". Er inspiriert die meisten Vokalensembles; der Männergesangverein Mendelssohn Bartholdy 1855 e.V. in Montabaur wählt ihn, angeregt durch die beim Mendelssohn-Gut Horchheim ansässigen Dernbacher Schwestern, zum Namenspatron. Zehnmal bereist er England, wo ihn die Queen empfängt, wo seine Spitzenpopularität den Heimatruhm noch übertrifft. Wegweisend ist er als Neuinterpret Bachs und Händels, stilbildend als erster Dirigent im heutigen Sinne.

Fanny Hensel: „Nach Süden." Aus dem Reisealbum 1839/1840. Vignette von Wilhelm Hensel.
Fanny Hensel: "To the South." From her Travel Album 1839/1840. Vignette by Wilhelm Hensel.

„Die Erste Walpurgisnacht“. Druck (1844) der Weltlichen Kantate von Felix Mendelssohn Bartholdy und J.W. von Goethe. Mit einer Widmung an den Freund Ignaz Moscheles. Die Uraufführung der Erstversion fand 1832 im Gartensaal der Leipziger Straße 3 statt.

"The First Walpurgis Night" (1844) from the Secular Cantata by Felix Mendelssohn Bartholdy and J.W. von Goethe. With a dedication to his friend Ignaz Moscheles. The premiere of the first version took place in 1832 in the Garden Room at Leipziger Strasse 3.

Fanny Hensel mit ihrem Sohn Sebastian am Klavier.
Zeichnung von Wilhelm Hensel (1840).

Fanny Hensel and her son Sebastian at the piano.
Drawing by Wilhelm Hensel (1840).

Berliner Künstler (Musiker).
Oben, von links nach rechts: der an Stelle Mendelssohn Bartholdys als Sing-Akademie-Direktor gewählte Carl Friedrich Rungenhagen (1778 – 1851); Gaspare Spontini (1774 – 1851), ein Pariser Bekannter Abraham Mendelssohn Bartholdys, der als Berlins Generalmusikdirektor Felix' Opern-Debüt zu verhindern suchte; Felix Mendelssohn Bartholdy. Unten: der Komponist Friedrich Wollank (1781 – 1831); der Komponist Bernhard Klein (1793 – 1832); der Sing-Akademie-Direktor Karl Friedrich Zelter (1758 – 1832). Lithographie von Wilhelm Devrient.

Artists of Berlin (musicians).
Above, left to right: Carl Friedrich Rungenhagen (1778 – 1851), elected Director of the *Sing-Akademie* instead of Mendelssohn Bartholdy; Gaspare Spontini (1774 – 1851), a Paris acquaintance of Abraham Mendelssohn Bartholdy – as Berlin's General Music Director, he attempted to prevent Felix' opera debut; Felix Mendelssohn Bartholdy. Below: the composer Friedrich Wollank (1781 – 1831); the composer Bernhard Klein (1793 – 1832); *Sing-Akademie* Director Karl Friedrich Zelter (1758 – 1832). Lithograph by Wilhelm Devrient.

Klaviertrio op. 49 von Felix Mendelssohn Bartholdy (1. Partiturseite).

Piano Trio, Opus 49 by Felix Mendelssohn Bartholdy (first page of the score).

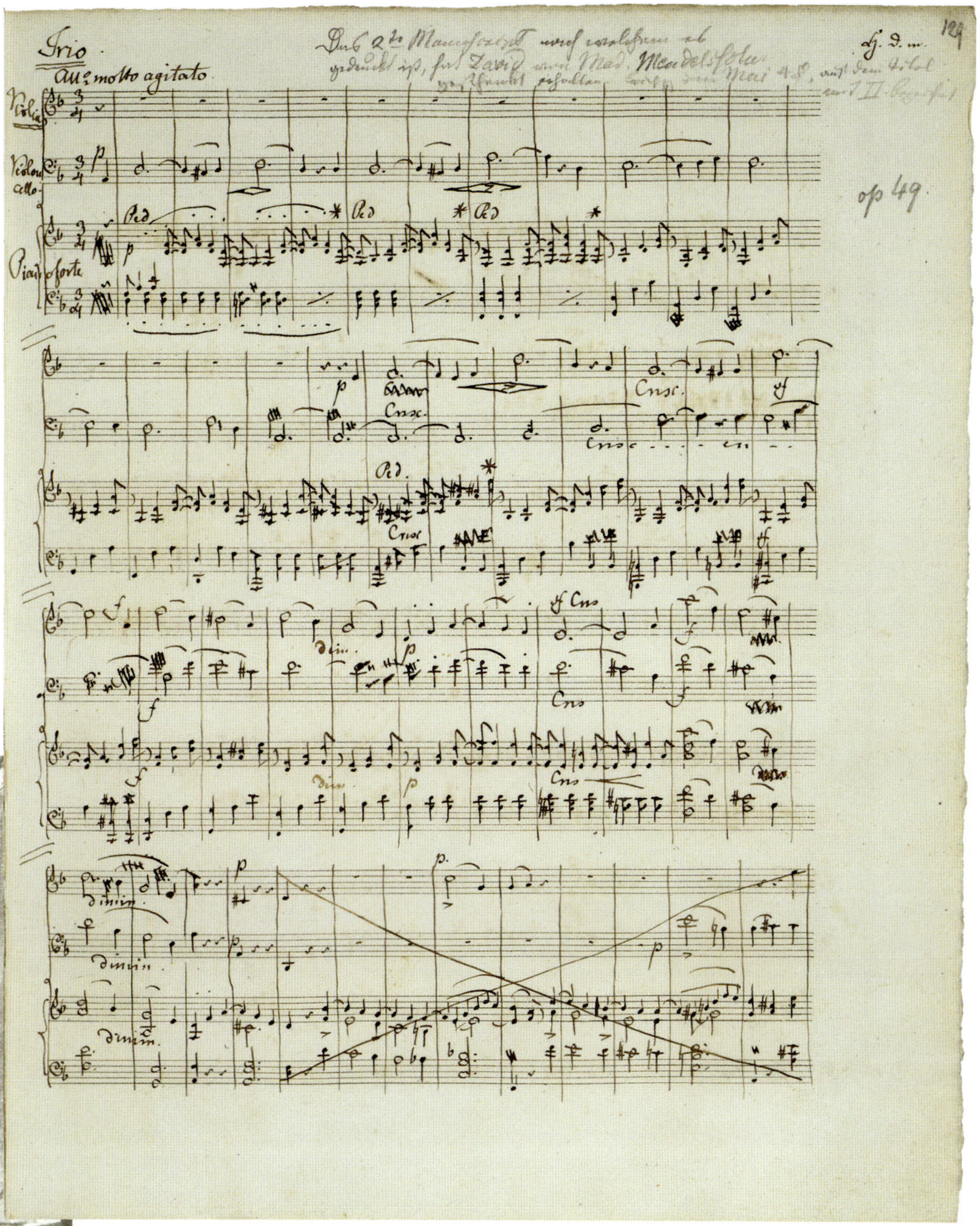

Mendelssohn Bartholdy spielt für die Queen und Prince Albert. Nach einem Gemälde von Carl Rohling.

Mendelssohn Bartholdy plays for Queen Victoria and Prince Albert. After a painting by Carl Rohling.

"One must uplift the listener to more subtle sentiments"

As Director of the Leipzig Gewandhaus Orchestra, Felix founded the first German conservatory (1843). Although Berlin's Sing-Akademie had refused to let him succeed Zelter as director, he later worked in the capital as Prussia's General Director for Musical Affairs. Even so, he proved unable to realize the reforms he had envisioned for Berlin's Academy of the Fine Arts and the Cathedral Choir, due to the cultural politics of the time (1842). His music, unfairly maligned as "overly sentimental" by later generations, was born from a fighting determination to express his serious artistic passions, even if this meant swimming against the tide. Some of this feisty spirit comes across in his critique of an operatic success by Meyerbeer, Berlin's other musical star at the time: "It had its effect, but it was no music to me, for it was vulgar; and if that is what our times demand and deem fitting, then I would rather write church music" (1831).

Felix and Fanny's circle of friends included Clara Wieck and Robert Schumann; unfortunately this did not keep the latter from harboring a certain degree of anti-Semitic prejudice. Felix had not long been dead when he and Meyerbeer came under vicious ideological attack in Richard Wagner's pamphlet "Jewishness in Music" (1850). This enmity would play itself out later in an incident between Felix' nephew Arnold Mendelssohn and Wagner's son Siegfried: Upon learning from his friend Humperdinck that Arnold was working on "Der Bärenhäuter" (The Bear Skinner), a fairy-tale opera in the late Romantic style, Siegfried decided to appropriate the same story for an opera of his own, which he completed in 1898. This was two years before Arnold could premiere his version at the Theater des Westens with the support of his banker nephews; Arnold struck back with a lawsuit for plagiarism. Though Arnold wrote three operas in all, they found limited favor with the public. On the other hand, he was highly regarded for breathing new life into Protestant sacred music through his work as organist, cantor, and conservatory teacher (in Cologne/Frankfurt), and as Director of sacred music for the court of Hessia. His choral works and 170 *Kunstlieder* would become better known than his symphonies and chamber pieces.

A re-discoverer of Heinrich Schütz and teacher to Paul Hindemith, he was also a disputatious conservative who went against the grain, rejecting Romanticism as a "disgustingly exhibitionistic expression of modern emotionality" – which included most of this uncle's works. In 1912, Arnold, began to jot down the first of the

„Man muß den Hörer zur zarteren Empfindung heben"

Als Leipzigs Gewandhausdirektor gründet Felix Mendelssohn Bartholdy das erste deutsche Conservatorium (1843). In Berlin, wo ihn die Sing-Akademie als Nachfolger des Direktors Zelter abgelehnt hatte, scheitern seine Reformen für die Akademie der Künste und den Domchor, die er als Preußischer Generalmusikdirektor plant, an der Kulturpolitik (1842). Entstanden ist seine von Nachgeborenen sentimental mißdeutete Musik aus kämpferisch-ernster Kunst-Liebe, gegen den Trend – wie es in seiner Kritik am Opernerfolg des anderen Berliner Stars, Meyerbeer, anklingt: „Es hat Effekt gemacht, aber ich habe keine Musik dafür. Denn es ist gemein, und wenn das heut die Zeit verlangte, und nothwendig fände, so will ich Kirchenmusik schreiben" (1831).

Befreundet sind Felix und Fanny mit Clara Wieck und Robert Schumann, der von antisemitischen Ressentiments nicht frei ist. Scharfe ideologische Angriffe auf Meyerbeer und Mendelssohn Bartholdy werden, nach dessen Tod, durch Richard Wagners Pamphlet „Das Judenthum in der Musik" (1850) verbreitet. Ein Nachspiel dazu findet zwischen Felix' Neffen Arnold Mendelssohn und dem Wagner-Sohn Siegfried statt. Daß Mendelssohn, der Spätromantiker, an einer Märchenoper arbeitet, erfährt Wagner von dessen Freund Humperdinck; er nimmt sich denselben Stoff vor, wird früher fertig (1898) – und von Arnold, dessen „Bärenhäuter"-Uraufführung am Theater des Westens (1900) durch seine Bankiers-Neffen unterstützt wird, wegen Plagiats verklagt. Arnolds insgesamt drei Opern finden nur begrenzt Beifall. Doch der Organist und Kantor, der Konservatoriumslehrer (in Köln/Frankfurt) und hessische Kirchenmusikmeister gilt als Erneuerer evangelischer Sakralmusik. Seine Chorwerke und 170 Kunstlieder werden bekannter als seine Sinfonien und Kammermusiken.

Der querköpfige Konservative, ein Neuentdecker von Heinrich Schütz und Lehrer Paul Hindemiths, lehnt den „ekelhaften Exhibitionismus" einer als romantisch verstandenen „Darstellung des modernen Seelenlebens" ab, ebenso die meisten Werke seines Onkels. 1912 beginnt Arnold, „Gedanken und Grillen" zu notieren: insgesamt 4488 Aphorismen. „Nicht Expressionsmusik tut not ... nicht Streben nach gefühlig schmelzender Auflösung, sondern nach Konstruktion, in der das Gefühl zwar pulsiert, aber gebunden ist", schreibt er 1919. Man müsse „den Hörer zu einer kräftigeren, zarteren, gesunderen Empfindung" heben: „Musik

Giacomo Meyerbeer (1791 – 1864) und Felix Mendelssohn Bartholdy (links) auf dem Fries am Roten Rathaus (1879) – die einzige öffentliche Darstellung der verfemten Musiker, die in Berlin das „Dritte Reich" überstand.

Giacomo Meyerbeer (1791 – 1864) and Felix Mendelssohn Bartholdy (left) as pictured on the frieze of Berlin's city hall, the Rotes Rathaus (1879). This was the only representation in Berlin of the two musicians to survive the Third Reich.

Langenau im Juli 1917

1228. Eine volkstümliche Melodie darf in der Grundharmonie durchaus nicht über die 3 Hauptstufen 1, 4, 5 hinausgehen. Sie muss trotzdem charakteristisch sein durch prägnante Melodieschritte und vor Allem durch ihre Rhythmisierung. Gelungen ist in dieser Hinsicht [illegible] — von 2 Akkorden! Dabei ist [illegible] Durgeschlecht nötig; Moll steht bedenklich. Selbst Zelters König von Thule ist trotz seiner Einfachheit nicht ins Volk gedrungen.

1229. Der Protestantismus wird durch den Katholizismus an Festigkeit, Überzeugung u. s. w. übertroffen; aber jener ist lebendiger, als dieser. Und ein lebendiger Hund ist nach [illegible] besser, denn ein toter Löwe.

1230. Langes Gespräch über den Materialismus gelesen. Der Materialist sieht in den geistigen Vorgängen nur Wirkungen, im Grunde sehr überflüssige Begleiterscheinungen körperlicher Prozesse. Diese bedeuten ihm letzte Realität. Der Idealist hält umgekehrt die ganze Körperwelt für eine durch unsere Sinnlichkeit erzeugte symbolische Erscheinung einer geistigen Wirklichkeit. Es versteht sich [illegible] für ihn, daß diese geistige letzte Wirklichkeit nicht ohne Weiteres mit dem menschlichen Seelenleben zusammenfällt. Sondern noch [illegible] verschiedener, als Goethes Geistesleben von dem eines Spulwurms ist, müssen die Formen des Geistes angenommen werden, die sich in so verschiedenen materiellen Erscheinungen darstellen, wie z. B. als [illegible] des Wassers, als Entfalten der Rose, die Milchbildung der Kuh, als Rosten des Eisens. Der Idealist fügt dieser Untersuchung hinzu, daß er den Geist zwar für als letzte Realität hält, sofern dieser erkennbar ist, nicht aber für die letzte Realität schlechthin: die tiefste Wurzel aller geistigen Vorgänge bleibt dunkel. Doch ist, sie materiell zu denken, ein größerer Fehler, als sie geistig zu denken, weil alles Materielle im Vergleich zum Geistigen [illegible] ist, [illegible] daher der Wurzel näher ist.

Der prinzipielle Fehler des Materialismus, ~~der~~ [illegible] für die Wissenschaft, sofern sie sich mit Körpern beschäftigt, völlig genügt, tritt sofort [illegible] der Erscheinung des Geistes [illegible]: dieser ist (ihm) unverständlich, überflüssig und [illegible], weil er ihn als äußere unmittelbarste Realität nicht ableugnen kann. Dagegen ist dem Idealisten die Körperwelt im Ganzen nicht rätselhaft: sie kann aus dem Geistesleben abgeleitet werden. Aber nicht umgekehrt.

Immer bildet für den Materialismus ein unlösbares Problem in der sog. Wechselwirkung zwischen Körper und Geist. Er zerhaut den Knoten freilich durch Verkennung des Geistes zu einem blassen Schatten des realen Körperlichen, wodurch dessen Schöpfung etwas [illegible] Gespenstisches erhält: ein Nervensystem, das aber fühlt, will, denkt! Dagegen dem Idealismus die Wechselwirkung geistiger Wesen

[illegible] Materialisten

4,488 aphorisms that would make up his "Gedanken und Grillen" (Whims and Ideas). "What is needed is not expressionistic music ... or an attempt to lose oneself in a meltdown of emotions; but rather structure, one in which feeling pulses yet remains harnessed," he noted in 1919. His aim was "to uplift the listener towards a more vigorous, yet also more subtle and salutary state of perception; what's needed today is music as a moral institution." Having achieved the status of an honored professor, Arnold passed away in 1933, on the eve of the Third Reich. During the Nazi period, neither Arnold's works nor those of his uncle Felix were performed in public. In fact, "Aryan" composers were hired to write substitute music for "A Mid-Summer Night's Dream."

‚als moralische Anstalt' ist heut an der Zeit." Seine Werke kommen im „Dritten Reich", nach dem Tod des hochgeehrten Professors (1933), ebenso wenig zur Aufführung wie die seines Onkels Felix. Für dessen „Sommernachtstraum" werden „arische" Tonsetzer beauftragt, einen Ersatz zu komponieren.

„Gedanken und Grillen". Aus Arnold Mendelssohns Aphorismen-Sammlung: „ ... Ferner bietet sich dem Materialismus ein unlösbares Problem in der sogenannten Wechselwirkung zwischen Körper und Geist. Er zerhaut den Knoten freilich durch Ernennung des Geistes zu einem bloßen Schatten des realen Körperlichen, wodurch unsere Existenz etwas grausenhaft Gespenstisches erhält ..." (Juli 1917).

"Gedanken und Grillen" (Whims and Ideas). From Arnold Mendelssohn's collection of aphorisms: "... and what is more, materialism faces an insoluble problem in the so-called 'reciprocal interaction between body and spirit.' It of course cuts through the knot of the problem by calling the spirit a mere shadow of what is real and corporeal, thereby giving our existence a grim and ghoulish cast..." (July 1917).

Leipziger Denkmal Felix Mendelssohn Bartholdys von Werner Stein, enthüllt 1892, zerstört 1936, wiederhergestellt 2008. Aufnahme von 1930.

The Felix Mendelssohn Bartholdy memorial in Leipzig by Werner Stein, dedicated in 1892, destroyed in 1936 and rebuilt in 2008. Photo from 1930.

Das Alte Leipziger Gewandhaus (Bibliotheksflügel).
Aquarell von Felix Mendelssohn Bartholdy (1836).

The old Leipziger Gewandhaus (library wing).
Water color by Felix Mendelssohn Bartholdy (1836).

„Das Judentum in der Musik, wie es Richard Wagner gefällt – wenn es nämlich 25 Gulden für einen Fauteuil bezahlt".
Karikatur in Kikeriki (1872).
Aus „Musik und Musiker in Karikatur und Satire" von Karl Storck (1910).

"Jewishness in music as its suits Richard Wagner: namely, when it pays 25 gulden for a seat."
Caricature in Kikeriki (1872).
From "Musik und Musiker in Karikatur und Satire" (Music and Musicians in Caricature and Satire) by Karl Storck (1910).

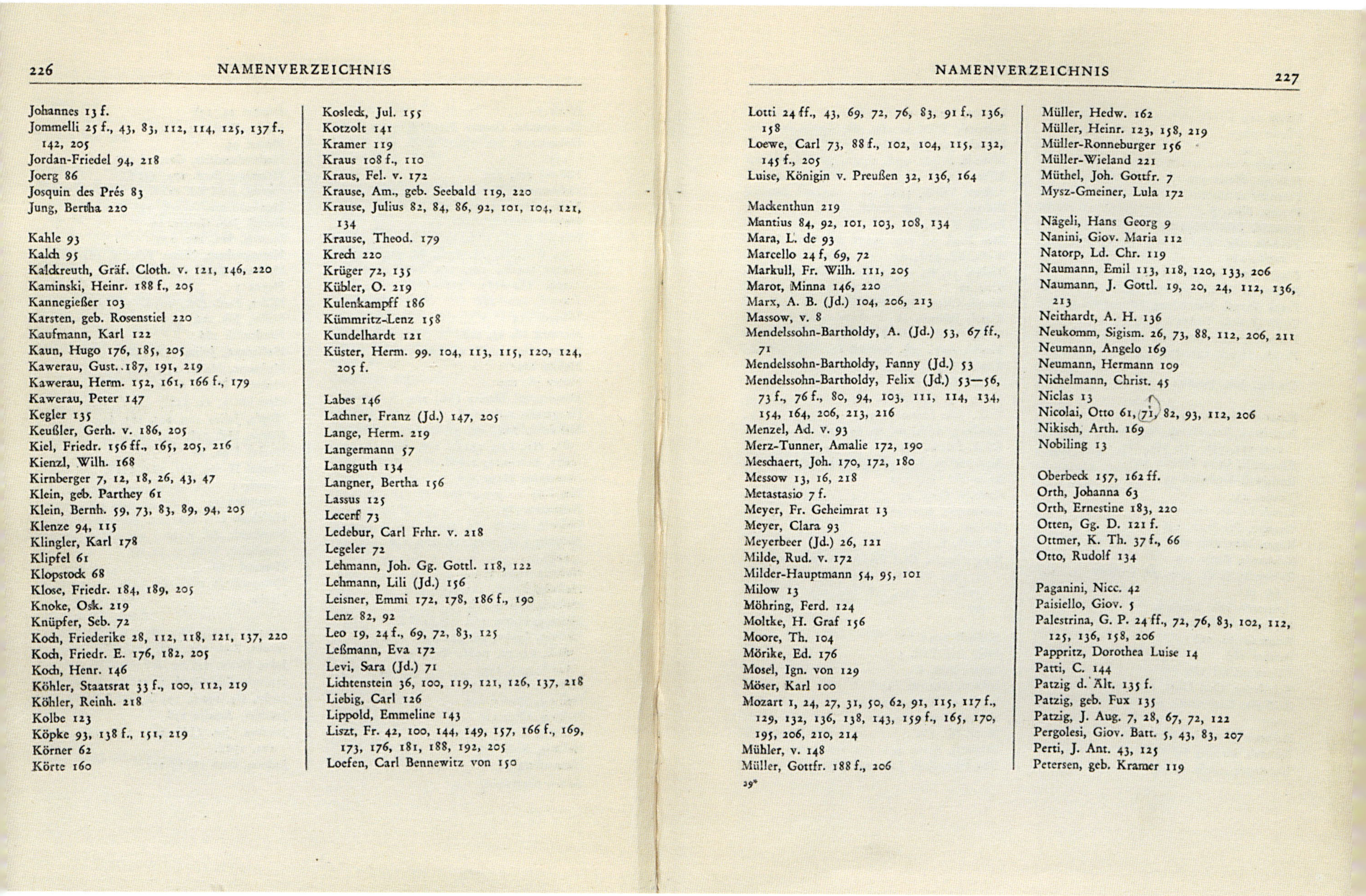
226 NAMENVERZEICHNIS

NAMENVERZEICHNIS 227

Markierungen der Musiker jüdischer Herkunft im Jubiläumsbuch Georg Schünemanns „Die Singakademie zu Berlin. 1791–1941“ (1941).

Markings identifying musicians of Jewish origin in Georg Schünemann's anniversary publication "Die Singakademie zu Berlin. 1791–1941" (1941).

The bankers' home concerts

Music would continue to play an outstanding role among the later descendants of Moses – as leisure enjoyment, on social occasions, and as a professional vocation. When the two musicians Enole Biarnez and Giulietta Gordigiani married into the fourth and fifth generations of Joseph Mendelssohn's line, they renewed the tradition of mounting highly ambitious private concerts. These were held at Jägerstrasse and in villas of the posh Grunewald district, with the active participation of the bankers and their sons who, being outstanding amateur musicians, were frequently accompanied by professional virtuosi. As a professional cellist, Francesco von Mendelssohn was a member of the Klingler and Busch Quartets, respectively. Emil Bohnke, who played viola in the latter ensemble, married violinist Lilli von Mendelssohn; he would later become Director of the Berlin's Symphony Orchestra and a composer of orchestral and chamber music. Emil and Lilli died in a car crash in 1928, and their children Robert-Alexander and Lilli would also become musicians. Felix's grandson Albrecht, a jurist, also wrote texts for musical theater and composed on the side; his cousin, the philosophy professor Herbert Mendelssohn-Bartholdy, was known as an exceptional violinist who performed with two string ensembles in Erlangen, and also with his wife Léonie, a piano teacher. In 1942, their children, the pianist Dorothea and the cellist Sebastian, would change their "Jewish" last name in order to escape professional discrimination. Dorothea was forbidden by the race laws from marrying the man of her choice, civil servant Otto Schollwoeck. After Otto had provided hiding places for Jews, relatives helped him to stay one step ahead of the Gestapo. Sebastian, whose final musical stint was that of solo cellist in the symphony orchestra of Lille, France, was killed in action as a Wehrmacht soldier in 1944 near Aachen.

Die Hauskonzerte der Bankiers

Musik spielt als Lebensglück, Geselligkeit und Broterwerb unter weiteren Moses-Nachkommen eine herausragende Rolle. Mit der Einheirat zweier Musikerinnen, der Enole Biarnez und der Giulietta Gordigiani in die Josephs-Linie IV. und V. Generation, entwickeln sich ambitionierte Hauskonzerte, unter aktiver Beteiligung der Bankiers und ihrer Söhne, an der Jägerstraße und in den Grunewaldvillen. Profi-Virtuosen scheuen sich nicht, mit diesen ausgezeichneten Freizeitkünstlern zu musizieren. Als professioneller Cellist gehört Francesco von Mendelssohn zum Klingler- und zum Busch-Quartett, an dem Emil Bohnke als Bratschist beteiligt ist; der heiratet die Geigerin Lilli von Mendelssohn, wird Dirigent des Berliner Symphonieorchesters, komponiert Orchester- und Kammermusik. Das Paar stirbt 1928 bei einem Autounfall; ihre Kinder Robert-Alexander und Lilli werden ebenfalls Musiker. Der Felix-Enkel Albrecht, ein Jurist, textet fürs Musiktheater und komponiert; sein Cousin, der Philosophie-Dozent Herbert Mendelssohn-Bartholdy, tritt als herausragender Geiger mit zwei Erlanger Streicher-Ensembles auf, wie auch mit seiner Frau Léonie, einer Klavierpädagogin. Ihre Kinder, die Pianistin Dorothea und der Cellist Sebastian, legen 1942, um beruflichen Schikanen zu entgehen, den „jüdischen" Namen ab. Dorothea darf den Beamten Otto Schollwoeck nicht heiraten; als er Juden versteckt, helfen Verwandte ihm, der Gestapo zu entkommen. Sebastian, zuletzt Solo-Cellist im Sinfonie-Orchester Lille, fällt als Wehrmachtssoldat 1944 bei Aachen.

Joseph Joachim (1831 – 1907), der Violinvirtuose, musiziert mit dem Bankier Franz von Mendelssohn d.J. (1901).

Joseph Joachim (1831 – 1907), the violin virtuoso, performs with the banker Franz von Mendelssohn Jr. (1901).

Hausmusik bei Franz und Marie von Mendelssohn an der Herthastraße im Grunewald (1930er Jahre).

Home recital at the home of Franz and Marie von Mendelssohn on Herthastrasse in the Grunewald district (1930s).

Francesco von Mendelssohn als Cellist des Klingler-Quartetts (1928).

Francesco von Mendelssohn as a cellist of the Klingler Quartet (1928).

Porträt des Komponisten Emil Bohnke (1888 – 1928), der seit 1919 mit Lilli von Mendelssohn (1897 – 1928) verheiratet war. Gemälde von Johann Walter-Kurau. Öl auf Papier.

Portrait of the composer Emil Bohnke (1888 – 1928), who married Lilli von Mendelssohn (1897 – 1928) in 1919. Painting by Johann Walter-Kurau. Oil on paper.

„Hausmusik“ im Hörsaal mit Herbert Mendelssohn-Bartholdy (1880 – 1940), zweiter von rechts, dem Vater von Dorothea und Sebastian Mendelssohn-Bartholdy, in Erlangen.

“Home recital” in the university of Erlangen with Herbert Mendelssohn-Bartholdy (1880 – 1940) (second from the right), the father of Dorothea and Sebastian Mendelssohn-Bartholdy.

Dorothea Mendelssohn-Bartholdy, Pianistin (1912 – 1997).

Dorothea Mendelssohn-Bartholdy, pianist (1912 – 1997).

Sebastian Mendelssohn-Bartholdy, Cellist (1914 – 1944).

Sebastian Mendelssohn-Bartholdy, cellist (1914 – 1944).

Robert-Alexander Bohnke, Pianist (1927 – 2004): „Die Kürze“ (1975). Text von Friedrich Hölderlin.

Robert-Alexander Bohnke, pianist (1927 – 2004): “Die Kürze” (1975). Text by Friedrich Hölderlin.

Florentin

Ein Roman

von Dorothea Schlegel.

herausgegeben

von

Friedrich Schlegel.

Varnhagen.

Erster Band.

(Mehr ist nicht im Druck erschienen.)

Lübeck und Leipzig,
bey Friedrich Bohn,
1801.

nahm ihr die Guitarre ab, und spielte einen raschen Tanz, sie drehte sich mit Eduard in schnellen Kreisen. Er hatte sich unter einem Baume niedergesetzt. Nachdem sie zu tanzen aufgehört hatten, setzten sich beyde neben ihn. — Es tanzt sich gut auf dem kurzen Grase. — Besser und erfreulicher als auf dem getäfelten Fußboden Eurer Säle, das ist gewiß. — Wenn man nun hier im Walde an eine Assemblee denkt! — Davon kein Wort, Juliane, ich mag eben so wenig von Assembleen hören, als Sie vom Tode. — Hiemit nahm er die Guitarre wieder auf, und sang:

Sie ist mir fern, wie soll ich Freude finden!
Ich kann dem Kummer nur mein Leben weihn.
Wie um den Baum sich üppig Ranken winden,
Die Nahrung raubend seiner Krone dräun,
So, fern von Dir, mich Sorg und Unmuth binden,
Daß keine Erdenlust mich kann erfreun.

Fragt nicht, warum mein Sinn so rastlos eilt;
Für mich ist nirgends Ruh, als wo sie weilt.

Juliane, erhitzt vom raschen Tanz, lehnte sich an Eduard, ein sanfter Wind, der hoch in den Wipfeln der jungen Birken rauschte, kühlte ihr das glühende Gesicht, und wehte die Locken zurück, die in der Bewegung durch ihre eigne Schwere sich von der Nadel losgemacht hatten, und nun bis tief auf die Hüften herabfielen. Eduard verlor sich ganz im Anschaun ihrer Schönheit, und die Töne der Guitarre, die dazu gesungenen Worte drangen in sein Innerstes. Er drückte Julianen mit Heftigkeit an seine Brust; die Gegenwart des Freundes vergessend hielt er sich nicht länger, seine Lippen waren fest auf die ihrigen gepreßt, seine Umarmung wurde kühner, er war ausser sich. — Juliane erschrack, wand sich geschickt aus seinen Armen, und stand auf, ihm einen zürnenden

The literati become literary subjects themselves

The literary salons of Brendel Mendelssohn, Henriette Herz and Rahel Levin, which had been inspired by the frequent gatherings in Moses' open house, helped to stimulate the development of a literary culture in Germany. The more than 1,000 critical reviews that Moses had written for three journals helped standard German evolve into a language of artistic criticism. Moses' eldest daughter Dorothea wrote novels ("Florentin," 1801) and, together with her father, also worked as a translator and occasional lyricist. Both father and daughter were also engaging letter writers – like so many of the other relatives in their own and succeeding generations. These included the multi-talented Felix (who as a twelve-year-old wrote a satirical verse epic about his brother), and his poetically inclined grandson Albrecht; between the two of them, they produced thousands of letters. Hermann, the forefather of banker Alexander Mendelssohn, published a broad range of literature in his Leipzig publishing house from 1850 onward: e.g. Kugler's biography of Frederick II, Felix' travel letters, Mirabeau's book "Sur Moses Mendelssohn," Kayserling's biography of Moses, as well as Sephardic poetry and synopses of the New Testament. In 1978, Hermann's great-grandson Albrecht Knaus founded a non-fiction and literary publishing house that issued, *inter alia*, Kempowski's "Echolot."

Above and beyond their own endeavors as writers, the Mendelssohns became literary subjects themselves. Thus, patriarch Moses and the members of his household inspired the characters in Lessing's "Nathan the Wise" (1779), while the scandalous love life of Moses' daughter Dorothea became the plot for Friedrich Schlegel's "Lucinde" (1799). Wilhelm Speyer's bestseller "Der Kampf der Tertia" (1928) ends on a moving note with Felix' evergreen "Abschied vom Walde;" his later novel about a Jewish merchant dynasty ("Das Glück der Andernachs," published in exile in 1947), takes in place in Jägerstrasse, the old neighborhood of the Mendelssohn bankers. Speyer's sister Edith was the widow of banker Ludwig Mendelssohn Bartholdy, who had fallen in action in 1918. Active in cultural politics, Edith was active as a publisher ("Die deutsche Künstlerin," 1933) for the Leipzig-based GEDOK, an association of female artists, 1933) and, after her return from emigration to England, in the field of elder care ("Der Lebensabend," 1959).

Literaten werden selbst zum Sujet

Literarische Salons der Brendel Mendelssohn, der Henriette Herz und der Rahel Levin, die durch Moses' offenes Haus inspiriert wurden, tragen dazu bei, daß eine literarische Kultur in Deutschland entsteht. Vor allem befördert Mendelssohn mit über 1000 Kritiken für drei Zeitschriften die Entwicklung des Hochdeutschen als Rezensionssprache. Er und seine Älteste wirken als Übersetzer und Gelegenheits-Lyriker; der Vater und die Romanautorin Dorothea („Florentin", 1801) sind zudem faszinierende Briefeschreiber – wie viele Verwandte ihrer und folgender Generationen. Unter denen ragen als Multitalente Felix (der mit zwölf Jahren ein spöttisches Vers-Epos auf seinen Bruder verfaßt hat) und sein ebenfalls dichtender Enkel Albrecht, mit jeweils tausenden von Briefen, hervor. Hermann Mendelssohn, der Stammhalter des Bankiers Alexander, präsentiert in seinem Leipziger Verlag (ab 1850) ein weites Spektrum: von Kuglers Friedrich II-Biographie über Felix' Reisebriefe, Mirabeaus Schrift „Sur Moses Mendelssohn" und Kayserlings Moses-Biographie zu Sephardischen Poesien und Synopsen des Neuen Testamentes. Hermanns Urenkel Albrecht Knaus begründet 1978 einen Belletristik- und Sachbuchverlag, in dem Kempowskis „Echolot" erscheint.

Die Mendelssohns sind außerdem selbst zum Sujet geworden: der Stammvater samt Hausgenossen als Charaktervorlagen für Lessings „Nathan der Weise" (1779); das Liebesleben der Skandaltochter Dorothea als Plot für Friedrich Schlegels „Lucinde" (1799). Wilhelm Speyers Jugendbestseller „Der Kampf der Tertia" (1928) endet bewegend mit Mendelssohn Bartholdys Evergreen „Abschied vom Walde"; sein im Exil verfaßter Roman einer jüdischen Kaufmannsfamilie („Das Glück der Andernachs", 1947) spielt in der Jägerstraße, dem Quartier der Mendelssohn-Bankiers. Speyers Schwester Edith Mendelssohn Bartholdy, die kulturpolitisch aktive Witwe des 1918 gefallenen Bankiers Ludwig, engagiert sich als Herausgeberin für den Künstlerinnen-Verband GEDOK („Die deutsche Künstlerin", 1933) in Leipzig, und, nach ihrer Rückkehr aus der englischen Emigration, in der Altenfürsorge („Der Lebensabend", 1959).

„Florentin" (1801). Dorothea Veits von Friedrich Schlegel herausgegebener Roman: ein Exemplar aus der Bibliothek Karl August Varnhagens von Ense, mit dessen Kommentar.

"Florentin" (1801). A novel by Dorothea Veit published by Friedrich Schlegel. This copy comes from the library of Karl August Varnhagen von Ense, who made annotations.

Rahel Varnhagen von Ense, geb. Levin (1771 – 1833), Salonière und Freundin der Moses-Kinder Henriette Maria Mendelssohn, Dorothea Schlegel und Abraham Mendelsohn Bartholdy. Sie ist mit ihrem Mann Karl August, einem Chronisten des 19. Jahrhunderts, vor dem Halleschen Tor begraben.

Rahel Varnhagen von Ense, née Levin (1771 – 1833), salon hostess and friend of the Moses children Henriette Maria Mendelssohn, Dorothea Schlegel, and Abraham Mendelsohn Bartholdy. She is buried alongside her husband Karl August, a chronicler of the 19th century, near Berlin's Hallesches Tor.

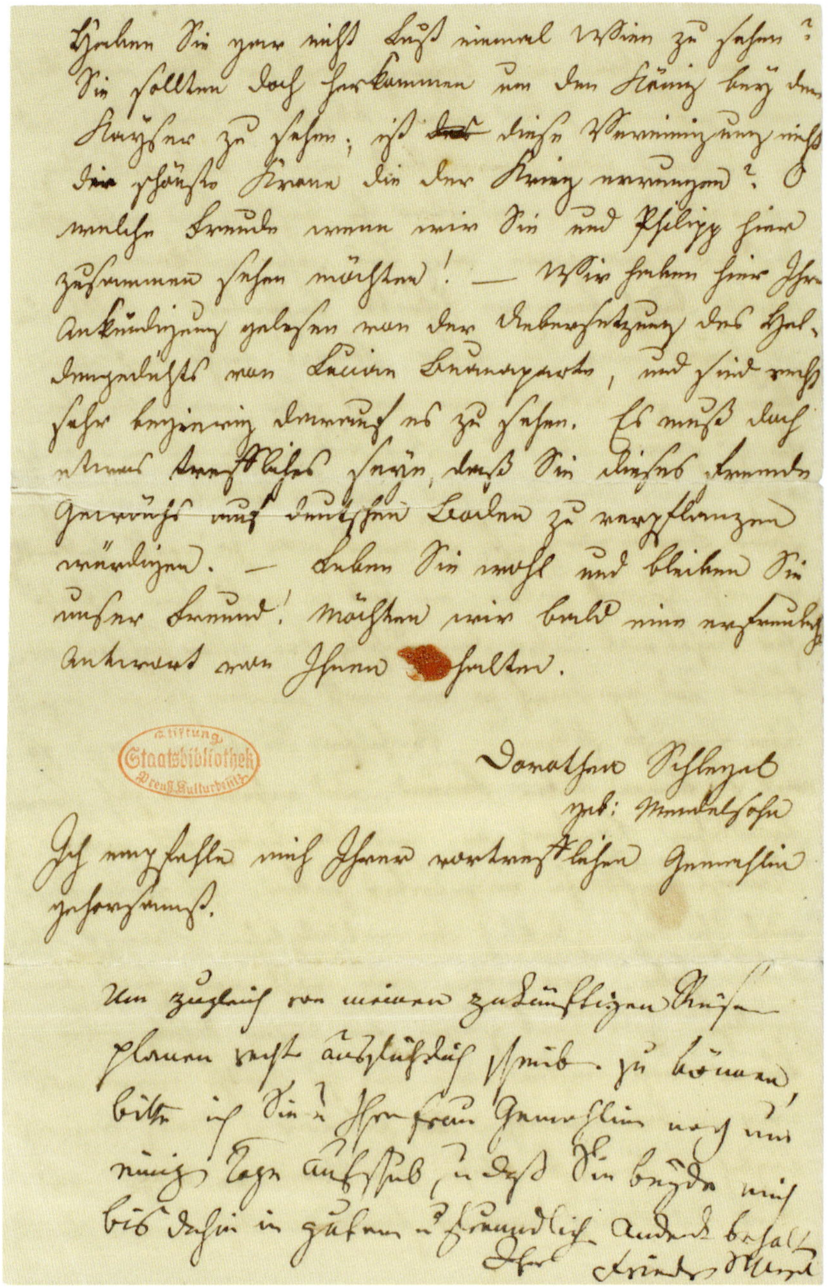

Friedrich Schlegel und Dorothea Schlegel, geb. Mendelssohn: Brief aus Wien (1. Juni 1814) an den Schriftsteller Friedrich de la Motte Fouqué.

Friedrich Schlegel and Dorothea Schlegel, née Mendelssohn: letter from Vienna (June 1, 1814) to the writer Friedrich de la Motte Fouqué.

Hermann Mendelssohn (1824 – 1891), Verlagsbuchhändler in Leipzig.

Hermann Mendelssohn (1824 – 1891), publisher in Leipzig.

Der Schriftsteller Wilhelm Speyer (1887 – 1952), Bruder Edith Mendelssohn-Bartholdys (1882 – 1969).

The author Wilhelm Speyer (1887 – 1952), brother of Edith Mendelssohn-Bartholdy (1882 – 1969).

Albrecht Knaus, Verleger (1913 – 2007), ein Urenkel des Verlegers Hermann Mendelssohn.

Albrecht Knaus, publisher (1913 – 2007), a great-grandson of Hermann Mendelssohn, also a publisher.

Die „Grünen Bücher“, in denen Felix Mendelssohn Bartholdy seine Korrespondenz sammelte.

The “Green Books” in which Felix Mendelssohn Bartholdy compiled his correspondence.

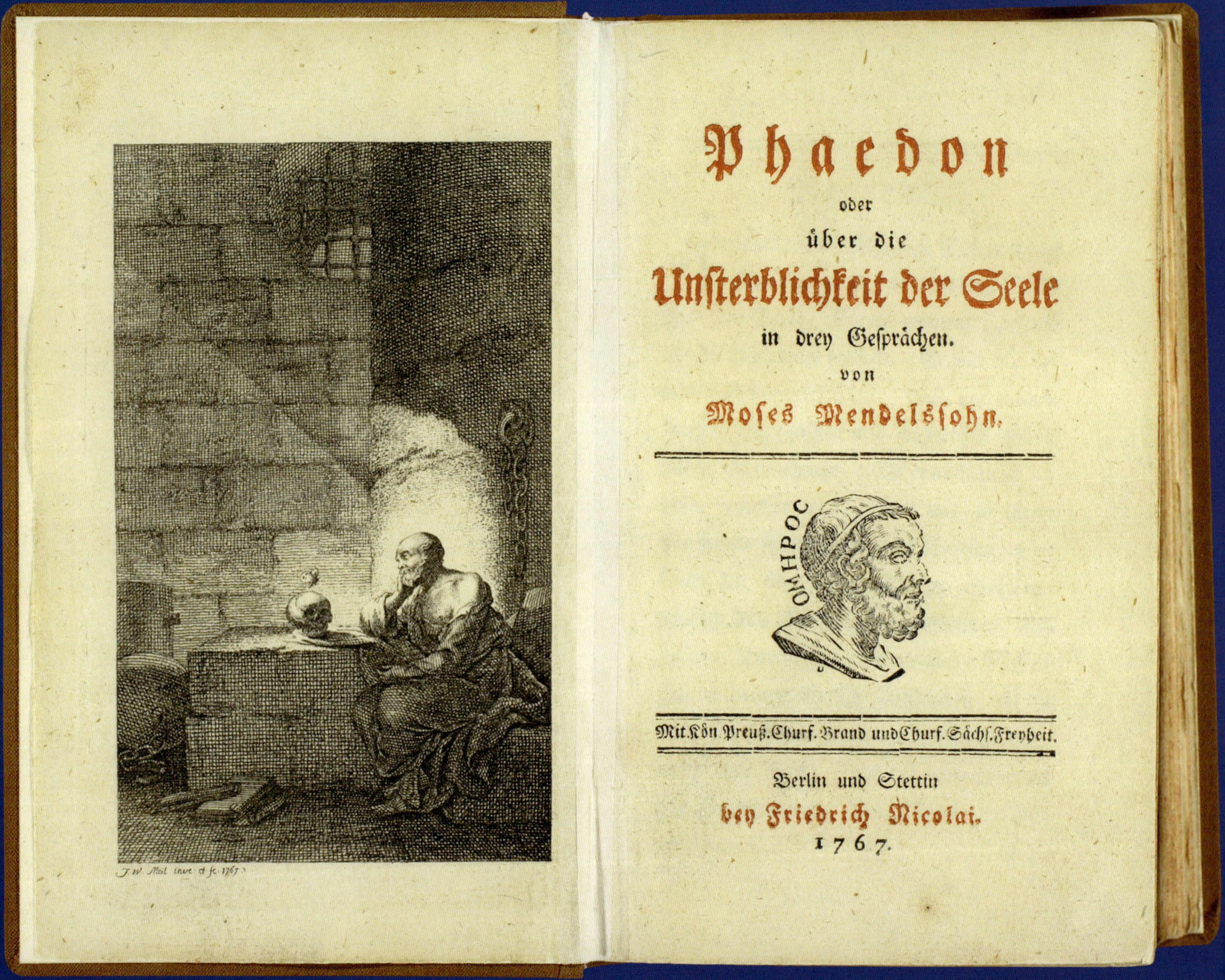
J. W. Meil inve. et fc. 1767.
Phaedon
oder
über die
Unsterblichkeit der Seele
in drey Gesprächen.
von
Moses Mendelssohn.
ΟΜΗΡΟϹ
Mit Kön. Preuß. Churf. Brand. und Churf. Sächs. Freyheit.
Berlin und Stettin
bey Friedrich Nicolai.
1767.

"To the end abides our love for images and stories"

In 1935, the Baltic-born writer Werner Bergengruen, husband of Charlotte Hensel (sixth generation), published "Der Grosstyrann and das Gericht" (The Great Tyrant and the Court). This novel was hailed as a key literary work of the resistance to Hitler and caused Bergengruen, a Catholic convert, to be excluded from the Reichschriftstumkammer (Reich Literature Chamber) in 1936. In an attempt to help his wife and children, as well as other relatives endangered under the race laws as *Mischlinge* ("half-breeds"), he would travel to Eastern Europe to perform genealogical research while negotiating with the Reichssippenamt (Reich Office of Genealogy).

On April 12, 1933 the Deutsche Studentenschaft (German Students' Union) launched a billboard campaign entitled "Against the Un-German Spirit." There followed over 94 book burnings all over the Reich – the rich German-Jewish culture that had evolved from the legacy of the "Moses of the German Jews" was to be isolated and rooted out. Till then, Moses' seminal works and Sebastian Hensel's "Die Familie Mendelssohn" had remained top sellers among the many works published by the family. 1879, the year Hensel's family chronicle first appeared, also marked the first time the term "anti-Semitism" was discussed by the general public; a half-century later, publication of the book came to an end entirely under the Third Reich.

The memorial plaque in honor of the composer Felix Mendelssohn Bartholdy at the family home on Leipziger Strasse was removed in September 1935 on the orders of Reich Marshal Hermann Göring. In his family chronicle, Hensel had described this address as a crossroads of culture during the Romantic age, a description that was echoed by a relative from the same generation, the author Paul Heyse: "An illustrious society filled the wide room, and almost every single one could claim a right to be there based on an intimate relationship with music ... the broad glass doors facing the garden stood open; at times, the birds would chime in with their song... Here, the 'First Walpurgis Night,' only recently completed by the composer, was premiered and, like many of his beautiful piano pieces and Lieder, was played and sung fresh from the hand-written page. ... I myself stood all the way back at the threshold of the adjoining room, behind my friend Sebastian, and stretched my long frame on tip-toes, so as to not miss a single note and to survey the faces arrayed around the piano."

„Was uns bis zuletzt gefällt, sind Bilder und Geschichten"

Der baltische Schriftsteller Werner Bergengruen, verheiratet mit Charlotte Hensel (VI. Generation), veröffentlicht 1935 „Der Großtyrann und das Gericht": Die Erzählung wird als Schlüsselroman des Widerstandes gelesen und führt zum Ausschluß des 1936 katholisch Konvertierten aus der Reichsschrifttumskammer. Für Verwandte, die wie seine Frau und seine Kinder als „Mischlinge" gefährdet sind, reist der Dichter zur Stammbaum-Recherche nach Osteuropa, verhandelt mit dem Reichssippenamt.

Die deutsch-jüdische Kultur, das Vermächtnis des „Moses der deutschen Juden" sollte ausgesondert, ausgemerzt werden, als am 12. April 1933 mit der Plakat-Aktion „Wider den undeutschen Geist" eine Kampagne der Deutschen Studentenschaft begann. In der Folge fanden reichsweit 94 Bücherverbrennungen statt. Bis dahin hatten, in puncto Auflage, an der Spitze der Publikationen aus dem Verwandtenkreis, Moses' Longseller und Sebastian Hensels „Die Familie Mendelssohn" gestanden. Im Erscheinungsjahr dieser Familienchronik, 1879, war erstmals von dem Begriff „Antisemitismus" die Rede gewesen. Im „Dritten Reich" wird das Buch nicht mehr verlegt.

Das Haus der Mendelssohn Bartholdys an der Leipziger Straße, von dem Reichsmarschall Göring im September 1935 eine an den Komponisten Felix erinnernde Gedenktafel entfernen läßt, hatte der Chronist Hensel noch in seinem Bestseller als romantischen Kultur-Treffpunkt geschildert. Auch sein gleichaltriger Verwandter, der Schriftsteller Paul Heyse, schwärmte von diesem Ort: „Eine illustre Gesellschaft füllte den weiten Raum, doch war kaum einer darunter, der nicht durch ein intimes Verhältnis zur Musik ein Anrecht auf seinen Platz beweisen konnte ... Die breiten Glastüren nach dem Garten zu standen offen; zuweilen schmetterte der Vogelgesang mit hinein. Hier wurde die „Letzte Walpurgisnacht", von dem Komponisten soeben vollendet, zuerst aufgeführt und wie manche der schönen Klavierstücke und Lieder noch im Manuskript frisch vom Blatt gespielt und gesungen. ... Ich selbst stand neben Freund Sebastian zuhinterst auf der Schwelle des Nebenzimmers und reckte meine lange Figur auf den Zehen, um keinen Ton zu verlieren und die Gesichter zu betrachten, die sich um den Flügel reihten." Heyses Vater war Hauslehrer bei den Humboldts und in der Leipziger Straße 3 gewesen; geheiratet hatte er Julie Saaling (Salomon), eine Cousine Lea Mendelssohn Bartholdys. Sein Sohn erhält als erster

Moses Mendelssohn: „Phädon oder über die Unsterblichkeit der Seele in drey Gesprächen" (1767).
Der europäische Bestseller des „Juden von Berlin".

Moses Mendelssohn: "Phaedon, or On the Immortality of the Soul in Three Dialogues" (1767).
This was the famous "Jew of Berlin's" Europe-wide bestseller.

Heyse's father had worked as private tutor in the home of the Humboldts and at Leipziger Strasse 3; he was married to Julie Saaling (Salomon), a cousin of Lea Mendelssohn Bartholdy. His son Paul would receive the Nobel Prize for Literature (1910). Paul Heyse's "Spruchbüchlein" (Booklet of Sayings), published in 1885, contains the following four-liner:

"In time, we by and by let go
Of many worldly joys and glories.
But to the end abides our love
For images and stories."

Autor für Belletristik den Nobelpreis (1910). Aus Paul Heyses „Spruchbüchlein" (1885) stammt auch der Vierzeiler:

„Auf so manche Lust der Welt
lernt man früh verzichten.
Was uns bis zuletzt gefällt,
sind Bilder und Geschichten."

Das Gartenhaus der Wohnung von Fanny Hensel und Felix Mendelssohn Bartholdy in Berlin, Leipziger Straße 3. Aquarell von Sebastian Hensel (10. Juni 1851).

The garden house of the Berlin town home of Fanny Hensel and Felix Mendelssohn Bartholdy at Leipziger Strasse 3. Water color by Sebastian Hensel (June 10, 1851).

Der Literaturnobelpreisträger Paul Heyse (1830 – 1914), ein Neffe Lea Mendelssohn Bartholdys. Fotografie von Franz Hanfstaengl.

The Nobel Prize Laureate for Literature Paul Heyse (1830 – 1914), a nephew of Lea Mendelssohn Bartholdy. Photo by Franz Hanfstaengl.

Werner Bergengruen (1892 – 1964) und seine durch die Nürnberger Rassengesetze betroffene Familie: links Luise, geb. 1924 (oben) und Maria, geb. 1928 (unten); Mitte: Ehefrau Charlotte, geb. Hensel (1896 – 1990); rechts: Alexander, geb. 1930. Aufnahme von 1934.

Werner Bergengruen (1892 – 1964) and his family, all of whom were affected by the Nuremberg Race Laws. Left: Luise, born 1924 (above) and Maria, born 1928 (below); middle: Werner's wife Charlotte, née Hensel (1896 – 1990); right: Alexander, born in 1930. Photo from 1934.

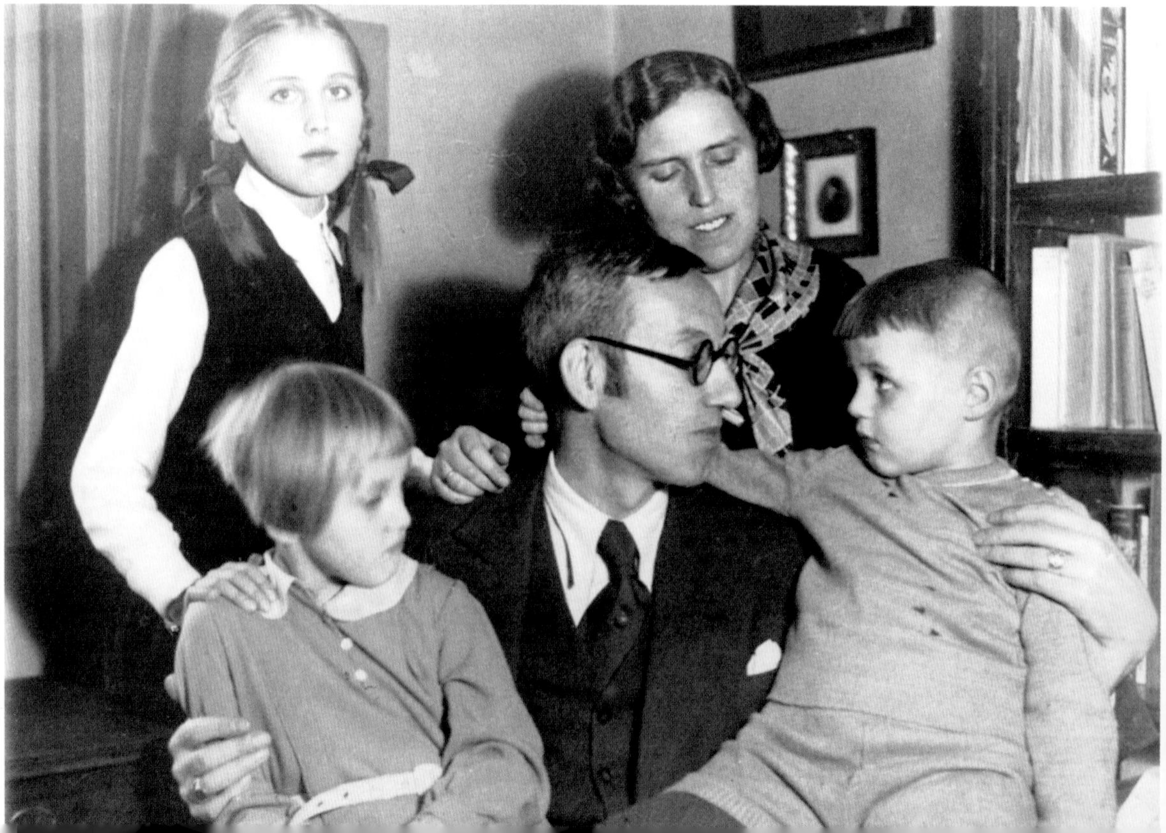

„Wider den undeutschen Geist“:
Plakat des NS-Studentenbundes zur Vorbereitung der Bücherverbrennung, April 1933.

“Against the Un-German Spirit”:
Billboard circulated by the Nazi Student Union in April 1933 as a prelude to the book burnings.

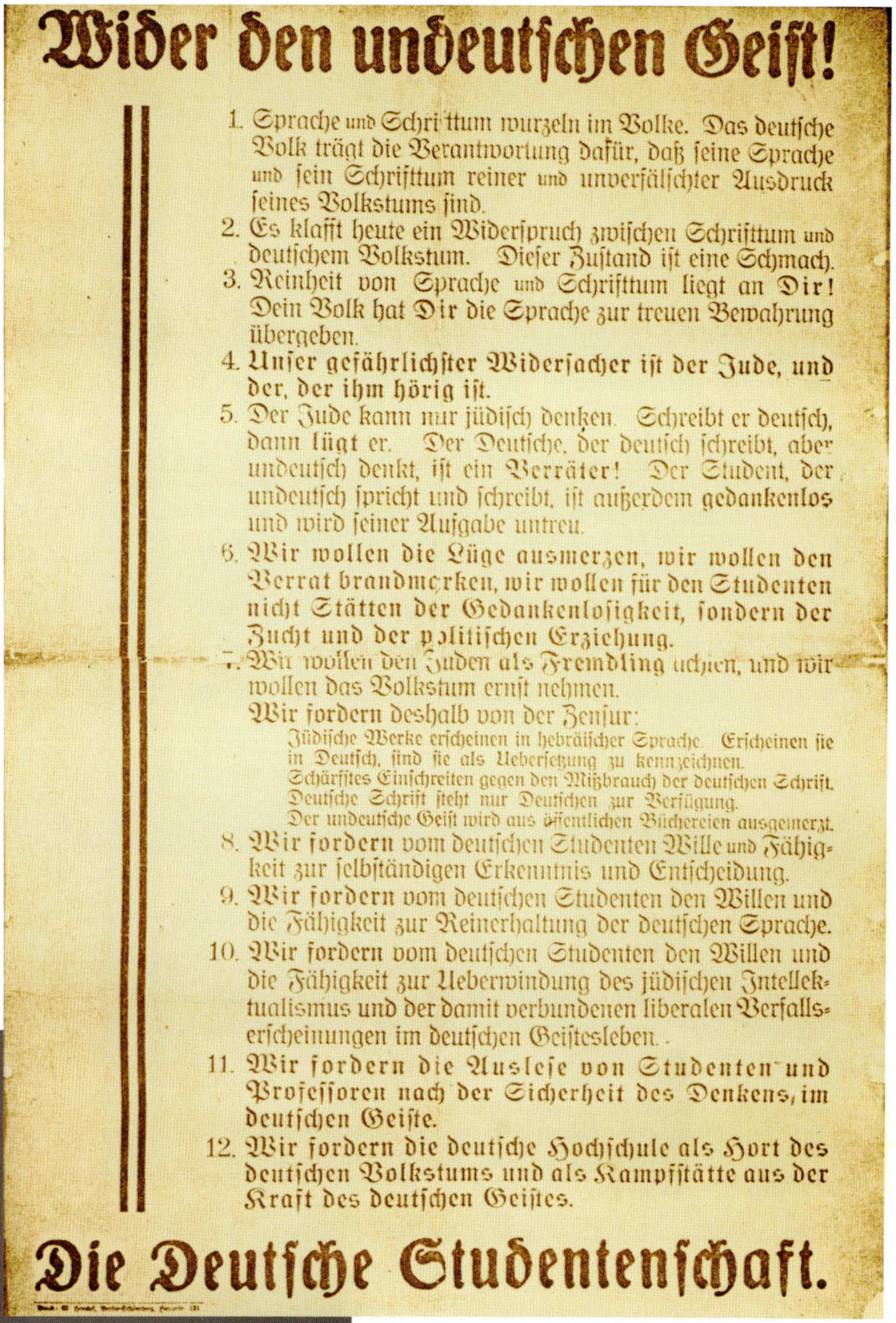

Wider den undeutschen Geist!

1. Sprache und Schrifttum wurzeln im Volke. Das deutsche Volk trägt die Verantwortung dafür, daß seine Sprache und sein Schrifttum reiner und unverfälschter Ausdruck seines Volkstums sind.
2. Es klafft heute ein Widerspruch zwischen Schrifttum und deutschem Volkstum. Dieser Zustand ist eine Schmach.
3. Reinheit von Sprache und Schrifttum liegt an Dir! Dein Volk hat Dir die Sprache zur treuen Bewahrung übergeben.
4. **Unser gefährlichster Widersacher ist der Jude, und der, der ihm hörig ist.**
5. Der Jude kann nur jüdisch denken. Schreibt er deutsch, dann lügt er. Der Deutsche, der deutsch schreibt, aber undeutsch denkt, ist ein Verräter! Der Student, der undeutsch spricht und schreibt, ist außerdem gedankenlos und wird seiner Aufgabe untreu.
6. **Wir wollen die Lüge ausmerzen, wir wollen den Verrat brandmarken, wir wollen für den Studenten nicht Stätten der Gedankenlosigkeit, sondern der Zucht und der politischen Erziehung.**
7. Wir wollen den Juden als Fremdling achten, und wir wollen das Volkstum ernst nehmen.
   Wir fordern deshalb von der Zensur:
   Jüdische Werke erscheinen in hebräischer Sprache. Erscheinen sie in Deutsch, sind sie als Uebersetzung zu kennzeichnen.
   Schärfstes Einschreiten gegen den Mißbrauch der deutschen Schrift.
   Deutsche Schrift steht nur Deutschen zur Verfügung.
   Der undeutsche Geist wird aus öffentlichen Büchereien ausgemerzt.
8. Wir fordern vom deutschen Studenten Wille und Fähigkeit zur selbständigen Erkenntnis und Entscheidung.
9. Wir fordern vom deutschen Studenten den Willen und die Fähigkeit zur Reinerhaltung der deutschen Sprache.
10. Wir fordern vom deutschen Studenten den Willen und die Fähigkeit zur Ueberwindung des jüdischen Intellektualismus und der damit verbundenen liberalen Verfallserscheinungen im deutschen Geistesleben.
11. **Wir fordern die Auslese von Studenten und Professoren nach der Sicherheit des Denkens im deutschen Geiste.**
12. **Wir fordern die deutsche Hochschule als Hort des deutschen Volkstums und als Kampfstätte aus der Kraft des deutschen Geistes.**

Die Deutsche Studentenschaft.

Bücherverbrennung auf dem Berliner Opernplatz am 10. Mai 1933.
Book burning on Berlin’s Opernplatz on May 10, 1933.

Abbildungsnachweis

Bettmann / CORBIS: 93 unten
Biblioteka Jagiellońska, Krakau: 47 rechts
Bodleian Library, Oxford: 34 unten, 46 unten, 48 unten, 139 links, 224 unten rechts, 247 unten
Bulletin Leo Baeck Institute 10 / 40 (1967): 10 Mitte
bpk: 11 unten, 18 oben links, 19 rechts, 118, 132 links, 200, 208 oben links, 209 oben links, 226, 238 links, 253 oben
bpk / Bayerische Staatsbibliothek / Archiv Heinrich Hoffmann: 92 oben, 253 unten
bpk / Lutz Braun: 44
bpk / Das Gleimhaus, Halberstadt / Ulrich Schrader: 126 oben rechts und unten rechts, 132 unten, 133 oben links, 170 oben
bpk / Kupferstichkabinett, SMB: 31 oben rechts, 132 oben rechts
bpk / Kupferstichkabinett, SMB / Jörg P. Anders: 32, 43 rechts, 55 oben links, 138 unten
bpk / Kupferstichkabinett, SMB / Volker-H. Schneider: 55 unten links, 229 unten
bpk / Loescher & Petsch: 198 oben rechts
bpk / Metzke: 216
bpk / Münzkabinett, SMB: 127 unten und rechts
bpk / Nationalgalerie, SMB: 16
bpk / Nationalgalerie, SMB / Jörg P. Anders: 212
bpk / Nationalgalerie, SMB / Klaus Göken: 204 oben
bpk / RMN – Grand Palais / Bulloz: 168
bpk / Staatsbibliothek zu Berlin: 8 und Umschlagabb. vorn 1. Bild, 11 oben, 11 rechts, 12, 14 oben, 20, 26 links, 26 unten, 36 links und Umschlagabb. vorn 4. Bild, 42 links, 43 oben links, 55 oben rechts, 60 rechts, 74 oben links, 78 oben, 84, 110 unten links, 151 links, 161 unten, 161 rechts, 166 unten, 171 unten, 179 oben rechts, 222 oben links, 225 oben, 231, 232 links und oben rechts, 233 oben, 238 oben rechts, 242 unten, 248
bpk / Staatsbibliothek zu Berlin / Johanna Eilert: 240
bpk / Staatsbibliothek zu Berlin / Ruth Schacht: 46 oben, 47 oben links, 47 unten links, 48 oben links und rechts und Umschlagabb. vorn 6. Bild, 228 unten rechts, 250
bpk / Staatsbibliothek zu Berlin / Carola Seifert: 219 links, 222 unten links, 223 unten, 246 oben rechts
bpk / Toumazet: 171 oben
Bundesarchiv, Bild 183-2008-0826-503: 107 oben
Manfred Claudi: 146 unten und rechts, 148, 234, Umschlagabb. hinten rechts
Cooper-Hewitt, National Design Museum, Smithsonian Institution / Art Resource, NY / Scala, Florenz: 43 unten
Depositum der Mendelssohn-Gesellschaft im Mendelssohn-Archiv der Staatsbibliothek zu Berlin: 39 links, 121, 142 oben, 144, 146 oben, 147 oben links, 147 rechts, 150 oben, 172, 174, 224 oben rechts
Depositum der Mendelssohn-Gesellschaft im Mendelssohn-Archiv der Staatsbibliothek zu Berlin / Foto: Manfred Claudi: 10 unten
Deutsches Literaturarchiv Marbach: 182
Hans-Joachim Dopfer, Sigmaringen: 18 rechts unten, 19 oben, 19 unten, 24, 58 unten, 120 links und Umschlagabb. vorn 2. Bild, 142 unten, 194 unten
Eleonora von Mendelssohn Papers, Manuscripts and Archives Division. The New York Public Library. Astor, Lenox, and Tilden Foundations: 66 rechts
Elisabeth-Stiftung: 31 links
Ev. Kirchengemeinde St. Petri / St. Marien: 42 unten
Ev.-Luth. Kirchgemeinde St. Thomas Leipzig: 220 links
Galerie Sabatier: 242 rechts
Geheimes Staatsarchiv – Preußischer Kulturbesitz: 63 oben links, 103 oben links
Gemäldegalerie der Stadt Mainz (Leihgabe an den Glaspalast in München): 194 oben links
Germanisches Nationalmuseum: 58 oben links
Heimatmuseum Treptow: 83 unten
IHK Berlin: 104
IHK / HWK Berlin: 167 oben rechts
Industrie- und Filmmuseum Wolfen: 164
Institut für die Geschichte der deutschen Juden: 134, 137
Judah L. Magnes Museum: 15 unten
Jüdisches Museum Berlin: 143 oben
Jüdisches Museum Berlin / Foto: Hans-Joachim Bartsch: 14 rechts, 54 oben rechts
Kunstverlag Josef Fink, Lindenberg / Foto: Klaus Baranenko: 143 unten
Kupferstichkabinett / SMB: 74 unten
Landesdenkmalamt Berlin: 179 links
Landeskirchliches Archiv Hannover: 184 unten
Landesmuseum Mainz (GDKE): 56 links, 56 rechts, 195 oben
Leo Baeck Institute New York / Greta Rapp Collection: 98 links
Leo Baeck Institute New York / Veit-Simon Family Collection: 15 rechts, 18 unten links, 22 rechts, 23 unten, 160, 194 oben rechts
August Lotz: Frankfurter historische Gestalten. Wandgemälde an der Bavaria, Schillerplatz & Schillerstraße nebst den Malereien im neuen

Restaurationssaal, Frankfurt am Main 1884, Tafel 1 (Institut für Stadtgeschichte Frankfurt am Main, Ort 285): 58 oben rechts
Mendelssohn-Gesellschaft: 62 rechts, 63 rechts, 67 unten, 87 unten links
Mendelssohn-Gesellschaft / Foto: Manfred Claudi: 66 oben links
Mendelssohn-Gesellschaft / Foto: Zeno Colantoni: 59 links
Mendelssohn-Gesellschaft / Foto: Anna Fischer: 175
Mendelssohn-Gesellschaft / Foto: Wolfgang Günzel: 139 rechts
Mendelssohn-Gesellschaft / Foto: Marco Popp: 59 rechts
Mendelssohn-Gesellschaft / Foto: Peter Steemann: 79 unten
Elsbeth Müller, Köln: 180
Museum Charlottenburg-Wilmersdorf: 215
Musikabteilung mit Mendelssohn-Archiv, Staatsbibliothek zu Berlin – Preußischer Kulturbesitz: 221, 224 oben links
Niedersächsisches Landesarchiv Bückeburg: 11 Mitte
Österreichische Nationalbibliothek, Bildarchiv Austria: 228 oben rechts
Österreichische Zentralbibliothek für Physik: 82 oben rechts
Sebastian Panwitz: 82 links
PK / Staatsbibliothek zu Berlin: 10 rechts
Stewart Pollens: 92 rechts
Privatbesitz: 14 unten, 18 oben rechts, 22 links, 26 rechts, 27 oben, 30 oben, 36 rechts, 64, 66 unten links, 67 oben, 68, 69, 70 und Umschlagabb. vorn 7. Bild, 71, 72, 75, 76, 78 links und unten, 82 unten, 83 oben, 86 rechts, 87 oben links, 88, 92 links, 94, 96, 97 oben, 98 rechts, 100, 102, 103 unten und rechts, 106, 107 unten, 110 unten rechts, 112, 114, 115, 116, 117, 119, 126 links, 147 unten links, 150 unten, 161 oben links, 166 oben, 167 oben links, 167 unten, 178, 184 oben, 185, 198 unten, 199 unten, 202, 204 unten links und rechts, 205, 208 oben rechts und unten, 209 rechts und unten, 210 rechts, 215 oben, 219 rechts, 222 rechts, 232 unten rechts, 242 oben, 243 oben und rechts, 246 unten, 247 oben rechts, 252 unten
Privatbesitz / Foto: Manfred Claudi: 35 unten, 54 oben links, 60 links, 62 links, 128
Privatbesitz / Foto: Anna Fischer: 10 oben, 26 oben
Privatbesitz / Foto: Wolfgang Günzel: 30 unten
Privatbesitz / Foto: Thilo Rückeis: 27 unten, 55 unten rechts, 97 unten, 120 rechts und Umschlagabb. vorn 3. Bild, 199 oben
Privatbesitz / Foto: Bernhard Thévoz: 38 oben
Radio Times Hulton Picture Library, London: 231 unten
Sammlung Bernoulli: 90 und Umschlagabb. vorn 8. Bild, 93 oben links
Bettina Speyer: 247 oben links
Staatsbibliothek zu Berlin – Preußischer Kulturbesitz, Musikabteilung mit Mendelssohn-Archiv: 28, 30 links, 31 unten, 34 oben rechts, 42 oben rechts, 74 unten, 86 links, 87 unten rechts, 110 oben, 140, 198 oben links, 229 oben, 243 unten links
Staatsbibliothek zu Berlin – Preußischer Kulturbesitz, Musikabteilung mit Mendelssohn-Archiv / Foto: Manfred Claudi: 79 oben, 151 rechts
Staatsbibliothek zu Berlin – Preußischer Kulturbesitz: 36 links, 124, 130, 206, 210 links und oben, 238 unten, 239, 244
Städel Museum – Artothek: 189 unten rechts, 192
Stiftung Historische Museen Hamburg – Altonaer Museum, Foto: Elke Schneider: 34 oben links
Stiftung „Neue Synagoge Centrum Judaicum": 2, 23 oben, 127 oben, 133 links, 138 oben, 228 links
Stiftung Preußischer Kulturbesitz – Staatsbibliothek zu Berlin / Foto: Jörg Anders: 196
Stiftung Stadtmuseum Berlin: 39 unten rechts, 54 unten, 162, 170 unten, 195 unten
Stiftung Stadtmuseum Berlin, Reproduktion: Hans-Joachim Bartsch, Berlin: 50 rechts
Stiftung Stadtmuseum Berlin, Reproduktion: Christel Lehmann, Berlin: 50 links
Stiftung Stadtmuseum Berlin, Reproduktion: Michael Setzpfand, Berlin: 52
Staats- und Universitätsbibliothek Hamburg: LA: Mendelssohn, Joseph 2-3: 214
The Jewish Museum / Art Resource / Scala, Florenz: 40 und Umschlagabb. vorn 5. Bild
The Trustees of the British Museum: 187 unten rechts
Bernhard Thévoz: 156, 158
Universität Hamburg, Arbeitsstelle für Universitätsgeschichte: 108, 111 oben
Universität Hamburg, Arbeitsstelle für Universitätsgeschichte / Foto: Sabine Krause: 111 unten und rechts
Universitäts- und Landesbibliothek Bonn: 38 unten
Universitäts-und Landesbibliothek TU Darmstadt: 223 oben, 236
VG Bild-Kunst, Bonn 2015 / Ev.-Luth. Kirchgemeinde St. Thomas Leipzig: 220 rechts
Yad Vashem: 225 unten

„Die Familie Mendelssohn und ihre Gräber vor dem Halleschen Tor“ ist der Katalog zu einer gleichnamigen Dauerausstellung, die 2013 mit Mitteln der Stiftung Deutsche Klassenlotterie Berlin, unterstützt von der Stiftung Historische Kirchhöfe und Friedhöfe in Berlin und Brandenburg, in einer ehemaligen Kapelle auf dem Dreifaltigkeitsfriedhof I in Berlin-Kreuzberg eröffnet wurde.

Herausgeber:
Evangelischer Friedhofsverband Berlin Stadtmitte

EV. FRIEDHOFSVERBAND
BERLIN STADTMITTE

Mendelssohn-Gesellschaft e.V.

MENDELSSOHN
GESELLSCHAFT e.V.

Konzeption & Gestaltung: Andreas Neumann
Texte & wissenschaftliche Konzeption: Thomas Lackmann
Wissenschaftliche Beratung: Hans-Günter Klein, Sebastian Panwitz
Übersetzungen: SAMSON-ÜBERSETZUNGEN GmbH

Die Herausgeber danken dem Bildarchiv Preußischer Kulturbesitz
für die großzügige Unterstützung der Ausstellung und der Katalog-Produktion.

b p k

Besonderer Dank gilt auch der Übersetzerin Carmen von Schöning und den Mitarbeitern von SAMSON, den Fotografen und Korrektoren aus dem Team der Mendelssohn-Remise sowie der Bodleian Library der University of Oxford, der Staatsbibliothek zu Berlin – Stiftung Preußischer Kulturbesitz, der Universität Hamburg – Abteilung für Universitätsgeschichte, dem Landesmuseum Mainz – Generaldirektion Kulturelles Erbe Rheinland-Pfalz, dem Leo Baeck Institute New York, der Stiftung Neue Synagoge Berlin – Centrum Judaicum, dem Jüdischen Museum Berlin, der Stiftung Stadtmuseum Berlin und allen Nachkommen Moses Mendelssohns, deren Dokumente zu dieser Publikation beigetragen haben.

www.mendelssohns-vor-dem-halleschen-tor.de
www.stiftung-historische-friedhoefe.de
www.evfbs.de
www.mendelssohn-gesellschaft.de

nicolai *Der Hauptstadtverlag*

Lektorat: Freia Schleyerbach
Herstellung: Melanie Walter

Printed in the EU

ISBN 978-3-89479-903-8